Colossus with Feet of Clay

LOW-WAGE CAPITALISM

What the new globalized,
high-tech imperialism means
for the class struggle
in the U.S.

By Fred Goldstein

Goldstein, Fred.
**Low-wage capitalism : colossus with feet of clay –
what the new globalized, high-tech imperialism
means for the class struggle in the U.S.**
Fred Goldstein. 1st ed. p. cm.
Includes index and bibliography.
ISBN-13: 978-0-89567-151-6
ISBN-10: 0-89567-151-6 (paperback : alk. paper)

1. Globalization – Economic aspects.

2. Information technology – Economic aspects – United States.

3. Employment – Effect of technological innovations on.

4. Contracting out.

5. Working class – United States.

6. Marxian economics.

HC 59 F67 2008

338   2008929963

World View Forum
55 W. 17th St., 5th Floor
New York, NY 10011

Available at discounted bulk rates for educational use
To place credit card orders or bookstore and university
invoice orders and discounts, contact: Leftbooks.com

Book fonts: Minion, Fenice and Myriad

Table of Contents

i

Tables and charts

About this book

Many books have been written about globalization, including many radical indictments of its devastating effects on the people of the world. In fact, a number of these sources have been used in writing the present work. This book, however, is not limited to issuing an indictment. An analysis of the comprehensive global restructuring of capitalism and the relentless leveling downward of wages going on in the United States, it uses Marxism to lay bare how these processes are laying the basis for a long-delayed social upheaval of the multinational U.S. working class.

Section I of the book deals with the basis for this prognosis. It analyzes the new international division of labor in the world capitalist economy that was conditioned by the two most important events of the late twentieth century: the scientific-technological revolution in production, communications, and transportation, and the demise of the Soviet Union and Eastern Europe.

Its premise is that the principal feature of the present stage of globalization is worldwide wage competition among the workers of the globe, organized by giant corporations that are orchestrating the depression of wages in a race to the bottom.

For the first time in the history of capitalism, technology has advanced to the point at which transnational corporations are able to pit workers in the rich, developed imperialist countries in a direct job-for-job wage competition with workers in poor, underdeveloped, low-wage countries on an ever-widening scale around the globe.

Autoworkers in Detroit are set in competition with autoworkers in Mexico. Customer service workers in Phoenix are set against customer service workers in Mumbai. The wages of legal secretaries in New York City are measured by law firms against those of legal secretaries in the Philippines. Computer programmers and engineers are set against their counterparts in Moscow or Bangalore.

The other side of offshoring for low wages abroad is the presence of millions of low-wage immigrant workers in the United States. Millions have been forced to flee the poverty imposed on their countries by corporate neo-liberalism and seek out meager wages in the U.S. Thus, the corporations have an expanded army of vulnerable workers. The threat of deportation hangs over them as a bludgeon, enabling employers to impose low wages and miserable working conditions. This is an integral part of the era of globalization.

This is not a temporary phase that world capitalism and the working classes are passing through. It is the result of changes that are as profound as the Industrial Revolution and the age of colonization.

From 1985 to 2000 the so-called "active work force" available to world capitalism and imperialism doubled from 1.5 billion to 3 billion, an unprecedented event in the history of capitalism.

This vast expansion of territory and low-wage labor newly available to the corporations coincided with the accelerated development of the scientific-technological revolution.

The transnational corporations are using technology to restructure production and services so that they can scour the globe to find the cheapest labor. Under this new international division of labor, wages are being determined based upon international competition, thus pushing downward national wage standards in the rich imperialist countries.

This book goes to press in the autumn of 2008, as the U.S. economy is in the beginning of a downturn. The downturn first emerged in the framework of a global credit crisis, but layoffs are growing. At this point it is impossible to know how the economic recession will end. But this much is certain: The masses are entering a period of impending capitalist crisis more impoverished, more in debt, more insecure, and bereft of any resources that might cushion the blows of a downturn than in decades.

Over the last three decades, workers have been forced to accept lower wages and the reduction or elimination of benefits; they have learned to live on less; they have submitted to harsh working conditions; they have relocated or traveled long distances to get jobs after having been laid off. Households have adjusted by their members working multiple jobs to supplement lost income.

Workers have resorted to unprecedented amounts of credit and borrowing to keep their heads above water. The personal debt of the workers has been used to stave off personal crises—daily, weekly, and monthly in millions of individual cases. All this individual borrowing to stay afloat has transformed itself into a crisis of the class as a whole and is part of the general economic crisis of the system. Millions of workers are faced with the prospect of losing their homes.

Section II of the book deals with the economic background to the present situation. It documents the thirty-year decline in the conditions of the working class and the oppressed peoples in the U.S. Capitalist restructuring began in the late 1970s and early 1980s, mostly within the country, and was heavily influenced by robotics and automated production. It progressed to the international level with advances in the Internet, software, electronic communications, and transportation.

The transformation of the U.S. economy to low-wage capitalism is symbolized by the fact that in the 1970s the largest employer was General Motors, where 600,000 mostly unionized workers earned relatively high pay with benefits. Today the largest employer in the U.S. is Wal-Mart, where 1.2 million workers get near poverty-level wages, many existing on food stamps and government assistance, in an environment utterly hostile to even the mention of unions.

Section III deals with the prospects for the revival of class struggle in the U.S. It draws on examples from history that illustrate the possibilities for the future.

The decline of the conditions of the workers, of union membership, and of oppressed communities has been driven first and foremost by the relentless attacks of the corporations, with the backing of the capitalist state and the big-business media.

But the official top labor leadership, including heads of unions in the AFL-CIO and the newly formed Change to Win, has been in retreat for more than three decades, giving concessions or organizing on the basis of low-wage contracts. Their orientation is to find common ground with business and government in an era when the bosses are fixated on one thing: obtaining more and more concessions.

The multinational working class in the U.S. is being pushed to the wall by low-wage capitalism. There is very little room for further concessions and adjustments to the exorbitant demands of capital—particularly for the most oppressed, but also for a growing number of white workers. A capitalist downturn could lead to the breaking point—either workers' rebellions, uprisings of the oppressed masses, or both.

The employers have made the need to remain "competitive" their universal bargaining weapon. They are attempting to make the workers, who create all the wealth in the first place, responsible for maintaining the profitability of capital. Corporate ideology has become so dominant that the bosses openly demand as a matter of course that the unions and the workers tie their wages, conditions, and their very jobs to fluctuations of the capitalist market. Combating these capitalist ideological positions goes hand in hand with fighting back.

If they are to stop the blood-letting and regain the initiative in this era of downsizing, offshoring, outsourcing, and plant closings, the workers must transcend the confines of capitalist anti-labor laws and the capital-labor relationship. There must be a fight for the right to a job as a worker's property right. The right to occupy the workplaces to defend jobs and defeat concessions must be put on the agenda. There must be a struggle for the right of workers to take over bankruptcy proceedings as the primary creditors.

The sit-down strikes of the 1930s and the great Civil Rights movement of the 1950s and 1960s defied unjust laws that had been on the books for generations. Beyond the South and the territory of legal segregation, there were urban uprisings against poverty, racism, and repression. The momentum of these struggles inspired the women's movement, the lesbian and gay movement, the disabled movement, and others. It ended up expanding democratic rights in the United States.

In the last thirty years workers have shown their willingness to struggle against concessions—from the Hormel strike of 1985 through the Detroit newspaper strike of 1995, the UPS strike of 1997, the New York City transit workers' strike of 2005, and the May Day Boycott of 2006 led by undocumented workers. This will to struggle needs to be mobilized.

Globalization, capitalist restructuring, the hardships of low-wage capitalism, and growing racism and national oppression are creating the material basis for a new era of rebellion and class unity. As the working class has become poorer, the proportion of African American, Latina/o, Asian, women, lesbian, gay, bi and trans workers has become greater. At the same time white workers have also become poorer. This change in the character of the working class, both its social make up and its increasing impoverishment, is laying the basis for a more militant, more left direction for the labor movement. At the same time it is destroying the basis for class collaboration and class compromise with the bosses. These changes are creating the foundation for building a broad working-class movement which fights for the multinational working class as a whole.

The rank and file of the workers' movement will be compelled by new conditions to assert itself and exercise leadership in the struggle. Such a movement, because it is rooted in the communities of the working class and the oppressed, will be able to go beyond narrow trade unionism, which limits itself to bargaining for wages and conditions, and fight for economic, social, and political justice on all fronts in the struggle against capitalism, and ultimately against the condition of wage slavery itself.

The workers and the warfare state

The focus of this book has been largely limited to a discussion of the advances in the productive forces, the global restructuring of capitalism, its effect on the working class, and the prospects for a revival of the class struggle. The treatment of politics and war has necessarily been omitted for the sake of analyzing the above developments.

The military aspect has been dealt with only in the appendix, "Imperialist war in the 21st century." It covers the post-Soviet phase of the U.S. war drive to reconquer spheres of influence and exploitation lost during the preceding three-quarters of a century due to the advance of socialism and national liberation movements. The appendix is an abbreviated version of a longer essay that will be published in the future. Some brief observations on the connection between worldwide wage competition and the growth of U.S. militarism are necessary, however. In fact, the Pentagon is the protector and enforcer of U.S. economic globalization and low wages.

The much-anticipated "peace dividend" that was supposed to follow the end of the Cold War has turned into invasions, occupations, wars, and military spending in preparation for future aggression. All this deeply affects the conditions of the workers and the oppressed in the United States.

As of mid-2008, the estimated cost of the Iraq war and occupation, both direct and indirect, present and future, ranges between $1 trillion and $2 trillion. The over-all military budget keeps growing in preparation for future wars. The Pentagon is modernizing its nuclear weapons—"nuclear bunker busters"—for tactical use; it is creating high-tech surveillance systems; it is building anti-missile systems in Eastern Europe, Alaska, and the Pacific; it is developing new missile ships, new generations of aircraft, and is working on space warfare capability. All this is for future wars and/or global intimidation. But while it encircles China, Russia, and Iran and reactivates the Fourth Fleet in the Caribbean, the Pentagon is also churning out "smart bombs," Predator and Reaper drones, explosive-proof armored vehicles, and other weapons to use in the present against forces of popular resistance.

The money goes into the coffers of Boeing, Lockheed, Halliburton, Northrop, and others, but it is the working class that bears the economic brunt of the war drive. Trillions of dollars in value that is created through the exploitation of the labor-power of workers is transferred through government contracts to the military-industrial complex, from the giant firms to the tens of thousands of military sub-contractors in their supply chains.

Meanwhile, the working class pays in blood on the battlefield. An economic draft based on growing pauperization and unemployment forces workers into the so-called "volunteer" army. Recruiters promise funding for education and career preparation to workers who cannot afford college and who have no prospects for the future. Low-wage workers accept signing bonuses that commit them to kill or be killed because there is no economic security in the capitalist job market. Immigrant workers who are desperate to work legally sign up for the military in exchange for promises of a green card. Others sign up under pressure or because they mistakenly believe that they are fighting for a just cause. But the rich don't go to the front lines. They get workers to fight their wars, one way or another.

Finally, the working class is ideologically and politically diverted from pursuing its own class interests by the steady drumbeat of war propaganda, churned out around the clock by every capitalist channel of communication: television networks, cable channels, newspapers, magazines, radio talk shows.

The fact is that every one of the transnational corporations cited in this book as part of the race to lower wages worldwide has a global empire. These corporations are the enemies of the workers. They are the exploiters who are cynically and systematically engineering the destruction of the workers' standard of living.

The Pentagon, the CIA, the State Department, and the entire warfare state promote war and intervention, from Colombia and Venezuela to Iran and the Philippines, to insure the protection and continued expansion of these very corporate empires. And the owners of these corporate empires are the architects of the worldwide wage competition and race to the bottom that are creating low-wage capitalism in the U.S.

There can be no sustained revival of the working class without a consciousness of the role of militarism and war in capitalist society. The working class must be inoculated against imperialist war propaganda and understand the role of the Pentagon. In social and economic crises, when facing a revival of the class struggle, the capitalist class is prone to resort to **war or the threat of war as a political weapon** to divert the masses. Bringing a class understanding of war and militarism to the workers' movement is indispensable.

A note on the current capitalist crisis and low wages

Most of this book was written prior to the development of the economic downturn in the United States. It is going to press as layoffs, short hours, foreclosures, and a decline in production and services are escalating. The thesis put forward about technology and global capitalist restructuring, worldwide wage competition, and the prospects for class struggle is not dependent on any particular crisis or event. Nevertheless, it is important to discuss the relationship of the new phase of low-wage capitalism to an economic crisis of the system.

Low wages, while they are a crisis for the working class in its day-to-day existence, are not the cause of the crisis of the capitalist system. This crisis, which has been repeated over and over throughout the history of capitalism, is characterized by rising inventories of unsold goods, a collapse of production, a sharp rise in bankruptcies, mass layoffs, closing down of workplaces, and the calamitous growth of unemployment.

Crises are caused by the inherent laws of capitalism. As we explain in the book, capitalist production is also the process of capitalist exploitation of labor, whose purpose is to increase profits. Each capitalist grouping struggles to increase its profits in order to keep from being vanquished by its rivals and to expand its own corporate or financial domain. Capital can never operate outside the framework of competition, whether it is a small garment shop or a transnational microchip giant like Intel. This competition drives each capitalist to increase profits by increasing the productivity of labor—i.e., increasing the exploitation of the workers.

This cycle dictates that, during periods of capitalist expansion, the powers of production increase ever more rapidly while the powers of consumption of society expand only gradually. Sooner or later production outstrips consumption. Profit does not arrive in corporate bank accounts until sales take place. If commodities cannot be sold at a profit, inventories pile up, production stops, workers are laid off, and a crisis ensues. That is the crude dynamic of the capitalist crisis of overproduction.

It is not that there is too much production over and above the needs of the people. On the contrary, the unmet needs are monumental. The rise in poverty and near poverty, homelessness, and hunger worldwide is dramatic testimony to this. But distribution under capitalism does not take place on the basis of human need. It takes place on the basis of selling for a profit. Thus capitalism is unique in history in having growing poverty and want at the same time as growing unsold inventories of everything from food to housing.

What is the place of low-wage capitalism in this picture? High wages alone cannot abolish the crisis of capitalism. And low wages alone do not, by themselves, cause the crisis. No matter what, production under capitalism eventually outstrips consumption, causing an economic downturn and a crisis for the working class and the oppressed.

But the present phase of globalization and the worldwide wage competition engineered by the giant transnational corporations, together with the scientific-technological revolution, has severely aggravated the chronic crisis of capitalism and is making the downturn more acute and damaging. This is conditioned by the vast expansion of the low-wage reserve labor force available to capital in the wake of the collapse of the USSR and Eastern Europe and the opening of China to foreign investment.

The impact of these developments has been to drive down the wages of the working class. Whether it is offshoring jobs to Mexico, Thailand, or Romania, or the bosses just shifting labor from the Midwest to the "right-to-work" South, or the presence of millions of documented and undocumented immigrant workers subjected to extreme exploitation and low wages, capitalism has entered an era of worldwide wage competition.

During the earlier history of capitalism, workers had gained ground during capitalist expansions for the simple reason that the bosses were in great need of exploitable labor-power to fuel the expansion of production and profits. Jobs were easier to find in a boom because of what capitalist economists call a "tight labor market." Competition among workers diminished and wages rose as the bosses had to fill orders.

However, in the last period of economic recovery, from 2000 to 2004, which was also the beginning of a renewed expansion of globalized restructuring, jobs were still hard to find in the United States and wages declined. It was dubbed the "jobless recovery." This was not just rhetorical exaggeration. The economy actually lost jobs during the first four years of economic expansion—an unprecedented development in U.S. capitalist history.

Of course, an underlying factor was the increasing productivity of labor. Workers produced more in less time. Job creation thus went slowly. Manufacturing went up but manufacturing employment went down.

But the other side of this is the worldwide wage competition that was promoted without pause by the transnational corporations during the recovery. The workers were under siege, threatened by offshoring, outsourcing, and a general increase in the reserve army of labor despite the expansion. To a large number of workers the "boom" felt more like a bust.

Even during the capitalist recovery, wages continued to decline. Depressed wages accentuated the gap between production and consumption and intensified the fundamental contradiction of capitalism.

How did the U.S. financial managers deal with this situation? Alan Greenspan, head of the Federal Reserve System, and the moneyed lords of Wall Street dealt with it by pouring money into the economy in the form of credit. Much of that money wound up in the housing boom, which was stimulated by a wave of fraudulent lending practices. Another large portion was directed at pushing consumer credit on the workers and the middle class in order to sustain consumption and keep production going. Finally, a large portion of the available capital went straight to pure, parasitic financial speculation schemes.

The doctrine of the capitalist economists is that consumers were carrying the economy. In fact, it was hundreds of billions of dollars of working-class and middle-class debt that kept the economy afloat and production and services going. One would have to live in Never-Never-Land not to notice that while the corporations were ramping up production, pushing the sales of everything from homes to iPods, they were simultaneously destroying the wages of the workers. What temporarily bridged the gap between declining wages and expanding production were credit card debt, mortgage debt, auto loan debt, and general personal borrowing in the hundreds of billions of dollars by workers trying to get by. This gap can no longer be bridged and the mechanism of capitalist crisis has taken over the economy.

The new international division of labor pits workers all around the world against each other in a race to the bottom. It depresses the wages of the working class in imperialist countries and expands the sweatshop, super-exploitation of the workers in low-wage countries. It makes each capitalist recovery more difficult and undermines the historic advantages accruing to the workers in a capitalist upturn. All this is aggravating the general crisis of capitalism. High technology and low-wage capitalism on a world scale are accelerating the crisis of overproduction and laying the basis for a massive counter-attack by the working class.

Postscript: the crisis within the crisis

A s this book goes to press (October 2008), the Congress, at the behest of Secretary of the Treasury Henry Paulson and Federal Reserve System Chair Ben Bernanke, has voted to give the banks more than $1 trillion in bailout money. The goal is to reimburse the bankers with social funds to make up for the bad debts they have on their books. These bad debts arise out of their attempt to swindle the workers through high-pressure, deceptive mortgage lending, usurious credit card loans, student loans, auto loans, and other loans that were bound to become unpayable.

The interest, fees, and principal on these loans constitute claims on the future wages of the workers and on the incomes of the middle class. These claims on future wages really amount to a raid on the shrinking consumption funds of the increasingly hard-pressed multinational working class. Most affected are women, African-American, Latina/o, and other oppressed workers and their families. The people are now being told they must pay the bill for the capitalists' orgy of speculation on mortgage-backed securities, other packaged loans, and so-called "exotic" financial instruments.

In addition to being exploited on the job and working for low wages, the workers are besieged in their personal lives on all sides by mortgage bankers, credit card companies, and other financial loan sharks. Millions have been sinking deeper into debt. Struggling to pay bills to keep from going under has become a way of life.

In the age of low-wage capitalism, this bloated financial edifice, built largely upon working-class debt, was bound to come crashing down.

The pretext behind the government bailout of the banks—really a handout—is that it was necessary to keep the U.S. economy from plunging into deep recession. But while the whole world is in the grip of a capitalist economic contraction, one that has been aggravated by the financial crisis, it arose independently of the turmoil in the financial markets.

Joblessness is rising and production is declining. The automatic capitalist process of downturn due to overproduction is in progress. In this latest crisis, overproduction reached its high point in the housing boom. Real estate developers, financed by the banks, sought to cash in on the speculative rise in housing prices. This led to a glut of housing on the market and a price collapse. Now homeowners are defaulting and an epidemic of foreclosures is sweeping the country. Tent cities are rising, from Seattle to San Diego; from Columbus, Ohio, to Athens, Georgia.

But it is not just housing that is in a state of overproduction. The auto industry is incurring record drops in sales, including the Big Three U.S. auto companies and such Japanese "powerhouses" as Toyota. Technology and other industries are also affected.

The corporate race for market share was fueled by the flow of cheap credit pumped into the economy by the Federal Reserve to keep consumption and production going. Now it has reached its limits and the government is trying to feed the banks in a futile attempt to ease the crisis.

No one knows where this contraction will end. The financial and economic crises are coming together as the ruling class tries to transfer the enormous cost onto the backs of the people.

As the crisis mounts there will be finger pointing by politicians and pundits alike, meant to assuage the anger of the masses. Official opinion is blaming the situation on greed and on a failure of regulation. To be sure, the bankers on Wall Street are voracious and greedy. And it is obvious that the destruction of regulatory restraint on finance capital opened the door wide to an escalation of gambling and speculation—to the "casino" economy.

This deregulation began with the Reagan administration, passed a milestone in the Clinton administration with the repeal of the Depression-era Glass-Steagall Act, and continued in the current Bush administration. Alan Greenspan, former head of the Federal Reserve System, presided over much of this deregulation during his reign of 19 years, from 1987 to 2006.

But to say that deregulation is the cause of capitalist excesses is to put the cart before the horse. It is the irrepressible capitalist lust for profit itself that leads to excesses. These excesses, such as the wild speculation in stocks and land deals that led up to the market crash of 1929, led to New Deal-era regulations restricting the financiers—but only after the speculative horse was out of the barn and millions had been ruined.

The gradually accumulating need of capital to engage in speculation inevitably results in the destruction of regulatory restraint. The system itself creates excess money capital and drives it more and more toward financial speculation and investment in paper wealth that has no relationship to underlying value.

The fact is that the bankers and the rich in general have vastly increased their fortunes in the last three decades. Income inequality in the U.S. has become notorious around the world. For example, in 1976 the top 1 percent of households received 8.9 percent of total income. In 2005 the top 1 percent received 21.8 percent—the highest percentage of total household income since 1928, the year before the stock market crashed. (Inequality.org)

From 2000 to 2007 the wealthiest 400 individuals in the U.S. got a $670-billion increase in their wealth and owned $1.5 trillion. While the top 1 percent of households earn more than the bottom 50 percent, they **own** more than 90 percent of the wealth. (Figures from Sen. Bernie Sanders' speech against the bailout.) These are truly staggering numbers and have profound implications for the profit system.

The working class produces all wealth, all value in society. The class struggle is really a struggle over which class will get a larger or smaller share in the social surplus created by labor. If the bosses get more, the workers get less, and vice versa. This is what makes class antagonisms irreconcilable.

Saying that there is growing income inequality in the U.S. is really a masked way of saying that there has been a broad redivision of the social surplus in favor of the capitalist class and to the detriment of the working class. The bosses and bankers have taken a larger and larger relative share and the working class has received a correspondingly smaller share.

However, the rate at which the owners of capital have accumulated this wealth exceeds the rate at which it can be reinvested profitably in productive capital. The scientific-technological revolution has made business more and more productive. The workers turn out more goods and services in less time with each new advance in technology.

Furthermore, the anarchy of production—that is, the unplanned and competitive nature of capitalist production—sends each capitalist grouping in search of greater and greater market share in pursuit of profit, to the point that they collectively produce a glut of commodities on the market and can no longer sell at a profit. This is a fundamental feature of capitalism and cannot be eliminated.

And after the rich spend billions on yachts, jets, mansions, servants, and every form of obscene luxury, they still have hundreds of billions in money capital left over. And, as Karl Marx showed, capital cannot rest, cannot remain idle. It seeks profit, and it seeks to maximize profit.

For example, the two largest industrial corporations in the United States—General Electric and General Motors—both have huge financial subdivisions. GE plows billions in profits into GE Capital, which invests tens of billions in loans all over the globe. GM's financial arm is GMAC. (In 2008, to raise capital, it sold 51 percent of GMAC to Cerberus, a private equity firm.) While GM has downsized its production and forced a large part of its workforce to take buyouts, the company has expanded its lending. The same goes for Ford, Chrysler, and other industrial giants. Instead of investing surplus capital in their own companies, they use it to make loans.

The collapse of the housing boom in August 2007, followed by turmoil in the capital markets, was only the latest in a series of capitalist crises.

During the Reagan administration, a severe recession in 1982 and 1983 sent unemployment above 11 percent. The capitalist class used the opportunity to begin the technological restructuring of industry, leading to millions of workers losing high-paying jobs. Reagan then stimulated the economy with $2 trillion in military spending, using Cold War propaganda to justify this huge handout to the military-industrial complex.

The economy expanded and the stock market boomed again—until it collapsed in October 1987 with record losses. Several trillion dollars of paper wealth were wiped out. An economic collapse was prevented only when Alan Greenspan, who was appointed head of the Federal Reserve in August 1987, poured tens of billions of dollars into the financial system to support the banks and the stock market on an emergency basis. This emergency rescue of the economy lasted only until 1991, when there was another recession.

However, the collapse of the USSR, also in 1991, stimulated a decade of capitalist expansion. Capital flooded into the former Soviet Union, Eastern Europe, India, and other places. The upturn in economic output accelerated in the mid 1990s with the development of the Internet and related technologies. From 1995 to 2000, venture capitalists, who are really fronts for the big banks, poured billions of dollars in speculative capital into technology companies. New companies were being created on a daily basis. The stock market boomed, creating the so-called "dot-com" bubble—until the overproduction of technology led to another collapse, beginning in March 2000. From that time until October 2002, $5 trillion in paper wealth was wiped out and an economic downturn developed simultaneously.

In the 110 years since the Spanish-American war of conquest, imperialist capitalism has brought an endless cycle of wars, recessions, depressions, and more wars. After each economic downturn, the system has had to resort to military expansion and financial manipulation to revive itself.

During the depression of the 1930s, Franklin D. Roosevelt tried to get the economy going with the Works Project Administration and by allowing workers' wages to rise. But by 1937-1938, after a brief uptick, there was a second depression. Only preparations for World War II and conquest in the Pacific and Europe revived the U.S. economy.

Throughout the entire Cold War period, U.S. capitalism was dependent on military spending to keep its economy going. The growth of the military-industrial complex, with its web of prime contractors and tens of thousands of subcontractors thriving on Pentagon appropriations for war and for arms exports, was the principal means of keeping the capitalist economy from sinking into stagnation and depression.

This history illustrates that since the turn of the twentieth century, capitalism, in order to sustain itself, has had to resort to artificial measures that bring disaster in their wake, in the form of war, depression or both.

The present economic crisis is descending upon the workers and the oppressed after they have already endured three decades of getting poorer; after they have been pushed to the wall by worldwide wage competition and technological attacks by the bosses.

What was a chronic erosion of the standard of living of the workers has taken a leap to become an acute crisis of unemployment, foreclosures, and national oppression. Thirty-five percent of the subprime mortgage loans were made to African Americans. Official Black unemployment has risen to more than 10 percent, as compared to 6 percent overall. The rise in Black unemployment is largely among women. Immigrant workers, especially Latina/os whose low-paid labor was the foundation of the construction boom, are now being rounded up, jailed, and deported—or they are leaving the country to escape persecution, because they cannot find jobs, or both.

There are two important points about the present economic crisis. First, it is not an aberration attributable to George W. Bush and his administration. This crisis is not simply the result of greed and deregulation. It is a dramatic and dangerous episode in the general crisis of capitalism, which is a century old. The capitalist system cannot function except by growing parasitism, militarism and oppression.

Wild speculation in pursuit of easy, rapid profits; war for oil profits in the Middle East; destruction of the environment in the interest of profit, and much more are all a natural outgrowth of capitalism.

The second and most important point to grasp in the present crisis is that the automatic processes of capitalism—that is, economic contraction, layoffs, unemployment, and war—remain on auto-pilot only so long as the multinational working class allows them to proceed without fighting back.

The politicians of both big-business parties, along with the media, are trying mightily to indoctrinate the workers in the way that credit works, in the way that capitalism works, both in order to exonerate the system of exploitation and so that the workers will feel overpowered by an impersonal machine that cannot be resisted—a machine that eats their jobs, their homes, and their very lives.

They are trying to shift the burden of the crisis onto the multinational working class, especially the African-American, Latina/o, Asian, and Native communities, the undocumented, the youth, the elderly, the disabled, and all who suffer from exploitation and oppression. The bosses do this on the assumption that the workers and the oppressed are the mere objects of history to be manipulated and, in the last resort, to be held in check by the power of the state.

But history, including U.S. history, is filled with examples of how the masses of people took destiny into their own hands, got organized, and became the subjects of history.

The object of this book is to make a contribution to this latter process.

–*October 3, 2008*

Imperialist globalization and worldwide wage competition

1

Doubling the global workforce

Political expansion after 74 years of contraction · The new international division of labor
Corporate design for worldwide wage competition · Marx on wages and competition

In an amazingly short time span, from the early 1980s to the turn of the century, the number of workers worldwide available to the transnational corporations for exploitation more than doubled.

The rapidity and magnitude of this growth is unprecedented in history. It has had profound effects on the working classes of the world, beginning long before the ominous economic crisis of 2008. Precisely for that reason, the corporations have sought to downplay this development publicly, while furiously racing to take advantage of it to pile up profits.

Their mouthpieces in the mass media have tried to minimize the damage and hide it, not only from the workers but from the general public, as much as possible. Announcements of layoffs or cutbacks in health care and pensions or wage reductions at various companies were for the most part either ignored or, when they did make the news, treated routinely as items of the day. When the layoffs or cutbacks were too large and too critical to overlook, such as the layoffs in auto or the airlines, the media adopted a mournful tone and gave sympathetic interviews to some of the victims. The bosses' line was then regurgitated about how layoffs are the inevitable and unavoidable result of the need to stay "competitive." Then the news abruptly moved on to the next thing.

The fate of hundreds, thousands or tens of thousands of workers and their families hit by the layoffs and left staring disaster in the face sank out of the reporters' line of sight. The bosses were let off the hook. Meanwhile, nothing was done and the media were silent until the next outrage was announced and there followed a renewed cycle of hypocritical sympathy, absolution of the bosses, and again silence.

Real discussions, however, have taken place in business publications, think tanks, and the academic world. But even there, the discussions are carried out in a most cautious fashion and it is difficult even for experts to unearth the real extent of developments.

Behind the scenes various researchers have been quietly trying to gauge the extent and potential impact of this explosive expansion of both labor and capital. Their explorations have been driven by fear of the economic, social, and political effects of this potentially earthshaking development.

One attempt that is widely known, not among workers but among those of the elite who concern themselves with the question of globalization, comes from Richard B. Freeman, an economics professor at Harvard University who is also associated with the National Bureau of Economic Research and the London School of Economics. In November 2004 Freeman made a presentation to the International Public Policy Institute entitled "Doubling the Global Work Force." He based his presentation on two ambitious studies, the first by the International Labor Organization (ILO) of the United Nations and the second by the Center for International Comparisons (CIC) at the University of Pennsylvania.

Freeman concerns himself, among other things, with the labor movement and economic issues involving youth. He gave population figures to dramatize the global expansion of the power of the advanced capitalist countries during the recent period—an expansion of which he fully approves.

He cited what he called the "One Big Fact": From 1985 to 2000, the population of the "global economic world"—that is, those fully within the grasp of the world capitalist market—grew from 2.5 billion to 6 billion people.[1]

Between 1985 and 2000, the world working class newly available for exploitation by the imperialist transnational corporations increased by 1.47 billion

And what happened in this period? The opening up of China to foreign capital, the collapse of the USSR, and the consequent ending of what he calls "autarky" in India—that is, the full-scale surrender by the Indian capitalist class in 1991 of their country's economic sovereignty to the International Monetary Fund and the penetration of foreign investment.

Aside from general population figures, most significant from a class point of view is that, according to the ILO study, the world working class newly available for exploitation by the imperialist transnational corporations by the year 2000 had increased by 1.47 billion because of the inclusion of China, India, the former Soviet Union, and Eastern Europe. With just 1.46 billion already in the rest of the world labor force (ILO), the opening up of these three regions doubled the size of the world working class potentially available to compete on the world labor market The ILO's global labor figure for the year 2000 is 2.93 billion.[2]

The figures from the University of Pennsylvania are comparable. The Penn World Tables (PWT), published by the CIC, give the same figure—2.93 billion —for the total world working class, dubbed the "economically active population." But, according to the PWT, China, India, and the former Soviet-bloc countries alone had added 1.383 billion workers to the pool by the year 2000.[3]

Of course, the figures given in both studies are crude estimates. Both studies say as much. Furthermore, the lumping together of the three regions without regard to their political and class differences requires numerous qualifications.

China had a socialist revolution and has allowed an excessive and dangerous growth of capitalism, but it still maintains broad controls over what imperialist corporations can and cannot do.

The Russian bourgeoisie, by contrast, opened up its economy to unrestricted capitalist investment and then began to pull back. The Eastern European countries have become satellites of Western capital.

The Indian government has been capitalist from birth but, while it was always somewhat penetrated by imperialist capital, for many years it allied itself with the USSR, from which it received aid. Until 1991, it exercised a considerable amount of state control over the flow of foreign capital.

In addition, Freeman underestimates the real expansion of the sway of imperialism by failing to take into account that the working classes and peasants of most of Latin America, Africa, and other parts of the underdeveloped world were subjected to intensified plunder as a result of the collapse of the USSR and Eastern Europe. The gradual neo-liberalist offensive of the IMF and the World Bank—that is, economic austerity programs, privatization of state industry, deregulation, and removing barriers to foreign imports and capital investment—accelerated during the 1990s. For example, NAFTA, which went into effect in January 1994, subjected the workers and peasants of Mexico (population over 100 million) to a wave of capital investment and super-exploitation from U.S. corporations.

Freeman, the ILO, and the CIC are struggling to portray the general order of magnitude of the drastic increase in the numbers of workers and peasants available to imperialist capital. They try not only to assess the numbers of toilers but also to analyze the growth of skilled, semi-skilled, and technically educated workers around the world. Such research has undoubtedly been undertaken on behalf of, or for the benefit of, financial and government officials or the upper echelons of bourgeois academia, who are well aware that this new world relationship of capital and labor has a potential for destabilizing the entire capitalist system.

All these regions of the world suffer from high unemployment and underemployment as well as poverty. The reinstitution of capitalism in the former USSR and Eastern Europe has drastically increased unemployment and reduced the standard of living of the masses. China is still struggling with the legacy of underdevelopment inherited from feudalism and colonialism. India has small islands of wealth amidst a sea of rural and urban poverty and unemployment. From Indonesia to Brazil, from Mexico to Thailand to South Africa, there exists a vast reserve population being drawn into the world proletariat.

Thomas Friedman, the *New York Times* columnist, author, and millionaire enthusiast of capitalism, has been thrilled by the prospects of globalization. In his recent book, *The World Is Flat*, Friedman waxes enthusiastic about how "the people of China, India, Russia, Eastern Europe, Latin America, and Central Asia" whose "economies and political systems opened up during the course of the 1990s" were "increasingly free to join the free-market game."[4]

Friedman spends much time gushing about the new age of globalization, what he calls Globalization 3.0, which is allegedly characterized by the "newfound power for *individuals* to collaborate and compete globally."[5] Commenting on the Freeman report, Friedman says, "As a result of this widening, another roughly 1.5 billion new workers entered the global economic labor force. ..."[6]

Friedman has a particular focus on the so-called professional section of the working class: service, engineering, and research. He virtually drools over the prospect of a new global competition within this sector of workers. If one-tenth of these workers "have the education and connectivity" to compete in the upper-level job market, "that is still 150 million people, roughly the size of the entire U.S. workforce,"[7] he says. And he quotes Craig Barrett, the chairperson of Intel, on the significance of opening up India, China, and Russia: "You don't bring three billion people into the world economy overnight without huge consequences, especially from three societies with rich educational heritages."[8] It is the capitalist world economy they are both referring to, of course, and the "consequences" they are looking forward to are the depression of wages.

Prior to the ILO and WPT studies, Alan Tonelson, a research fellow for the U.S. Business and Industrial Council (USBIC), speculated in 2002 in his book *The Race to the Bottom* about "the continuing, unprecedented surge in the number of workers around the world available to U.S. business." He described this as a significant factor in "globalization's corrosive impact on U.S. living standards."[9]

Without the benefit of any overall studies, Tonelson made an attempt to show the scope of the expansion of the labor exploitable by globalizing monopolies or, as he says, "how the world's economic labor supply began to explode":

> The actual numbers involved are staggering. At present, seven countries with populations of 100 million or greater (as of mid 1999) are rapidly entering world markets—China (1.25 billion), India (987 million), Indonesia (212 million), Brazil (168 million), Russia (147 million), Bangladesh (126 million), and Mexico (100 million). The former Communist countries of Eastern Europe—excluding the former Yugoslav republics—and the former Soviet republics represent two more roughly 100-million regions joining the global economy. Right behind them in size are Vietnam (80 million), the Philippines (75 million), and Turkey (66 million).[10]

Tonelson had pointed out earlier in the book, "Until roughly 1980, the flow of workers into the international trading system was relatively gradual, and the wage and employment effects of much industrialization were **mainly national, not global**."[11] [Emphasis added.]

Tonelson writes for various publications and testifies before congressional committees on trade. He talks about protecting manufacturing workers in order to bolster his arguments for protecting small U.S. manufacturers because the USBIC is an association of small businesses, mostly manufacturers who are being undermined by the offshoring policies of the monopolies. They have allied at times with the official labor movement to promote bourgeois protectionism and stand for the exploitation of U.S. workers at "decent wages." Hence, Tonelson's concern for jobs and wages. Nevertheless, his findings contain information that can be useful to the workers.

Thomas Palley, assistant director of public policy at the AFL-CIO, alludes to the potential crisis for the working class posed by these new developments. While too much of his writing reflects the labor leadership's chauvinist anti-China rhetoric, he nevertheless also sees the broader picture:

> Much attention has been devoted to adverse impacts of the U.S. trade deficit, particularly with China…. However, no one in Washington is talking about the deeper question of what happens to wages when two billion people from low-wage countries join the global labor market.
> Such an event is unprecedented in history.[12]

It is not clear what Palley's source for the two billion is. What is more important than the accuracy of his estimates is how the obviously undeniable explosion of the global workforce since the collapse of the USSR is seen by an economic policy adviser to the labor leadership. In the past what Palley and all bourgeois economists call "integration" of the expanding working class was gradual and, this is a key phrase, "production was largely immobile across countries."

Globalization has changed this by accelerating the process of international integration. It has also made capital, technology, and methods of production mobile, marking a watershed with the past....

... Manufacturing has already been placed in competition across countries, with dire consequences for manufacturing workers. The internet promises to do the same for previously un-tradable services, and higher-paid knowledge workers will start feeling similar effects.

Not since the industrial revolution has there been a transformation of this magnitude, and that revolution took one hundred and fifty years to complete. By comparison the new revolution is only twenty-five years old. These developments have a significance that goes far beyond the currency manipulation and WTO rules violations.... **There is no reason to think that the end is in sight, and American workers can look forward to the international economy exerting downward pressure on wages and work conditions for the next several decades.** [13] [Emphasis added.]

Ben Bernanke, the principal manager of U.S. finance capital as chairperson of the Federal Reserve System since the retirement of Alan Greenspan, dealt with the same phenomenon in a surprise speech to central bankers at a retreat in Jackson Hole, Wyoming, in August 2006.[14]

Bernanke gave his quick survey of globalization, beginning with the Roman Empire, continuing through Christopher Columbus and the post-Napoleonic era up until today. After going over what he considered to be similar threads running through the ages, he zeroed in on what he saw as new elements.

Among the factors he cited were "the emergence of China, India, and the former communist-bloc countries [which] implies that the greater part of the earth's population is now engaged, at least potentially, in the global economy. There are no historical antecedents for this development."[15] Columbus's voyage led to vast economic changes, but they took centuries. By contrast, the imperialists got an opening to China less than three decades ago.

Furthermore, Bernanke noted, "the traditional distinction between core and periphery is becoming increasingly less relevant, as mature industrial economies and emerging-market economies become more integrated and interdependent. **Notably, the nineteenth-century pattern, in which the core exported manufactures to the periphery in exchange for commodi-**

ties, no longer holds, as an increasing share of world manufacturing capacity is now found in emerging markets." [16] [Emphasis added.]

Bernanke also stressed,

> [P]roduction processes are becoming geographically fragmented to an unprecedented degree. Rather than producing goods in a single process in a single location, firms are increasingly breaking the production process into discrete steps and performing each step in whatever location allows them to minimize costs. For example, the U.S. chip producer AMD locates most of its research and development in California; produces in Texas, Germany, and Japan; does final processing and testing in Thailand, Singapore, Malaysia, and China; and then sells in markets around the globe."[17]

Finally, Bernanke spoke of the enormously disproportionate flow of foreign investment and how international investors hold "an array of debt instruments, equities, and derivatives, including claims on a broad range of sectors."

In a low-key, understated way, which spoke volumes to his banker audience, he said that the ruling class could not take the present situation for granted: "[A]s in the past, the social and political opposition to openness can be strong. Although that opposition has many sources, I have suggested that much of it arises because changes in the patterns of production are likely to threaten the livelihoods of some workers and the profits of some firms, even when these changes lead to greater productivity and output overall."[18]

So, experts from academia, the top echelons of the labor movement, small business, and the central banker of U.S. finance capital, all from their own points of view, have zeroed in on the change in the condition of the economy of world imperialism in the post-Soviet era. They all view these changes with different shades of trepidation.

What emerges from this cross section of views, either explicitly or by implication, is that:

- The world working class that is available for imperialist capital to exploit has taken a quantum leap of unprecedented, historic proportions— not just in China, India, and the former Soviet Union and Eastern Europe, but well beyond.

- This expansion has been in low-wage regions of the globe—i.e., regions that have been colonized or dominated by colonialism and imperialism at some point in history and are still living at various stages of underdevelopment as a result of that legacy, whether those countries are today socialist or capitalist, semi-independent or totally dependent neo-colonies.

- Low-wage workers from these regions are increasingly being brought under the domination of imperialist monopoly capitalism, dubbed by bourgeois commentators as "the global economy." The ownership and/or control of these giant monopolies is centered in the U.S. and other imperialist countries.
- The scientific-technological revolution has enabled the giant corporations with global reach and huge reserves of capital to restructure production and services, to "fragment" them, to quote Bernanke. This means that the bosses can spread out production internationally and pay much lower wages to workers in manufacturing and services abroad than they would pay for the same work at home.
- Because of the creation of so-called global production chains, offshoring of services, and immigration—the migration of low-wage, oppressed workers, which is an integral part of the "globalization" process—wages in any particular country are no longer determined primarily by a national standard but, to an increasing degree, are determined internationally.

Thus, it is not just the numerical growth of this reserve army of labor that constitutes the potential for crisis and struggle. It is the fact that the doubling of the reserve army of workers subject to exploitation by imperialist finance capital has taken place simultaneously with the breakdown of the old world social division of labor and the evolution of a new global arrangement.

Political expansion after 74 years of contraction

The decisive event in the rapid expansion of the power of imperialist capital over the workers and the oppressed of the world is certainly the fall of the Soviet Union and Eastern Europe. Prior to their collapse, world imperialism's political control over the geography and economic spheres of exploitation in the world had been contracting for 74 years, since the Russian Revolution of 1917.

With the seizure of power by the Bolsheviks, one sixth of the globe had been lost to capitalism. In the period after World War II, socialism spread to Korea and the countries of Eastern Europe. One-fourth of the human race was added with the triumph of the Chinese Revolution in 1949, followed by Vietnam, Cuba, Cambodia, Laos, Angola, Mozambique, Guinea-Bissau, Ethiopia, and Yemen. Imperialism was being challenged from Nicaragua to El Salvador to Palestine. The bourgeois nationalist revolutions in Iraq and later Iran freed those countries from the grip of the oil companies.

In addition to the expansion of socialism and the rise of the national liberation struggles, various nationalist regimes seeking to sustain political independence and to reduce their vulnerability to economic penetration by transnational corporations and banks were able to lean on the socialist camp for support to counteract the overbearing influence of the imperialist camp.

The world became divided into two class camps: the socialist camp allied with the formerly colonial countries versus the imperialist camp and its puppets, clients, and agents around the world. However, with the collapse of the USSR, imperialism reversed the historic trend of its contraction and began a rapid expansion not seen since the "scramble for Africa" at the end of the nineteenth century.

Not only did the transnational corporations and banks, operating through the IMF, the World Bank, and other agencies, gain access to the former Soviet republics and Eastern Europe, but the removal of the economic and political force of the socialist camp as one able to retard the advance of the corporate ruling class into the so-called Third World paved the way for an escalation of the neo-liberalist offensive.

Among the more profound effects of the collapse was the strengthening of those elements in the People's Republic of China (PRC) that were moving in the direction of relying on capitalism to build up the productive forces. There was also a major shift of the Indian ruling class away from neutralism in foreign policy and state capitalism in economic policy, which had been designed to limit the influence of the transnationals. In 1991 India moved toward Washington, opening up to the IMF and to expanded foreign investment.

Thus, in the short span between the early 1980s, when the PRC carried out a controlled but expanded opening up to imperialist foreign capital, and 1991, when the capitalist counter-revolution triumphed in the USSR, the imperialist ruling classes in the U.S., Europe, and Japan struck it rich. To put it plainly, the imperialists' sphere of exploitation grew during this period by leaps and bounds.

The new international division of labor

The international division of labor that existed under imperialism until the latter part of the twentieth century confined the workers and peasants of the oppressed countries overwhelmingly to mining, production of export crops, and carrying out the hard labor that went into building and maintaining the infrastructure required for extraction and transport of all raw material and agricultural commodities to the imperialist centers.

Suzanne Berger, the team leader of a major research study by the MIT Industrial Performance Center about the competitive business practices of 500 corporations around the world, found that in 2004 the developing countries' share in world merchandise trade rose to 31 percent of the total; of that trade, more than 70 percent was in manufactured goods.[19] This amounted to slightly under $2 trillion out of $8.9 trillion worldwide.[20]

The new, developing division of labor certainly does not eliminate the plunder of the raw materials, natural resources, and agriculture of the oppressed countries. On the contrary, it expands the corporate search for natural resources of all kinds as the industrial processes expand and grow more sophisticated.

Capitalist restructuring has drawn workers in the underdeveloped regions into direct wage competition with workers in the imperialist countries

But the capitalist restructuring of the economy has also made it possible to draw the surplus workers in the underdeveloped regions into the most advanced manufacturing and service processes in direct competition with workers in the imperialist countries. This is a competition that was impossible under the old division of labor and the previous technological level.

The bosses have used offshoring, outsourcing, and the super-exploitation of immigrant labor, with all its accompanying racism, to intensify the exploitation of this new, expanded global labor supply. They have used every technological weapon at their disposal to restructure world capitalist production and services in order to ensnare more and more layers of workers over wider and wider territories into an ever-extending global chain of exploitation and wage competition. This ruthless campaign has the benign, non-class designation of "globalization."

In the United States the bosses have played a double game. On the one hand, they have used the opportunity to whittle away piecemeal the rights and living conditions of the workers at home—industry by industry, factory by factory, and office by office. On the other hand, for fear of provoking a rebellion, they have carefully tried to conceal the fact that they are engaged in a general, all-out offensive against the working class and the oppressed.

Tonelson summarizes this offensive as follows:

> [The] current globalization policies have plunged the great majority of U.S. workers into a great worldwide race to the bottom, into a no-win scramble for work and livelihoods with hundreds of millions of their already impoverished counterparts across the globe.[21]

Corporate design for worldwide wage competition

In the process of striving after profits, the capitalist class, as Karl Marx pointed out in *The Communist Manifesto*, "constantly revolutionizes the means of production." Indeed, since the dawn of capitalism, the driving force of every technological and organizational advance in the processes of production, communication, transportation, and commerce has been not for the betterment of humankind or the creation of wealth for society in general, but for an increase in the profits of the class of capitalists.

With all their lofty and breathtaking achievements, whether putting two billion transistors on a microchip or performing long-distance surgery by computer-operated robot, the current scientific-technological revolution and the consequent reorganization of global capitalism are in the hands of the capitalist class. They are therefore powered by one motive every step along the way: advancing and intensifying the exploitation of labor and speeding up the plunder of the world's resources with the aim of increasing profits.

Authoritative figures who have studied the new phase of imperialist economic expansion and reorganization have independently come to a common conclusion and have stated more bluntly what Bernanke expressed in vague language.

Barry Lynn, a business journalist, consultant to various capitalist governments, and a senior fellow at a prestigious business think tank, the New America Foundation, referred to the debate in the establishment about "outsourcing" in his book *End of the Line*. After criticizing mainstream economists for being oblivious to the fate of U.S. workers, he wrote:

> For anyone listening to this debate, the prime lesson from outsourcing would seem clear enough. It is that Americans must now compete for their jobs to a degree we never had to before, with people in Guangdong, in Karnataka, in Kuala Lumpur. And if we look honestly at outsourcing, we will see that it does tend naturally, to some degree intentionally, to set workers into more intense competition with one another, not only across borders but often right here at home within the borders of the United States.[22]

In a study calculated to warn the government and the ruling class that the giant monopolies are running wild and creating a fragile system of "interdependence," Lynn adds:

> [T]he global communications and transportation revolution has in the past few years enabled companies to hire suppliers located not simply on the far side of town or the far side of America but on the far side of the earth. And inspired by 'just-in-time' production strategies, these companies have often linked these scattered operations together far more efficiently than

was true even when they were all within the walls of a vertically integrated factory of yore.... They were designing a system that set American workers more and more into competition against one another and with workers overseas....[23]

Suzanne Berger of the MIT research team elaborated on this trend:

The deep reserves of unskilled and skilled labor of emerging economies have now become available for hire to producers from high-wage countries. Over the past twenty years, countries on the periphery of the advanced industrial world have educated large numbers of semiskilled and skilled workers, technicians and engineers, making it possible to carry out sophisticated manufacturing processes like semiconductor fabrication just about anywhere. For example, two new semiconductor-fabrication plants (frequently referred to as 'fabs'), Semiconductor Manufacturing International Corporation (SMIC) and Grace, with near cutting-edge capabilities, were opened in China in 2001 by Taiwanese engineers operating with foreign capital and American and Japanese technology.

Today, manufacturing and services can be handed off from Western countries to workers and technicians in India, China, Romania, and elsewhere with **wages that may be as low as a tenth of the wage** in the more advanced country. Europeans shift production from high-wage plants in Germany and France into low-cost sites in Romania, Hungary, or Poland and reimport the goods made there back into the European Union without any tariff duties; Americans can do the same thing with goods that are processed in Mexico or the Caribbean. Software and telecom companies with a scarcity of educated workers who will work for low wages at home can open facilities in places like Bangalore, India. The global market makes it possible for firms to access resources like manufacturing, a low-cost, semiskilled workforce, skilled technicians, and innovation around the world and to incorporate them in the home company in new ways.[24] [Emphasis added.]

Tonelson cites the massive imbalance between the world's unemployed and the available jobs.

These global labor surpluses undermine American wages in two principal ways. First, the bleak economic prospects of many emerging market workers have led millions to emigrate to their more prosperous third world neighbors or to industrialized countries like the United States. In the latter case, by artificially increasing the U.S. labor supply, these movements give U.S. employers the same options as their foreign counterparts of restraining wages—and not only for the unskilled and uneducated.

Second, the worldwide reach of U.S. multinational corporations also greatly expands the pool of workers potentially available to U.S. business. These companies perform much of their production abroad, either through affiliates they own in whole or in part, or through independent foreign subcontractors. As a result, many have foreign workforces that have long been significant percentages of their domestic workforces. In addition, multinationals can easily choose among either U.S. or foreign subcontractors in the numerous industries that supply them, thereby sending downward wage pressure rippling far into the U.S. economy.[25]

Finally, it is worth quoting Friedman, the most celebrated journalistic phrasemaker and cheerleader for imperialist globalization. He unashamedly boasted: "There is almost nothing about Globalization 3.0 that is not good for capital. Capitalists can sit back, buy up any innovation, and then hire the best, cheapest labor input from anywhere in the world to research it, develop it, produce, and distribute it.... All the things related to capital do fine." Workers and communities, however, "will feel the pain."[26]

Marx on wages and competition

This brutal effort to set up global wage competition has profound implications for the class struggle. In this connection it is worthwhile recalling one of the most famous passages in *The Communist Manifesto*. In the final paragraph of the first section, Marx concluded:

> The essential condition for the existence, and for the sway of the bourgeois class, is the formation and augmentation of capital; the condition for capital is wage labor. Wage-labor rests **exclusively on competition between the laborers**. The advance of industry, whose involuntary promoter is the bourgeoisie, replaces the isolation of the laborers, due to competition, by their revolutionary combination due to association. The development of modern industry, therefore, cuts from under its feet the very foundation on which the bourgeoisie produces and appropriates products. What the bourgeoisie therefore produces, above all, are its own gravediggers. Its fall and the victory of the proletariat are equally inevitable.[27] [Emphasis added.]

The present phase of world capitalist development encompasses both processes described in this passage. The ruling class is today, more than ever, required by the force of competition to revolutionize the means of production as a way of both vanquishing its rivals and protecting itself from being vanquished by those very rivals. As the owners of capital, they can behave in no other way. In that sense they are the involuntary (but eager and energetic) promoters of a new global structure of production. But they are also creating a newly expanded international working class, which will be compelled to struggle against not only its own growing local exploiters but transnational corporate masters.

In addition, the giant monopolies, as they expand everywhere, are feverishly trying to set up a wage competition between the higher-paid workers in the imperialist countries and the growing working class in the low-wage countries, as well as between workers at different wage levels in the low-wage countries themselves. In doing so they are gradually but relentlessly cutting the ground out from under capitalist stability. For, as this process deepens, it is changing the structure of the working class in the imperialist countries. It will eventually confront the workers with their true condition as wage slaves, whose only salvation is to unite against the bosses, not only on a national but on an international basis.

At the moment, the working class in the imperialist countries, in the United States especially, is on the defensive. Nevertheless, the law of the value of labor power discovered by Marx is operating to eventually arouse their struggle instincts, to evoke their natural tendency to combat the bosses. This tendency to struggle has been shown in the past but has been choked off since the 1930s and suppressed by all institutions of capitalist society—not the least of which is the labor bureaucracy.

In *Capital*, Volume I, Marx analyzed the true nature of wages in his explanation of the "buying and selling of labor power."[28]

Wages are the purchase price paid by the capitalists for the labor power of workers. That price, Marx showed, is equal to what it takes to keep the workers and their families alive—i.e., to be able to go to work in conditions healthy enough to perform their labor for the capitalists and to be able to return to work repeatedly during the most productive years of their lives to serve as exploitable labor—so long as the bosses need them. But not only do they have to remain fit for work, they have to produce the next generation of workers for future exploitation. The price that the capitalists have to pay for the sum total of this is the value of labor power, called wages.

But Marx also explained that every country has its historically determined level of what is considered the necessary means of subsistence for the workers.[29]

It depends on the degree of comfort to which the working class and society in general are accustomed, based on the degree of economic development of the country and the class struggle within that country. In what we today would call a country with a legacy of oppression, the masses are forced to accept less; in a more privileged country, particularly where the labor unions are strong, the masses are accustomed to more. In each case, accordingly, the bosses will pay less or more **based upon national conditions**.

The revolution in technology and the globalization of capitalist production and services is eroding the national determination of wages.

The wage level of the working class in the imperial- *__The globalization__*
ist countries, under pressure of the global competition *__of capitalist production__*
set up by the giant monopolies, is being **increasingly** *__is eroding the national__*
determined internationally and under the down- *__determination__*
ward pressure of the wage level in the low-wage coun- *__of wages__*
tries. From the point of view of the bosses, a worker in
Detroit with health care, a pension, vacation, and a living wage is overpriced,
given the world labor market. Stating it from a Marxist point of view, the boss
views wages paid that worker to be above the socially necessary value of labor
power. The value of labor power, as far as General Motors, IBM, or General
Electric are concerned, should be closer to the wages in China, Mexico, or
the Philippines than to the wages in Detroit, New York, or Chicago. And the
bosses will continue to push in this direction until the workers stop them.

To the bosses the workers in the United States are getting wages above the
international norm, as computed by the corporate planners of global economic empires. In a word, Marx's labor law of value and its corollary, the law
of maximization of profits, is the driving force of the new phase of globalization and worldwide wage competition.

Marx long ago explained that it is the development of the productive forces that creates new classes and destroys outmoded ones. Capitalism is compelled to constantly revolutionize the means of production, and as a consequence the character and relationships of existing classes constantly undergo
transformation. The transformation of the world working class is underway
in the post-Soviet era in a direction that must produce a momentous reawak-
ening and upsurge of the class struggle.

2

New global networks of exploitation

Dell: 'Collaboration of individuals' or global regimentation of workers? • Toyota, the pioneer
Hewlett-Packard • IBM • Liz Claiborne • U.S. auto companies • Boeing • Making stuff cheap

Over the past ten to fifteen years the giant monopolies of the United States, Europe, and Japan have been systematically adopting the major technological advances of the period. They have been reorganizing world production processes and, more recently, services so as to streamline and accelerate the process of global capitalist exploitation and super-exploitation.

In stages they have developed and utilized the technology to increasingly segment the labor process and relocate its various segments to low-wage areas around the globe, including in their own countries, and they have constructed vast, interconnected, worldwide networks of wage slavery, dominated by corporate giants. This latest evolution of world capitalism is calculated to incorporate the newly available global workforce into the process of capitalist exploitation.

This segmented labor process is referred to by bourgeois economists and officials variously as "production chains," "production networks," "value chains," and so on. Federal Reserve System chairperson Bernanke and others describe this economic expansion into India, China, the former USSR, Eastern Europe, and elsewhere as a process of "global integration." But this benign terminology is meant to conceal and prettify the brutal class essence of the process, which is not only integration but also **subjugation** of hundreds of millions of workers into chains or networks of **exploitation and super-exploitation**, an expansion of finance capital's enslavement of wage labor.

Dell: 'Collaboration of individuals' or global regimentation of workers?

A textbook description of this restructuring, written from the capitalist point of view, is provided in a section of Thomas Friedman's book *The World Is Flat*, which has become a bible for the bourgeoisie.

Friedman was so enamored of the age of the "collaboration of individuals," as he puts it, that he went to the Dell management center in Austin, Texas, before he wrote the book to research the process by which the Dell computer on which he was going to write his book was made. Dell at the time sold about 140,000 to 150,000 computers a day and was the largest maker of personal computers in the world. It has recently been surpassed by Hewlett-Packard.

Here are some of the highlights of the detailed information he presented.

Once his order was placed by phone it went to Penang, Malaysia, one of the six Dell factories in the world (the others were in Limerick, Ireland; Xiamen, China; Eldorado do Sul, Brazil; Nashville, Tennessee; and Austin, Texas). Surrounding every Dell factory are numerous parts supply centers, called Supplier Logistic Centers (SLCs), owned by different suppliers. They are like staging areas. "If you are a Dell supplier anywhere in the world, your job is to keep your SLC full of your specific parts so they can constantly be trucked over to the Dell factory for just-in-time manufacturing."[30]

Dell Malaysia sends an e-mail every two hours to its SLC telling it what parts it wants within the next ninety minutes. Trucks from the SLCs pull up, a bar code for each part is recorded, and the parts are loaded into bins for assembly. It was not possible to tell precisely where the parts for Friedman's notebook came from without taking it apart. But even an account of the various possibilities is revealing.

The Intel processor came from an Intel factory located in either the Philippines, Costa Rica, Malaysia, or China. The memory came from locally owned factories in south Korea, Taiwan, Germany, or Japan. The graphics card could have come from a Taiwanese-owned factory in China, the motherboard from a Korean-owned factory in Shanghai, and the hard disk from a Japanese-owned factory in Indonesia or Malaysia, and so on.

Each component, including the modem, battery, LCD, power cord, memory stick, carrying bag, etc., could have been made at any one of multiple suppliers throughout the region, including Thailand, Indonesia, or Singapore. Dell makes sure it has a stable of suppliers on hand to compete with each other and have parts available at all times. It is the suppliers that must keep the inventory on hand in order to keep Dell's business from going elsewhere.

With breathless wonder Friedman recounts how the parts were picked and screwed together, the software was downloaded, the computer was boxed and coded, specially placed on a pallet for transportation, and put on a nightly chartered Dell 747, along with 25,000 other notebooks, total weight a quarter of a million pounds, to land at the Dell airport in Nashville, Tennessee, the next day. There it was put in a larger box and shipped by UPS to Bethesda, Maryland. Under optimal conditions it would take four days from placing the telephoned order to delivery.

The total "supply chain" for this computer, including suppliers of suppliers, came to about 400 companies in North America, Europe, and Asia, mostly the latter, with about thirty prime suppliers.

Friedman, true to character, thinks only of suppliers, companies, parts, and logistics. While he did inquire about the names of the workers who took his order and helped create his computer, this had nothing to do with any concern for the workers themselves. He never asked about or described the conditions of labor, the wages, hours, job security, health benefits, vacation, safety, or union status of the workers, who actually constitute the living supply chain, the living labor that makes it all happen—even if it is orchestrated by Dell and managed by the supply companies. Friedman's interest in the names of particular workers arose because he was dazzled, as any boss would be, by the information-gathering, i.e., overseeing capability of Dell's workflow software, which can track every worker from Texas to Singapore to Brazil. Other than that, the workers in this Asia-wide regional production do not rate a mention.

Barry Lynn, on the other hand, who gives a more summarized overview of Dell's operations, at least includes the workers in his description and gives a sense of Dell's empire.

Lynn describes the Dell facilities in Austin and Nashville as "storefronts" that conceal an assembly line stretching more than 10,000 miles.

> Dell in the 1990s was one of the first manufacturers to come of age in a world fully familiar with Toyota's just-in-time production system, very much at ease with the idea of employing workers and engineers and managers in many nations in a single common effort, fully able to take advantage of the highly advanced logistics services managed by others. Blended together, the result was that Dell learned how to coordinate manufacturing done in its name by hundreds or even thousands of companies around the world, thereby commanding the labor of tens of thousands if not hundreds of thousands of workers, and then choreographed the overall operation as neatly as if it were all happening under one roof.[31]

Trucks line up outside the Dell assembly plants to insure the steady flow of parts from all around the world, which, in turn, insures the steady process of production and exploitation. The workers in the assembly plants screw, bolt, or snap together the parts and download the software. One person can assemble a computer in about four and a half minutes.[32]

Toyota, the pioneer

Lynn's reference to Toyota involves the Japanese auto giant's pioneering of the system of organizing a vast network of suppliers owned by outside companies but linked to the so-called "lead firm." This network organizes the capital, including the workers, and has to meet Toyota's short-term demand for components and subassemblies. Toyota's main suppliers are clustered around its assembly plants. It can order parts as needed so that it does not have to invest in large inventories and can supply its assembly lines with parts "just in time." If there is a reduction in the sales of a model, the method of just-in-time production enables Toyota to reduce production quickly so as to minimize any loss of profit due to unsold vehicles. Toyota has made numerous innovations, including the reduction of down time for changing dies, aimed at minimizing time lost and maximizing time in which to exploit the workers.

This method was perfected by the 1980s, when the Toyota empire already had 168 first-tier subcontractors, 4,700 second-tier subcontractors, and 31,600 third-tier suppliers.[33] In addition to the Big Three auto companies, numerous corporate giants in the U.S. studied the Toyota model, including General Electric, Westinghouse, and Wal-Mart.

Unlike Dell, Toyota owned or partially funded some of its major suppliers. But like Dell, it had dozens of suppliers clustered around its assembly plants, which were spread out, mostly throughout Asia. Toyota continued to build networks of "captive suppliers" who were subject to "constant pressure to improve their performance, both through constant comparison with other suppliers and contracts based on falling costs and (therefore) delivery prices."[34] Virtually all the big Japanese monopolies—Toshiba, Matsushita, NEC, Panasonic, Mitsubishi, Sony—sit on top of tiers of dependent and subordinate suppliers and subcontractors regionally and globally disbursed.

Hewlett-Packard

By the mid-1990s Hewlett-Packard, which recently passed Dell as the world's number one supplier of personal computers, was laying off production workers and selling off most of its manufacturing plants and engineering design activities. Jobs that were once carried out within HP were sent to contract manufacturers, mostly in Asia.[35] This was hardly a prelude to the company's decline. Today HP has 150,000 workers in 178 countries, in addition to the workers who turn out HP computers and printers in the contract manufacturing firms.

Using Internet technology (IT) to coordinate its production made HP an expert in its use. Today, boosted by massive, subcontracted low-wage labor, it has become a $50-billion global colossus. It is now the largest supplier of electronic consumer technology in the world. But it is also, according to Friedman, the largest IT company in Europe, Russia, the Middle East, and South Africa.[36] It is also getting a stranglehold in India, where it has recently taken over the entire in-house technology operation of the Bank of India in Mumbai. It has three transaction processing centers—in Bangalore, Barcelona, and Guadalajara—and workflow software that allows it to process its billing transactions from 178 countries. HP now derives the majority of its profits from outside the United States.[37]

International Business Machines

In 1996 IBM began shedding its factories and moving production work to contract manufacturing. The degree of reliance on labor from low-wage countries is illustrated by a breakdown of the production of components for the IBM ThinkPad X31. The breakdown is for a model assembled in 2004 by the contract manufacturer Sanmina-SCI, which further subcontracted out the production. Assembly took place in Mexico. The memory and the display screen were made in south Korea; the case, the keyboard, and the hard drive in Thailand; the battery in Malaysia; the graphics controller in Taiwan. The microprocessor was the only component made in the U.S., by Intel. Other laptops were being assembled in Scotland and Shenzen, China. There were 4,000 workers in the Shenzen assembly plant, representing 40 percent of the IBM PC workforce.

IBM sold its PC unit to the Chinese company Lenovo in December 2004, but it kept 18.9 percent ownership in the company. The two main manufacturing facilities were to be in Shenzen and Raleigh, North Carolina, a right-to-work, anti-union, low-wage state in the U.S.[38]

Liz Claiborne

Liz Claiborne is a giant apparel company that did more than $4 billion in sales in 2004. It owns and markets numerous brand names. Claiborne keeps its high-end designer brands here in the U.S. For example, Lucky jeans, which sell for about $100, are designed here. The zippers, denim, and trim are purchased from suppliers. They are sewn and given a stonewashed and sanded finish by Latina/o workers in Los Angeles factories owned by south Koreans and supervised by Lucky managers.

But it also makes low-end, mass-marketed Faded Glory jeans, which sold at Wal-Mart for $11 in 2004 and were made in Mexico. In fact, Liz Claiborne had 512 contractors in forty-five different countries in 1995. The strategy of having so many suppliers was based upon fomenting competition among them in order to keep the cost at the absolute minimum. Gradually, Claiborne sifted out the best and overcame the inefficiency involved in having so many suppliers, so that the number has now been reduced to 250 in thirty-five countries. As of 2004 the company was planning to offshore more of the jobs still left in the United States.[39]

U.S. auto companies

Automobiles are heavy. Shipping is costly and each model is uniquely designed, in part at least—unlike computers, apparel/textiles, shoes, etc. Nevertheless, the auto barons, in pursuit of maximum profit, are attempting to utilize the new structure of capitalist production to lower wages wherever possible.

General Motors, Ford, and Chrysler are all restructuring. As of early 2008, they had announced plans to get rid of more than 70,000 union jobs and shut down twenty assembly plants in the United States. But as they close unionized plants, destroying workers' lives and entire communities in the U.S., they are going offshore to seek out low-wage labor.

For example, GM is spending $600 million to build a new assembly plant in San Luis Potosi, Mexico, that will employ 2,000 workers by 2008. Mexican assembly workers average $3.50 an hour compared to $27.00 an hour in Detroit. But that is only part of the story. The GM and Ford assembly plants in Mexico are themselves outsourcing to suppliers who deliver pre-assembled pieces of cars directly to the factory floor. At the Mexican plant of auto parts maker Delphi, skilled workers get $1.50 an hour.

Ford, which is shutting down fourteen plants in the U.S., recently spent $1 billion expanding its Mexican plant in Hermasillo to create 2,000 new jobs, in addition to the 1,200 workers already at the plant. As a price for making the investment in Mexico, the company forced concessions from the Ford Auto Workers Union in Mexico, demanding more flexible work rules and lower starting wages. As a result, half of the factory's 3,000 workers make $2.00 an hour.[40]

Delphi and Visteon are the two largest auto parts suppliers in the world. That is because they previously belonged to GM and Ford, respectively. Both were "spun off" as part of the auto companies' plans to reduce labor costs. Delphi has declared bankruptcy for its U.S. operations, which are unionized by the UAW. Its overseas operations employ 115,000 workers. Many of these branches operate in low-wage countries like Mexico and China and are not part of the bankruptcy procedure. The company's immediate goal is to reduce U.S. workers' wages from $27.00 an hour to $16.50 an hour. Its long-term goal is to reduce its U.S. workforce from 32,000 to 7,000, destroying 25,000 union jobs.[41]

In 2006 Visteon had 49,000 workers at 170 locations in twenty-six countries.[42] In November of that year the company announced it was cutting 13.9 percent of its salaried workforce in North America and Europe—6,900 workers—and relocating to low-wage countries at an annual savings of $75 million in labor costs. The company recently opened a 110,000-square-foot software engineering center in India and new climate control facilities in China, Turkey, and Slovakia. Visteon's goal is to have 50 percent of its engineering workforce in low-wage countries by 2008, up from a third, and 75 percent of its hourly workers in low-wage countries, up from 68 percent, also by 2008.

Boeing

The search for cheap engineering labor and speed-up of production at Boeing intensified after the fall of the Berlin Wall, when the counter-revolution in the USSR was coming to a climax. In 1991 Boeing started to farm out work to Soviet scientists who had designed high-quality aircraft for the Ilyushin, Tupolev, and Sukhoi divisions of the state-owned industry. By 1998, when Russia had become capitalist, Boeing set up a twenty-four-hour operation, with two shifts in Moscow and one in the U.S., in both Seattle and Wichita, Kansas, using fiber-optic cable, workflow software, and videoconferencing to connect them.

Russian engineering labor was $40 an hour compared to $120 an hour in the U.S. But as important as it was to get cheap Russian labor, the ultimate aim of the design work was to increase the rate of exploitation, i.e., productiveness, of the assembly workers, and to fight Boeing's European corporate rival, Airbus. The time it took to produce a Boeing 737 was brought down from twenty-eight days to eleven days. The next generation of aircraft will be built in three days, according to Friedman.[43]

Of course, the new Russian bourgeoisie had converted the aircraft industry from branches of planned socialist production into individual profit-making companies. So the Russian bosses, in order to increase their cut of the profits, emulated Boeing by outsourcing part of their work to an even lower-wage supplier in Bangalore, India.

Making stuff cheap

A typical example of the bourgeois spirit of greed expressed in the new-found craze for low wages is reported by Suzanne Berger, leader of the MIT study mentioned earlier. She cited the example of a London clothing manufacturer, which refused to be named, as did its CEO (with good reason).

This "manufacturer," whom Berger calls Alpha, like Dell, has no factories. About eighty people work in its London offices but it outsources to Romanian subcontractors with giant plants that employ about 10,000 workers. Alpha "makes" about 120,000 tailored jackets, slacks, and skirts a week.

The London CEO was reading an article one day about Airbus and its outsourcing system. "For me it was a life-changing idea," he told Berger. The article explained that as long as Britain kept the technology for making the wings of the plane, and let the seats and all the rest be made in the cheapest places, Britain would always have good profits and jobs from the wings.

So, ten years ago, Alpha closed its apparel factories in Britain and moved its production to Romanian contractors who work only for British corporations. Alpha used its worldwide "supply chain" to buy zippers, lining, buttons, hangers, plastic bags, etc. If one garment has twenty components and there are 4 million garments, then 80 million pieces must be brought from the lowest-wage places available and delivered to the Romanian subcontractors.

Alpha has its overseers in the factories, but its control over the process goes way beyond that. Using workflow software, the company sets up a private network so that factory managers, customers, and the London office can all be in the same virtual room. If, for example, a certain type of sleeve is wanted, the pattern for the sleeve is picked up from an electronic company library by the cutting machine in the factory, which then cuts the sleeve according to the specifications.

Berger asked the head of Alpha why he doesn't contract out to Asia, where labor costs are low. At first he talked about "quality" and how you "develop factories you now love." But then he blurted out his racist, chauvinist, bourgeois bottom line. "To be fair, in Romania they are earning about three bowls of rice and a cup of tea every day. For how much less are you going to find anyone to make stuff for you?"[44] This is the true voice of imperialist "globalization."

And this is the spirit that is sweeping the boardrooms from Wall Street to London, Paris, Berlin, Rome, and Tokyo. They are intoxicated with the opening for increased profits unleashed by and inherent in the new technology. Levi's has shut down sixty-plus plants, mostly in the southwest of the U.S., in order to seek sweatshop labor from Indonesia to the Caribbean. Wal-Mart has forced its suppliers to go all over the world to get the lowest price and then come back next year with an even lower price. Apple is moving its overseas center to Singapore; Alcoa is moving to Iceland, Brazil, Russia, and China.

3

Supply chains: vassals of the lords of capitalism

Flextronics, the lead vassal · Solectron · Boeing and 'reverse auctions' · Cisco
sheds factories · Contracting out for super-profits · Price-setters and price-takers:
workers are on the bottom · Fears of the overseers and secrecy of the monopolies

The basis for the new global restructuring is the creation of hundreds of thousands of large, medium, and small capitalist firms that compete to serve the giant monopolies. These suppliers are linked to the giant corporations in a variety of relationships. Some serve to make one or a few components. Others make entire commodities and are committed to only one monopoly or one industry. Others do design or engineering work. Still others do partial or even complete assembly work, and so on.

But what they all have in common is that they are modern-day vassals of the giant lords of capital. They are vassals in the sense that they are dependents. Their relationship to the monopolies may be contractual, but they are as much an integral part of the global corporate empires of the companies they serve as if they were owned directly by them.

Like the vassals of the feudal lords, they gather around IBM, General Electric, Motorola, Procter & Gamble, Nike, Citibank, JPMorgan Chase, and most of the Fortune 500, in addition to the European and Japanese transnationals, and are granted a share of the surplus value—i.e., profit—extracted from the growing global networks of wage slaves.

In feudal times, the higher vassals were granted the use of land belonging to the lords with the right to exploit the serfs or land slaves attached to it, in return for service in the dynastic wars. The higher vassals, in turn, granted parts of these lands, along with their serfs, to subordinates in return for allegiance, and these subordinates further divided their lands and their land slaves to even lower orders.

In the same way today, these subordinate exploiters, called "first-tier" suppliers, subcontract out the work to second-tier capitalists, who take their cut of the profit from the exploitation of the workers while contracting out to lower tiers of suppliers.

Flextronics, the lead vassal

A prime example of a supply organizer that serves the multinationals is a company that is little known, either to the general public or the working class. Its name is Flextronics. It has more than 100,000 workers of its own, aside from those exploited by the lower-level suppliers it deals with. Its headquarters is in Singapore, although it was founded out of Silicon Valley by a Harvard-educated MBA. If it were on the Fortune 500 list it would be number 138. In 2006 it had $15.3 billion in revenue.

Flextronics promotes itself on its Web site as a true supplicant to the giants of the electronics industry, having "established an extensive network of design, manufacturing and logistics facilities in the world's major electronics markets ... to serve the growing outsourcing needs of both multinational and regional OEMs [original engineering manufacturers, or giant multinational corporations, FG]."[45]

> We are a global industry leader in low-cost production capabilities. Our significant investments in manufacturing facilities in low-cost regions of the world enable us to provide our customers with competitive manufacturing costs. The majority of our manufacturing capacity is located in low-cost regions such as Mexico, Brazil, Poland, Hungary, China, India, Malaysia, and other parts of Asia.[46]

In 2006 Flextronics had factories in more than thirty countries on five continents, including in South Africa. It established industrial "parks" for its clients. It has given this cheery name to nine gigantic facilities where it provides "total supply chain management by co-locating our manufacturing and logistics [supplying and shipping—FG] operations with our suppliers at a single low-cost location." The industrial "parks" are located in Gdansk, Poland; eastern and western Hungary; Guadalajara and Juarez in Mexico; Sorocaba, Brazil; Chennai, India; and Doumen and Shanghai in China.[47] In February 2007 Flextronics set up an Internet supply portal in Tczew, Poland, that offers its corporate customers on-line ordering. Some twenty-three production facilities can order 60,000 different parts from 1,400 suppliers.[48]

As of 2004, according to Jeff Ferry in the magazine *strategy+business*, Flextronics made all of Microsoft's Xbox games (for a contract worth $750 million a year), most of Hewlett-Packard's inkjet printers ($1 billion), all of

Xerox's desktop copiers ($1 billion), and all of Sony Ericsson's cell phones ($2 billion). In early 2004 Nortel made Flextronics its largest supplier, farming out much of its production of telecommunications equipment ($2 billion).[49]

Sun Microsystems made Flextronics one of its major suppliers, among 26 others, when it outsourced 90 percent of its production. Flextronics designed cell phones for Motorola and then got the manufacturing contract for more than $1 billion.[50]

Michael Marks, its founder and CEO, explains the strategy of a subordinate capitalist navigating the new structure of the imperialist competition. "If you boil it down, there's one principle, and it's the age-old 'listen to the customer.' Each service and each geography we added, we added because that's what our customers told us to do."[51,*]

It is of interest that Flextronics got its real start as a major supplier in 1993 when it bought an Austrian-based firm, Neutronics, from the Dutch electronics giant Philips. It thereby acquired four large industrial facilities in Hungary, where production workers were getting three dollars an hour compared with twenty dollars an hour in countries like France, Germany, and Austria.[52] Flextronics is a living beneficiary of the capitalist counter-revolution, as further illustrated by its major facilities near the city of Gdansk, Poland. It was at the Gdansk shipyards, now closed, where the overthrow of socialism began its initial phase.

The value of the contract suppliers to the ruling class was directly and brutally stated by the head of HP's global Imaging and Printing Division. Mike Fawkes, a senior vice president, told Ferry that "a couple of years ago Mexico got very expensive for consumer products, and we moved our production to the Flex factory in Shanghai. To be able to do that is a beautiful thing. If I had to build or shut down my own factories, the lead times would be very long."[53]

Marks displayed the same calloused indifference to the fate of the workers in describing how the company revamped its business during the downturn after the tech bubble burst in March, 2000 followed by the recession of 2001 . From 2001 to 2004 it shifted toward consumer electronics. In the process "our net employment went up, but we had to let 10,000 people go. Our business shifted away from the U.S. and Western Europe. The growth was in Asia, Eastern Europe, and Mexico." Thus, between 2001 and 2004,

---

* The monopolies have their pick of suppliers and make them prove themselves before being selected. For example, Nortel first began testing Flextronics' manufacturing capabilities (its workers' abilities, that is) in 2003, using it to do some wireless and switching work. Flextronics passed the cost-reduction test and was awarded a major contract in 2004.

Flextronics **laid off** workers in high-wage, i.e., imperialist countries, while it **increased** the number of jobs in low-wage countries by a number exceeding the layoffs.[54]

The dominance of the giants and the fact that they take the lion's share of the surplus value produced by the workers shows up in the difference in profit margins between them and the contract suppliers. Flextronics, for all its global efforts and with 100,000 workers, made 6 percent profit in 2004. The giant electronics firms, however, typically earn double-digit super-profits. "The margins are slender in contract manufacturing," wrote Ferry, who contrasted General Electric's 36 percent profit margins with the paltry take of Flextronics.[55]

Solectron

The next largest electronics contract manufacturer is Solectron. It has a similar profile, with more than 50,000 workers, $10 billion in revenue, and a global network of more than fifty facilities in twenty countries. It is based in Portland, Oregon, and has plants in the major imperialist countries in Europe and Japan. But its presence is heavily weighted toward low-wage countries (and in the low-wage South in the U.S.). It has plants in Sao Paulo, Brazil; Chihuahua, Mexico; and Aguadilla, Puerto Rico. In Asia, it has nine plants in China alone and is also in India, Indonesia, Malaysia, Singapore, and Taiwan. In Eastern Europe it is in the Czech Republic, Hungary, and Romania. It also has a plant in Turkey.

Solectron has numerous plants in the U.S. but the majority of them are in the low-wage Southern states: Alabama, Georgia, Kentucky, three plants in the right-to-work state of North Carolina, and others in South Carolina, Tennessee, and Texas.[56]

The system of contracting out production is dominant in the global electronics industry in many forms. The Taiwan Semiconductor Manufacturing Company (TSMC) is the largest dedicated foundry for the production of semiconductors. It produces semiconductor chips for the industry but does not develop its own products. In 2004 it had revenues of $2.7 billion with foundries in Taiwan, China, and Singapore. It makes chips for the monopolies that used to make their own—companies like Texas Instruments, IBM, and Philips—saving them the huge capital investment in fabrication foundries, which now cost up to $3 billion apiece.[57] A whole host of similar dedicated chip-makers sprang up to serve the transnationals in the wake of TSMC's success. In fact, TSMC was founded by a partnership between Philips and the Taiwanese government.

Quanta, another Taiwanese company, is Dell's supplier and in 2004 made one out of every four PC laptops in the world. In that year its revenue was $10 billion. "In order to produce final goods," writes Berger, "companies like Dell, Broadcom, Cisco, the Gap, Nike need to link up with these nonbrand contract manufacturers like Quanta, Hon Hai, Solectron, Flextronics, Fang Brothers, Pou Chen. These names are mostly unknown to the public, but they make our computers, our MP3 players, our sweatshirts, and our sneakers."[58] What she really means is that low-wage workers around the world make these commodities, which bring in handsome profits to the so-called "lead firms," i.e., monopolies that dominate the industries.

As Berger indicated, this structure applies not only to the electronics industry. For example, one Taiwanese company, Pou Chen, with factories in the People's Republic of China, owns a subsidiary in Hong Kong that is the world's largest contract manufacturer of sneakers. In 2002, it produced 130 million pairs of shoes and sneakers for Nike, New Balance, Reebok, and Adidas.[59]

Boeing and 'reverse auctions'

Boeing, together with Europe's Airbus, sits atop the aircraft industry. It can dictate to suppliers of structures, systems, interiors, raw materials, and so on. Boeing Commercial Aircraft (BCA) is constantly trying to drive down costs, especially labor costs, and speed up production. Key or first-tier suppliers have been reduced by BCA from 3,800 to 1,200. Just as in the auto industry, Boeing is demanding subassemblies in kits. The role of suppliers is taken right to the production line. For example, the moving production line for the Boeing 737 signals suppliers, who have been brought to the site, when workers on the production line need parts, mainly subassemblies. The supplier is supposed to deliver the kit right to the line. Just as in auto, the workers employed by the suppliers may or may not be unionized. In any case, so-called "parts" workers, who are doing more and more assembly work, have lower wages than workers on the final assembly line, even if they are in the same plant.[60]

The vice president of BCA's Global Partners, Steve Schaffer, told Reed Business Information about how highly the company regards its suppliers—thus the name Global Partners. But the fact is that Boeing puts maximum pressure on suppliers. Thomas Friedman describes Boeing's "reverse auction." Boeing has an Internet site that all the suppliers have to monitor. The company announces a date and time for the auction. It posts its starting price for each item, everything from toilet paper to nuts and bolts—all off-the-shelf parts. Everyone can see everyone else's bid. Then Boeing sits back and watches everyone bid everyone else down. "It's like watching a horse race," says Friedman.[61] But this "horse race" ends up with the ultimate pressure being put on the workers in the so-called supply chain.

Barry Lynn, writing in 2004, shows how fiercely the monopolies have seized upon the contract manufacturing system as the path to cheap labor and reduction of constant capital costs. Lynn describes how, at many of the Flextronics plants, the company has set up multiple assembly lines to serve multiple customers, locating the product runs of even vicious rivals right next to each other on the factory floor. "A telecom product stamped with the Cisco brand may be assembled within a few feet of a product stamped Nortel, in a process overseen by a single group of workers and technicians. But even the most paranoid of the big branded companies have learned quickly to accept this arrangement, as such pooling of people [low-wage workers—FG] and machines reduces the cost of manufacturing by between 10 and 20 percent compared to a single company."[62] Lynn failed to add, compared to a single company in a high-wage country.

"Not surprisingly," he continues, "contract manufacturers have emerged in many other industries, including clothes, toys, shoes, pharmaceuticals, and semiconductors, even brewing and the processing of food. The model is increasingly common in aerospace and is growing especially fast in the automotive industry."[63]

Cisco sheds factories

Cisco is a technology company that had $28.5 billion in sales and 54,500 workers directly employed in 2007. It markets routers, switches, and many other devices and software, all of which direct the flow of information on the Internet. Cisco built its leading position in the world by abandoning the ownership of most manufacturing facilities and instead outsourcing most of its production all over the globe. In the mid-1990s, as the technology boom gathered increasing momentum and the market for routers was rapidly expanding, Cisco was doing most of its manufacturing in California. Its strategy for capturing the growing markets was to begin searching the world for outside manufacturers to make its products. Between 1994 and 1996 Cisco got rid of 75 percent of the company-owned manufacturing and thereafter even contracted out its assembly operations.

By the year 2000, 90 percent of Cisco's subassembly work took place outside California in thirty-four plants around the world, only two of which were owned by Cisco. Of the workers who produced Cisco products, only 15 percent were Cisco workers. Cisco "estimated that turning over manufacturing to outside contractors each year cuts ... production costs by between $900 million and $1.3 billion."[64]

When the technology boom turned into a bust in 2001, Cisco cut its payroll from 38,400 workers to 34,440. But most of the workers who made Cisco products labored for contractors that Cisco could "cut at will."[65] Many of the contract manufacturers kept more than half their workers on as temporaries. So during the collapse of 2001 many tens of thousands of workers did lose their jobs without making any headlines in the U.S. They were spread out among small outsourcing contractors in the U.S. and offshore in countries like Brazil, China, Mexico, and Hungary.[66]

Contracting out for super-profits

This example of Cisco can be extended to virtually all the giant monopolies. It clearly illustrates several major strategic advantages for the bosses of the new global restructuring. During times of capitalist expansion, the bosses can quickly expand production by putting out more work to contract suppliers without increasing their investment in plant and equipment. During times of capitalist overproduction and crisis, the global networking of production allows the transnationals to push much of their crisis onto the backs of oppressed workers far from the shores of the so-called "lead firms."

Furthermore, the arrangement of tiers of low-wage suppliers, contract manufacturers, and other subordinates hampers the ability of the workers to unite and resist the central economic decision makers and principal beneficiaries of these networks of super-exploitation—namely the Ciscos, Dells, IBMs, etc.

The production networks act as a shield for the masters of capital.

The network arrangement diffuses the crisis of layoffs or cutbacks over a wide region and spreads the local responsibility to many different owners. Furthermore, and most importantly, it transfers much of the crisis onto the backs of the low-wage workers, while it eases the social crisis in the imperialist centers. In addition it pushes a great deal of the economic loss onto the backs of the suppliers, generally producing a ripple effect among the workers and small businesses, and spreads much of the secondary damage to the low-wage countries. Thus not only are the layoffs at the lead firm accompanied by layoffs among its suppliers, but the multiplier effect brings even wider layoffs in the affected communities in the low-wage countries.

Lynn, who is clearly critical of the monopolies and sympathetic to the workers but is hardly a radical, gives the following assessment of the significance of contract manufacturers for the giant corporations:

When a company like Cisco accelerates the disintegration of manufacturing activity within the lead corporation, the results mean very different things for the shareholder and for the worker. For the shareholder, one of the prime benefits of off-loading work from the lead firm onto other companies is to transform fixed costs into variable costs. Any firm able to slough off plants and workers in bad times is better able to protect its margins, hence its return on investment, and highly outsourced companies are obviously much more able to do this. Such flexibility is one of the oldest and most enduring dreams of capital, and it has been pursued often with great vigor by the salesmen and financial experts who dominate the ranks of CEOs today.[67]

Later in the book, Lynn writes:

In many senses, Flextronics and the other contract manufacturers are the powers that made possible Cisco's power. But theirs is a limited power, that of a valued but always expendable employee. In a new global economy populated by ever more aristocratic and even dilettantish lead firms, Flextronics and its colleagues have come to serve increasingly as the foremen, responsible for rounding up the workers and getting them to work.[68]

Earlier in the same work, Lynn had observed:

Another way to understand what has happened is to look not at the process of outsourcing but at the network of production that results naturally from any system-wide outsourcing. In a sense, any such network can be viewed as common property that belongs to all the companies that rely on it.[69]

Lynn bemoans the fact that since no one entity owns this network, no one is in charge of watching out for the risks, etc. He does point out that "the nature of competition results in a race among users to exploit the common system most effectively."[70] But being a bourgeois himself, he cannot lay the responsibility at the feet of capitalism. He regards the anarchy of production and the vicious, anti-worker corporate competition for global dominance as a failure of governmental regulatory policy, rather than as the inevitable results of the profit system itself.

But Lynn's characterization of the production networks and the "foremen[,] responsible for rounding up the workers" as "the common property that belongs to the companies" which rely on them is the key to the new structure of imperialist super-exploitation by contract.

The United Nations Industrial Development Organization (UNIDO) did a study of globalization with reference to sub-Saharan Africa in the year 2000. It described this key new feature—of the economic structure of super-profits by contract—in a section entitled "From physical to digital markets." The document, using elliptical language, actually refutes the idea of a so-called global marketplace of classical capitalist competition and describes the market dominated by monopolies. It discusses the difference between the classical supply-and-demand capitalist economic theory of the free marketplace and what it calls "market discipline" imposed by the corporate giants.[71]

The study puts forward "the theoretical proposition that the difference between a global market place and a global market discipline is that whereas, in the case of the former, the market price is the outcome of the interplay between supply and demand, in which supply has always been a function of so-called **cost price plus** calculations, in the case of a global market discipline, prices are determined on the **market price minus** principle." [72] [Emphasis in original.]

The document then cites the process previously described in the case of Boeing and its subcontractors.

> In the "real time" world of digital markets we see, for example, the emergence of what have been termed "reverse markets" or "auction" markets in which consumers post on-line what they are willing to pay for products or services. *Priceline.com,* for example, is an on-line auction place that allows consumers to set the price at which they will buy an airplane ticket. Airlines can then decide if they want to "hit the bid" and fill a consumer's order. **On a big scale** producer/manufacturing companies, such as General Electric, Ford, Chrysler have web-based links to their suppliers that enable these to make bids for component contracts. For example, *FreeMarkets Online* has developed software that enables large industrial buyers to organize on-line auctions for qualified suppliers of semi-standardized parts like fabricated electronic components. Auction bidding drives the cost down to the purchaser by about 15-40%. The cost-reducing potential of digital (real time) markets constitutes the core of the claims by globalists and new economy enthusiasts of all-round growth and prosperity.[73] [Emphasis added.]

Subcontractors are like foremen rounding up the workers of the world on behalf of the big monopolies

This was in the year 2000; the process has since progressed further.

Thus is laid bare one of the key mechanisms of garnering super-profits from low-wage workers. Under the international division of labor in the earlier period of imperialism, prior to the leap forward in communications and Internet technology, General Electric, Ford, Chrysler, and any other giant transnational corporation garnered super-profits, i.e., profits over and above those extracted from "their own" working class, by simply forcing workers they employed in the oppressed countries to work for low, colonial-level wages and then keeping the extra surplus value in the form of fabulous profits.

In the present stage, the monopolies derive super-profits by forcing their capitalist contractors and subcontractors to surrender to the corporate overlords part of the normal profits derived from the exploitation of low-wage workers in their employ. This is in addition to the super-profits made by the large firms from the super-exploitation of workers whom they employ directly. The transnationals force the prices down, driving their contractors to bring greater pressure on the workers. Meanwhile, the monopolies pocket the extra profits. They accomplish this because they control the end markets, the brands, the key technology, and sometimes the financing needed.

Price-setters and price-takers: workers are on the bottom

Some of the giant brand-name companies send teams of engineers to "live" in the contractor's plant to monitor operations and keep the pressure on. Others set up pilot factories and learn the manufacturing process so they can always have a credible threat to take business away from the contractor. Still others make sure to maintain multiple suppliers so they can threaten to move production around and keep their vassals in line. Berger shows how U.S. apparel giants like Ralph Lauren, Jones NY, Liz Claiborne, the Gap, and Calvin Klein, among others, give their suppliers such large orders that these suppliers become dependent on the giant monopolies for most of their business and are forced to accept their terms or risk going under.

An unnamed apparel executive in an interview with Berger's MIT team explained how it works. "The CEO of Liz Claiborne or of Jones or one of the others will say to Kenneth Fang, president of Fang Brothers, Hong Kong, one of the world's largest manufacturers of apparel, 'We'll give you an order for 30,000 units per month; which factory will you give us?' If you're a Liz Claiborne or a Jones NY or a Kellwood, and you find a good factory, you want to control it, hence to do the lion's share of the manufacturing in that plant. Say it's Liz. They'll say, 'We have to control our own destiny.' The physical plant Liz is in, Liz controls. Fang may own it, but to all intents and purposes it is your plant."[74]

The giant firms use this power to completely dominate the manufacturing process. Cisco outsources most of its production yet maintains control over the process. "Cisco controls databases, quality control, and production monitoring even when outsourced," writes Berger. "For instance, data from contract manufacturers' quality-control systems can be pulled by Cisco at any time to find out everything about the product—who made it, where it was made, and when."[75]

Of course, Berger leaves out the fact that this gives Cisco control over the workers, their speed of production, etc., as well as over the supplier capitalists.

An executive from Timisoarawear, a Romanian apparel company, re-counts: "Our German clients ... continually watch over our shoulders and tell us how to do everything. The Germans have their own technicians who are in the plant every day....

"Even with long-standing German customers, we have endless negotiations about every conceivable problem that could come up. One of these German brand-name firms had 60 percent of our capacity. Two years ago, they wanted to place a big order and insisted on a lower price. We hesitated, and they cut us off with a single fax—even though we'd been doing business with them for years."[76]

A prominent Taiwanese laptop computer maker told an MIT interviewer that, no matter how much travel his engineers did, he dared not let them use business-class seats, for fear that they would be seen on the plane by a customer who would conclude that there was still "fat" that could be shaved off his prices. Berger concluded: "Although they may negotiate over price, essentially the lead firms are price-setters and the outsourcers are price-takers, and the wishes and whims of the lead firms ordinarily win out...."[77] So much for the "free market" under the domination of the monopolies.

Thus, while the transnationals make high, "above-normal" profits, the subcontractors make below-normal profits. At the bottom are the low-wage workers, whose labor has supplied all the surplus value with the sweat of their brow, while the lion's share goes into the vaults of super-rich imperialists. This is how it works out that Flextronics, a $15-billion contract manufacturer, the largest in the world, makes 6 percent profit while General Electric, a $300-billion monopoly, makes 36 percent.

This is a new global form of imperialist super-exploitation, carried out through subordinate capitalist intermediaries and enforced by contract backed up by monopoly power. It is these intermediaries that run the sweatshops, enforce unsafe, unsanitary working conditions with low wages, speed-up, anti-union policies, reduced or no benefits, and so on. Squeezing the workers is the only way these capitalist "foremen" can bolster their profits so there is enough to satisfy the giant firms and still have some margin of the loot left over for themselves.

Fears of the overseers and secrecy of the monopolies

The question on the minds of the managers of capitalism is: Where is all this leading? Of course, this question should also be on the minds of every labor leader and all leaders of the workers and the oppressed. However, the extent of this development is being kept secret by the bosses, precisely because it is such an explosive issue for the working class.

The bosses have told the federal government not to collect data on offshoring and not to release whatever data they have.[78,*] The Department of Labor surveys the corporations and workers but will not reveal anything about its findings.[79,†] In fact, the U.S. Department of Commerce would not release a 200-page report made by its Technology Administration experts on the impact of offshoring. In 2006 the House Science Committee voted down a resolution that would have forced release of the report to Congress[80] and in August 2007 the TA was abolished under the America Competes Act. Thus, the Bush administration no longer has to be embarrassed about suppressing information, since the agency tasked with compiling it has been liquidated.

This conspiracy of the bosses to keep the workers in the dark is causing deep concern in the highest echelons of the capitalist establishment. Governmental and financial authorities are afraid that the trend is leading in the direction of crisis, but they have no clue as to how large or the timing. The think tanks and researchers have been reduced to trying to tabulate data from the press releases that big corporations decide to release.

---

* Harrison's work, written in 1994, was devoted to debunking the false notion that the "new era" of high-tech capitalism opened the way for small, "creative" firms to lead the world forward into prosperity. He demonstrated the old-style dominance of the monopolies in the age of high tech. Much of his work depended on showing the outsourcing crisis. But he had great difficulty in compiling information. At that time he wrote, "Much of the most revealing information about globalization's course, impact, and probable future is locked away in the records of the world's multinational corporations. U.S.-owned multinationals have dissuaded the government from seeking much of the data and from releasing much of the data that Washington does possess." The corporations use the excuse of the need for competitive secrecy to hide their schemes to search for low-wage labor. Harrison shows that it would be a "public relations disaster" for them if their deeds got out.

† Ten years after Harrison's work, nothing had changed. Uchitelle, the chief *Times* economic writer, referred to the debate over the jobless recovery two years after the recession of 2000-2001 ended. The debate was raging "but in all the heated back and forth, an essential statistic is missing: the number of jobs that would exist in the United States today if so many had not escaped abroad." And he noted that, while experts were still trying to find a way to gauge the impact with wide-ranging estimates, the so-called "expert consensus" was that 15 percent of the 2.81 million jobs officially listed as lost since the downturn had been offshored to low-wage countries. Yet the Labor Department, in its numerous surveys of employers and employees, has never tried to calculate the number.

4

Offshoring: millions of service jobs at risk

Offshoring fever rises in boardrooms • White-collar outsourcing by Europe and Japan • Blinder comes up with miserly 'solutions'

Alan Blinder, once a member of President Bill Clinton's Council of Economic Advisers and a vice chair of the Board of Governors of the Federal Reserve System, who is now back at his position as professor of economics at Princeton, broke onto the front page of the *Wall Street Journal* in March 2007 with a projection that between 30 million and 40 million service jobs in the U.S. were at risk.[81] He hastened to tell the reporter he was not predicting that this number of jobs would actually be moved abroad. Rather, his concern was that, given the development of technology and the current push to offshore, the bosses can now choose from a wide variety of higher-paid service jobs, should they move more aggressively in the direction of offshoring them within the next decade or so. Blinder expected the bosses would be straining at the bit to offshore service jobs of all types.

Blinder had first declared his anxiety a year earlier in an article in *Foreign Affairs* magazine dramatically entitled "Offshoring: The Next Industrial Revolution?"[82] Blinder is the leader of a faction among the economic overseers of the imperialist economy who feel they are watching the slow-motion development of the material for a social explosion. They express their anxiety and flounder around for preemptive solutions, trying to ring alarm bells to wake up the rest of the ruling class establishment.

The Blinder faction is answering the "globalize at all costs" school, one of whose principal advocates is N. Gregory Mankiw, a former chair of the Council of Economic Advisers appointed by President George W. Bush. The Bush-Mankiw faction are cheerleaders for offshoring and play the tunes of mindless optimism. Mankiw caused a stir at the top echelons of the labor movement and embarrassed the Bush administration in February 2004 by "appearing indifferent to the pain caused to those whose jobs go overseas," wrote the fiercely anti-labor *Wall Street Journal* in the same article that reported on Blinder's expectations on the offshoring of service jobs. "Does it matter from an economic [meaning profit—FG] standpoint whether items produced abroad come on planes and ships or over fiber-optic cables?" asked Mankiw. "Well, no, the economics is basically the same.... More things are tradable than ... in the past, and that's a good thing."[83]

Blinder, like the entire economic establishment, suffers from lack of information and has stated that there are no reliable national data. Of course, he does not mention that this is because of the secretiveness of the corporations. Such information would be readily attainable if the bosses cared to divulge it and/or if the capitalist government were inclined to collect and classify it.

Offshoring fever rises in the boardrooms

Blinder was in Davos, Switzerland, at the World Economic Forum in January 2004, a month before Mankiw's statement. At this gathering of the global ruling class, he heard executives talking excitedly about moving jobs overseas that not long ago had seemed anchored in the U.S.

What Blinder observed at Davos corresponds to anecdotal reports about what has been transpiring in the boardrooms of the ruling class. In a 2003 PowerPoint presentation, Microsoft Senior Vice President Brian Valentine urged managers to "pick something to move offshore today." In India, he said, you can get "quality work at 50 percent to 60 percent of the cost. That's two heads for the price of one."[84]

The big job migration is in its very early stages. One of the chief corporate research companies, Gartner, Inc., wrote in 2003 that "Globalization trailblazers, such as GE, AmEx, and Citibank, have spent a decade going through the learning curve and now are ramping up fast. More cautious companies—insurers, utilities, and the like—are entering the fray." Gartner expected 40 percent of the top 1,000 companies in the U.S. to begin their own pilot offshoring projects between 2003 and 2005. The projection is that offshoring will really accelerate by 2010, by which time global white-collar outsourcing practices are expected to be standardized.[85]

In May 2004, Forrester Research, Inc., a major adviser to big business on the trends in technology and how to take advantage of them, made a projection that 3.3 million white-collar jobs would go offshore by 2015. The Forrester report also estimated that $136 billion in wages would shift from the United States to "low-cost countries" in that time period. "Europe is joining the trend too. British banks like HSBC Securities Inc. have huge back offices in China and India; French companies are using call centers in Mauritius; and German multinationals from Siemens to roller-bearing maker INA-Schaeffer are hiring in Russia, the Baltics, and Eastern Europe."[86]

According to a press summary of the report, "New figures on offshore outsourcing suggest that American companies are sending even more white-collar jobs to low-wage countries such as India, China, and Russia than researchers had originally estimated."[87] Forrester gave as an example that computer programmers averaged $10 an hour in India compared to more than $60 an hour in the United States. The report predicted that the trend would further devastate the Midwest as agribusiness, auto parts suppliers, and other giant manufacturers began to offshore accountants, programmers, analysts, and other white-collar jobs.

These numbers are entirely speculative, straight-line projections based upon the trend of the moment. Given the anarchic, unplanned character of capitalist production, bourgeois researchers and economists can never go beyond such methods, which amount to wild guessing about the future. Economic crisis, trade wars, imperialist war, and especially the class struggle of the workers, among any number of currents inherent in the profit system, could drastically overturn these projections. But what is important for the working class is that Forrester was basing its report on what was going on in the boardrooms at the time—and that trend seems to have deepened, if anything, since 2004. Gross numbers remain the secrets of the corporations. But examples abound.

The Philippines is a country of nearly 80 million people that produces about 380,000 college graduates a year. U.S. accounting houses and corporations are zeroing in on the abundance of Filipino accounting graduates trained in U.S. standards, making them targets for offshoring.

> *By 2004 some 10,000 Filipinos, almost all with college degrees, were staffing forty-five call centers for the transnationals*

As of 2004 there were 10,000 Filipinos, almost all with college degrees, staffing forty-five call centers to provide 24/7 customer service for the transnationals. Companies like American Express, Eastman Kodak, Intel, Microsoft, and Dell are flocking to the Philippines, lured by the country's low wages, generous tax breaks, and ample supply of English speakers.

Fluor Corporation of California (an Iraq War contractor and favorite of the Pentagon) in 2004 employed 1,200 engineers and drafters in the Philippines, Poland, and India to work on some of the 50,000 separate construction plans involved in the building of a multi-billion-dollar petrochemical plant in Saudi Arabia. Two hundred young Filipino engineers, each earning less than $3,000 a year, worked over the Web with elite U.S. and British engineers earning up to $90,000. Its Manila operations, according to the head of Fluor, reduce the company's project costs by 15 percent.[88]

India had 520,000 Internet technology (IT) engineers in 2004; their starting salary is $5,000. It graduates 260,000 engineers every year. A top chemical or electrical engineering graduate will earn about $10,000 a year compared to $80,000 in the United States. OfficeTiger, the service equivalent of the contracting manufacturers, has analysts in Madras writing research papers for Wall Street firms. In a 140-acre city within a city in Mumbai, Morgan Stanley, JPMorgan Chase, Goldman Sachs, and other big investment banks are hiring their own armies of analysts and back-office staff. Here they pile up super-profits surrounded by the poverty and misery of the urban poor.

In 2003 some 25,000 U.S. tax returns were processed in India. By 2005 the number was about 400,000. This number is expected to rise dramatically. About 70,000 accountants graduate in India every year, many of whom go to work for $100 a month. They are ripe for U.S. offshoring. There are about 245,000 Indians answering phones or dialing out at call centers, soliciting people for credit cards or cell phone bargains, notifying of overdue bills or offering customer service.[89] General Electric has thousands of technicians, scientists, and engineers working directly or indirectly for its numerous companies, both in India and around the world.

Indian companies like Infosys, Wypro, and Tata Consultancy Services, Ltd. among others, are firms that provide outsourcing of everything from Internet technology to back-office work for the transnational giants. IBM Services has become a major outsourcing adviser to other giant firms. The organization of outsourcing has become a big business in itself as corporations seek to find low-wage labor but want to short-circuit the trial-and-error process.

A *BusinessWeek* special feature on "The Future of Outsourcing" in 2006 gave a summary description of the process. "Here's what such transformations typically entail: Genpact (formerly a GE company), Accenture, IBM Services or another big outsourcing specialist dispatches teams to meticulously dissect the workflow on an entire human resources, finance or info tech department. The team then helps build a new IT platform, redesigns all the processes, and administers programs, acting as a virtual subsidiary. The contractor then disperses work among global networks of staff ranging from the U.S. to Asia to Eastern Europe."[90]

Giants such as Procter & Gamble, DuPont, Cisco Systems, ABN AMRO, Unilever, and Marriott were among the firms that signed contracts worth billions. Procter & Gamble, a $57-billion company, outsourced everything from IT infrastructure and human resources to management of its offices, from Cincinnati to Moscow. DuPont gave management of the payroll and benefit records for its 60,000 workers in seventy countries to Convergys, one of the largest call-center operations in the world.[91]

Eli Lilly, the pharmaceutical giant, is now doing 20 percent of its chemistry work in China for one-quarter of the U.S. cost and is trying to cut the cost of clinical trials for drugs by outsourcing them to Brazil, Russia, China, and India. Other pharmaceuticals are making similar moves.[92]

Penske Truck Leasing, a joint venture with General Electric that has 216,000 trucks, hired Genpact (40-percent owned by GE) to restructure its office work. The restructuring resulted in an international speedup of drivers in addition to outsourcing to low-wage office workers. For example, if a Penske driver is detained at a weigh station for lack of certain papers, the driver calls an 800 number. Genpact staff in India obtain the papers over the Web. The weigh station is notified electronically and the truck is back on the road within thirty minutes. Previously, Penske thought it did well if it accomplished that in two hours. And when a driver finishes the job, his/her entire log, including records of mileage, tolls, and fuel purchases, is shipped to Mexico, punched into computers, and processed in Hyderabad. In all, 60 percent of the 1,000 workers handling Penske back-office processes are in India or Mexico. The low-wage office workers in India also help with scheduling, billing, and invoices. Penske saves $15 million annually in direct labor costs.[93]

In 2006 Texas-based Electronic Data Systems (EDS) was losing top clients because it lacked low-cost offshore capabilities. It bought up a Bangalore software and back-office services firm, MphasiS, for $380 million and quickly boosted its Indian work force from 3,000 to 11,000. Oracle Corporation paid $900 million to buy the controlling share in a Mumbai banking software company. R.R. Donnelly & Sons, which already has 2,000 workers in India doing its back-office work, bought OfficeTiger, an Indian accounting and analytic outsourcer, for $250 million. IBM, Hewlett-Packard, and Accenture have added thousands of workers in India. In 2004 IBM bought a New Delhi call center and by 2007 had 38,500 workers in India.

According to Forrester Research, $70 billion in existing outsourcing contracts were up for renewal in 2008 and billions more in new contracts were expected to be signed. The key for outsource providers in the competition to sign up corporate customers is to have masses of low-wage workers either under their employ or in their outsourcing networks.[94]

White-collar outsourcing by Europe and Japan

The trend is taking hold in the imperialist world as a whole. Accenture, the giant outsourcing company with $19.7 billion in revenue in 2007, has taken thirteen stories in an eighteen-story skyscraper in a corporate park in Prague, capital of the Czech Republic. Accenture has 180,000 employees in 150 cities in 49 countries and does business with two-thirds of the Fortune 500 as well as with European corporations.[95] It is rounding up white-collar labor in Eastern Europe for the transnationals, such as the French chemical giant Rhodia and the global German software company SAP, among others. "Commerzbank of Germany does its data processing in Prague; Siemens, the electrical giant, does bookkeeping, research, and development here; Philips, the Dutch electrical conglomerate, operates a shared services center outside Warsaw."[96]

Accenture came to Prague in 2001 and has since expanded into the second-largest Czech city, Brno; to Bratislava, capital of Slovakia; and to Budapest in Hungary. In 2007 it opened offices in Warsaw and in Bucharest, capital of Romania. The corporations seem thrilled with the fact that they can have skilled workers who speak English, French, German, Russian, and other local languages. But the real attraction is that workers in Hungary and the Czech Republic earn a quarter of what workers make in Western Europe. Pay rates in Slovakia are even lower: about a fifth of Western wages. In 2004, when Germany's SAP chose to move accounting and personnel services to Prague, the company could hire five workers for the price of one in Germany. In addition, the governments offer tax breaks and subsidize office construction as an enticement.

When the British food and personal-care giant Unilever, in 2005, announced that it was going to move its accounting, personnel, and computer divisions to Eastern Europe, Unilever workers in Germany called a one-day work stoppage, fearing the loss of 4,000 jobs. The company retreated, but the next year called in IBM and Accenture to organize the outsourcing over time, declaring that it would kill the jobs by attrition.

Not to be outdone, IBM, Dell, and Morgan Stanley, among others, have outsourced services to Eastern Europe or helped other U.S. companies to outsource. Last summer Morgan Stanley announced it was opening a business services and technology center in Budapest, in addition to a mathematical center established there in 2005.

The Japanese imperialists are following the same pattern. To deal with the language issue for outsourcing white-collar work, they have pushed work through intermediaries into the northern port city of Dalian, China, where about one-third of students take Japanese as a second language. "Dalian has become for Japan what Bangalore has become for America and the other English-speaking countries: outsourcing central," says Friedman.[97] Kenichi Ohmae, an author and former corporate consultant who champions globalization, established his own outsourcing company in Japan to promote shifting work to China, mostly data entry. The company has branched out into architecture. In addition to its regular workforce, it has contracts with 70,000 Chinese housewives who work at home.

Japanese firms can hire three Chinese software engineers for the cost of one in Japan. Chinese call center operators get $90 a month starting salary. Some 2,800 Japanese companies have either set up operations in Dalian or formed joint ventures. Dalian has twenty-two universities and the students take either Japanese or English. Thus, Chinese white-collar workers are also equipped to work for U.S. monopolies with back-office operations in Dalian, such as General Electric, Microsoft, Dell, and Accenture, among others.

The offshoring of white-collar service jobs is generalized throughout the imperialist world. As in manufacturing, the corporations have their intermediaries who become the overseers, rounding up service labor of all types to meet the needs of the multinationals, taking their cut, and trying to profit by getting the lowest possible labor costs at the skill level required by the global corporate bosses. Whether it is working Chinese software engineers for one-third of what it would cost in Japan, or Eastern European bookkeepers for one-fifth of what workers get in Western Europe, whatever they call it, it is imperialist super-exploitation and the corporations are garnering super-profits.

Blinder comes up with miserly 'solutions'

As each monopoly plunges ahead to gain a profit advantage or an advantage of position that will lead to more profits in the long run, the already ferocious competition is only bound to intensify. That competition among the monopolies is won by whichever corporate grouping can wring more profit out of the workers and accumulate more surplus value, one way or the other. Given that U.S. companies are the leaders in the process of outsourcing service work, just as they were in the outsourcing of manufacturing, and given that the union resistance to offshoring is barely visible, Blinder's urge to get a measure of the problem is understandable.

His method was to study jobs in the economy in order to determine the types of jobs that will be under threat in the next decade and beyond. His starting point is that any service that can be delivered electronically, that does not require person-to-person contact, can potentially be offshored.

On that basis he analyzed 817 job categories set up by the Bureau of Labor Statistics and arrived at the figure of 30 million to 40 million jobs. The list includes bookkeepers and accountants, computer programmers, data entry keyers, graphic designers, film and video editors, medical transcriptionists, and others. He warned that "tens of millions of additional American workers will start to experience an element of job insecurity that has heretofore been reserved for manufacturing workers." He continues: "This is something factory workers have understood for a generation.... It's now coming down on the heads of highly educated, politically vocal people, and they're not going to take it."[98]

In fact, Blinder was one of the champions of the anti-labor North American Free Trade Agreement, which went a long way to increase that "element of job insecurity" among the workers. As a member of Clinton's Council of Economic Advisers, he supported the legislation that opened up Mexico to food exports by U.S. agribusiness and relaxed conditions for capital investment by U.S. manufacturers. NAFTA did away with manufacturing jobs in the United States and brought devastation to Mexican peasants and super-exploitation to Mexican workers. (For more on NAFTA, see Chapter 9, "Globalization and Immigration.")

Blinder does not seem to concern himself with the hundreds of thousands of workers in call centers and others doing so-called low-end "back-office work" around the world for the banks and big corporations at low wages. Perhaps he has no fear of call-center workers in the United States rising up, either. Nor does he concern himself with the conditions of the workers who are going to get the jobs abroad. He makes no mention of the one-sided development imposed upon low-wage countries or how they are forced to distort their economies in order to accommodate the outsourcing requirements of the imperialist monopolies, just to attract investment.

Blinder's calculation is that the manufacturing and lower-paid workers have been taking it on the chin for the last three decades and have not been able to mount a mass rebellion. But his vision of the future, based upon his studies and those of others, forms a firm basis for his anxiety. He says that "… manufacturing workers in the rich countries have grown accustomed to the idea that they compete with foreign labor. But … many service workers will also have to accept the new, and not very pleasant, reality that they too must compete with workers in other countries. And there are many more service than manufacturing workers."[99]

What he does not say is that, if service workers rebel, it could easily spill over to manufacturing workers. On the other hand, if the industrial workers begin to resist, it could infect the service sector of the working class. Blinder's concern and anxiety reflect the ambivalence of those in the upper echelons who can see the trends in capitalist global restructuring. On the one hand, they are completely wedded to the super-profits to be garnered from offshoring. On the other, they fear the social crisis that is inherent in the processes of the profit system. In general, Blinder is guided primarily by the desire to head off any such future social upheaval.

He cites a 2003 Berkeley study and a later one by the prestigious business consulting firm McKinsey Global Institute dealing with the Fortune 500. Both estimated that 11 percent of U.S. jobs were at risk for being offshored. And then he goes on to say that he thinks "this is the currently visible tip of the offshoring iceberg. The future will reveal much more."[100]

Blinder cites figures showing that the trend away from manufacturing work toward services is a phenomenon affecting all the imperialist countries. The scenario he arrives at is approximately as follows: Blanket education and "upskilling" the workers are not really the answer. You need to educate workers, not in general, but for jobs available. That means educating workers for jobs that cannot be offshored, i.e., that cannot be delivered electronically and require personal contact—child care, health care, etc. But the projections for job growth are heavily weighted toward low-wage jobs. "Major readjustments" will have to be made, moving people from one industry to another. This will create wage competition in the service industries and "will show up in real wages. As more and more rich-country workers seek employment in personal services, real wages for those jobs are likely to decline…. Thus, the wage prognosis is brighter for luxury personal-service jobs (such as plastic surgery and chauffeuring) than for ordinary personal-service jobs (such as cutting hair and teaching elementary school)."[101]

At the end of the *Foreign Affairs* article Blinder admits that while there must be transformation of the nature of work and of education, "the rich countries will retain many jobs which require very little education." He polemicizes against Thomas Friedman, who promotes the fantasy that "creative jobs" will abound and will rescue the offshoring corporate profiteers from social disaster. Says Blinder, "It is hard to imagine that truly creative positions will ever constitute anything close to the majority of jobs. What will everyone else do?" [102]

But Blinder's solution to what he sees as "wrenching social changes" in the enforced "transformation in the nature of work" is miserly: "We may have to repair and thicken the tattered safety net that supports workers who fall off the labor market trapeze—improving programs ranging from unemployment insurance to job retraining, health insurance, pensions, and right down to public assistance."[103]

Of course, under capitalist wage slavery in which profit and profiteers rule, the bosses create only those jobs that will help them to accumulate capital, beat out their rivals, and get rich at the same time. Thus, wages have nothing to do with the actual usefulness of work performed, the creativity on the job, or the needs of the workers and their families. The bosses do not recognize any "creativity" on the job unless it is the type that leads to selling more, reducing labor costs, speeding up the capitalist process of exploitation through revolutions in technology, or in other ways boosting profits.

In general, the capitalist class rewards the creativity of the elite who devise ways to increase the productivity of labor of the workers, either directly or indirectly, who find ways to reduce down time, squeeze more labor time out of the labor process, eliminate jobs altogether, and in general increase the rate of exploitation and the extraction of surplus value.

Capitalism spurs the creativity of the few to increase the hardship of the many

Capitalism spurs the creativity of the few to increase the hardship of the many.

The not-so-novel idea of creating good jobs at good pay in both the service and manufacturing industries and using technology to make those jobs easier and more fulfilling could never occur to Blinder. Nor could the simple idea of paying good wages to workers abroad who are doing vital jobs and need the income, most of all in order to make up for centuries of colonialist- and imperialist-imposed underdevelopment. That rational idea is unthinkable to Blinder because it is rational only from a general social point of view, from a human point of view, not from a capitalist point of view—and of course not from the point of view of an imperialist financial official who sometimes wears the hat of a professor.

Capitalism, the system of production for profit instead of human need, is incompatible with such notions as making the health and well-being of those who produce all the wealth and perform all the services the priority of social and economic organization.

These tasks and goals are compatible only with socialism, which finally brings about harmony between collective, consciously cooperative production for human need and consumption for the well-being of humanity.

5

Marxism and globalization

Lenin on 20th-century imperialism • The dual character of imperialism • Three factors behind new 'globalization' • Marx on technology and international division of labor • Lenin on the previous imperialist division of labor • International solidarity and globalization An irony that helped the globalizing exploiters • Impact on U.S. workers of defeat of socialist bloc • Anti-communist crusade showed ruling-class fear • Socialist camp set standard for working-class security • Global expansion can't dispel crisis of overproduction

> The bourgeoisie cannot exist without constantly revolutionizing the instruments of production, and thereby the relations of production, and with them the whole relations of society. Conservation of the old modes of production in unaltered form was, on the contrary, the first condition of existence for all earlier industrial classes. Constant revolutionizing of production, uninterrupted disturbance of all social conditions, everlasting uncertainty and agitation distinguish the bourgeois epoch from all earlier ones....
>
> The need of constantly expanding markets for its products chases the bourgeoisie over the whole surface of the globe. It must nestle everywhere, settle everywhere, establish connections everywhere.
>
> —**Karl Marx,** *The Communist Manifesto*

The above quote from Karl Marx is perhaps the most concise and at the same time comprehensive description of the globalizing tendencies of capitalism yet penned. It so profoundly captures both the spirit and the essence of ever-expanding capitalism that it is often quoted by even the fiercest opponents of Marxism. It is unsurpassed as a historical depiction of capitalism as it was developing 160 years ago, when the *Manifesto* was written. At the same time it renders a vivid picture of the process going on today before our very eyes.

After all, is not current-day imperialist "globalization" accompanied by the revolutionizing of the means of production, communication, and transportation, and driven by the need of the profiteers to chase over the entire surface of the globe? Are they not destroying social relations as they go everywhere—reaching into remote towns and villages as well as teeming cities, drawing tens and hundreds of millions into their ever-widening web of exploitation?

Marx described the globalizing tendency of capitalism in its most general form. In its earliest stages, capitalism's irrepressibly expansive character already stood out in bold relief to societies that preceded it. But Marxism, in its efforts to explain and promote the class struggle, is the doctrine that sees all things in their development. Society, like all natural phenomena, can only be understood in motion. It is important to grasp the specific stage of capitalist globalization we are in at the moment, in order to gain the proper perspective in the struggle against imperialism and for socialism. It is necessary to see what forces led up to the present and those at work now that will propel society forward to the next stage.

Prior to the age of imperialism, as Marx's quote from the *Manifesto* indicates, capitalist globalization was primarily driven by the search for trade and markets. The quest for gold and other precious metals, as well as luxuries and articles of consumption—spices, sugar, coffee, indigo, cotton, wool—had been driving capitalist enterprises to expand at the very dawn of capitalism. Christopher Columbus set out looking for trade routes to India, but the conquistadors wound up looting the indigenous peoples of the Western Hemisphere. The Portuguese, the British East India Company, the Dutch East India Company, and later the French East India Company were among the early "globalizers" whose merchant capital penetrated India and Indonesia, among other regions of the globe, in search of trade and profit.

Most importantly, the African slave trade became fully integrated into the newly developing capitalist system and served to generate massive wealth for the European and U.S. financiers and merchants, who profited both from transporting and selling slaves and from marketing the commodities created by slave labor.

This penetration of commercial capital laid the basis for future colonization. But it was the full-blown development of massive large-scale industry—based on railroads, steamships, the generation of electricity, the telegraph, metallurgy, and other technological advances—that led to the insatiable need of the giant capitalists for industrial raw materials. Coal, iron ore, tin, bauxite, petroleum and lumber, as well as rubber, jute, and other agricultural commodities were required for the developing factory-based profit system.

With superior firepower and technology, and backed by their respective capitalist governments, the new multinational corporations were able to overcome anti-colonial resistance and impose massive forced labor in the mines, on plantations, building roads, railroad tracks, ports, and transporting and loading freight.

By the end of the nineteenth century, as the larger and stronger capitalists swallowed up the weaker ones, giant industrial firms and financial institutions were created that dominated national and, eventually, world markets. This process led to the transformation of competitive capitalism into monopoly capitalism—i.e., imperialism—and the export of capital as the new expansionary force driving the profit system.

Karl Marx and Frederick Engels, the founders of modern scientific socialism, analyzed the fundamental economic laws and class contradictions of capitalism as a social system. These contradictions discovered by Marx and Engels still govern the development of capitalism—such as the labor law of value, for example, and its corollaries, including the maximization of profit. (The labor law of value demonstrates that the exchange value of everything sold is determined by how much socially necessary labor is embedded in it, not by how much people need it. While supply and demand may push prices up and down, they do so within a range dictated by the amount of labor in a commodity.)

In the age of capitalist monopoly, which grew enormously in the twentieth century, changes occurred in the economic and political forms by which these laws played out on a world scale. These changes profoundly affected the class struggle, requiring fresh analysis and updating in light of new developments.

Monopoly capitalism ushered in, among other things, a vast expansion of the global export of investment capital and, with this, the age of imperialist war and the widening and deepening of national oppression.

Lenin on twentieth-century imperialism

Vladimir Lenin, the leader of the Russian Revolution of October 1917, came to political maturity in the late nineteenth and early twentieth centuries. This was the very period during which competitive capitalism was transformed into fully developed monopoly capitalism—that is, capitalism's imperialist stage. It was Lenin who brought Marxism up to date to take into account the vast changes in capitalism brought about by the growth of global monopolies since the time of Marx and Engels.

Among Lenin's wide-ranging contributions to the updating of Marxism was his crucial analysis of imperialism. In his groundbreaking work *Imperialism, the Highest Stage of Capitalism*, written in 1916 at the height of the first imperialist world war, he laid out the anatomy of the system. He demonstrated that the essence of monopoly capitalism was the development and domination of finance capital, that is, the merger of giant industrial capital with bank capital. He showed how the imperialist powers had divided the entire globe into spheres of influence or outright colonies and how they were in a constant struggle to re-divide territories for plunder. Giant cartels and syndicates of the international monopolies had taken control of the world markets.

Lenin focused on the role of the export of capital as a dominant feature of imperialism. He showed that finance capital drove foreign corporate investment and the expansion of imperialism into the underdeveloped world. The corporations made vast profits from these ventures because they paid the workers in the oppressed countries far less than the workers in the imperialist countries. He called the extra profits made because of these super-low wages "super-profits" and the process of exploitation at such low wages "super-exploitation." The quest for super-profits led to the flow of capital from the giant corporations into low-wage areas of the globe, in much the same way as today. In Lenin's time, however, the bosses sought these super-profits primarily through investment in mining, plantations, and the infrastructure needed to bring out raw materials and other products.

The dominant technology of the time—railroads, the telegraph and later the telephone, steamships, canals, heavy industrial manufacturing, etc.— determined the development of the structure of world capitalism. The gigantic, integrated industrial factories and administrative offices that centralized production and business processes existed almost exclusively in the imperialist countries. Slow-moving freighters, cumbersome international telephonic communication, etc., dictated the form of division of labor within the world, which left the oppressed workers and peasants in the colonies and semi-colonies primarily limited to performing relatively unskilled and backbreaking physical labor. This labor largely involved providing the riches of the earth that would be transformed into manufactured products in the distant imperialist countries. There was a clear separation of function in the world capitalist system between the workers in the imperialist countries and the super-exploited workers in the oppressed countries.

Even with the invention of air travel and telephonic communication, it was still possible, during the first century of imperialism, to have an approximate demarcation between the economic activity in the "domestic economy"— that is, the imperialist centers—and the expanded capitalist economy represented by foreign investment or, as Lenin accurately described it, the export of capital. The domestic economy consisted mostly of high-level manufacturing and services as well as increasingly mechanized and concentrated agriculture. Foreign holdings might include textile mills, even some auto plants and light manufacturing, but by and large it referred to such occupations as mining for gold, diamonds, tin, copper, bauxite, etc., or plantation labor producing tea, cocoa, coffee, palm oil, oranges, bananas, and so on. All demanded hard labor at low wages necessary to support imperialist plunder.

While one part of this picture still remains the same—the plunder of the resources of the formerly colonial countries—the scientific-technological revolution has added a whole new dimension to world economic processes that is having revolutionary implications. Lenin's thesis must be expanded to take into account the current phase of imperialism as conditioned by the new technology.

The dual character of imperialism

Lenin's Marxist analysis of imperialism, as it arose at the end of the nineteenth century and developed thereafter, showed that it had a two-fold effect. On the one hand, imperialism, by extending the capitalist system and wage slavery everywhere, has spread modern means of production across the globe and created a vast productive network involving hundreds of millions of workers. The single aim of this ever-growing network was to increase capitalist exploitation and expand profit. That is why poverty and inequality grow along with it.

On the other hand, imperialism also tends to create greater division between the upper and lower layers of the working class, both on a world scale and within each imperialist country. The bosses have used this division to blunt the class struggle, particularly in the imperialist countries.

To make his point about how imperialism softened the class struggle at home, Lenin quoted from the British colonialist Cecil Rhodes, who wrote:

> I was in the East End of London (working-class quarter) yesterday and attended a meeting of the unemployed. I listened to the wild speeches, which were just a cry for 'Bread! Bread!' and on my way home I pondered over the scene and I became more than ever convinced of the importance of imperialism.... My cherished idea is a solution for the social problem, i.e., in order to save the 40,000,000 inhabitants of the United Kingdom from a bloody civil war, we colonial statesmen must acquire new lands to settle the surplus population, to provide new markets for the goods produced in the factories and mines. The Empire, as I have always said, is a bread and butter question. If you want to avoid civil war, you must become imperialists.[104]

Because the multinational corporations and banks have such a stranglehold over the underdeveloped countries—which are underdeveloped because they are held back by imperialism and colonialism—they are able to bring in vast profits, some of which they have historically used to make concessions to sections of the workers in the "home" country.

Lenin observed that imperialism, with its monopoly profits, creates a minority of privileged nations where it "has a tendency to create privileged sections also among the workers and to detach them from the broad masses of the proletariat."[105]

"Obviously," wrote Lenin in 1920 in a preface to the French and German editions of the book, "out of such enormous **super-profits** (since they are obtained over and above the profits which capitalists squeeze out of the workers of their 'own country') it is **possible to bribe** the labor leaders and the upper stratum of the labor aristocracy. And the capitalists of the 'advanced' countries are bribing them; they bribe them in a thousand different ways, direct and indirect, overt and covert." [106] [Emphasis in the original.]

Three factors behind new 'globalization'

In the age of the scientific-technological revolution, however, the export of capital is sharply countering this feature of imperialism that Lenin described. It is pushing downward the standard of living of the vast majority of workers in the imperialist countries. The process of building up privileged layers of the working class as a loyal social and political base for the imperialist bourgeoisie is being steadily eroded. This turn-about is the result of three deeply related developments within the last two decades.

Most important is the enormous expansion of the number of low-wage workers available to direct exploitation and super-exploitation by the giant transnational corporations and banks after the political victory of imperialism over the USSR and Eastern Europe. Even earlier, a faction in the Chinese Communist Party had come to power that argued for utilizing market mechanisms as a major lever for development—a political current that Mao Zedong characterized as "capitalist roaders." These victories for imperialism had ramifications for the workers in both the low-wage countries and the imperialist countries.

Next is the profound scientific-technological revolution that enabled the capitalist class to make a leap forward in the creation of new labor processes in both production and services, including advances in automation, robotization, and computerization. This has created new automated processes in the factories, mines, offices, ports, etc., in which tens of millions of higher-wage jobs simply disappeared while a small number of high-skill jobs took their place and low-wage jobs mushroomed. As the skills required by capital were wiped out, layoffs, large and small, became the rule.

Thirdly, in the most recent phase of the scientific-technological revolution, advances in transportation, communications, internet technology, and software development have permitted the giant capitalist companies, with huge treasuries and links to the giant banks, to create **a new division of labor in the world**, or what Marx called the social division of labor, as distinct from the division of labor in the workplace.

The new technology opened up to the capitalist class the ability to reorganize and relocate production processes around the globe, using both new and old methods. This process accelerated a worldwide corporate race to find the cheapest labor in the less-developed countries (and in low-wage areas at home) and incorporate them into the networks of the most modern productive processes, as well as import low-wage labor from abroad.

The process of imperialist super-exploitation was freed from all geographical limits by the scientific-technological revolution

The process of imperialist super-exploitation was freed from all geographical limits by the scientific-technological revolution. It could now be carried out wherever workers could be rounded up on the globe.

Marx on technology and the international division of labor

Marx showed how the revolution in the means of production that took place with the development of machinery and the factory system, i.e., a new division of labor within the workplace, gave great impetus to a new world social division of labor.

> So soon, however, as the factory system has gained a certain breadth of footing and a definite degree of maturity, and, especially, so soon as its technical basis, machinery, is itself produced by machinery; so soon as coal mining and iron mining, the metal industries, and the means of transport have been revolutionized; so soon, in short, as the general conditions requisite for production by the modern industrial system have been established, this mode of production acquires an elasticity, a capacity for sudden extension by leaps and bounds that finds no hindrance except in the supply of raw material and in the disposal of the produce. On the one hand, the immediate effect of machinery is to increase the supply of raw material in the same way, for example, as the cotton gin augmented the production of cotton. On the other hand, the cheapness of the articles produced by machinery, and the improved means of transport and communication furnish the weapons for conquering foreign markets. By ruining handicraft production in other countries, machinery forcibly converts them into fields for the supply of its raw material. In this way East India was compelled to produce cotton, wool, hemp, jute, and indigo for Great Britain.... A new and international division of labor, a division suited to the requirements of

the chief centers of modern industry springs up, and **converts one part of the globe into a chiefly agricultural field of production for supplying the other part, which remains a chiefly industrial field.** [107] [Emphasis added.]

Thus the age of machine tools, advanced metallurgy, railroads, the telegraph, etc., and the industrial factory system led to the subordination of the colonial peoples to the needs of the industrial ruling class of developing capitalism for raw materials. Under the impact of automatic, digitally controlled, production, revolutions in communications and transportation, control systems and the like, a similar process is going on today, but it has been drastically modified under contemporary economic and political conditions.

Lenin on the previous imperialist division of labor

In 1916 Lenin gave a general description of the extent of the socialization of production and world division of labor. Until the 1970s, Lenin's description of what were the main features of imperialism continued to apply: the obtaining of raw materials and agricultural products to be shipped hundreds or thousands of miles from the oppressed countries to central points of production in the imperialist countries and then distributed, all according to central corporate plans, either by a single giant monopoly or a cartel.

> When a big enterprise assumes gigantic proportions, and, on the basis of an exact computation of mass data, organizes according to plan the **supply of primary raw materials** to the extent of two-thirds, or three-fourths, of all that is necessary for tens of millions of people; when the raw materials are transported in a systematic and organized manner to the most suitable places of production, sometimes situated hundreds or thousands of miles from each other; when a single center directs all the consecutive stages of processing the material right up to the manufacture of numerous varieties of finished articles; when these products are distributed according to a single plan among tens and hundreds of millions of consumers (the marketing of oil in America and Germany by the American oil trust)—then it becomes evident that we have socialization of production.... [108] [Emphasis added]

The important point to note is the emphasis on the shipping of raw materials and agricultural products from the colonies to production centers in the imperialist countries. With the exception of some neo-colonial countries, such as Argentina, most workers in the oppressed countries labored in the mines, on plantations, in agricultural settings, or in transportation and the ports. Thus direct competition for manufacturing and service jobs between workers in the colonies and in the imperialist countries was limited.

In the United States chattel slavery in the South had provided the equivalent of colonial labor, an internal colony that produced vast wealth. Much of that wealth flowed into the coffers of the bankers, merchants, shipping lines, insurers, etc., in the North. It was the totally unpaid labor of generations of enslaved African people that formed much of the basis of the commercial and industrial wealth of the U.S. capitalist class.

The early stages of plunder of Latin America also added to U.S. capital accumulation. Washington entered the full-fledged stage of imperialism with the conquest of Cuba, Puerto Rico, and the Philippines in 1898 in the so-called Spanish-American War. The U.S. ruling class took possession of their agricultural and mineral wealth and super-exploited the newly conquered colonial labor.

In the present era the scientific-technological revolution has brought about development of the productive forces—in electronics, computerization, transportation, communication, and Internet technology—that has enabled the monopolies to reorganize world production, bringing hundreds of millions of low-wage workers into global manufacturing and services and thus, in direct wage competition, job for job, with the working class in the imperialist countries.

Whereas the export of capital was once used to foster an upper stratum of the working class in the imperialist countries, to soften the class struggle, and to promote social stability, with the new world division of labor the export of capital is being used to drive down the living standards of the workers in the imperialist countries, decimate the upper layers of the workers and sections of the middle class, and destroy job security and social benefits. This will inevitably undermine the foundation of social stability. It will lay the basis for the revival of class warfare in the heartland of the giant corporate exploiters. Furthermore, the expanding worldwide socialization of the labor process and the rapidly growing international working class is making class solidarity across borders against imperialism an imperative.

International solidarity and globalization

The first imperative in establishing international solidarity is for workers and their leaders in the United States to take a global view of the entire working class. The problem of international wage competition is a dangerous one for the working class in the imperialist countries, especially here. Dealing with it could easily lead down the path of national chauvinism, if not outright racism. The reflex of sections of capital that are losing out in the global competition is to call for protectionism. This falls right in line with right-wing populist demagogy of the Lou Dobbs type.

But the top labor leadership in the United States has also leaned toward narrow-minded bourgeois protectionism, allegedly to "protect American workers." In the fight against the treacherous tactic of capitalist-inspired international wage competition that pits workers in this country against low-wage workers in the rest of the world, the first premise must be that the enemies are the globalizing bosses, not the workers in low-wage countries who are suffering poverty and unemployment and desperately need jobs. The hundreds of millions of unemployed or low-wage workers in the rest of the world live in countries whose resources were plundered, whose labor was brutally exploited, and whose very civilizations were trampled upon by colonialism and imperialism. And it was this process of robbery and plunder that greatly contributed to the creation of the wealth of the United States, including everything from railroads to coast-to-coast highways, auto plants, machine shops, skyscrapers, laboratories, educational institutions—and television sets, iPods, and the Hollywood film industry.

This plunder, which has made the United States the richest country in the world and given it a high standard of living, has also created under-development—the source of poverty and unemployment in those low-wage countries to which jobs are being outsourced.

The greatest part of the wealth of the United States is owned by the capitalists, and it is growing greater every day. That wealth was created by workers. But not just by the working class in this country. The final production processes and the performance of services that take place here are links in an unending, intricate chain of labor performed by the working class of the world. This chain of labor abroad has contributed in untold ways to the provision, shaping, and transporting of the materials used to create the wealth and standard of living in the United States—as much as by the workers in this country, if not more. Before anyone can do their job on a production line in Detroit, in an office building on Wall Street, or in a laboratory at MIT—or even attend a university in Boston—the basis for it was in large part created by millions of workers the world over who were exploited by some boss.

An irony that helped the globalizing exploiters

In addition, it must be stated that the latest phase in the expansion of world capitalism, what has been dubbed "globalization" and is driven by imperialist investment, has been made possible by global advances in the educational and technical levels of large sections of the formerly oppressed and colonized peoples. But these gains came largely as a result of the socialist revolutions, national liberation movements, and anti-colonialist victories of the past century.

For example, the Bolshevik Revolution in Russia lifted up the cultural and technical level of not only the proletariat in the cities but the huge rural population of the tsarist empire, particularly in the formerly subject nations. It brought schools and literacy in many languages to peasants just one generation away from serfdom and to small nations that were still nomadic or hunted in the vast forests of Siberia.

The Chinese Revolution, which liberated one fourth of the human race from imperialism, brought education to the countryside in a land where literacy had been restricted for centuries to the Confucian bureaucracy. That revolution laid the basis for the educational strides of present-day China; without it the present-day economic advances would not have been possible. People's China, the USSR, the German Democratic Republic, and the Czechoslovak People's Republic, among other socialist countries, set up programs to educate and train people from newly liberated or newly independent countries, as well as cadre from national liberation movements fighting imperialism.

After mass pressure brought an end to centuries-long British economic and colonial domination in India, the post-independence bourgeois nationalist regime of Jawaharlal Nehru set up the country's first university system.

Why do Taiwan and south Korea, two of the so-called Asian Tigers, today occupy such a prominent position in the world economy? Because both were built up by U.S. imperialism: Taiwan in order to oppose the socialism of the People's Republic of China; south Korea as a bulwark against the Democratic People's Republic of Korea in the north. In Vietnam, it was the revolution that put an end to the status of the country as basically a rubber plantation for French imperialism. The revolution, including the final victory over U.S. neocolonial war and occupation, allowed Vietnam to become a forward-looking country focused on national development.

The present-day advancement of global capitalism was made possible by the previous struggles of oppressed peoples for the right to knowledge

All the countries that are now providing skilled and semi-skilled labor power to the expanding empire of finance capital, including Singapore, Malaysia, Thailand, Indonesia, and all the new offshore subordinates of the giant transnational corporations, were once kept in a state of enforced mass illiteracy in order to use them as colonial labor on the plantations and in the mines.

Ironically, the entire present-day advancement of global capitalism is only possible because of the previous struggles of the oppressed peoples of the world for the right to knowledge, struggles that were waged against the very imperialist powers that are now penetrating their countries with advanced capitalist processes with the sole aim of widening and deepening exploitation.

The propagandists for globalization constantly rub their hands with glee over the masses of educated workers who just "happen" to be available, without explaining that this is because the masses fought against the imperialist powers to gain the right to enter the modern world. The truth is that no matter how much scientific and technical knowledge has become accessible through the Internet, no matter how eager the imperialists are to spread their productive processes and service industries to low-wage countries, none of this could be happening were it not for the previous victories in the anti-imperialist struggles by the oppressed and the world working class. That is what prepared the former colonies to enter the modern technological stage.

Nor do the worshippers of "globalization" explain the class basis for the technological advancement in the centers of imperialism. Wealth stolen over generations from the oppressed countries created the support for the universities, the scientific elite in the Stanfords and MITs, and the laboratories of the transnational corporations where the technology was created.

In addition, an incalculable contribution was made through the brain drain from the former colonial countries. Hundreds of thousands of special visas were given to professionals from India and China, for example. They contributed to the new technology while working at below-par salaries in Silicon Valley, Route 128 around Boston, and the technological "triangle" in North Carolina, just to name the main centers. Many other skilled professionals in various fields—medicine, for example—were drawn from countries like the Philippines and parts of Africa. This not only boosted science and technology in the centers of imperialism but in many cases further underdeveloped the countries from which this specialized labor was lured.

Impact on U.S. workers of defeat of socialist bloc

During most of the period in which the U.S. and the USSR were competing throughout the world as rival social systems, particularly during the Cold War era after World War II, the existence of the socialist camp acted as a restraint on the ruling class's attacks on the working class here. This was similar to the preventive concessions non-union employers often make when unions are strong and growing.

The globalization of production and the intensification of international wage competition fomented by imperialism is just one facet of a more general phenomenon that both preceded and followed the collapse of the USSR: the drive by the capitalist class to reverse a century of advances made by the working class. Just as the drive toward war in the post-Soviet era is fueled by the attempt to reconquer lost territories and spheres of influence, the tendency in domestic class policy is to retake ground the bosses lost due to the working-class struggle and the resistance of the oppressed. This reactionary tendency is particularly pronounced in the United States and was given a great impetus by the demise of the USSR, giving the ruling class a new sense of freedom from restraint in its assaults on the workers and the oppressed.

Competition with the rival socialist system, and how to contain and ultimately destroy that system, dominated the thinking and policy of imperialism from the time of the 1917 Bolshevik Revolution in Russia until the end of the Cold War. Indeed, the early reaction after World War I was to send armies against that revolution. When that failed, the U.S. ruling class joined in the campaign of economic and political isolation of the USSR. There followed the Red Scare, the Palmer Raids on immigrants suspected of radicalism, mass deportations, the frame-up and execution of Sacco and Vanzetti, and many other acts of anti-communist and anti-radical hysteria.

This preoccupation became a virtual life-and-death obsession of Wall Street after World War II. The USSR had lost between 20 million and 30 million people in the war. Nevertheless, the Red Army not only defeated the core of Hitler's legions but drove the Nazi armies back to Berlin. The triumph of the Chinese Revolution in 1949 was a veritable social earthquake that shook the foundations of world capitalism. It consummated a twenty-five-year struggle of the Chinese people, led by the Communist Party, to oust the imperialists—first Japan and then the U.S.—and led to the establishment of a socialist government.

After World War II, revolutions advanced in the colonial world. The USSR, which gained in scientific, industrial, and military strength despite the horrendous devastation it had suffered from the German fascist onslaught during the war, became a powerful material center for world socialism and was able to aid the national liberation struggles.

The supreme class-consciousness of the imperialist bourgeoisie came through in its never-ending, crude, anti-communist tirades during the Cold War (read class war), which revealed that the ruling class lived in fear of the spread of socialism. There was never a moment when it failed to attack socialism and the socialist countries in one way or another, during periods of both "détente" and accommodation and periods of violent confrontation as well.

The present-day tirades against revolutionary Cuba and the Democratic People's Republic of Korea, as well as attacks on the socialist features that remain in China and Vietnam, give a small sense of the unbending hostility and slanderous anti-communist propaganda waged against the USSR and the entire socialist world. It flooded the airwaves, blanketed the print media, and was deeply interwoven in the entire culture, from Hollywood to the universities to elementary school. During the McCarthy period in the United States, persecution of the Communist Party and all communists and their sympathizers in political organizations, in anti-racist organizations, in the unions, in the fields of academia and culture was particularly severe. Capitalist democracy was thrown out the window for the sake of rooting out anyone who would try to bring the socialist message to the masses. The broad anti-communist campaign during the Cold War was all-encompassing, universally applied to all struggles, energetically embraced, and sustained even more widely than the current "war on terrorism."

Anti-communist crusade showed ruling-class fear

The fear that the socialist message generated in the ruling class was akin to the fear among the landed feudal aristocracy and Catholic Church hierarchy created by the Protestant Reformation and the rise of capitalism and the bourgeois class in Europe. The witch hunt against communists and communist sympathizers and the demand that they renounce their associations and beliefs or suffer social banishment, imprisonment, and being barred from employment is rightfully regarded as a milder, modern-day version of the Spanish Inquisition. The witch hunt in the U.S. was accompanied by slanderous attacks on communism as a system. The analogy with the Inquisition holds most strongly in that both were driven by the fear felt by an old, outmoded ruling class toward a new, rising revolutionary challenge to its decadent social system.

All this anti-communist vilification and persecution was laid on so heavily precisely because socialism was a historically superior social system, from the point of view of the working class and all oppressed people. Capitalist propaganda was aimed against the fairly basic argument that those who produce the wealth should own and dispose of it for the benefit of society and to meet human need; that wealth produced collectively should be owned collectively. The inhumanity of producing for profit to increase the wealth of a tiny minority could easily be exposed.

The capitalist propaganda machine, which was beamed to all continents, had to struggle to drown out this argument twenty-four hours a day, seven days a week. It was an implicit admission that socialism had a natural attraction for the workers and the oppressed—an attraction that had to be eradicated by a deluge of lies and slanders. (Of course, the ruling class resorted to force where arguments failed.) After all, despite the severe material limitations of the USSR and Eastern Europe, the workers there were guaranteed jobs as a political right. Pensions, free health care, free education, childcare, vacations, paid maternity leave, early retirement in hazardous occupations, etc., were fundamental rights—in everyday life, not just on paper.

However, the economic limitations imposed by underdevelopment, severely aggravated by worldwide imperialist economic blockades and sanctions, put limits on the abilities of the socialist countries to afford the workers and peasants the standard of living attained by the upper echelons of the working class and the middle class in the imperialist countries.

Nevertheless, the social and economic rights in the socialist countries made life far more secure for the working class in general. By contrast, every capitalist recession and depression made it excruciatingly obvious to the bourgeoisie that their system was vulnerable to socialist criticism. In the capitalist world, there would be a sudden and seemingly irrational collapse of the economy, in which poverty appeared to be caused by too much production. Sweeping layoffs were always taking place, causing dislocation and suffering for millions of workers. It was widely known that the USSR never had a single year of decline in production, except during the worst period of the Nazi invasion. That decline, unlike capitalist depressions, was not caused by economic mechanisms inherent in the system itself.

Similarly, the Chinese Revolution empowered hundreds of millions of workers and peasants to overthrow capitalism, break all ties with imperialism, and set out to accomplish national development by mass mobilization and socialist economic planning. China, formerly known as "the land of hunger" where millions perished in frequent famines, served as a socialist model for the oppressed countries in Asia, Africa, the Middle East, and Latin America that were throwing off the shackles of colonialism.

Thus imperialism, headed by Wall Street, was engaged in a global struggle to discredit socialism and, above all, to defend capitalism as a superior system to the workers and the oppressed in both the Third World countries and in the advanced capitalist countries.

However, the State Department, the U.S. Information Service, Voice of America, Radio Free Europe, and all the other organs conveying anti-communist and pro-capitalist propaganda faced major challenges because of the exploitive and oppressive nature of capitalism. In the competition to entice the allegiance of the masses of the world in the direction of capitalism and away from socialism, they were burdened with having to sell a poisonous product that was being offered up as medicine.

To be sure, the imperialists did not rely on ideology alone to secure their interests in the struggle with the socialist camp. The fundamental instruments were the Pentagon, the CIA, the National Security Agency, and a host of "dirty tricks" as well as coordination with the corporations to deny the socialist camp the necessary economic means to succeed in socialist construction. But the ideological and political struggle was a key factor in the overall strategy of defeating socialism. They devoted vast resources to spreading pro-imperialist, pro-capitalist propaganda.

Both the USSR and China, two socialist powers in the period after World War II, while being vastly inferior to the United States in industrial development and infrastructure, nevertheless had the capacity to expose the racism, the poverty, the huge class inequalities of capitalism. They could point to the perennial hardships for the working class created by the boom-and-bust cycle in the imperialist countries, particularly in the U.S., which was supposed to be the pinnacle of world capitalism. They published millions of volumes of Marxist literature annually in over a hundred languages and distributed them throughout the world at prices workers could afford.

The socialist countries had magazines and newspapers popularly written that covered events in the capitalist countries, the struggles for national liberation, news of development aid and assistance given to newly independent countries, and so on. The USSR and China had news agencies that sent daily dispatches around the world. They had radio stations that broadcast in many languages. They had the capacity to expose the capitalist system and wage a political and ideological struggle for the allegiance of political leaders and mass organizations worldwide.

Information about domestic events or the domestic situation in the imperialist countries could readily be used in the ideological and political struggle for influence in a country, a region, or around the world. A major strike in the United States, a mine disaster caused by corporate greed and negligence, a police atrocity in the Black community, a political frame-up, such as that of Angela Davis, or the rebellions after the assassination of Dr. Martin Luther King Jr.—all could quickly become world news written from a socialist perspective and therefore represent a setback for the capitalist propaganda machine. One of the reasons that government economic reports in the United States had to be so carefully considered and shaped for world consumption was that a major exposure could be used against Washington and Wall Street and put forward as an argument for socialism.

Socialist camp set standard for working-class security

The most important point is that the world struggle between the rival social systems acted as a restraint upon the ruling class in the United States in its treatment of the workers and the oppressed, so long as the USSR and the socialist countries set the world standard for the rights of the working class. Perhaps the most fundamental of these rights was the right to a job, something contrary to the very essence of capitalism. Shedding labor is part of the automatic mechanism of capitalism, and the creation of a reserve army of unemployed is an essential condition for the advance of capital accumulation.

Louis Uchitelle, a long-time authoritative writer on capitalist labor economics for the *New York Times*, wrote a book entitled *The Disposable American* that is largely about the evolution of the practice of layoffs in the United States. In it he gives an example of the effect of the collapse of the USSR on the working class. In explaining the escalation of U.S. layoffs, Uchitelle traces their evolution over the last decades of the twentieth century.

"The collapse of the Soviet Union in 1991, ending the Cold War," wrote Uchitelle, "relieved the pressure on companies to preserve job security. Or, as Richard Freeman, a labor economist at Harvard, put it: 'You had a different attitude toward your employees when you thought that Communism was still out there as an alternative.'"[109]

'You had a different attitude toward your employees when you thought that Communism was still out there as an alternative'

The USSR, in addition to guaranteeing job security, also set the standard on guaranteed pensions, free health care, and many other rights. Every capitalist country had to take this into consideration in dealing with its own working class.

Jeff Faux, in his book *The Global Class War*, described the pressure exerted by the Russian Revolution on the capitalist world:

> In 1916 Wilson had promised the electorate that he would not enter World War I. He broke the promise the next year. The socialist Eugene Debs, who had received almost a million votes in the election of 1912, publicly denounced Wilson for sending the working class to fight a rich man's war. He was promptly sent to the penitentiary.

> The appeal of utopian socialism receded in the boom of the 1920s, but when the Great Depression struck, capitalism's governing class faced a graver challenge; the real-world alternative of communism. From the Russian Revolution in 1917 to the fall of the Berlin Wall in 1989, the distribution of income and wealth—and therefore political power—in the capitalist countries was constrained by the competition for **the hearts and minds of the working class**. Given the Soviet Union, communism was no longer just talk. [110] [Emphasis added.]

The need to placate the working class was strongest in Western Europe and Japan, where consciousness and working-class organization was very high. Nowhere was this more evident than in West Germany, which was in direct competition with the German Democratic Republic in the East, the most economically advanced country in the socialist camp. The West German industrial working class and its unions were granted major concessions regarding representation on industrial councils along with the bosses, protections against layoffs, social insurance, and so forth. This German ruling class was indirectly subsidized by not having the burden of military spending—it took shelter under the military and nuclear umbrella of the Pentagon. Once the USSR collapsed, the German ruling class began an offensive to take back the concessions given during the Cold War. Needless to say, layoffs, which had been unknown in socialist East Germany, have now become rampant throughout capitalist Germany, east and west.

The existence of the USSR and the socialist camp set a standard for working-class rights, even in the United States. It set a floor under which the capitalist class could not go and still hold the position, both internationally and domestically, that capitalism was better than socialism for the workers. As Uchitelle observed elsewhere, during the Cold War competition with the USSR, "American workers in a market economy had to be better off than their Soviet counterparts in a government-run system...."[111]

In many ways the relationship of the USSR to the working class in the capitalist countries was similar to the relationship of a strong union movement to non-union workers in the same country. A strong union movement forces the capitalists to grant wages and conditions high enough to keep the union out. In this way, a strong union movement keeps the standards of the entire working class, even the unorganized, higher than they would ordinarily be without the unions.

This, of course, does not prevent large sections of the African-American working class and other oppressed nationalities from being super-exploited and subjected to racism and national oppression.

The capitalist class was compelled, however, to put limits on its exploitation and repression sufficient to keep its own working class from turning against capitalism as a system and responding to socialist agitation. But the collapse of the USSR was comparable to the demise of a powerful union movement in a capitalist country. It relieved all pressure on the bosses to meet any standards of job security, decent pay, vacations, health care, pensions, etc. There were no longer any limits to the concessions that could be demanded of the workers and their unions. The only limiting factor could be the struggle of the workers themselves.

Global expansion cannot dispel crisis of overproduction

Those who thought that, after the fall of the USSR, capitalism had somehow entered a new era that freed it from its fundamental contradictions and the prospect of crises, were deluding themselves. The all-around expansion of the new, streamlined system of global exploitation, which rapidly progressed in the wake of the collapse of the Soviet Union, for a while relieved the general crisis of overproduction endemic to the capitalist system. (It is no accident that the nine-year boom that followed the USSR's collapse was the longest in U.S. history.) But this expansion had only temporarily hidden this profound, unavoidable contradiction.

Under the capitalist system, no matter how wide the scope of its operation, production is driven forward by leaps and bounds under the impact of competition for profits. The bosses look for new, more productive technology and economies of scale to cut their labor costs, and this leads to ever-expanding production, which outpaces the slow development of the consumer power of society. The workers and peasants of the world number in the billions. It is their wages and revenues that overwhelmingly determine the consuming power of society. The consuming power of the tiny minority of the rich and the upper middle class, no matter how extravagant, is a small part of the overall consumption of society.

No matter how many times bourgeois ideologists declare Marxism to be obsolete, no matter how many times bourgeois economists declare that capitalism has entered a new era, they cannot change this law of capitalism— namely, that production must eventually outstrip consumption and that this contradiction cannot but end up in a crisis of overproduction. This is the inevitable result of the profit system.

At the time of this writing, a full-blown global financial crisis of capitalism shows menacing signs of becoming a massive economic crisis. Unemployment is rising and capitalist investment in the U.S. is declining. This takes place in the midst of a global credit crisis that was triggered by the subprime mortgage crisis, the home-loan second-mortgage crisis, the credit card crisis, and other credit schemes engineered by U.S. finance capital. These profit schemes are now coming home to roost, with the potential of defaults worth trillions of dollars.

No one knows at this point how rapidly the crisis will develop and how severe it will be. There are mountains of speculation in the capitalist media. The

Employment growth
61 months after peak

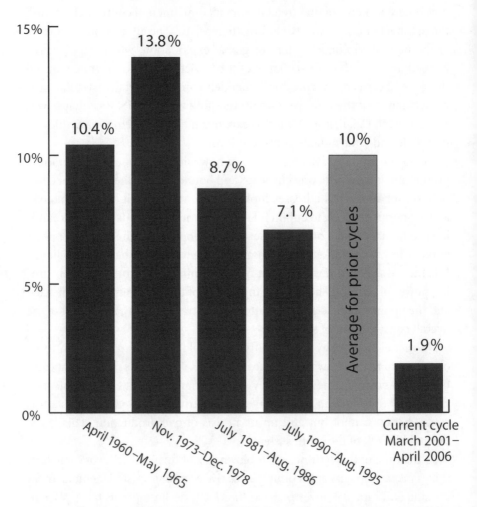

Reprinted from Lawrence Mishel, Jared Bernstein and Sylvia Allegretto, *The State of Working America, 2006/2007*. Copyright 2007 by Cornell University. Used by permission of the publisher, Cornell University Press.

Percentage of growth in employment created in each recovery 61 months (five years) after the highest level of employment in the previous recovery period. For more than a quarter of a century U.S. capitalism has put fewer and fewer workers to work with each recovery. [FG] assessments range from a mild recession, to a recession with a soft landing, all the way to a financial collapse on the scale of 1929. Whatever the case turns out to be, the present situation is rooted in the inevitable crisis of capitalist overproduction. The bosses will seek to unload the crisis on the backs of the workers, just as they unloaded the subprime mortgage crisis on the backs of working class homeowners. The workers had been swindled by greedy mortgage lenders, who in turn were backed up by the biggest commercial and investment banks on Wall Street—from Citigroup to Morgan Stanley, Bear Stearns, and Merrill Lynch, among others.

The present credit crisis arises out of the policies pursued by Alan Greenspan, former head of the Federal Reserve System, who presided over a series of interest rate cuts for the banks following the collapse of the high-tech bubble of 2000. The collapse of 2000 precipitated an economic downturn, a rise in unemployment, and a decline in corporate investment and profits. By 2001 the automatic processes of the normal capitalist boom-to-bust cycle, followed by a recovery, had failed to reignite the economy sufficiently to get things going again.

Economic growth was so sluggish during the so-called recovery that no new jobs were being created. In its first 27 months, that is, **in the period of expansion** of the economy from November 2001 to March 2004, there was a **net loss of 594,000 job**s. From the point of view of the workers, this was the worst "recovery" since the government began tracking these numbers in 1940. According to Stephen Roach, chief economist at Morgan Stanley, the job growth by 2004 was 8 million less than in a "normal" recovery. It took a record 61 months for the job level to reach where it had been when the downturn started in March 2001. Finally, when job growth did begin, most of it was in low-wage industries.[112]

It is significant that the only other "jobless recovery" in U.S. history was the recovery from the previous recession, in 1991. And a study of job growth in previous recoveries shows a steady trend downward in the rate of jobs created during the recovery. In the "normal" down cycle during a recession, inventories of excess goods that piled up by the end of the boom are slowly sold off or destroyed altogether. Then industry gradually starts on an upward course again, creating jobs as capitalists invest for the new round of struggle for markets, which have opened up again.

By 2002, however, U.S. capitalism had reached the stage where it could not create jobs by the automatic process that drives a capitalist upturn. The productivity of labor due to technology was so high that the markets for goods and services were insufficient for the capitalists to make big investments in new productive capital. In addition, an undetermined number of jobs were being created in low-wage countries or in overseas markets.

The answer dictated by Wall Street was for Greenspan to funnel government money to the banks by lowering the interest rates they paid for it and for Bush to hand out tax breaks to the corporations and the rich. The aim was to pump up production and profits—and in the process to create jobs. But because the markets were not expanding fast enough, all the efforts to overcome capitalist overproduction by pumping credit and tax breaks into the economy could not send the bosses rushing to borrow money to invest.

The housing boom was insufficient to absorb all the fictitious capital created by the Federal Reserve System

The subprime mortgage boom was part of the answer. Greenspan gave a wink and a nod to the schemes concocted by the banks to create a housing boom on the basis of tricky loan offers. The housing boom, made even more profitable by hiring low-paid, undocumented construction workers, was a way to help ward off the crisis of capitalist overproduction and overcome the jobless recovery.

But the housing boom was insufficient to absorb all the fictitious capital created by the Federal Reserve System. Therefore, much of the trillions of dollars pumped into Wall Street by Greenspan and Bush wound up in stock market speculation and credit schemes to fleece the masses rather than in job-creating investment in production. In other words, parasitic activity among the bankers had run amok.

Interest—whether on subprime mortgages, on credit cards, or on the $1.2 trillion advanced for refinanced home equity loans—is a kind of tax workers pay bankers for the "privilege" of borrowing funds for their survival because they cannot live on their pay. This is another way for capitalists to enrich themselves at the workers' expense in addition to direct exploitation on the job.

But the current economic situation threatens to go beyond the subprime mortgage crisis to a more general economic crisis. After three decades of declining income and increasing debt, the workers and large sections of the middle class have little or no reserves to withstand even a short-term capitalist downturn, let alone a protracted crisis or a major crash.

So long as the accumulation of surplus value (or profits) is the aim of all economic activity, so long as the distribution (sale) of the huge quantities of the means of life—food, clothing, housing, social services, and other elements of everyday need—to the broad masses of people depends on the ability of the bosses to sell them at a profit, then shutdowns, layoffs, slashing of wages, mass unemployment, and suffering and hardship on a mass scale are inevitable. Globalizing capitalism cannot change this one iota. It can only delay the appearance of the crisis, but it will expand its scope and depth when the crisis does come. This is something bourgeois economists do not want to openly contemplate, but the working class needs to understand.

Today the new division of labor within the workplace has made possible a new worldwide social division of labor. And while the giant corporations are reaping super-profits from the initial stages of this process, they are also multiplying their own gravediggers—the world working class.

Three decades of getting poorer

6

Where high tech is leading

High tech and the military · Role of technological offensive in weakening unions · Changed social composition of working class · Declining rate of profit and capitalist crisis · The era of permanent layoffs · 30 million lose their jobs · 'A ceaseless bloodletting' · The end of 'safe' jobs · Law of capitalist accumulation applied to U.S. · High tech and increased exploitation of labor Manufacturing jobs down, manufacturing up · From manufacturing jobs to low-wage service jobs

The transformation of the capitalist economy in the electronic age of automation and the communications revolution flows from the same drive for competitive advantage that drove previous transformations of capitalism. It goes hand in hand with the bosses' increasing the exploitation of labor. This compulsion to shed labor, to take its skills away, to cheapen the worker, to get more production per labor hour, and to increase surplus value is the force that propelled capitalism from the stage of simple cooperation to manufacturing to the industrial revolution and then to mass production and the assembly line, sometimes referred to as Fordism.

At each stage the working class was transformed and subjected to shocks. The generations that were subjected to the initial assaults were disoriented by capitalist reorganization. But subsequent generations were able to recover and reconstitute themselves for renewed struggle.

For example, when the steel industry began mass production in the U.S. in the late 1880s, only the skilled crafts were organized. Then the craft unions were broken in the bloody Homestead lockout of 1892. An attempt to get union recognition was defeated in the steel strike of 1919. It was not until 1937 that the masses of semi-skilled steel workers got a union, as part of the general upsurge of industrial unionism of the 1930s.

Henry Ford opened up his Highland Park assembly line for production of the Model T in 1913. Thousands of skilled workers were pushed aside by the assembly lines. It took the new generation of semi-skilled assembly-line autoworkers until 1937 to win their industrial union in the great Flint sit-down strike.

Assembly-line mass production eventually spread to the rest of the auto, truck, and farm machinery industries, meatpacking, and the production of refrigerators, sewing machines, radios, etc. Production expanded as the electrification of the country spread, roads and highways were built, and the capitalists put in place an overall infrastructure.

The present stage, the so-called "digital" or "information" age of automat-ed production and advanced communications, has temporarily changed the relationship of class forces in favor of the bosses, as did all previous quali-tative advances in technology under capitalism. This change, however, has been aggravated by the collapse of the USSR and the consequent economic and political strengthening of the bourgeoisie on a worldwide basis against the workers.

It was not only the strikebreaking, union-busting offensive headed by Pres-ident Ronald Reagan in the 1980s that pushed back the working class. Simul-taneously there was a profound technological attack aimed at reducing labor costs and increasing surplus value. While they were attacking the unions, the bosses were promoting the development of technological innovation that would undermine the position of the working class in numerous ways.

New computerized and robotized factories would eliminate massive num-bers of jobs and reduce the skills needed for many others because the skill formerly exercised by the worker would now be embedded in a machine; thus it would be easier to employ lower-skilled workers and reduce wages based on increased competition for lower-skilled jobs. In the absence of a significant fight-back, the technological offensive would create a climate of fear and insecurity among the workers. This situation was played upon by the labor leadership of the AFL-CIO to depict retreat as the only course. It led to a decade of unprecedented concessions.

In individual strikes the workers showed their determined willingness to fight back and stop the concessionary juggernaut. (See Chapter 11, "Decades of rank-and-file fight-back.") But the labor leadership left each battle to be fought out separately and made no attempt to mobilize the workers and the communities in the kind of mass struggle necessary to meet the challenge. It would have required a class-wide mobilization to meet the unified ruling class assault, which had the full backing and encouragement of the Reagan administration and the Carter administration before it. Thus the technologi-cal onslaught went forth relatively unhindered. Modernization meant inten-sified exploitation and increasing the strength of capital over labor.

High tech and the military

Much of the early scientific-technological revolution was rooted in the militarization of U.S. capitalism. The Pentagon commissioned the first computers for the purpose of computing the trajectory of shells. Later this technology was handed over to IBM, which was reluctant to develop it at first.

When the Soviet Union inaugurated the space age in 1957 by launching Sputnik, the first satellite to orbit the earth, the Pentagon and the ruling class went into a virtual panic. The Eisenhower administration reorganized the entire educational system in the U.S., from elementary to post-graduate schools. Billions were poured into the sciences. Grants and subsidies flowed generously from Washington and science competitions were organized for students.

Again, it was the Pentagon that funded much of the early technology that led to the Internet. Once the World Wide Web was developed by the Geneva-based European Organization for Nuclear Research (CERN) in 1990, the U.S. military used it not only for global communications but also in order to decentralize the entire communications system so that it could not be easily disabled in a major war—most importantly, in a nuclear war with the USSR. The microchip and the integrated circuit, the bases of the computer revolution, were also promoted by the Pentagon for the advancement of missile technology.

After the launching of Sputnik, the Pentagon formed the Defense Advanced Research Projects Agency (DARPA), linking together the top scientists and developers of technology. It expanded the military-university complex, linking major science-teaching and research institutions such as MIT, Stanford, Duke, and others—all to insure U.S. military superiority.

This gave great impetus to a new development in monopoly capitalism that, in Lenin's time, had been comparatively undeveloped: the institutionalization on a massive scale of permanent state-organized, military-guided research and development as an integral part of capitalist big business.

Lenin had noted, however, that parasitic monopoly capitalism, which could also rely on its dominant position in control of the world's resources and markets, could use its position of power to inhibit or retard the development of any technical innovation that might undermine a profitable industry. This feature of imperialism is still operative.

For example, the oil monopolies have for generations fought against any and all attempts to develop non-fossil fuel or renewable energy sources. The auto barons and all their allied industries have fought against the development of mass transportation.

However, by and large the global class struggle against the socialist camp accelerated the development of militarism and the military-industrial complex, which in turn drove the scientific-technological revolution. The generals, being but businessmen in uniform who become captains of industry when they return to civilian life, made the technology developed through government programs available to the capitalists in order to multiply their exploitation of labor and strengthen their competitive position on the world arena. Of course, the workers paid for all this.

As the scientific-technological revolution matured and early advances in computerization, miniaturization, and communications were perfected, the bosses channeled these developments into business applications in order to improve their position against their imperialist rivals. However, the German and Japanese imperialists were getting back onto their feet and cutting deeply into the world market share of the U.S. corporations.

The technological offensive was particularly powerful in Michigan, the bastion of the Big Three automakers. In 1981, shortly after the air traffic controllers' strike was crushed by the Reagan administration, Governor William Milliken created a task force that strategized on how to strengthen the Big Three auto monopolies in their struggle against their rivals. The program was sold to the public as focused on keeping jobs in Michigan. In fact, its real purpose was to cut labor costs for the auto barons.

The bosses created "automation alley," the road M-14 that connects the University of Michigan at Ann Arbor with Detroit. They developed computer-integrated technology, robotics (GM soon became the largest single user of robots in the world), and other technological innovations that spread from the Big Three to their growing army of outsourcing suppliers, as part of the general offensive against the workers in the auto industry.

Similar processes went on in steel with the development of the so-called mini-mills and electric furnaces. To create steel, these mills used scrap iron instead of the iron ore and coke (made from coal) used in the large, integrated, and unionized mills. With the new technology the bosses could put electric-furnace steel mills anywhere because scrap iron is easily obtainable in any location, unlike coal and iron ore, which had to be shipped from the mines. The cost of capital was far lower than for the giant integrated mills. Thus the bosses were able to set up non-union plants far away from union environments and from the concentrations of Black workers in urban industrial centers.

The large, integrated mills also introduced automation. Employment in the steel industry has plummeted in the past three decades, while steel production rose.

The technological offensive, combined with union busting, strengthened the bosses' hand in the demands for concessions; the long slide in the general standard of living of the working class in the United States was underway.

Role of technological offensive in weakening unions

In order to prepare for a truly broad fight-back, it is first necessary to grasp the overall situation presently faced by the workers. It is characteristic of this new stage of low-wage imperialism that the working class has felt extraordinarily weak and on the defensive, even during a capitalist upturn. It has been generally understood that a capitalist upturn increases the need for labor by the bosses. It has historically been the most favorable environment for the workers in the struggle over wages and conditions.

But in spite of the capitalist expansions that have taken place in the last three decades, the workers have been subjected to multiple economic pressures that have robbed them of much of their advantage. We restrict ourselves for the moment to the purely economic causes and leave aside all other factors—the state, the political situation, the labor leadership, etc.—that influence the economic situation of the workers.

The expansion of capital investment inside the United States has been weak. The consequent advantage to the workers of capital's increased need for labor-power to fuel its expansion has been diminished by the demand being satisfied either abroad, through offshoring, or by increasing use of low-wage labor at home, including immigrant labor. It has been further diminished by the replacement of labor by machinery through the development of technology.

During a downturn, on the other hand, what weakens the workers and generally enables the bosses to drive down wages is the increase in unemployment. The contraction of capitalism brought about by the crisis of overproduction brings plant closings and reduction in shifts, re- *Worldwide wage competition makes the working class feel great economic pressure even during a capitalist economic boom* sulting in layoffs and adding new battalions to what Marx called the reserve army of labor—the unemployed workers who are forced to compete for the diminished number of jobs during a downturn.

The expansion of the capitalist class into low-wage, high-unemployment regions abroad, and the importation of low-wage immigrant labor from those same areas around the world, has the effect of putting the same type of pressure on the workers inside the imperialist countries as they would normally be feeling during a downturn.

Furthermore, past capitalist downturns have been the primary occasion for the bosses to swallow up their rivals, concentrate ownership, and retool with whatever new technology was available. As the capitalist cycle moved from its bust period and began a renewed expansion, the bosses would re-hire based upon expanded productive capacity.

In the last three decades, however, the continuous and unrestrained introduction of labor-reducing technology has been widespread throughout the economy, even during a capitalist boom. Outsourcing and offshoring have also proceeded without letup, independently of the capitalist cycle. Layoffs have become massive and permanent, particularly in high-paying manufacturing jobs, and are now becoming permanent even in medium-paying office jobs.

The availability of this vast reserve army for direct exploitation by the U.S. capitalists has been made possible by technology. The workers understand this and fear it—rightfully so. The threats of outsourcing, of offshoring, of companies threatening to go out of business, are credible to the workers, who have seen these threats carried out all around them. This acts as a severe deterrent and a form of class intimidation by the employers, particularly when stable jobs even at low wages are hard to come by.

And no one is helping the workers find ways to turn the situation around. All they feel is negative, competitive pressure. They are unaware of their latent power to use their strategic position in the new global, "just-in-time" production and retailing economy, unaware that they can turn the situation around by using the very technology that is being used against them. (More will be said on this later.)

This negative pressure is not nearly as dramatic as the effect of sudden mass unemployment. But over three decades of outsourcing, offshoring, and immigration, the pressure has become more insidious than a market crash. The confidence of the workers has been slowly and imperceptibly undermined by the bosses' gradualist, piecemeal tactics: layoffs in one plant or a group of plants, staggered over time and in different industries and regions. Production is shifted to low-wage areas behind the backs of the workers. Over time, concessions have been made to the bosses in increments. It all adds up to a massive attack on the entire class, but in slow motion.

The workers are influenced by what has become known as the "fear factor" and their leadership has shown no way out. It has helped condition them to accept the capitalist "realities" of corporate "competitiveness," instead of fighting to change those realities through the struggle for basic workers' rights.

These are the global economic conditions that have shaped an almost continuous, thirty-year slide of living and working conditions for the vast majority of workers and oppressed people in the United States. The results are creating privation among the workers and pushing them back to pre-New Deal conditions, the kinds of conditions that led to class rebellion in the 1930s and to the upheavals of the 1950s and 1960s.

The late Sam Marcy, chairperson and founder of Workers World Party, in a very important book entitled *High Tech, Low Pay: A Marxist Analysis of the Changing Character of the Working Class*, published in 1986, analyzed the early stages of the high-tech revolution and its effect on the working class in the United States.

In a section devoted to its impact on the unions, he traced the phases of development of the productive forces under capitalism from the manufacturing phase of simple cooperation to the industrial revolution and large-scale machinery to mass production— primarily assembly line production—in the early twentieth century. He then described the high-tech phase:

> This [mass production] stage has now given way to another phase of technological development. The mass production period which began with Ford and continued for a period of time after the Second World War was characterized by expansion. But the current stage, the scientific-technological stage, while continuing some of the earlier tendencies of development, contracts the workforce.
>
> Like all the previous stages of capitalist development, the current phase is based on the utilization of workers as labor power. But its whole tendency is to diminish the labor force while attempting to increase production. The technological revolution is therefore a quantum jump whose devastating effects require a revolutionary strategy to overcome.[113]

Marx's studies had shown that the advance of capitalist technology subordinated the workers more and more to the machine, made work more and more monotonous, increased the division of labor, and reduced the skills of the workers. The final result was to lower the wages of more and more workers by setting them in competition with one another, all to increase the profits of capital. The high-tech revolution, Marcy showed, has accorded completely with Marx's analysis.

Marcy noted the decline of manufacturing jobs and the growth of service jobs. But he did not simply talk about them as a bourgeois category. The main aspect of the shift from manufacturing to service was, for the vast majority of workers forced into this change, a shift from high-wage jobs to low-wage jobs.

Changed social composition of the working class

Marcy promoted various tactics and strategies for the struggle against the anti-labor assault, many of which are completely applicable today. But also important were the sociological observations he made and the political conclusions he drew.

> It is this highly significant shift from the higher paid to the lower paid which is dramatically changing the social composition of the working class, greatly increasing the importance of the so-called ethnic composition of the working class, that is, the number of Black, Latin, Asian, women and other oppressed groups, particularly the millions of undocumented workers.[114]

The changed social composition of the working class—both from the point of view of the growing numerical significance of the oppressed and the increasing preponderance of low-wage workers over the higher-paid, more privileged workers—"matters a great deal," wrote Marcy, "because in terms of political struggle, the objective basis is laid for political leadership to be assumed by the more numerous segment of the class..."[115]

Quoting from an earlier piece he had written on the effect of high technology on the workers, Marcy wrote:

> What has happened, particularly in the last decade, is that the very speed of the introduction of high technology, the very sophisticated type, has undermined the privileged sectors of the working class (such as those in steel and auto) on a world scale and has begun a leveling process which has undermined the living standard of the working class as a whole....
>
> ... While it continues to ravage the living standards of the workers, at the same time it lays the objective basis for the politicization of the workers, for moving in a more leftward direction and for organization on a broad scale. The political consciousness that ought to correspond to the new material conditions of life has lagged behind, as it almost always does.[116]

The tendency of imperialism to build up the privileged layers of the working class at home, which Lenin had observed, was already in the 1980s beginning to be counteracted by the application of automation, robotization, and new industrial processes, mini-mills, etc. The higher-paid workers in heavy industry—such as steel, auto, rubber, and electric, the bastions of the AFL-CIO—were being undermined by capitalist technology and pushed into the lower-paying service industries or long-term unemployment.

Marcy and other communists were rightfully anticipating that the high-tech assault on the workers would lead to an upsurge of the class struggle in the near period. The basis for this prognosis was both subjective and objective. The process of pauperization of the working class would project forward the more militant sections of the workers, while the increase in the productivity of labor would turn out more and more commodities which would be harder and harder to sell in the limited world capitalist markets. This would intensify the classical capitalist malady of overproduction, accelerate an economic crisis, and stimulate the class struggle.

But the collapse of the USSR transformed the world situation and postponed the immediate prospects for class struggle in the United States and the imperialist camp as a whole.

Declining rate of profit and capitalist crisis

Marcy's work was designed to show the destruction of working-class living standards wrought by the development of the productive forces, the subsequent change in the composition of the working class, and how these developments formed the basis for the revolutionary revival of the class struggle. His focus was on the spread of technology by the ruling class inside the United States. He analyzed the internal restructuring of U.S. capitalism and charted the early stages of the widening pauperization of the proletariat.

Marcy shone a spotlight on new trends in the development of capitalism in the age of the scientific-technological revolution. He explained the laws of its development flowing from the innermost features of capitalism, as they had existed since its inception—the struggle to increase surplus value and to reduce labor. And he catalogued their effects on the workers and the oppressed, with an emphasis on how this affected the labor unions.

In analyzing the decline of the labor unions and the rise of technology, Marcy invoked Marx's law on the decline in the rate of profit.

> The bourgeois press is full of the wonders of high technology and the introduction of robots in almost fully automated factories. But they neglect to mention an extremely important element in the economic laws of motion governing capitalist society: robots do not produce surplus value.

> As Marx demonstrated long ago, machinery or constant capital is the result of past labor and past surplus value. Profit does not come from machinery itself. It is the labor of a worker, known in Marxist terms as variable capital, that produces surplus value, from which profit is derived. Workers produce a greater value than they receive back in wages, and it is the unpaid portion of their labor that produces surplus value. But a robot is not a worker. A robot is fixed or constant capital, which does not produce profit. Only unpaid human labor produces profit.[117]

The entire purpose of introducing new technology is to have fewer and fewer workers producing more and more commodities in shorter and shorter time. But new technology is usually very expensive and the high cost can outweigh the savings on labor. Since the rate of profit is calculated by dividing the total profit by the total investment in both constant and variable capital—that is, in machinery and raw materials as well as wages—costly new means of production reduce the rate of profit.

The capitalists who are willing to spend money on new technology before their rivals get it temporarily escape this problem. In fact, new technology produces a great leap in how much unpaid labor can be gotten from the workers. The capitalists who get it first garner super-profits, i.e., profits above the level of the rival capitalists using the older technology. The first capitalists using the new technology sell at or slightly below the general price of the commodity and still make extra profit.

Following Marx's argument in *Capital*, Marcy wrote,

> With fewer workers and more constant capital, the organic composition of capital changes, resulting in a falling rate of profit. This is an invariable law of the capitalist process of production. It cannot be gotten around.
>
> The more dead or constant capital and the less human or variable capital used in production, the higher the organic composition of capital. This invariably leads to a decline in [the rate of] profit.
>
> Despite this, the individual capitalists are driven to substitute labor-saving machinery for workers because it gives them a competitive advantage. For a certain period, the capitalist who is able to utilize the new technology and lower the unit cost of his product can actually enjoy a greater profit because the market reflects a generalized cost still based on the old technology. Eventually, however, the new technology itself becomes generalized and the rate of profit falls.
>
> The advantage to a higher composition of constant capital [new technology—FG] is always temporary. It spurs on destructive competition, in which much equipment that could still be socially useful is made prematurely obsolete.
>
> In order to compensate for the falling rate of profit, the owners are forced to increase the volume of profit. This can only be done by further increasing production.[118]

This is what leads to capitalist overproduction and economic crisis.

The example of General Motors is illustrative. GM early on invested huge sums in robots. It became the largest user of robots in the world during its heyday as the totally dominant auto manufacturer in the capitalist world. But this advantage gradually evaporated as the robotization spread to Japan, West Germany, and the other two of the Big Three. GM has long been closing plants and laying off workers despite its early lead in technology. These plants, under a socialist system of production for human use instead of profit, could be producing cars at affordable prices, or could be switched over to produce vehicles for a much-needed mass transportation system, employing the hundreds of thousands of GM workers who instead have been laid off purely to boost profit margins.

As Marcy pointed out, "automation does not solve the problem of the capitalist contradiction that leads to economic crisis. On the contrary, it exacerbates it precisely because of the decline in the rate of profit."[119]

This explanation was made as a preamble to understanding the decline in union strength in the United States. Marcy was showing what the workers were up against and how the only way out was to break out of the narrow limitations of labor relations that have been dominated by a leadership that accepted the capitalist profit motive and the bosses' arguments about "competitiveness." Marcy showed that the race to introduce new technology amounted to "an intensification of the exploitation of labor" and urged a class-wide counteroffensive.

Marcy was writing before the new phase of global restructuring, but the essence of his Marxist analysis applies completely to the current worldwide wage competition generated by the capitalists.

Marx developed his analysis of the law of the declining rate of profit much earlier, during the competitive phase of capitalism. He showed that the underlying tendency for the rate of profit to decline, as a result of the insatiable need to accumulate capital and profit, promoted capitalist crisis and would contribute to its ultimate destruction.

Lenin later pointed out that, in the monopoly stage, capitalist competition continued but on a higher and more intense level. Monopoly and competition exist side by side under imperialism. Each monopoly grouping seeks to vanquish or absorb its rivals. In the age of monopoly, competition becomes more deadly and dangerous for the working class as unbridled competition reaches into every corner of the globe by use of the most advanced technological means.

The neo-liberal drive to destroy all vestiges of economic sovereignty in countries of Asia, Africa, and Latin America is driven by the competition for super-profits. The special economic zones in the oppressed countries, where the imperialist corporations practice virtual extra-territoriality—suspending local laws that protect labor, curtailing or outlawing unions, expropriating peasants and seizing land for development—are all part of the relentless competition of the imperialists to expand their profits.

At the root of the current technology-driven worldwide wage competition is the cutthroat competition of tiny groups of owners and directors who operate behind closed doors, unelected and largely anonymous to the masses. These corporate barons secretly decide the fate of millions of workers the world over as they carry out the ruthless restructuring of world capitalist exploitation.

The era of permanent layoffs

In the late 1970s, the capitalist class and the state turned sharply toward an era of escalating confrontation with the labor movement and with the workers in general. This attack began on the economic front with a technological assault and on the political front with a state-backed anti-union campaign by the bosses.

The capitalist ruling class opened up the restructuring of its manufacturing apparatus: so-called reindustrialization. Downsizing, plant closings, outsourcing, and layoffs were rife as this process got underway. And as the campaign progressed, it became clear that U.S. capitalism was entering a new phase of forcing down the wages and general standard of living of the working class.

For the bosses, the freedom to increase the rate of exploitation of labor means the freedom to reorganize the labor force, whether to accommodate new job-destroying or speed-up technology or to outsource or offshore. This means freedom to lay off workers at will. The labor movement has been the only real obstacle to this freedom, both directly through union contracts and indirectly by setting the standard for job security for broad sections of the workers.

Nothing has so profoundly shaken the labor movement and the working class in general as capital's successful imposition of the regime of permanent mass layoffs. It is a temporary triumph of capitalist ideology that layoffs of 5,000 or 10,000 workers no longer merit anything but passing mention in the capitalist press and no longer evoke protest and resistance. The argument made by the corporations that the workers must help them to remain "competitive" and succeed in boosting their profits has become an ideological battering ram used for three decades to justify layoffs. The labor leadership has come to accept this practice, much to the detriment of the rank and file.

Over the past thirty years layoffs have become a way of life for the vast majority of workers and business as usual for the bosses

The degree to which permanent layoffs have become a standard practice and principal strategy among corporate managers was illustrated by the layoff of 3,400 workers in 2007 by Circuit City, the second-largest retailer of consumer electronics in the United States. It has more than 600 superstores in forty-five states and more than 40,000 workers, in addition to larger operations in Canada.

In April of 2007 the company announced it was laying off 8 percent of its workforce—not because they were doing a bad job or because the company was doing away with their jobs, but in order to lower wages. This was Circuit City's brutal answer to its competition with Best Buy, number one in the industry. The workers, mainly sales clerks and warehouse workers who earned $10 to $20 an hour, were fired. The company announced it would immediately start hiring at lower wages and that the fired workers, many of whom had years of seniority, could apply for their old jobs after ten weeks.[120]

The crude, unapologetic manner in which this cruel act of replacing workers who were just getting by with workers who are to receive poverty-level wages merited nothing more than passing articles in the capitalist media. It was duly noted and then promptly forgotten. There was similar non-response a month later to the announcement by Citigroup that it would cut 17,000 jobs and move 9,500 others from various points around the globe to lower-cost locations. Around the same time Ford Motors announced the intended layoff of 70,000 workers; this announcement made one or two news cycles. Over the past three decades, layoffs have become a way of life for the majority of workers in the United States and business as usual for the bosses.

30 million lose their jobs

Louis Uchitelle, the *New York Times* reporter referred to earlier, is considered the expert on layoffs among liberal* bourgeois journalists. In the mid-nineties he followed the downsizing of the "rust belt" industries and wrote a best-seller entitled *The Downsizing of America* based upon a major series by the same name in the *Times*. Now another book, *The Disposable American: Layoffs and Their Consequences*, written a decade later, continues his coverage of this deep trend, which has alarmed his particular current in the establishment.

In an April 2007 article, following up on the findings in his book, Uchitelle described the regime of permanent layoffs and its role in pushing down the

---

* The term "liberal" is used in this book in the sense that it is generally understood in the United States, as distinguished from its interpretation in Europe, Latin America, and elsewhere. On the spectrum of bourgeois politics, liberalism in the U.S. has been generally associated with defense of civil liberties, civil rights, fighting poverty, limiting repressive measures of the state, and so on—i.e., with more progressive politics. In Europe, Latin America, and elsewhere the term is more associated with neo-liberalism, the worship of the capitalist market, imposition of austerity for the masses, and political reaction in general. U.S. liberalism, because it is a bourgeois ideology and does not base itself on a class analysis or an anti-imperialist analysis, is inconsistent and can take reactionary positions. Nevertheless, the right-wing mood in the U.S. ruling class over the past three decades has been so severe that bourgeois politicians nowadays run from being labeled as liberals.

standard of living of the workers. "Across America, more than 30 million [full-time workers] have been forced out of their jobs since the early 1980s, the Bureau of Labor Statistics (BLS) reports, and regaining lost incomes has not been easy."[121] The incomes of a quarter of these workers had declined by at least 30 percent.[122]

To arrive at the number of 30 million, Uchitelle took unpublished statistics on displaced workers from the Bureau of Labor Statistics and added his own estimates. He says he did not include part-time workers, who are far more easily forced out of their jobs.[123]

In *The Disposable American*, Uchitelle expands on the subject. He shows that the BLS biennial survey of displaced workers found that between 3.3 percent and 5.9 percent of full-time workers at least twenty years of age were permanently laid off every two years from 1981 to 2003. Uchitelle acknowledges that the official figure is an undercount. It is based on a survey of 60,000 households. Only one layoff is counted, even if the person has been laid off more than once in the previous three years. Forced buy-outs are not counted. Tens of thousands of forced early retirements are not counted. Contract workers whose contracts have ended are not counted. Temporary workers, who are terminated when their work runs out, are also left out of the statistics, even if they had been on the job for several years.

"Whatever the reason," concludes Uchitelle, "the growing presence of temps and contract workers—they constitute more than 10 percent of the nation's workforce, up from 2 or 3 percent thirty years ago—is evidence of a reorganization of the workplace to accommodate layoffs without having to call them that."[124]

Another form of disguised layoffs is growing more and more common. "Many companies outsource food service or building maintenance or computer services or payroll preparation or sales or some other function, and the employees who did this work in-house are transferred to the payrolls of the outsourcing companies. An unknown number then quit rather than accept the lower pay and reduced benefits so often forced on them by their new employers. They lay themselves off in effect."[125]

Uchitelle discusses "the netherworld of jobs that are so poorly paid and so stripped of opportunity (no promotions, no raises, no training) that quitting them and being laid off are roughly the same thing. The message from management is that your value is minimal, not worth preserving. The people in these jobs are drawn from the 25 percent of the workforce earning $9 an hour or less [in 2004] in fast-food restaurants, discount stores, supermarkets, telephone centers, and elsewhere. Turnover is frequently 100 percent a year or more: indeed, the jobs are designed for turnover. People lay themselves off out of discouragement and exhaustion."[126]

'A ceaseless bloodletting'

Cyclical layoffs have always been present in the capitalist system. The boom-and-bust cycle, the result of periodic crises of capitalist overproduction, has always resulted in layoffs. In the decades after World War II, there were always permanent technological layoffs in the bust periods of low production as U.S. capitalists upgraded their technology. Capitalism always expels workers from the workforce by destroying jobs through technology and reorganization. But until the late 1970s, permanent layoffs due to technological innovation grew only gradually alongside cyclical unemployment.

A permanent layoff is when a job is permanently destroyed, either by technology or other means. Cyclical layoffs mean that workers are laid off during the downturns, or recessions as they are called, but the majority are rehired during the upturn.

Capitalist overproduction entails a race among capitalist groupings against one another to capture markets and enhance profits. This dictates that each corporation expand production and investment in plant and equipment. Since they all try to outdo each other, the total productive capacity of each industry outstrips the ability of society to purchase the masses of commodities produced. Markets become saturated and the bosses are unable to sell off their inventories at a price yielding a profit. Production slows, workers are laid off. They struggle to get by on unemployment insurance, their savings, and/or side jobs.

In past crises, the overstocked inventories would eventually be reduced, orders would start coming in, and expanded production would require the rehiring of workers laid off during the downturn. The upturn phase of the cycle would start again. As the bosses resumed a higher and higher level of production, many of the workers would eventually come back **to the same jobs that they had been laid off from, with the same pay and benefits** and at the same or similar plant, using equipment based upon the same general technology. This applied to union jobs, but also to many non-union jobs where the capitalists followed the pattern set by the unions in order to keep them out.

This cyclical type of unemployment, in spite of the traumatic hardships and suffering imposed upon the working class, nevertheless permitted a certain degree of continuity and stability, particularly among the organized workers. And this, in turn, made it easier to carry on the class struggle.

Permanent layoffs, on the other hand, lead to the dispersal and disorganization of the workers. Thus, they not only benefit the bosses in the immediate sense of directly increasing the mass of profits, but they also give the capitalists advantages in the struggle. The union leadership can never reverse the situation unless they stem the tide of this disorganization and develop strategies for reuniting the workers in mass, class-wide mobilizations.

Unlike cyclical layoffs, the mass layoffs in the age of globalization and the scientific-technological revolution, in addition to being permanent, **take place during the boom period as well as the bust period**. To be sure, declines in capitalist production during the 1981, 1991, and 2001 downturns made the mass layoffs shoot up. The layoffs in the next phase of capitalist crisis, which has already begun, are sure to be catastrophic. But what is distinctive is that, during the last three capitalist revivals that followed the downturns, the layoffs continued.

For example, the steel industry had continuous layoffs from 1973 to 1995, through boom and bust alike, which reduced steel industry employment from 600,000 to 180,000. Uchitelle describes it as "ceaseless bloodletting." Youngstown Sheet & Tube opened up an assault in 1977 by firing 5,000 workers at its Campbell, Ohio, works. United States Steel fired its first shot with the announcement of fourteen plant closings in 1979, during a period of capitalist expansion. Steel workers occupied U.S. Steel's headquarters in Youngstown, Ohio, but the international union and the labor officials in general let the protest remain isolated.[127]

The steel barons were changing over from open hearths and blast furnaces, which took ten to twelve hours to produce a batch of steel, to oxygen furnaces, which could produce the same amount of steel in forty-five minutes. They then added electric furnaces, which were even more efficient for the production of specially hardened steel. The last two methods were already being used in Europe and Japan, whose older steel industries had been largely destroyed in World War II. Wall Street's corporate rivals had a higher rate of exploitation of labor and the bosses in the United States were determined to catch up. They shut down serviceable factories that could have lasted many years and produced high-quality steel, but the pursuit of profit came first and the workers had to pay the price.

When Ronald Reagan became president in January 1981, he put the capitalist state firmly behind the bosses' campaign to lay off workers and restructure industry. He implemented a plan, devised by President Jimmy Carter before he left office, to break the air traffic controllers' union, PATCO. Reagan fired 11,400 workers and barred them for life from federal employment.

The ruling class got the signal. Jack Welch took over the helm of General Electric in 1981 in the wake of the PATCO attack. In his first two years, which was a time of capitalist downturn, Welch fired 72,000 workers. The company bought RCA and, during the following period of capitalist upturn, Welch fired 51,000 RCA workers and then 31,000 more.[128] (His nickname by then was Neutron Jack, after the neutron bomb, which killed people but left structures standing.) Throughout the recovery of the 1980s, U.S. capitalists continued their layoffs and restructuring. The auto industry alone shut down over thirty-five plants.

The layoffs continued into the 1990s, again through both recessions and revivals. According to Uchitelle, when the numbers of workers displaced were tabulated in 1995, it turned out that layoffs occurred at a higher rate during the first half of the nineties, a recovery period, than in the first half of the eighties. "These were comparable years of recovery from recessions," writes Uchitelle. "The layoff rate was higher, in fact, in almost every year of the nineties expansion than in the nearly as long eighties expansion—a signal that layoffs were spreading even in good times."[129]

The end of 'safe' jobs

Cyclical unemployment was the predominant cause of layoffs during the post-World War II period, when U.S. capitalism dominated world production and had a stranglehold on technology. The rise of inter-imperialist economic competition and the scientific-technological revolution qualitatively transformed the situation.

As Marcy noted in *High Tech, Low Pay* in 1986: "This latest phase in the development of capitalism has to be seen in light of its evolution of more than half a century and the role of the U.S. in the global economy at the end of the Second World War. At the time this country held a predominant position in both science and technology. It controlled the fundamental levers of capitalist development in the West and had gained political and diplomatic predominance over Japan."[130]

Marcy showed how the United States was responsible for 50 percent of the world's industrial production after World War II but, because of the revival of German and Japanese capitalism, that proportion had shrunk to 25 to 30 percent by the end of the Vietnam War. It slipped further to 20 to 25 percent by the mid-eighties.

World War II had destroyed so much of the industrial infrastructure of Europe and Japan that the capitalist classes there had to rebuild from scratch. This lent itself to the renewal of industry on the basis of high technology.

The technology of the U.S. was being diverted into military production while Washington's imperialist rivals were pouring all their know-how into civilian industry. Before long, Germany and Japan were eating into the U.S. monopoly over the world capitalist economy.[131]

Immediately after World War II, the European central banks were pushed to purchase large quantities of dollars and make them available for buying U.S. factories, machinery, distribution centers, and offices. U.S. capitalist production expanded both at home and abroad with the additional stimulation of military spending. Without competition, profits poured into Wall Street.

Strikes reached a high in the U.S. during this period. The bosses resisted the workers' demands and some of the strikes were long and hard fought. But with their flowing profits, with the Cold War against the Soviet Union consuming the ruling class, and with the civil rights movement rising in the 1950s, the bosses thought it the better part of wisdom not to open up another front by declaring war on the workers at home. This tactical, conditional restraint by the bosses is what some labor historians refer to as the "social contract."

According to Uchitelle, nearly 20 percent of the workforce had relative job stability working in areas like telephone companies, electric utilities, banks, trucking companies, airlines, railroads, and insurance companies. These monopolies were either protected from price competition by the government or had monopoly pricing power in their industry. If they raised wages, they could pass on the cost in the form of price increases for the whole working class. Other giant corporations that had few or no unions—such as Eastman Kodak, Sears, IBM, Hewlett-Packard, and Procter & Gamble—maintained funded pensions and health insurance and offered raises and promotions in order to keep the unions out.

Uchitelle's reference to job stability must be seen in a strictly relative light. Job stability under capitalism, even in the best of circumstances, is precarious. No one is considered to have the right to their job. No boss is required to keep the plant open and workers working. No worker's living is protected by anything other than a union contract and/or the company's fear of the class struggle. Layoffs can come at any time. These decisions are made by the owners, not the workers. Workers' security is always subject to financial decisions made by the bosses, based upon considerations of maximizing profit.

To be sure, as early as the 1950s, workers in light industry—such as New England textile workers, shoe manufacturers, furniture workers, and others— were under constant pressure of permanent layoffs as company after company moved to the South, where so-called "right-to-work" laws kept unions out. This movement picked up steam under President Dwight D. Eisenhower when the national highway system was built and it was easier to put equipment on a truck and move, even if it meant going far from the company's traditional customer base.

Of course, Uchitelle was talking mainly about white, male workers—the upper layers of the working class—who had relative job stability and livable wages and benefits. The vast majority of African-American workers (not to mention the impoverished Black population of the rural South), Latina/o workers laboring in agriculture and sweatshops, Asian, and Native workers had little if any job security. They were shut out of the unions and of higher-paid employment in general. They were the last hired and first fired. They suffered from low wages, high unemployment, and semi-employment; held menial jobs for the most part, and in addition suffered the oppression of racism and discrimination. They constituted a significant part of the working class and were deliberately and consciously marginalized by the racist ruling class; their plight was largely ignored by the upper echelons of the labor leadership.

But by the mid-1970s, with the end of the monopoly economic and technological position the United States had held in the world capitalist economy since World War II, whatever job stability did exist came under sharp pressure as the restructuring of U.S. capitalism got underway.

Deregulation exposed 13 percent of the workforce, employed in 'safe' industries, to layoffs

President Jimmy Carter deregulated the airlines in 1978, setting off a competition in the industry followed by mergers and bankruptcies that led to tens of thousands of workers losing their jobs—a process still underway in 2008. "Deregulation in airlines and soon after in trucking, banking, telephones, railroads, and utilities exposed to layoffs nearly 13 percent of the national workforce employed in these once safe industries," wrote Uchitelle.[132] During the same period, Reagan not only signaled encouragement for a broad anti-labor offensive by breaking the PATCO strike but also gave the stamp of approval for a new wave of mergers and acquisitions among the monopolies, which led to tens of thousands of additional layoffs.

Law of capitalist accumulation applied to U.S.

Marcy opened *High Tech, Low Pay* with the following paragraph:

> Beginning in the late 1970s, U.S. big business and the government launched a coordinated assault on the wages and living conditions of the working class which, at the time this is being written [1986], has lasted nearly six years. The magnitude of this drive, judged by previous historical standards, makes it the longest and most severe ever.[133]

Thus, in 1986 the offensive against the economic condition of the working class was half a decade long and was considered the "longest ever." In retrospect, it is clear that by the mid-1980s the unfolding attack was still in its early stages. U.S. and world capitalism had entered a period of capitalist restructuring that has continued virtually and is now in its third decade.

The political setbacks for the working class on the world arena—the collapse of the USSR and Eastern Europe plus the dangerous encroachments of capitalism and imperialist investment into the Chinese socialist revolution—and the aggressiveness of the U.S. ruling class, backed by the capitalist state, have created the objective political basis for the protracted extension of this anti-labor offensive.

Marcy discussed the changed composition of capital—the tendency of constant capital to rise in comparison to the rise in variable capital. And he raised Marx's important analysis of this issue in relation to the inevitability of capitalist crises of overproduction.

But the underlying law—the law of capitalist accumulation—is what drives the entire process. And it is impossible to understand the last thirty years of perpetual layoffs, the contraction of high-wage manufacturing jobs, and the growth of the low-wage service industry without taking this law into consideration. It is necessary to deal with this in relation to the present phase of the scientific-technological revolution in order to get a proper grasp on what the working class is facing and the crisis of the labor movement.

The law of capitalist accumulation discovered and elaborated by Marx in *Capital* explains how, especially since the beginning of the industrial revolution, capitalism has continuously created a reserve army of labor that is always available, in greater or lesser numbers, to satisfy the steadily expanding needs of capital for exploitable labor-power. The internal force within the capitalist system that continually creates and recreates this reserve army of labor is the struggle for greater productivity of labor; that is, the permanent quest by the bosses to increase the rate of exploitation, to increase surplus value and profits by using technology to get more and more unpaid labor from the workers.

To do this, they employ more and more expensive means of production whose aim is both to shed labor and to make the remaining workers produce more in less time. As the system grows, each new cycle of reinvestment requires larger and more complex means of production. At each new stage the larger, more productive machinery creates two important effects: first, more sales are required because more commodities are produced per unit of labor-time; second, and most important for the working class, with each new round of labor-saving technology, fewer workers are employed relative to the new, larger means of production. This means that the employed labor force may grow in absolute numbers, but nevertheless expand slowly compared to the expansion of capital overall. If the capitalist economy slows sufficiently, then the absolute number of employed workers declines. In either case, there is an excess number of workers compared to the needs of capital.

Thus, the unceasing struggle by the bosses to increase profits by increasing productivity is the permanent, systemic cause of the reserve army of labor under capitalist relations of production. Full employment, in the true sense of the word, where every worker who can work has a job, is possible only in a planned socialist economy where production is geared to satisfy the consumption needs of society and not to create surplus value for an exploiting class of profiteers.

High tech and increased exploitation of labor

Capitalists have always used multiple methods of increasing surplus value, i.e., of increasing the rate of exploitation in pursuit of an increased mass of profits. The key to increasing the rate of exploitation is to increase the unpaid labor time of the workers. This can be done by lowering wages, by forcing workers to work longer hours without a proportional increase in pay, or by speeding up work—all methods that are rampant across the globe and in use constantly in the United States.

Workers who do not have unions or contracts to protect them have no recourse to enforce any conditions on the boss, except for whatever federal or state labor regulations may exist with regard to overtime pay, legal limits on the workday, minimum wage laws, etc. This is the situation faced by a growing mass of the workers. Enforcing those laws often necessitates cumbersome legal processes pursued through an unsympathetic capitalist state bureaucracy and judicial system. It is a lengthy, costly process, which, in the absence of a union, requires legal representation and organization that is most difficult to get, especially for the low-wage workers who need it the most.

Furthermore, millions of workers have no knowledge of these minimally protective labor laws and regulations. The bosses and the government do as little as possible to promote the knowledge of the legal rights of workers. In fact, they do as much as possible to obstruct their implementation.

All these methods of increasing exploitation—cutting wages, speeding up the work process, prolonging working hours—have been resisted historically by the class struggle of the workers. All the protective legislation—including laws regarding wages, hours, child labor, the right to organize, occupational safety, among others—originated in the class struggle, from the beginning of the twentieth century through the 1930s. Great victories were won.

As a stark reminder of what it was like when the bosses had full sway, unrestricted by organized labor, union activists sometimes carry signs at labor demonstrations that say, "We are the people who brought you the weekend."

However, the all-important struggle against widespread technological assaults by the bosses has not been part and parcel of the unions' struggle. Such battles have been intermittent, rearguard, delaying tactics, such as the attempt to slow down the use of automated cranes on the docks or "piggy-backing" trailers and containers in the trucking industry. The concept of a class-wide struggle to stop a tidal wave of technological layoffs must be put on the agenda of the labor movement, not just as a peripheral item but as a central feature of labor's program. And it will not be enough just to put it on the agenda. Strategy, tactics, and the appropriate propagandistic and ideological support for the tactics must be paramount in the effort. We will say more about this later on.

Historically, the tactics of lowering wages, speeding up production, and prolonging the workday have been employed at every stage of capitalism. But the fundamental method used historically to increase the rate of exploitation has been the development of labor-saving technology. It is by this means that capitalism has advanced from stage to stage.

The entire *raison d'être* of capitalism—in fact, its very role in history as a social system—has been to develop the productivity of labor through the advancement of technology. By so doing, in 600 years it has raised the standard of living of society in general and of the working classes compared to the slow or stagnant economic development during the preceding thousands of years of slavery and feudalism. By developing technology, capitalism created the potential for abundance and material security for all humanity. This is the material premise for socialism, communism, and the abolition of class exploitation forever.

But the bourgeoisie hardly did this for the benefit of humanity. On the contrary, the capitalist class developed technology, from the earliest stages of cooperation to the space age, because it was the fundamental means to more and more thoroughly exploit labor.

The law of capitalist accumulation explains why technology in the hands of the capitalist class has always been the enemy of the working class. It explains how the capitalist class, in pursuit of increasing profits, continually generates a surplus of workers available for exploitation and for the expansion of capital, regardless of the rate of growth of the overall population.

It explains why "full employment" under capitalism never means that all the workers potentially available in the population have jobs; it means there is a perpetual reserve army of unemployed or semi-employed workers available for additional exploitation when the bosses need them.

Bourgeois economists openly admit this fact when they refer to "full employment" in the same breath as 3 or 4 percent unemployment. These numbers are "acceptable" to them as so-called full employment. In a workforce of 150 million, 4 percent unemployment means a minimum of 6 million workers without jobs. And then, even under the best of circumstances, millions more are not even considered part of the workforce and are not included when calculating the rate of unemployment.

An extreme example of this phenomenon in the United States was the situation during World War II. During the war 15 million people, mainly male, were inducted into the military, producing an artificial labor shortage. Nevertheless, employment went up from 40 million in 1940 to 53 million in 1945. Before the war the official unemployment had been 17 percent—meaning a reserve army of unemployed of about 8 million. When, in 1943, the traditional male workforce began to be depleted, the ruling class opened up job opportunities for women workers. Jobs in industry were also opened up to African Americans, and Mexicans were brought into the country to work on the farms and railroads. More older workers got jobs and so did many youth. It is not as if these millions of workers had not needed jobs and additional income before the war started. It is just that capitalism kept them on the margins as part of the reserve army of labor.

So even with a sudden and artificial reduction in the workforce caused by sending millions of workers into the military on an emergency basis, U.S. capitalism had a reserve to call on. It had created enough surplus workers to enormously increase production (and capital) sufficient to wage an imperialist war on two fronts, from Asia to Europe. Of course, when the war was over, many of the women and other oppressed workers were abruptly pushed out of production to make room for the returning soldiers, most of whom were white males.

A more contemporary anecdote in connection with the hidden reserve army is worthy of note. In January 2006, some 25,000 people lined up for 325 jobs at Wal-Mart in a suburb just outside Chicago. All but 500 were Chicago residents. The *Chicago Sun-Times* quoted the manager of public affairs for the region as saying: "In our typical hiring process we have 3,000 applicants. They were really crowing about 11,000 in Oakland, Calif., last year. So to get 25,000-plus applications and counting I think is astonishing."[134]

It should also be noted that this line of workers desperate for low-paying, low-benefit jobs came at the height of the so-called recovery, during a period of what bourgeois economists refer to as "low unemployment."

Manufacturing jobs down, manufacturing up

In recent years there has been much talk about the decline of manufacturing employment in the United States and in the imperialist countries in general. To be sure, the offshoring of production plays a role in this decline. But offshoring plays more of a role in lowering wages here by threatening to send plants overseas and setting up a worldwide wage competition.

Offshoring is only part of the story in the decline of manufacturing jobs. The fact is that while manufacturing **employment** in the U.S. has **decreased,** manufacturing **output** has **increased.** According to the *Survey of Current Business*, the gross domestic product in manufacturing, measured in the year 2000 dollars, rose from $1.426 trillion in 2000 to $1.536 trillion in 2005—an increase of $110 billion (in constant 2000 dollars).[135] Manufacturing employment in the same period went down from 17.263 million to 14.232 million—a decline of 3.5 million jobs. In percentages, manufacturing production **increased** by 7.7 percent while manufacturing employment **dropped** by 17.6 percent![136] In just five years, 3.5 million workers, according to government figures, were expelled from manufacturing, even as manufacturing output was increasing.

The goal of technological innovation by the capitalists is to expand surplus value and increase the mass of profits. In the manufacturing industries, according to the U.S. Census Bureau, profits went from $158 billion in 1990 to $381 billion in 2000 and $524 billion in 2005.[137] **The vast rise in the mass of profits was based upon increasing the rate of exploitation of labor through technology and the simultaneous steady expulsion of workers from manufacturing.**

According to Uchitelle, "Starting in 1979 the manufacturing labor force steadily declined, mainly through layoffs, from a peak of 19.4 million in 1979 to 17.6 million in 1998 and then precipitously to 14.3 million in 2005, as more and more efficiencies kicked in and more and more merchandise once made in America came from abroad."[138]

The steel industry illustrates the ravages of technology upon the workers. In 1990 the industry produced 95.5 million tons. Production went up and down over the years, but rose to 131 million tons of steel by 2004. Employment, on the other hand, declined from 187,000 steelworkers in 1990 to 95,000 in 2004. But most importantly, whereas it took 350 million work

Manufacturing increases & employment decreases

Output and profits between 2000 and 2005
in constant 2000 dollars*

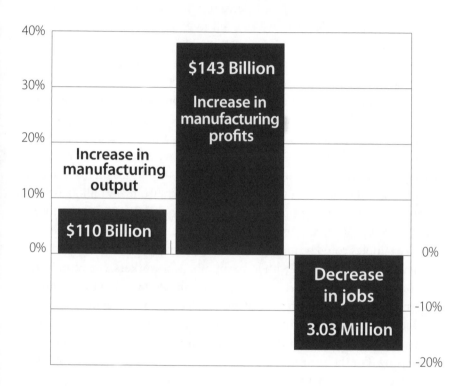

* Data from U.S. Census Bureau, *Statistical Abstract of the United States: 2007* (126th Edition), Washington, DC, 2006. (See endnotes 135-137.)

hours to produce 95.5 million tons of steel in 1990, it took 87.8 million hours to produce 131 million tons in 2004.[139] The steel workers were ravaged by technology; oxygen and electric furnaces decimated the steelworkers and weakened the union immeasurably.

The aerospace industry is another case in point. In 1990 it had sales, measured in constant 1987 dollars, of $123.5 billion. That figure declined to $114.4 billion in 2005, a drop of 7 percent.[140] Employment in the aerospace industry, which was 841,000 in 1990, fell to 456,000 by 2005, a net loss of 385,000 jobs, or a decline of 45 percent![141]

In the paper and paper products industry, sales measured in 2000 dollars hovered around $50 billion between 2000 and 2004, while employment in the industry during that same period dropped from 605,000 to 496,000, a net loss of 109,000 jobs or 18 percent. In the food, beverage, and tobacco products industry, combined sales in constant dollars remained around $155 billion during the five-year period 2000 through 2004. Yet employment dropped 4 percent, from 1.76 million to 1.689 million—71,000 jobs lost in five years. In the printing and related industries, production went from $49 billion to $44.4 billion, a drop of 9 percent in the same five years, while employment went from 807,000 to 663,000—an 18 percent decline, with 144,000 jobs lost.

Such examples could be multiplied in most industries. But the point is that manufacturing can **expand** with lower numbers of workers, can **remain the same** but with lower numbers of workers, or can **decline**—but the decline in the number of jobs completely outstrips the decline in production.

Uchitelle regards the permanent layoff of 30 million full-time workers over twenty years as a matter of bad policy, of corporate insensitivity, of capitalism gone wrong. On the contrary, the expulsion of workers from industry after industry under the impact of technology is a law of capitalist development.

Workers are made superfluous in relation to the needs of capital and are forced onto the unemployment rolls or into semi-employment. Many more are forced to go from higher-paying jobs to lower-paying jobs, going from job to job, uprooting themselves and their families to move from one location to another in search of work, or are forced into unwanted, premature retirement.

From manufacturing jobs to low-wage service jobs

It is an axiom of Marxism that increased competition among workers is the source of low wages. This is true on a world scale in the age of globalization, and it is certainly true on a national scale in the United States. Marcy characterized the period that was unfolding in the 1980s and has dramatically advanced up to the present. He wrote:

> The distinctive feature of this particular phase of capitalist development, the scientific-technological phase, is that while it enormously raises the productivity of labor, it simultaneously lowers the general wage patterns and demolishes the more high-skilled, high-paid workers. It enhances the pauperization of the working class.[142]

Since Marcy wrote this, the destruction of high-wage manufacturing jobs by technology has continued relentlessly, resulting in millions of workers competing for a diminishing number of remaining high-wage jobs. In the absence of the organized, united resistance of the workers, the bosses utilize this competition in order to lower wages in manufacturing. They not only apply pressure to the organized workers and force union concessions, but they also create new low-wage, non-union manufacturing jobs. Witness the massive growth of non-union parts plants in the auto industry.

The bosses applied high-tech innovation to manufacturing in the earliest stages of the scientific-technological revolution. But the drive to restructure high-wage jobs out of existence through downsizing, consolidations, etc., has been rife throughout U.S. capitalism.

Manufacturing lends itself to sweeping changes through computerized production, robotization, sensor technology, and so forth. Furthermore, manufacturing was the bastion of high wages; eliminating high-paying jobs and increasing the rate of exploitation in manufacturing was a priority for the bosses. Thus, manufacturing workers were the first to be laid on the technological chopping block by the exploiters in their global competition for profits.

The effect of this process in manufacturing, which had a relatively high concentration of African-American workers, was objectively racist in character and increased national oppression and suffering by the Black community.

The law of capitalist accumulation operated with particular force in the manufacturing industries, thus creating a large reserve army of workers ripe for exploitation by the growing low-wage service industry. Many of those 30 million workers and more cited by Uchitelle, who were laid off in the twenty years between the early 1980s and early 2000s, were driven into low-wage service jobs. Furthermore, each new generation entering the workforce was less able to get high-paid manufacturing jobs and wound up behind a fast-food counter, working as retail clerks, or in other low-paying jobs.

Uchitelle, who came up with the calculation of 30 million full-time workers permanently laid off, has close ties to experts in the Bureau of Labor Statistics. He described a national survey showing that two years after a layoff "two-thirds of the victims say they are working again. Of those two-thirds,

only 40 percent, on average, are making as much as they had in the old job....
The rest are making less, often much less. Out of a hundred laid-off workers,
then, twenty-seven are making their old salary again, or more, and seventy-
three are making less, or are not working at all. That downward pull con-
tributes mightily to the wage stagnation that has persisted,
Out of every 100 with only occasional relief, since the early seventies."[143]
workers who had A report by McKinsey Global Institute found that only
been laid off, 73 36 percent of U.S. workers displaced in the past two de-
were either making cades found jobs at the same or higher pay; 64 percent, or
less money or not almost two-thirds of the workers displaced, had a decline
working at all in income, and 25 percent of those whose income declined
had a reduction of 30 percent or more.[144]

Uchitelle says that 50 million jobs were created during the same period.
But these were mostly low-paying jobs. Tonelson had written previously,
in *The Race to the Bottom*, that 2.4 million manufacturing jobs were lost
between 1979 and 1999. "Employment in the typically lower-paying service
sector, however, jumped by some 37 million jobs, with the two biggest job-
creating service sectors being the two lowest-paying: wholesale and retail
trade and a category including business personnel and health services."[145]

Thus, while the law of capitalist accumulation—the creation of a larger and
larger reserve army along with the application of labor-saving technology—
was operating strenuously in manufacturing and other high-wage sectors,
the growing low-wage sectors of the service industry were absorbing waves
of the expelled manufacturing workers, as well as younger workers increasingly unable to find jobs with a living wage. The Wal-Marts, the McDonald's,
the hotel chains, the call centers, etc., were profiting from the growing competition among the workers.

In the Economic Policy Institute's bi-annual study, *The State of Working
America, 2006/2007,* authors Mishel, Bernstein, and Allegretto calculated
that what they call "goods producing" industries—mining, construction, and
manufacturing—made up 28 percent of all industry in 1979 but dropped
to 16.6 percent by 2005. The corresponding rise in the "service producing"
industry—defined as transportation, utilities, wholesale trade, retail trade,
information, finance, insurance, real estate, and then a general category of
services—went from 72 percent in 1979 to 83.4 percent in 2005.[146]

Most significantly, the study of contracting versus expanding industries
shows that from 1979 to 2005 those industries with high wages were contracting at a significant rate and those with low wages were expanding.

Mishel and his co-authors, liberal, pro-labor statisticians, calculated that "expanding industries have paid annual wages roughly 20 percent lower than the industries that were contracting. The gap in pay between expanding and contracting industries has been somewhat larger for compensation (wages plus benefits) than wages alone, indicating that the benefits gap is wider than the wage gap."[147]

This trend has accelerated in the recent period. Not only did manufacturing lose over 3 million jobs from 2000 to 2005, but high-paying information technology jobs declined by 565,000, while the service sector gained 3.6 million jobs during the same period.

While technology under capitalism is a nightmare that brings speed-up, job elimination, and lower wages, under a planned economy, where production takes place for social use rather than profit, the simplification of the labor process and the rise in productivity can make it possible to lighten the burden of the workers, to steadily reduce the workweek, and to take stultifying repetition and life-long specialization and one-sidedness out of the labor process.

Under socialism the goal of increasing the productivity of labor in society as a whole would be in order to increase leisure time, improve and expand the quality of life of the workers who produce all wealth, and set free their creativity instead of destroying it. Technology would serve humanity rather than the working class serving the profiteering owners of technology.

7

Globalization and low pay

44 million low-wage jobs in 2006 · Deskilling jobs and the 'education' scam · Marx on wages and growing poverty · More multi-earner working-class households · Costs rise, men's wages fall—women take up the burden · Driving down the value of labor power As real poverty goes up, official poverty goes down · Why the bosses need Wal-Mart

Paul Krugman, a liberal economist who writes for the *New York Times* and who has hailed globalization in the past, in September 2006 wrote an understated description of the last period, so far as the majority of workers are concerned. In a column called "The Big Disconnect," he asserted: "The stagnation of real wages—wages adjusted for inflation—actually goes back more than 30 years. The real wage of nonsupervisory workers reached a peak in the early 1970s at the end of the postwar boom. Since then workers have sometimes gained ground, sometimes lost it, but they have never earned as much per hour as they did in 1973."[148]

Krugman did not supply any figures for his assertion, but there are statistical studies to back up his findings. Such studies, whether carried out by bourgeois analysts or working-class analysts, are totally reliant on the capitalist government for data. The Bureau of Labor Statistics (BLS), the Census Bureau, the Commerce Department, and like agencies are the only institutions with the apparatus to collect national and international statistics. Researchers are at the mercy of decisions they make on what to disclose and how to slant their published findings. And, of course, the heads of these agencies have a strong class bias.

Statistics are highly political. What is put down in black and white by the capitalist government can be used against the ruling class by its liberal opponents or by revolutionaries. Government statistics can be used by unions in negotiations. They can be used by community organizers to agitate, organize, and press their demands, or by anti-racist or women's organizations. They can be used by legislators at every level of government in arguing for progressive programs. And they can be used by socialist or anti-imperialist forces around the world to condemn U.S. capitalism. For example, statistics on infant mortality rates show that the people in socialist Cuba, as poor as that country is, have better health care than the masses in the central cities and rural areas of the United States.

Poverty statistics can be politically embarrassing for any administration. If they are given in such a way as to draw a true picture of the hardships of the masses, these statistics can become material for an indictment of capitalism itself. The same holds true for trends in wages, in unemployment or under-employment, in economic racism, in the conditions of unionized workers versus non-unionized workers, in on-the-job safety, etc.

On the other hand, government economic statistics are also used by the Federal Reserve System, the Treasury, the President's Council of Economic Advisers, and other financial officials. The task of the government agencies is to inform the bourgeoisie and policy makers of trends. At the same time, the statisticians are under pressure to blunt or conceal public findings that depict the real results of capitalist exploitation.

Nevertheless, statistics compiled over decades cannot conceal the deep trends in capitalism and the declining condition of the workers and the op-pressed, even if they conceal the full extent of that decline.

One of the few measurements that comes closest to revealing the condition of working-class wages is that of the wages of "private production and non-su-pervisory workers." This category, according to *The State of Working America, 2006/2007* and other sources, includes about 80 percent of the workforce—factory workers, construction workers, and "a wide variety of service-sector workers ranging from restaurant and clerical workers to nurses and teachers." High-paid managers and supervisors were left out of the study.

The *SWA* study showed that the average weekly wage of a worker in 1973 was $581.67 (measured in 2005 dollars). It dropped steadily until 1995, rose during the capitalist upturn until 2000, and then began to drop again. In 2005 it was $543.65 a week, even as the upturn continued. Thus, with ups and downs, the study's analysis of government statistics concludes that in a little more than three decades there was a drop of close to $40 in the weekly earnings of four-fifths of the working class, or almost 7 percent.

This trend is confirmed by a hard-to-find chart from the BLS called "Wag-es and Benefits: Real Wages (1964-2004)." Calculating this time in 1982 dol-lars, the BLS records show that the average weekly earnings of all non-farm workers were $331.59 in 1973, declined steadily until 1992, rose until 2003, and then began to fall again to $277.57 a week in 2004—a drop of $55 a week in 1982 dollars, or over 16 percent!

Despite the dramatic differences between these two sets of statistics, the trend is undeniable. The wages of the working class are going down. Neither set of statistics reveals the figures for annual wages for this group of workers. The only statistics for annual wages available in the *SWA* survey and in typical BLS tables include salaried employees who are not workers but get paychecks in six figures. These big paychecks pull the averages up to such an extent that it is not possible to recognize in these high averages the true condition of the mass of the workers.

But the weekly earnings statistics for the vast majority of workers over three decades point in a direction that is intuitively sensed by the entire working class and the oppressed: things have been going down for a long time. The capitalist economy has shot up. Vast wealth has multiplied. The stock market has risen to undreamed-of heights. But the workers who are watching this rise of new ranks of billionaires and staggering sums spent on mergers and acquisitions are doing so from a descending escalator of declining living conditions.

The decline in wages has been aggravated by the loss of fixed-benefit pensions, the higher cost of health care or the loss of health-care coverage altogether, as well as the general rise in the cost of housing. Longer hours, more people in a family working, the frequency of layoffs, shut downs, expansion of part-time work, temporary work, and so on—all these factors constitute part of a hidden decline in wages.

44 million low-wage jobs in 2006

All the trends in capitalist development—whether it is globalization and offshoring, outsourcing, technological destruction of jobs, or the deskilling of the working class—are moving in the consistent direction of lowering the wages and standard of living of the workers. A recent study of low wages by a liberal think tank, the Center for Economic and Policy Research (CEPR), gave a snapshot of this development as of 2006. Their study, entitled "Understanding Low-Wage Work in the United States," defined a low-wage job as one paying $11.11 an hour or less.[149] This is a highly conservative definition of low wages, considering that the poverty-level wage for a family of four is considered by the government as $9.83 an hour, assuming a 40-hour week for 52 weeks of work a year, or an annual income of $20,447.

But even if we accept this conservative number, the study showed that 44 million jobs in the United States paid $11.11 or less. By another measure, taking the bottom third of the workers by wages earned, 47 million workers earned $11.64 or less.

The calculation of $11.11 an hour was arrived at by taking two-thirds of the median income of male workers. The median wage is that at which half of all workers make more and half make less. The median wage of male workers was $16.66 an hour. The reason the study chose two-thirds of male workers' median instead of the national median was because women earn such low wages that if they were included it would have brought the median down and consequently made the definition of low wages even lower!

The author points out that "inadequate wages are only the beginning. Low-wage jobs also mean few or no benefits, rigid schedules, late-night shifts, unsafe and unhealthy conditions, and lack of respect."[150] The study cites statistics showing the inadequacy or complete lack of health-care coverage, short-term and long-term disability insurance, life insurance, retirement benefits, paid time off for sick days or vacations, training, education, and other benefits.

The study also included a list of what it defined as low-wage occupations—those in which at least half the workers earn less than $11.11 an hour. The list includes only occupations with 500,000 workers or more. It covers 23 occupations, including 4.3 million retail sales people with a median wage of $9.20 an hour; 3.5 million cashiers with a median of $7.82 an hour; 3 million general office clerks with a median of $11.09 an hour; 2.36 million laborers and freight, stock, and material movers with a median of $9.91 an hour; 2.3 million food preparation and serving workers, including fast food, with a median of $7.11 an hour; 2.27 million waiters with a median of $6.83 an hour; 2.1 million janitors and cleaners, not including housekeepers, at a median of $9.82 an hour: stock clerks, nurses' aides and orderlies, receptionists, security guards, groundskeepers, maids, and so on. Furthermore, although the figures for wages are for the median, the likelihood is very high that those above the median in these low-wage industries are making very close to the median and are thus fully part of the low-wage workforce.

This list is significant because it is precisely these low-wage occupations that are slated for the fastest growth in the economy. In the Labor Department's job-growth projections for the decade 2004-2014 in the U.S. among the top areas of growth are the following: retail salespersons, customer service representatives [call centers–FG], janitors and cleaners, waiters and waitresses, food preparation (includes fast food), home health aides, orderlies and attendants, and general and operations managers.[151]

Deskilling jobs and the 'education' scam

All the apologists for the system have been touting education as the way for workers to raise themselves up. But the entire trend of capitalist development moves in the direction of deskilling workers and lowering wages. The bosses want to lower skills in order to reduce the need for training, to render workers virtually disposable by making them almost interchangeable, and thus to increase the competition among individual workers.

Increasing the division of labor and the application of technology has as its goal simplifying the labor process. Thus, under capitalism the relative need for higher education and higher skills in the workforce goes **down**, not up, with the advance of technology. Of course, some workers with higher education and complex skills are required by the new technology. But the proportion of the jobs created that require higher education and higher skills and offer higher pay goes down relative to the creation of lower-skilled or unskilled jobs at low wages.

While failing to analyze the systemic cause of this essential feature of capitalism, Uchitelle nevertheless unmasks the training-and-education-are-the-answer smokescreen created by the ruling class and their advisors.

He shows how the Comprehensive Employment and Training Act of 1973 led to the creation by state and city governments of 750,000 full-time jobs for adults at federally subsidized wages. The CETA program was the result of the struggles of the sixties and seventies. The program paid to train workers and then to provide them with jobs with subsidized wages. It did not provide high wages and it barely made a dent in unemployment and underemployment in the Black and Latina/o communities, to which the program was directed. But in 1982, CETA was destroyed anyway (by a then Democrat-controlled Congress) to be replaced by the Job Training Partnership Act. This marked the end of even limited government job creation.

While the CETA program recognized that job training without jobs creation was useless, the Reagan administration, and later on the Clinton administration, at the behest of big business, sold job training and education alone as the answer to the growing epidemic of layoffs.

Rather than a skills shortage existing, millions of workers in the U.S. have more skills than their jobs require

This became "part of every politician's stump speech," wrote Uchitelle. But training for what? "Rather than a skills shortage, millions of American workers have more skills than their jobs require. That is particularly true of the college educated, who make up 30 percent of the population today, up from 10 percent in the 1960s. College graduates now often find themselves working as salespeople, office administrators, taking jobs in hotels and restaurants, or becoming carpenters, flight attendants, and word processors to make a living. The number of jobs that require a bachelor's degree has indeed been growing, but more slowly than the number of graduates, according to the Labor Department, and that trend is likely to continue through this decade."[152]

Uchitelle shows that, in 2003 and 2004, about half of hiring was at $13.25 an hour or less: hotel and restaurant workers, health-care workers, temporary workers, and so on. "The $13.25 is important. More than 45 percent of the nation's workers, whatever their skills, earned less than $13.25 an hour in 2004, or $27,600 a year for a full-time worker. That is roughly the income that a family of four must have in many parts of the country to maintain a standard of living minimally above the poverty level. Surely lack of skill and education does not hold down the wages of nearly half the workforce. Something quite different seems to be true: the oversupply of skilled workers is driving people into jobs beneath their skills and driving down the pay of jobs equal to their skills."

No matter what level of skill workers have, the bosses strive to reduce it, from fast food work to office work to industry and highly technical occupations. Fast food restaurants have taken all skill out of cooking. According to *Fast Food Nation* by Eric Schlosser, "At Burger King restaurants, frozen hamburger patties are placed on a conveyer belt and emerge from a broiler ninety seconds later fully cooked. The ovens at Pizza Hut and Domino's also use conveyor belts to ensure standardized cooking times. The ovens at McDonald's look like commercial laundry presses, with big steel hoods that swing down and grill hamburgers on both sides at once."[153]

In 1999 the top executives of Burger King, McDonald's, and Tricon Global Restaurants (which by 2002 owned Taco Bell, Pizza Hut, and KFC), gathered at a conference to discuss labor shortages, employee training, computerization, and the latest kitchen technology, according to Schlosser. At the time, these three corporations employed 3.7 million workers worldwide, operated 60,000 stores and opened a new fast food restaurant every two hours.

"Putting aside their intense rivalry for customers, the executives had realized ... that when it came to labor issues, they were in complete agreement." They were unified in wanting to redesign kitchen equipment so less money would be spent on training workers. The goal was to make equipment that only worked in one way and then simplify instructions "to the fifth-grade level" and write them in Spanish and English. "All of the executives agreed that 'zero training' was the fast food industry's ideal, though it may never be attained."[154]

In a similar trend, Xerox has been experimenting with a system of artificial intelligence to eliminate skilled repair technicians. The company believed that repairs could be handled by customer service over the phone by walking the customer through the repairs, according to Simon Head's work, *The*

New Ruthless Economy.[155] But the company did not want to "invest in training or support for customer service representatives that would increase their knowledgeability. Instead, the company believed that reducing dependency on people knowledge and skills through expert artificial intelligence systems offered the best approach."

The company turned over transcripts of all previous conversations between customer service agents and customers to a "re-engineering" firm to automate the exchanges by creating scripted answers to all possible questions. "With the expert system containing most, if not all, of the knowledge required to perform a task or solve a problem, the knowledgeability of the agent could be confined largely to data entry and information retrieval procedures."

Another example of how highly skilled technical jobs are being destroyed is the process of making designs for integrated circuits on microchips. "Today, the circuit is drawn on a computer so that digital instructions for the mask [pattern] can be transmitted from one machine to another. The circuits on the chip are etched by an electron beam. In contrast, until the middle of the 1970s, the mask, much like a dressmaker's pattern, used to be cut out by hand with a razor by a skilled technician working together with the circuit designer and a draftsman."[156]

In the auto industry, skilled tool and die makers used to take rough shapes cut out by machine tools and work on them to perfect their shape and bring them within the required tolerances. Today, robots work the dies to final shape and tolerance.

Thus, whether it involves lowering the fast food industry, repair personnel, skilled crafts in electronic manufacturing, or skilled metalworking, the capitalists seek at every turn to reduce the skills of the working class and the training required for any and every job. This universal tendency to eliminate labor costs in the quest for higher profits has the society-wide effect of lowering wages across the board.

Marx on wages and growing poverty

The decline in the wages of the working class as a whole cannot be measured by bourgeois statistical methods alone, but must take into account the Marxist definition of wages. Bourgeois methods of calculating hourly pay do not, by themselves, give the true measure of the burdens that have befallen the workers in the last thirty years or more.

Marx began his analysis with the basics. Because workers do not own any means of production, any means of keeping themselves alive, and because those means are all owned by the bosses, the workers must sell what Marx calls their "labor-power," their ability to work and create new value. They must do this over and over all their lives. For the boss, hiring labor is like buying any commodity on the market. It is no different than buying a machine, iron ore, a hospital bed, or a computer. There is one special commodity that is a vital exception, the commodity that creates new value and hence surplus value: the commodity labor power.

Workers have to sell their labor-power, their ability to work, to the capitalists just as a vendor would sell any other commodity. And once the workers' labor-power is sold, the bosses get to use it the way they see fit—which always means to maximize profits. That's what happens when a worker gets hired. Under a union contract there are specified restrictions regarding pay, hours, work rules, etc., beyond which the boss is not supposed to go. Enforcing these rules is a constant struggle.

When there is no union contract, then the workers basically "work at will," that is, at the will of the boss. The owners decide the pay, hire or fire, make and change all the rules, etc. The only limits on the capitalists are whatever labor laws are in force. But the capitalist government is a laggard when it comes to enforcing workers' rights on the job where there is no union.

So when the worker sells his or her labor-power, the capitalist gets to use it to the maximum for the minimum pay. In both cases, union and non-union, the bosses sell what the workers produce, get the money, pay the workers wages, and pocket the difference. The larger the difference, the greater the profits.

What is the cost of the commodity "labor-power"? The cost starts from the amount of money it takes for the worker to support herself or himself. Workers must have a minimum on which to live and stay reasonably healthy so that they can continue working from the time they are old enough to work effectively and produce profit for the bosses until they get too old to continue. The minimum that it takes to keep a worker going Marx calls the basic means of subsistence.

In his presentation Marx mocks the "scientific," detached style of bourgeois political economists. He adopts a dry, sarcastic manner, in which he assumes the impersonal and heartless vantage point of the bosses, who view the worker as nothing more than a living instrument for exploitation and the production of profit.

> [T]he value of labor-power is the value of the means of subsistence necessary for the maintenance of the laborer.... If the owner of labor-power works today, tomorrow he must again be able to repeat the same process in the same conditions as regards health and strength. ... [The worker's] means of subsistence must therefore be sufficient to maintain him in his normal

state as a laboring individual. His natural wants, such as food, clothing, fuel, and housing, vary according to the climatic and other physical conditions of his country.[157]

But the cost of labor-power has at least two other components—the cost of bringing up children and the cost of their education. Marx deals with capitalists' need for the working class to perpetuate itself and keep filling the ranks generation after generation with workers available for exploitation. Young children, the future workers, cannot work and must be supported, but until what age? Child labor remains an integral part of capitalism in many parts of the world today.

Aside from the fact that many workers want children, love them, and want to bring them up, the capitalists look at the working class family from the point of view of constantly replenishing the future labor supply. The bosses, given the chance, will almost always have the urge to pay the workers less than they need to live on. But years of struggle and the fact that there must be workers in the future if there is going to be capital in the future have forced them to factor into wages what it takes to support a family.

Marx continued:

> The owner of labor-power is mortal. If then his appearance in the market is to be continuous … the seller of labor-power must perpetuate himself, "in the way every living individual perpetuates himself, by procreation." The labor-power withdrawn from the market by wear and tear and death, must continually be replaced by, at the very least, an equal amount of fresh labor-power. Hence the sum of the means of subsistence necessary for the production of labor-power must include the means necessary for the laborer's substitutes, i.e., his children.[158]

Marx also takes into consideration that different segments of the working class must have different levels of skill and that acquiring that skill requires varying degrees of education, which costs money. The amount of money depends upon the level of skill and training required. Thus, wages—that is, the cost of labor-power—include, for some sections of the workers who have the ability to command it, a portion to be used for the education of their children.

As Marx puts it, again adopting the laboratory attitude of the capitalist who views the working class purely as an instrument of exploitation:

> In order to modify the human organism, so that it may acquire skill and handiness in a given branch of industry, and become labor-power of a special kind, a special education or training is requisite, and this, on its part, costs an equivalent in commodities of a greater or lesser amount. This amount varies according to the more or less complicated character

of the labor-power. The expenses of this education (excessively small in the case of ordinary labor-power) enter ... into the total value spent in its production.[159]

Taken altogether, and considering that workers sell their labor-power as a commodity to the bosses, the cost of keeping a minimal level of health, the basic cost of supporting a family, the cost of educating the next generation of workers, are all called by Marx the "value of labor-power." Expressed in terms of money, labor-power has a price. The price of labor-power—that is, the price that the bosses pay for the right to exploit labor—is wages.

Wages do not necessarily reflect the actual value of labor-power, i.e., do not necessarily reflect the precise amount of money that it takes to buy the basic necessities of life. Wages of the individual worker can be above or below what is generally accepted as a basic wage necessary to sustain workers and their families. The variations can be caused by many factors. On the one hand, the most decisive factor, shown long ago by Marx in *Capital* and earlier works, is the class struggle and the ability of the workers to resist the bosses in their constant pressure to lower wages and benefits. By organization and struggle workers can push wages significantly above the basic average—above the value of labor-power. Conversely, lack of union organization, racism, sexism, witch-hunting in the case of undocumented workers, anti-union laws, excessive wage competition, and the innumerable situations that make workers vulnerable in capitalist society can drive wages toward the absolute basic minimum of a bare-bones existence. The tendency of each capitalist, if completely unhindered by the resistance of the workers, is to drive wages below the minimum.

The working class is vast in the United States, estimated at anywhere from 150 to 160 million. There are great variations in the standard of living of the workers. There is a numerically narrow stratum (which is shrinking) at the upper end that is highly paid; the price it commands for its labor-power, measured in wages or salary, is far above the basic level required to get by. There is a much broader section (which is growing in number) of workers at the bottom who live at or near the poverty level—meaning they suffer constant hardship and privation. These workers are disproportionately Black, Latina/o, Asian, and Native, and more likely to be women in general.

Thus, when wages are considered as the price of labor-power, and when the price of labor-power is considered as the amount of money it takes to keep the worker alive, a much starker light is shone on the general conditions facing the majority of workers than is indicated by bourgeois statistics on hourly wages alone. In fact, the Marxist view confirms what every worker knows. Things are getting worse year by year and the workers are besieged on all sides by high rents, high mortgages, massive credit card debt, high cost of health care, high cost of education—all while they are being subjected to wage pressure.

More multi-earner working-class households

Considering that wages represent more or less what it takes to keep a working-class family alive, the working class in the U.S. has taken a drastic wage cut across the board over the last thirty years, far greater than is reflected in government statistics.

According to *The State of Working America*, using even distorted government statistics, the ratio of families in which the wife was part of the paid labor force was about 20 percent in 1951; it rose to 40 percent in 1979 and then to 47.4 percent in 2000, before dropping to 45.4 percent in 2004—still a sharp jump over the last two generations. By the same token, families in which the wife was not working fell from 42 percent in 1979 to 30 percent in 2004.[160] (The use of the term "wife" follows the narrow classifications used in government statistics, which consider a two-earner household to consist of a legally married man and woman.)

It should be emphasized that the *SWA* definition of a two-earner family is taken from the narrow, patriarchal construct used by the various government statistical agencies from which it gets its information. For example, the category "two-earner families" specifically refers to married couples with a husband and a wife who are both working. It therefore significantly understates the problem. This definition excludes unmarried couples; gay and lesbian couples; families in which the children are grown but remain at home, in many cases working to support the family, and cannot afford to move out on their own; families where a working grandparent or other relative moves in, and households in which low-income workers with no familial relationship simply team up and move in together to cut expenses. [See Barbara Ehrenreich's *Nickled and Dimed: On (Not) Getting By in America*.[161]]*

Since such statistics either are not kept or are not available, our analysis must rely on the narrow, bourgeois definition of the family. But even within the patriarchal definition, the long-term trend of changes in family earnings illuminates the growing stress on working-class households.

---

* Ehrenreich's best-selling book is about spending three months trying to work and live on low wages. She worked a month each in Florida, Maine, and Minnesota waitressing, cleaning, working in retail, and being a health assistant. The book gives a far clearer picture of the plight of low-income workers than the selective statistics of bourgeois statisticians.

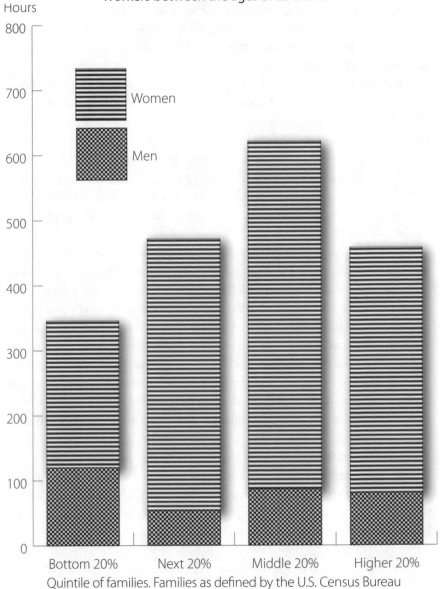

Additional hours worked
per two-earner family per year

In the year 2000 compared to 1979
Workers between the ages of 25 and 54

Hours

Women

Men

Bottom 20%   Next 20%   Middle 20%   Higher 20%

Quintile of families. Families as defined by the U.S. Census Bureau

Source: Data taken from *State of Working America 2006/2007*, Table 1.24, p. 91.

The fact is that under the capitalist patriarchal, heterosexist family structure, many male workers, especially white men, had good-paying jobs in the post-World War II era. In 1951 female partners (categorized as "wives" by the Census Bureau) were working in only 20 percent of married-couple families; in 70 percent of households women were not in the labor force and men were the only wage earners.

During World War II, it should be remembered, this patriarchal family structure had been temporarily modified when women flooded into the plants because the capitalists needed them for wartime production. The bosses allowed them all sorts of assistance, including childcare—in some cases twenty-four-hour childcare. But the moment the war was over, childcare and other services that had made it possible for women to work at industrial jobs were ended and the women were pushed out of the plants to make way for men returning from the war. Thus, the patriarchal family was fully restored to its pre-war condition.

That being said, the *SWA*'s presentation of the figures is still illuminating.

The annual number of hours worked per family has steadily risen since 1979. In some 80 percent of working-class families, the wage earners are between the ages of twenty-five and fifty-four. Of these, the lowest 20 percent by family income put in an extra 346 hours of work (the equivalent of 8.65 full-time weeks) in the year 2000 as compared to 1979. Of these 346 additional hours, women worked 226.

The next 20 percent by family income worked 472 hours more (11.8 full-time weeks). Of the 472 additional hours, women worked 418. The middle 20 percent by income worked 622 hours more a year (15.5 full-time weeks). Of the 622 additional hours, women worked 535. And the 20 percent above them worked 458 more hours a year (11.5 full-time weeks). Of the 458 additional hours, women worked 377.[162]

As men's real wages decline, women in two-earner households are working hundreds more hours per year than in 1979

Similar findings were revealed in a book by Elizabeth Warren and Amelia Warren Tyagi entitled *The Two-Income Trap*.[163] This study of divorce and bankruptcy records led to an analysis of the decline of real income among middle-income working families. In the early 1970s a typical single-income family with two children earned $38,000 a year (adjusted to reflect the year 2000 dollars). After paying off its fixed costs for mortgage, health care, insurance, auto, taxes, etc., it had $17,800, or $1,500 a month, left for other living expenses.

However, a typical dual-income family of four in the early years of the present decade, making $67,800 a year, had only $17,045 left after paying off fixed costs—less than a single-earner family thirty years ago! The two-income family had just over $1,400 a month to cover food, clothing, utilities, furniture, appliances, any vacation, any savings, any debt payments, etc. This family has to pay more for transportation, childcare, health insurance, education, and so on.

Jeff Faux finds that "fixed costs of running a family—items that cannot be legally or easily cut back, such as mortgage payments, health care, the cost of sending children to school, transportation, and health insurance—now come to about 75 percent of family income compared to 50 percent in the 1970s."[164]

Marx discussed the question of multiple-earner households in his investigation of the effect of machinery and industrialization on the condition of the working class:

> The value of labor-power was determined, not only by the labor-time necessary to maintain the individual adult laborer, but also by that necessary to maintain his family. Machinery, by throwing every member of that family onto the labor-market, spreads the value of the man's labor-power over his whole family. It thus depreciates his labor-power. The purchase of the labor-power of a family of four workers may, perhaps, cost more than it formerly did to purchase the labor-power of the head of the family, but, in return, four days' labor takes the place of one, and their price falls in proportion to the excess of the surplus-labor of four over the surplus-labor of one. In order that the family may live, four people must now, not only labor, but expend surplus-labor for the capitalist. Thus we see, that machinery, while augmenting the human material that forms the principal object of capital's exploiting power, at the same time raises the degree of exploitation."[165]

Women have come into manufacturing and services in vast numbers in the last three decades. Young people of high school and college age work in retail, fast food, and other service jobs all across the country. These youth are either helping to supplement the household income or helping to pay their way through school or both. The individual members of the household may not work for the same capitalist, but they all work for the capitalist class as a whole and contribute additional collective profits to the bosses. The household has to work more hours to stay alive.

Statistics that track three-earner and four-earner families, if they are kept, are not made available to the public. But it is clear that the rise of the two-earner and multi-earner household are modern forms of lowering the value of labor-power, that is, lowering real wages of individual workers and raising the degree of exploitation, as Marx described.

A Census Bureau report confirmed the continuation of this trend. It said that median household income rose 0.7 percent in 2006 to $48,200 (a statistically insignificant number). But "more people had to be at work in each household to get there. That's because median earnings for individuals working full-time, year-round actually fell for the third consecutive year. For men, earnings slipped 1.1 percent to a median of $42,300, while for women, earnings sank 1.2 percent to a median of $32,500."[166]

Median family income or earnings refers to the point at which half of families earn above that level and half earn below. To include hundreds of thousands of super-rich families, whose earnings have been soaring, in this calculation distorts the picture of the hardships workers face.

Thus, regardless of all government statistics about wages, the fact of the matter is that over the last three decades, the number of hours of labor-power that a working-class family must sell to the bosses in order to live has grown steadily. And the main way to increase that labor-power is for more people to work. Workers do not subject themselves to additional hours of exploitation in such a massive and dramatic fashion consistently over time unless they are compelled to do so by economic pressures.

Costs rise, men's wages fall—women take up the burden

The additional labor time came almost entirely from women workers. The entry of women into the workforce has a progressive side, from the point of view of women becoming part of the social labor process, having the opportunity to get away from isolation at home, and gaining a measure of economic independence. Nevertheless, much of the participation in the workforce is driven by dire economic necessity and subjects women to onerous conditions and great personal hardship.

Ruth Rosen, an author and teacher at the University of California, Berkeley, wrote an article entitled "The Care Crisis"[167] in which she pointed out that in 1950, less than one fifth of mothers with children under age six worked in the paid labor market. By 2000 this figure had jumped to two thirds. (It is worth noting that in the 1950s many of the mothers with children under six who went out to work were Black women who had to leave their own children in order to care for the children and clean the homes of well-off white couples.)

Rosen dubbed the crisis of home care "the problem that has no name"—a phrase coined by Betty Friedan in *The Feminine Mystique*. Commenting that men do somewhat more housework nowadays, Rosen wrote, "But women still manage and organize much of family life, returning home after work to a 'second shift' of housework and childcare—often compounded by a 'third shift,' caring for aging parents."

Rosen forthrightly raises the class character of the "care crisis" and the plight of immigrant women workers. "For the wealthy, the care crisis is not so dire. They solve their care deficit by hiring full-time nannies or home-care attendants, often from developing countries, to care for their children or parents. The irony is that even as these immigrant women make it easier for well-off Americans to ease their own care burdens, their long hours of paid care-giving often force them to leave their own children with relatives in other countries. They also suffer from extremely low wages, job insecurity, and employer exploitation."

Rosen shows that trying to solve the problem through demanding that men do more, a demand originating in the 1960s and 1970s, while progressive and needed, is insufficient to deal with such a massive economic and social problem. Furthermore, it ignores the responsibilities of the government. "A few decades later, America's working women feel burdened and exhausted, desperate for sleep and leisure, but they have made few collective protests for government-funded childcare or family-friendly workplace policies. As American corporations compete for profits through layoffs and outsourcing, most workers hesitate to make waves for fear of losing their jobs."

Further data on the subject is provided in *The Two-Income Trap*, which showed that in 1965 only 21 percent of working women had gone back to their jobs within six months after the birth of their first child. Today that figure is higher than 70 percent! Similarly, a modern mother with a three-month-old infant is more likely to be working outside the home than was a 1960s woman with a five-year-old child.

Women in two-earner families were driven into the workforce over the last three decades primarily by the falling wages of men and the rising cost of living referred to by both Warren and Faux. This suited the bosses well. Those laid off during the 1980s and 1990s from medium- and high-paying jobs, many in manufacturing, were mostly men. At the same time, their wives or partners, forced to make up for the loss of income, became a new source of low-wage labor.

Louis Uchitelle, in a segment of a book regarding layoffs in the post-Soviet era, commented about how important the role of women was in enabling bosses to carry out wave after wave of layoffs during the period of industrial restructuring. "[W]omen piled into the labor force, adding to the pool of available workers and making it easier for the family to struggle through the layoff of a husband, now that many wives brought home second incomes. That extra paycheck became a means of accommodating layoffs."[168]

But women who thought they were just "temporarily" holding the line during a layoff were mainly forced to remain in the workforce, for the simple reason that most of their husbands or partners were forced into lower-paying jobs.

Driving down the value of labor power

From a Marxist point of view, that is, from a genuine working-class point of view, wages are going down in an historic way for the working class as a whole, regardless of the statistics put forward by the capitalist government. The fact of the matter is that more and more often workers are earning less than what is necessary to support a family. The ability to support a family was the historic post-World War II standard for determining the value of labor-power and of a "living wage." The bosses are pushing things backwards by lowering men's wages and forcing women into the workforce at low wages to make up the difference. Two low-wage earners per family are becoming the norm—with the male workers paid less than they used to be and the women workers paid even lower wages.

The measurable facts, not the distorted bourgeois statistics, regarding the material life of the working class—how hard and how long they have to work and what they get in return—are the ultimate criteria by which to judge what real wages are, that is, what the real price of labor-power is. That was Marx's approach to wages.

Nothing can refute the decades-long downward slide or overcome the evidence of the growing need of working-class families to pool income and take second and sometimes third jobs. Nothing can refute the fall in leisure time, the longer working hours, the growth of enforced part-time work, of temporary labor, the ever-increasing demands of the capitalists for greater productivity in the name of "competitiveness." No one can deny that many students who graduate from college have to either stay at home or move back in with their families because they cannot afford to live on their own. And it is widely known that nowadays, older workers are often forced to move back in with their children when they lose a job or get an unaffordable medical bill.

In the new era of low-wage U.S. capitalism—accomplished by globalization, worldwide wage competition, technological attacks, offshoring, outsourcing, anti-union strategies, super-exploitation of immigrant workers, intensified racist economic discrimination, wage discrimination against women, the intervention of the capitalist state and its agencies, and a host of other anti-labor practices—the ruling class is forcing down the value of labor-power to a new level. This new level is based upon a drastically reduced standard of living. This economic aggression by the ruling class is being carried out steadily, by attrition, workplace by workplace, union contract by union contract, in a way that the workers in the United States have not experienced as a class in generations.

Marx explained that the value of labor-power, which every worker has to sell, is different from "other commodities" because "there enters into the determination of labor-power an historical and moral element. Nevertheless, in every given country, at a given period, the average quantity of the means of subsistence necessary for the laborer is known."[169] The "historical element" concerns the economic development of the country; the "moral" element concerns the standards that are considered necessary.

But here is where the question of the class struggle and the resistance to capital becomes vital. The value of labor-power is the basic minimum that it takes to keep workers working, raise their children, and give them enough education to enter the working class at some level—in a given country in a given period. The workers and the oppressed in the United States have fought for generations to achieve a general standard of living that exceeds this bare minimum, although many Black, Latina/o, Asian, Native, Arab, and poor white workers have always lived near or at the bare minimum.

The workers and the oppressed in general reached the peak of their standard of living by the end of the 1960s and the beginning of the 1970s, after a century of up-and-down struggle including open class warfare and uprisings of the oppressed. In Marxist terms, by resisting the exploiters, by organizing unions, by uniting and overcoming the competition between workers perpetually created by capitalism, the workers had raised the price of labor-power above its rock-bottom value.

When wages go below the bare minimum, disproportionately common in the case of Black, Latina/o, Asian, and Native peoples and single mothers, the capitalist government has been forced by past struggles to step in and make up the difference with some form of assistance to create a subsistence-level income. Aid to Families with Dependent Children, food stamp programs, student grants, poverty programs, free breakfast programs for children, disability benefits, etc., were gained through the struggle. All these programs were calculated to produce the equivalent of the wages missing from poor families whose income was below even the bare necessary minimum value of labor-power.

These past three decades have also seen, in addition to the lowering of real wages, a systematic effort by the rich to reduce economic assistance to the poorest sectors of the working class and appropriate the funds into the coffers of the financiers and corporations. This cruel process of the transfer of wealth, the robbery of the poor by the rich, took giant leaps forward under both Ronald Reagan and Bill Clinton and is continuing apace under George W. Bush.

As real poverty goes up, official poverty goes down

Before going any further, it is important to discuss the deceptive and utterly useless definition of "poverty" devised by the capitalist government. The definition is used repeatedly—shamefacedly by some liberal economists, gladly by reactionary commentators. It is calculated to hide a great portion of true poverty that lies outside the official definition. It conceals rather than reveals a monumental amount of suffering and privation because of the way it is constructed.

There is a complete disconnect between the official numbers and what workers experience and see around them in their everyday lives. On the one hand, tens of millions have been suffering declining wages, higher rents, and other crucial components affecting the real cost of living for three decades. Yet the capitalist government reports the numbers of people living in poverty as either going down, remaining stable, or rising slightly. The origin of this disconnect, this totally false picture, is in the manner in which the government calculates poverty.

The standard for a poverty-level income was set by the government in 1965 under the Lyndon B. Johnson administration's so-called "war on poverty." It was set at three times what the family spent on food. The level of food expenditure was taken from the Department of Agriculture's lowest-priced diet that still provided proper nutrition. The standard was inadequate then, and it is far more inadequate now.

The government has deliberately held the definition to such a low income that the proportion of people officially living in poverty always remains within a range of approximately 11 percent to 13 percent, regardless of economic reality.

For example, the official poverty-level income for a family of four, with two adults and two children, was set at $20,444 a year in 2006. This figure requires that one full-time worker, working a forty-hour week for fifty-two weeks a year, or 2,080 hours, make no more than $9.83 an hour for the family to be considered within the poverty level. It excludes work-related expenses and necessities such as childcare, transportation, housing, and health-care costs. Even with this narrow definition, there were 36.5 million people living in poverty in 2006. The fact is that this level of income for a family of four means living in the most dire straits, at the very edge of subsistence level.

The self-sufficiency standard*
for Philadelphia in 2004

Monthly costs	Adult	Adult + infant preschooler	Adult + preschooler & school age	2 Adults + infant and preschooler
Housing	$639	$791	$791	$791
Child care	0	1,078	977	1,078
Food	182	358	411	515
Transportation	106	106	106	212
Health care	90	217	225	259
Miscellaneous	102	255	251	285
Taxes	316	767	752	804
Child-care tax credit	0	-110	-115	-100
Child tax credit	0	-167	-167	-167
Self-sufficiency wage				
Hourly	$8.14	$18.71	$18.35	$10.45
Monthly	1,433	3,294	3,230	$3,677
Annual	17,201	39,526	38,759	$44,123

* The "self-sufficiency standard" represents a bare-bones budget. It does not allow for entertainment, carryout or fast food (not even a pizza), savings, credit card debt, or emergency expenses such as car repairs. In each wage category for different families, the wage is more than double the official poverty level. The calculated costs were unrealistically low, even for a budget that barely provides for survival. Thirteen cities were included in the study, "Coming Up Short." All had similar findings, adjusted for the cost of living in each city. See endnote 171.

Reprinted from "Coming Up Short: A Comparison of Wages and Work Supports in 10 American Communities. Used by permission of the publisher, Wider Opportunities for Women (WOW).

Twice the official poverty level is considered the threshold of "low income"; 40 percent of the households in the U.S. live within this category.

But what "low-income" really means is another story. For example, a 2005 study by the California Budget Project (CBP) entitled "Making Ends Meet," on what it costs to support a family in California is revealing.[170] California is the most populous state in the country, with a vast working class engaged in heavy industry and light manufacturing, including high tech, agriculture, white-collar work, and services of all kinds. Its millions of workers include many oppressed people and immigrants of all nationalities, who labor amid extremes of wealth and poverty.

Twice the official poverty level is considered the threshold of 'low income.' Some 40 percent of the households in the U.S. live within this category

The CBP report studied the whole state with a view to arriving at a budget that would support what it calls a "modest standard of living." This standard of living includes a typical cost for housing. It assumes rental (not owned) housing and crowded living conditions for a family of four. It includes the cost of food, childcare (baby sitters and not outside childcare), utilities (it assumes that housing and utilities come to 20 percent of income, which is way below the current average), low-cost health care, transportation, income taxes, and miscellaneous expenses.

This standard of living does not include any "extras" like college savings, insurance, vacations, unpaid days off, or any emergencies like an illness, an accident, assisting a relative, or any of the other things that impinge on the real lives of the masses.

This stringent budget, which is basically a paycheck-to-paycheck existence, requires in California anywhere from $51,551 a year to $70,708 for a family of four, depending upon where you live. According to the CBP, the average family in the state as a whole needs an income of $63,921 a year. To achieve this, both parents must work full-time, forty hours a week, and be paid for the full fifty-two weeks at a rate of at least $15.37 an hour each.

In other words, a family of four in California has to earn three times the official poverty-level income just to survive. For higher-cost states like Massachusetts and New York, the required income would be higher; for low-cost states in the South it would be lower. But wages are also lower in the "right-to-work" South, which makes up for the lower cost of living.

Another study, carried out by Wider Opportunities for Women, is entitled, "Coming Up Short."[171] The study was geared to getting government assistance for women who have been pushed off welfare since President Clinton's so-called welfare reform. This study devised a draconian budget, called the "self-sufficiency" standard, and applied it to ten cities. It shows that poverty-level wages as defined by the government are completely insufficient to support a family.

The "self-sufficiency" standard, described as "bare-bones," provides for the bare essentials of survival and nothing more. It does "not allow for entertainment, carry-out or fast food (not even a pizza), savings, credit card debt, or emergency expenses such as car repairs."[172]

In the city of Philadelphia, this budget for a family of four required full-time work, fifty-two weeks a year, by two wage earners, each making $10.45 per hour, in order to earn $44,123 a year in 2004, which is more than double the so-called poverty level.

The official poverty standards fly in the face of findings on "extreme poverty" in a *McClatchy Newspapers* analysis of 2005 Census Bureau figures.[173] The number of people living in extreme poverty increased 26 percent between 2000 and 2005, more than twice as fast as the population. Extreme poverty is considered to be half the already low official poverty level. Of the more than 16 million people officially at this inhumanly low level of existence, 10.3 million are white, 4.3 million are Black, and 3.7 million are Latina/o.* These figures do not count undocumented workers.[174]

"Severe poverty is worst near the Mexican border and in some areas of the South, where 6.5 million severely poor residents are struggling to find work as manufacturing jobs in the textile industry, apparel, and furniture-making industries disappear," said the analysis. "The Midwestern Rust Belt and areas of the Northeast also have been hard hit as economic restructuring and foreign competition have forced numerous plant closings."[175]

Mark Rank, a professor of social welfare at the University of Wisconsin, Madison, is quoted in the *McClatchy* article by Tony Pugh as estimating that one in every three people in the United States will experience a full year of poverty. This figure includes children. But Rank also found that 58 percent of people in the U.S. between the ages of twenty and seventy-five will spend at least a year in poverty. Two out of three will use a public assistance program between the ages of twenty and sixty-five, and 40 percent will do so for five years or more. This number excludes undocumented workers. If they were included, the figure would go even higher.

"It would appear that for most Americans the question is no longer if, but

---

* The figures for each nationality/race add up to more than 16 million. The reason is that the Census Bureau form requires that all registrants declare whether or not they are "Hispanic or Latino." In addition they have to declare their "race." Thus Latinas/os can be double counted as "Hispanic" and white or Black, etc.

rather when, they will experience poverty," Rank said. "In short, poverty has become a routine and unfortunate part of the American life course."[176]

The *McClatchy* study emphasized that extreme poverty has increased significantly in 65 of 215 large counties across the country and there are similar increases in 28 states. The report noted that Washington, D.C., a majority Black city where an overwhelmingly white federal government doles out hundreds of billions of dollars to the corporations, has a higher concentration of extreme poverty than any of the fifty states. In 2005 extreme poverty in the District of Columbia was about 10 percent higher than even Mississippi and Louisiana. This extreme poverty extends to rural and suburban areas as well.

The *McClatchy* article, which summarized highlights of the Census Bureau report, noted:

> The plight of the severely poor is a distressing sidebar to an unusual economic expansion. Worker productivity has increased dramatically since the brief recession of 2001, but wages and job growth have lagged behind. At the same time, the share of national income going to corporate profits has dwarfed the amount going to wages and salaries. That helps explain why the median household income of working-age families, adjusted for inflation, has fallen for five straight years.
>
> These and other factors have helped push 43 percent of the nation's 37 million poor people into deep poverty–the highest rate since at least 1975. [177]

It is important to note that these alarming figures are based on a report that uses the inadequate government definitions of "poverty" and "poor people." And it does not point out a major factor in the rise of desperate poverty—namely, that the Clinton administration destroyed welfare and put a five-year lifetime limit on family assistance, in addition to making that assistance harder to get. This has further aggravated the economic hardships already being suffered by the workers as a consequence of the relentless pursuit of low wages by the capitalist class.

Of course, any immediate assistance to the impoverished sections of the working class is vital. And those who fight for it are engaging in a progressive cause. But the goal should be not to find some minimal income that will keep workers who have been reduced to poverty by the exploiters from going under. The goal should be to get rid of poverty altogether and forever. And the only way to do that is to get rid of capitalist exploitation, which is what gives the bosses the power over wages, work, and life itself.

Why the bosses need Wal-Mart

Not only does Wal-Mart pay low wages, but its low prices allow the entire capitalist class to pay low wages to a large section of the working class.

Wal-Mart has been considered one of the engines driving the process of low-wage capitalism. The company in 2006 employed 1.2 million workers in the United States and 400,000 workers abroad, making it the biggest private employer in the world. Its rise to power has been on the basis of high technology, low prices, and low wages. Wal-Mart is the pre-eminent low-wage company in the U.S. capitalist establishment. Its wages have been declining since 1970, driving down wages throughout the retail industry.[178]

But Wal-Mart not only drives down the wages of its own workers. By using its leverage as the world's largest retailer, it pressures its suppliers to lower costs. This can only be done by increasing the exploitation of the suppliers' own workers or by offshoring to low-wage countries.

Wal-Mart spreads its monopoly power by destroying its competition with its famous "lowest prices." But it achieves these low prices by impoverishing its own workers and the workers of its suppliers and by forcing its suppliers to super-exploit low-wage labor across the globe. Wal-Mart and its apologists claim that these low prices are saving people hundreds of billions of dollars a year. But the truth is that Wal-Mart's low prices serve the entire capitalist class in the United States. They drive down the cost of the means of subsistence and thus make it easier for all the bosses to lower wages.

Wages at Wal-Mart have been variously estimated at anywhere from $8 to $10 per hour. It considers a full-time job to be thirty-four hours a week. But even at $10 an hour with a forty-hour week, a Wal-Mart worker would take home $1,280 a month after taxes. No one can support a family on Wal-Mart pay; even a single worker can barely survive on these wages. By 2005 the company faced forty different lawsuits filed by workers all across the country for making them work off the clock, work through scheduled breaks, or punch out and continue to work for no pay. Wal-Mart has been sued for sex discrimination (two-thirds of its workers are women). It has abused undocumented workers. In fact, Wal-Mart workers are so poor that many of them have to use Medicaid, food stamps, and other forms of government assistance just to survive.

The company is fiercely anti-union. In 2000, when eleven butchers at a Wal-Mart in Jacksonville, Texas, voted to join the United Food and Commercial Workers (UFCW), Wal-Mart announced that henceforth it would buy only pre-wrapped meat. It then eliminated butchers in all of its hundreds of supercenters.[179] When the UFCW, after a long and successful organizing drive, opened up bargaining at a store in Jonquière, Quebec, Wal-Mart shut the store down after five months at the negotiating table.[180] It is constantly on the lookout for any signs of union sympathy among its workers and fires them on trumped-up charges.

When Wal-Mart moves into an area, it puts unionized supermarkets out of business or gives the bosses of its competitors leverage at the bargaining table to demand concessions based on not being able to compete with Wal-Mart. The important grocery workers' strike in southern California of 2003-2004, waged by the UFCW, was triggered by Wal-Mart's threat to put forty supercenters in the state and drive wages down in the entire area.

In 2004 Wal-Mart accounted for 2.3 percent of the U.S. gross domestic product (GDP). It sold 14 percent of the groceries in the country and 20 percent of the toys. It racks up $300 billion in sales, running neck-and-neck with ExxonMobil for first place. Wal-Mart has close to 4,000 stores in the U.S. and hundreds abroad. It is the largest retailer in Mexico and Canada. It is the second-largest grocer in England.[181] A typical Wal-Mart has 60,000 different items on the shelf. A typical supercenter carries 120,000.[182] With this kind of leverage, suppliers don't tell Wal-Mart what price an item should sell for; Wal-Mart tells them. Even the largest monopolies, such as Procter & Gamble and Levi's, have lost out in the struggle over pricing with Wal-Mart. Furthermore, Wal-Mart is famous for telling its suppliers to cut prices by 5 percent year over year.[183]

Wal-Mart drives down prices by driving down wages at its 60,000 suppliers in the United States—and also in China, Singapore, Mexico, Indonesia, and Sri Lanka. It puts suppliers in all these countries in competition with each other to get their products onto Wal-Mart's shelves. Wal-Mart has such dominance in some industries that it can play a major role in establishing sweatshop wages that affect entire countries or regions. By 2003 Wal-Mart had over 3,000 factory suppliers in southern China at low wages. Wal-Mart is Bangladesh's most important customer. Bangladeshi sweatshop workers, most of them women, supply clothing to Wal-Mart.

The cost of Wal-Mart's low prices is illustrated by the plight of workers at the Western Dresses factory in Dhaka, Bangladesh. In 2003 a sixteen-year-old junior sewing machine operator, Robina Akther—whose job was to sew flaps on the back pockets of pants destined for Wal-Mart—worked for thirteen cents an hour, fourteen hours a day, making $26.98 a month. If she did not sew the required 120 pairs of pants per hour she was beaten. "They slapped you and lashed you hard on the face with the pants. This happens very often. It is no joke."[184] The work went on from 8:00 a.m. to 10:00 or 11:00 p.m., seven days a week, with ten days off in the whole year. Charles Fishman, the author of this account, calculated that it would take half a century for Akther to earn $16,200, while in 2003 Wal-Mart's profits were $19,597 a minute!

Akther brought a lawsuit against Wal-Mart in the United States for failure to provide basic wages, overtime pay, and protection from physical abuse that Bangladeshi law provides. Fourteen other workers were plaintiffs in the lawsuit—from China, Indonesia, Swaziland, and Nicaragua. According to Fishman, "all make merchandise for Wal-Mart, and all have nearly identical claims."[185]

On the home front, Wal-Mart tracks every item rung up on every cash register by every cashier. It has central communications and its loading workers must wear headsets for perpetual monitoring. It owns the largest private satellite communications system in the United States and links every store location to its central office. Combining communications technology with software, Wal-Mart tracks every item sold. It compels many of its suppliers to adopt similar technology in order to speed up workers—what the bosses call "achieving efficiency"—so the suppliers can come in with the lowest prices.

Wal-Mart and its capitalist admirers continually wax eloquent about the company's low prices, as if it were giving away money to the masses. The estimates of how much money consumers save goes all the way from $100 billion a year to $300 billion a year, depending upon which authority is used. All the bourgeois experts say it's a tradeoff, low wages for low prices. Wal-Mart CEO H. Lee Scott bragged, "In effect it gives them a raise every time they shop with us."[186]

Wal-Mart pays low wages and charges low prices, thus making it easier for all the bosses to pay low wages

But this argument flies in the face of intuition. After all, if every time workers shopped at Wal-Mart they were getting a raise and saving so much money, then why are the vast majority of the workers who shop there living from paycheck to paycheck? Why are so many of the customers of Wal-Mart (and other low-price discount retailers) in personal debt? In fact, CEO Scott contradicted himself in virtually the same sentence when he declared how much of a benefactor his company was to the working class.

"These savings are a lifeline for millions of middle- and lower-income families who live from payday to payday," he declared. Customers shopped at Wal-Mart 7.2 billion different times in the year 2006.[187] The masses should be rolling in wealth if they got a raise every time they went there. The fact is, however, that the average annual income of the people who shop at Wal-Mart is $35,000 a year. An article in the *Washington Post* that reported this figure called Wal-Mart a "force for poverty relief," saying its "$200 billion-plus assistance to consumers may rival many federal programs."[188]

Of course workers can benefit from lower prices for the necessities of life, but only if their wages do not go down at the same time. But workers in the U.S. are getting poorer. The truth is that tens of millions of workers who shop at Wal-Mart cannot pay higher prices at the declining wage levels. Life is getting harder. Yet Wal-Mart's low prices are "saving money." Where is all that money going, if everyone is still poor?

Marx's analysis of wages explains that the real beneficiary of Wal-Mart's low prices is the capitalist class as a whole.

In Marx's explanation of the bosses' drive to increase their surplus value, i.e., to increase the unpaid labor of the workers and thus increase profits, he showed the different ways the capitalists go about it. One way to get more profits from the workers is to simply make them work longer hours without increasing their pay. This elongation of the workday Marx called absolute surplus value. (Wal-Mart used this method by making workers work off the clock.)

But another way the bosses can get more surplus value, without making the workday longer, is to lower wages. However, wages have to be high enough to keep workers alive, so there is a limit to how low the bosses can push them and still retain the labor force without a mass rebellion. The limit of how low wages for the majority of workers can go is what Marx terms the price of necessary labor.

Necessary labor time is the hours it takes a worker to earn the wages necessary to sustain herself or himself and family. Let's assume the worker is paid by the week. As soon as the worker puts in the hours on the job needed to produce a value equivalent in money to his or her weekly wage, then the rest of the time worked, and the value the worker adds to the product or service during that time, the boss gets for free. This is the source of all profit. The value added to the product, or to the service rendered, during this time is unpaid labor-time.

For example, suppose a worker on a production line producing shoes adds $500 a week in new value to the shoes on which he or she works. That comes to $100 a day for five days. And further suppose that the worker receives $300 a week in wages to live on. But the worker has added labor to the shoes worth $300 in value in just three days. The money equivalent of value produced for the rest of the week—$200 for the last two days—goes into the boss's pocket once the shoes are sold. The worker has given two free days of labor to the boss.

The wage form of payment conceals the fact that only part of the workday represents paid labor; the rest is unpaid. That is the secret, uncovered by Marx, that has concealed the real nature of capitalist exploitation. Because of the form of capitalist production and the wage system—whether the pay or salary is calculated hourly, weekly, or monthly—workers are led to believe that they are being paid for the entire time that they work. They may get high wages, middle wages, or low wages, but whatever their pay, the capitalist myth is that the workers are getting paid for the entire day, week, or month, as the case may be.

Most auto workers know, because they see the prices of the cars they work on and they know how many come off the assembly line, that their labor produces vehicles worth hundreds of times what they get paid. In the case of automobiles, because they are so key to the entire capitalist economy, these figures are public and constantly in the press. But because of capitalist secrecy, most workers have to guess at the relationship between their wages and the wealth that they produce. Every worker needs to know that their wages come to only a fraction of the value they add to products with their labor. Otherwise, there would be no profit. That fraction of the total value of the product, representing the time it took to earn their wages, is the paid labor time; the other fraction is the unpaid labor time taken by the capitalist. If wages can be reduced because prices for the means of subsistence go down, then the boss gains the difference.

The bottom line is that Wal-Mart's low prices are at the expense of the low wages of their 1.2 million workers, as well as at the expense of the millions of workers in the United States and in sweatshops around the world who work for Wal-Mart's suppliers. In fact, these low prices have made it possible for the capitalist class to lower wages without driving all the workers to absolute hunger and rebellion. Lowering the price for the necessities of life has the objective economic effect of cheapening labor-power and reducing necessary labor time. When this happens, the bosses get more unpaid labor-time, more surplus value.

Only a class struggle that stops the slide in wages can allow workers to take advantage of lower prices. Otherwise, that $200 billion in "savings" goes into the pockets of the bosses, because the lower prices allow bosses all over the United States to pay lower wages.

8

Sexism, racism, and low wages

Women in the workforce · The class nature of Clinton's welfare 'reform' · National oppression and low-wage labor · African Americans and capitalist restructuring
Racism and low wages in the prison-industrial complex

If the rise in the cost of supporting a family together with the decline of wages hits a two-earner family hard and keeps them treading water, the pressure on single-parent families is, of course, even greater. The number of families headed by women has been increasing steadily for decades. It has gone from 10 percent of families in 1951 to 15 percent in 1979 to almost 20 percent, or one out of every five families in the United States, by 2004. (Families headed by single men doubled from 3 percent in 1979 to 6.4 percent in 2004.)[189] Being a single parent—because of divorce, separation, death of a partner, or other circumstances—drives women into the workforce in large numbers. With mouths to feed they are in a particularly vulnerable and desperate situation. Bosses have an overwhelming advantage in setting low wages under these circumstances.

Women in the workforce

Government statistics measure "labor force participation." The labor force is defined as all those who have jobs, plus all those who have no job but are reported as looking for one. It is the sum of official employment plus unemployment. Everyone else is considered to be out of the labor force. Labor force participation is a percentage of the "non-institutional" population over the age of sixteen. That means it excludes full-time students, those of working age who are in the military, in prison, in nursing or elder care homes, in hospitals, etc. Thus, in 2005, 149 million workers were officially in the labor force. Of those workers, 142 million were classified as employed. (To be classified as employed, they had to work only one hour in the week before they were surveyed.) The "non-institutional" civilian population was 226 million. So

The proportion of working women has steadily risen. By 2005 there were 80 million men and 70 million women in the workforce

the labor force participation, the proportion of the population over sixteen counted as officially in the labor force, was 66 percent.

But the rise in the number of women compared to men in the workforce over the last three decades is telling. In 1970, 79 percent of all men participated in the labor force as opposed to 43 percent of all women. In 2005, men's participation dropped to 72 percent while women's climbed to 60 percent. Women's participation in the labor force has steadily risen since 1980 and men's participation has steadily declined. By 2005 there were 80 million men and 70 million women in the workforce.

The influx of women into the workforce saw a rise in low- and poverty-level wages. "Overall trends in the share of workers earning poverty-level wages," wrote the authors of the SWA, "are primarily driven by trends among women, since women are disproportionately the ones earning these low wages....

"Women are much more likely to earn low wages than men. In 2005, 29.4 percent of women earned poverty-level wages or less, significantly more than the share of men (19.9 percent). Women are also less likely to earn very high wages. In 2005 only 10.1 percent of women, but 17.6 percent of men earned at least three times the poverty-level wage."[190]

The class nature of Clinton's welfare 'reform'

President Clinton's Welfare Reform Act of 1996 drove between 3 million and 4 million poor women into the workforce all at once. Clinton and Newt Gingrich, the rightwing Republican Majority leader at the time, teamed up to destroy Aid to Families with Dependent Children (AFDC). The legislation forced poor, single-parent families to try to survive on poverty-level wages, which, in many cases, amounted to less than the pitiful amount they had received from AFDC. The women were disproportionately Black and Latina, but many were poor white women, too, all of whom had families. This vicious act directed at the poor was a politically reactionary campaign to spread the idea that those on welfare were lazy people who just wanted to "live off the dole." It was racist in character because the racist regime of U.S. capitalism has left so many Black single parents in poverty and almost all references to the poor focus in on African Americans (even though the majority of the poor in the U.S. are white).

But this teamwork by Clinton and Gingrich also created a new massive pressure on wages as the women were at first forced to work for benefits and were then forced off assistance altogether. This mass expulsion not only created hardship and suffering for the single parents driven off AFDC but it also intensified wage competition among low-wage workers everywhere.

The Clinton forces and the entire stable of centrist capitalist politicians and even liberal economists justified the denial of basic assistance to millions of single mothers by pointing to the fact that their loss of AFDC was to be compensated by a rise in the Earned Income Tax Credit for low-wage workers.

For example, the authors of the *SWA 2006/2007* are enthusiastic about the results of welfare reform and declare that "policy changes significantly improved the returns to work for low-income families." Referring to single mothers, the authors state, "Their living standards have been particularly affected by changes in both market outcomes and poverty policy—such as welfare reform—over the last few decades."

In particular they single out the increase in the Earned Income Tax Credit (EITC). They show that public assistance for single mothers with at least two children who have incomes below twice the poverty level has declined. Under welfare reform these mothers have made the great "improvement" of achieving a "typical" income of $16,353 a year! But that includes a number of possible benefits that the mother may or may not be able to get. And here's another catch. Their AFDC declined from an average of $4,000 a year in 1979 to $671 a year in 2004, while the EITC increased from $350 a year to $1,700. But their actual wages earned on the job averaged $9,660 and the hours they worked, on average, increased to 1,092 a year—almost 300 more hours a year in which they could not attend to their children.[191]

Stated plainly, so-called welfare-to-work meant that henceforth assistance to poor single mothers and their children became dependent on the mother submitting to low-wage capitalist exploitation. The tax credit only applies if you earn wages; if you get no wages, you and your children get no aid. This was slightly modified by some of the states, which left a little room for assistance without work. But studies have been done showing that many of the people who left welfare fell below subsistence-level income, leading many to become homeless.

It is important to note that the capitalist government was willing to give assistance to poor families, but only in a different form. Prior to the welfare reform, poor families could get assistance without working. The burden of raising a family when you have no decent job is hard enough. To add hours of forced labor to a single parent's job of bringing up a family just piles hardship on hardship. The capitalist economy never has enough jobs for all the workers, and certainly not enough decent-paying jobs, and the government does not offer affordable, quality child care to allow single mothers to work.

The government was willing to provide tax subsidies, but it was really subsidizing the capitalists. In 2005, for example, Washington spent $40 billion on the EITC and $33 billion on food stamps. The tax credit allowed bosses to pay below-subsistence wages and make extra profits from the low-wage labor of vulnerable single mothers. With the tax credit, food stamps, and a minimal childcare allowance, the capitalist government makes up the difference between below-subsistence, "extreme poverty" wages and what it takes to allow a single mother and her children to barely survive. So single mothers have to bear the burden of a family on the insecure basis of the EITC, which will end or be reduced if they lose their jobs. This means these families often live with hunger. The real beneficiaries are the employers, who get a ready supply of workers for below-subsistence wages.

National oppression and low-wage labor

African Americans, Latina/os, Native people, and Asians have been a source of slave labor and low-wage labor since the earliest stages of U.S. capitalism.

Native Americans suffered attempted genocide in a naked land grab by landowners and capitalists over a 300-year period. Those who survived the dozens of so-called "Indian wars"—wave after wave of aggression by the settler government—were consigned to the U.S. version of Bantustans. National oppression, extreme racism, and ruthless super-exploitation were features of U.S. capitalism long before it became an imperialist power. Indeed, the U.S. early on earned the title that was given to Russia under the tsars: "a prison house of nations."

African Americans were ripped from diverse cultures in Africa, cut off from their lands of origin, and forced to adopt the culture dictated by the slave masters. Thus an internal oppressed nation was forged in the hell fires of slavery.

Two-thirds of Mexico was annexed by conquest in the Treaty of Hidalgo Guadalupe in 1846 and a subjugated population was added to the land and cattle barons' empire in the West and Southwest.

Chinese workers were brought to the West Coast after the Civil War to labor on the railroads. After the railroads were built and U.S. capitalism went into an economic crisis in the 1870s, the Chinese workers were then scapegoated, attacked in racist riots, and pushed out of their homes.

Thus, when the U.S. entered into its imperialist phase in 1898, in the Spanish-American War, it was already a preeminently racist power that relegated millions of oppressed people to backbreaking work, mostly in the fields at first, but gradually in the factories as U.S. capitalism expanded and industrialization and mass production gained ground.

Just as oppressed peoples—enslaved African Americans, captive Latina/os, Asian immigrant workers, and Native peoples—bore the brunt of the rise of capitalism and imperialism in the United States, so too they are now bearing the brunt of capitalist globalization, restructuring, and the world-wide wage competition. The war on the working class in the last three decades has taken an especially heavy toll on all its oppressed sectors. The attacks that have evolved over the recent period flow from the historic racism of U.S. capitalism. They have developed in different ways, but with similar results of poverty and increased super-exploitation.

These new conditions are going to require class-wide solidarity, which can only be achieved through a profound and determined struggle against racism by the white workers. This requires a solid understanding of how racism is used to undermine the workers' struggle and how vital such class solidarity is to the struggle to reverse the historic offensive by the bosses against all workers.

African Americans and capitalist restructuring

The African-American working class has been heavily hit by the restructuring of U.S. capitalism, both at home and abroad. The technological assault, the offshoring, and the domestic outsourcing have hurt the entire working class, but have done disproportionate damage to Black workers and their families.

The restructuring by the bosses devastated Black workers, partly as a result of a deliberate effort starting in the 1960s and 1970s to relocate plants away from the industrial central cities, where there were great concentrations of the African-American proletariat. But this devastation was also the result of a general decline in manufacturing and particularly of the general attack on the union movement.

Beginning with World War I, millions of Black people left the South to get jobs in Northern and Midwestern factories. They were fleeing Southern racism and poverty that were the legacy of slavery. They then had to face white racism in the North and Midwest and had great difficulty getting into relatively high-paying jobs in manufacturing. When they did, they were largely kept out of the skilled sectors and given the hardest and dirtiest jobs. Nevertheless, by the 1970s they had gained a foothold in manufacturing and other occupations and achieved some modicum of temporary material security.

One of the key elements in achieving this level of economic security was the fact that the manufacturing industries were heavily unionized. And Black workers, despite the racism of the almost entirely white union leadership, were the most union-oriented sector of the working class—precisely because of the protections and benefits that came with union representation. Pensions, health care, a contract, raises, work rules, etc., put a foundation under the lives of a section of African-American workers and their families for the first time. The legacy of slavery and then sharecropping had consigned the vast majority to low-paying menial labor.

When oppressed people in the U.S. are pushed out or kept out of unions, it has drastic effects. The authors of the *SWA* attempted to gauge the importance to workers of being in a union, using a measure that they call a "union premium."[192] This method measures the difference in hourly wages between union and non-union workers who are otherwise comparable in experience, education, region, industry, occupation, and marital status. The "union premium" is the extra dollars per hour earned by those covered by a collective bargaining contract.

In 2005 all workers covered by a collective bargaining contract earned an average of $1.52 an hour more than non-union workers—an increase of 14.7 percent. This number would have been significantly higher if pensions, health care, paid vacations, and other benefits had been added to the calculation, because union jobs have a much higher level of benefits, and thus overall compensation, than non-union jobs.

The benefits of being in a union in any given job and region are clearly shown for all workers. But even the cautious statisticians who put out the *SWA* showed that for Black and Latina/o workers the union premium amounts to much more than for white workers.

Because of racism, Black workers suffer far greater hardships than white workers once they are stripped of union protection

There are sizeable differences in union wage premiums across demographic groups, with Black and Latina/o workers "having union premiums of 20.3 percent and 21.9 percent, respectively, far higher than the 13.1 percent for whites. Consequently, unions raise the wages of minorities more than of whites ... helping to close racial/ethnic wage gaps."[193]

The union hourly wage premium is $2.31 an hour for African Americans and $3.02 for Latina/os. For those who work a full-time job all year-round, without overtime, the difference comes to $4,800 and $6,200 a year, respectively. That is without calculating benefits, which can add up to many more thousands of dollars a year.

In other words, racism is so bad that once oppressed workers are stripped of union protection by layoffs, plant closings, or just plain union busting, they suffer far greater hardships at the hands of the bosses than do white workers. Figures show that Black and Latina/o workers have lower savings, fewer assets, and fewer relatives and friends with resources to help them through hard times than do white workers. Thus, the loss of a union job, a hardship for all workers, is often a devastating blow to oppressed workers.

Effects of anti-labor offensive and restructuring on African-American workers*

- In the 1980s a Black worker was 50% more likely to be in a union than a white worker.

  By 2006 this had fallen to 30%.

- Between 1983 and 2006 the proportion of Black workers represented by a union fell from 31.7% to 16%.

- In 2005 the average full-time African-American union member earned $4,800 a year more than a non-union Black worker.

- Up to the 1990s Black workers were just as likely to have manufacturing jobs as white workers.

  By 2006 they were 15 percent less likely to have a manufacturing job than whites.

- In the year 2004 union membership fell by 304,000.

  African Americans accounted for 55% of the drop, even though whites outnumbered Blacks by 6 to 1 in the unions.

- In 2003 in NYC, out of the entire employable African-American population—**only 51.8% of Black men and 57.1% of Black women had jobs.**

- Privatization of government services, automation, and downsizing of the postal service, as well as corporate moves to the suburbs away from the inner cities, have all contributed to the decline of the condition of African-American workers and communities.

*For sources on data, see endnotes 193 to 199.

The Center for Economic and Policy Research, a liberal think-tank, did a study entitled "The Decline in African-American Representation in Unions and Manufacturing, 1979-2006." It found that

> For much of the postwar period, a higher share of African-American workers have been in unions than workers for other racial and ethnic backgrounds. As union representation and union coverage have declined for the country as a whole, unionization rates for African Americans have fallen more quickly than for the rest of the workforce. Black workers are still 30 percent more likely than the rest of the workforce to be in a union today, but as recently as the mid-1980s, black workers were almost 50 percent more likely to be in a union or covered by a union at their workplace.[194]

The study also found that since the early 1990s, the share of Black workers in manufacturing has been falling faster than for the workforce as a whole. "From the end of the 1970s to the early 1990s, African Americans were just as likely as workers from other racial and ethnic groups to have manufacturing jobs." Since the early 1990s, however, Black workers have lost considerable ground and by 2006 were about 15 percent less likely than other workers to have a manufacturing job.

Thus, between 1983 and 2006, the share of Black workers represented by a union fell from 31.7 percent to 16 percent! However, they were still more likely to be in a union than whites: the percentage belonging to unions was 15.7 percent for Black workers and 8.9 percent for white workers.

Uchitelle gave a dramatic example of the racist nature of the restructuring in a 2005 article. Discussing the decline of Black workers in unions—from one out of four in the 1980s to one out of seven in 2005—he cites a startling statistic for the year 2004.

> Overall union membership fell by 304,000, and blacks accounted for 55 percent of that drop, the Bureau of Labor Statistics reports, even though whites outnumber blacks by six to one in unions (12.4 million to 2.1 million). The trend seems likely to continue and perhaps accelerate as General Motors and its principal parts supplier, Delphi, cut costs in their struggle to be profitable.[195]

Uchitelle shows that it is not just manufacturing.

> On another front, privatization and outsourcing have eaten away at federal employment of black workers represented by the American Federation of Government Employees, which says that nearly 25 percent of its 211,000 members are black.
>
> African Americans make up an even higher percentage of the union's members at the operations that the Bush administration is turning over to private contractors. These include laundries at veterans' hospitals, ground maintenance and food service at government installations, and security guards at numerous federal buildings—much of it work that paid only $15,000 to $20,000 a year, but that came with pensions and health insurance.[196]

Similar attrition is going on through automation at the U.S. Postal Service. The installation of sorting machines is cutting into the heavily Black membership of the National Association of Letter Carriers and the American Postal Workers Union.

Another process that pushes Black workers down is the trend of companies to move out to the suburbs, away from downtown locations. In many of these cases white non-union workers replace unionized Black workers. The housing costs in the suburbs are high and there is a lack of public transportation, making it difficult or impossible for Black workers to reach these locations. The director of collective bargaining of the Communications Workers, George Kohl, told Uchitelle about the rise of call centers: "They gradually move to the suburbs, eliminating African-American union members in the city."

Locating jobs away from heavily African-American areas is a development that goes back to the earlier period of capitalist restructuring in the 1970s. The majority of manufacturing jobs lost to plant closings in urban areas with high concentrations of Black workers were relocated in suburban areas. Manufacturing employment fell almost 10 percent in the central cities. This was reported in a 2004 article by Betsy Leondar-Wright entitled "Black Job Loss Déjà Vu."[197]

One study of the causes of Black unemployment in 45 urban areas found that 20 percent to 50 percent resulted from jobs being shifted to the suburbs. A study of companies in Illinois that moved to the suburbs between 1975 and 1978 showed that Black employment in the area fell 24 percent while white employment fell less than 10 percent.

The U.S. Commission on Civil Rights found that, during the recession of 1973 to 1974, 60 percent to 70 percent of laid-off workers were African-American in areas where they were only 10 to 12 percent of the workforce. In five cities in the Great Lakes region, the majority of Black men employed in manufacturing lost their jobs between 1979 and 1984. Examples for the period can be easily multiplied. In cases of downsizing, Black workers often lost their jobs because they did not have as much seniority as the white workers. During earlier periods, racism had kept their numbers low in the plants and unions. Now it was a case of "last hired, first fired."

Leondar-Wright talks about the Great Migration, when millions of Black people got jobs up North but then lost them as "the U.S. economy began to deindustrialize and many of those jobs disappeared—in some cases shifted to the low-wage, nonunion South." But jobs that moved to the South during the earlier era of deindustrialization "are now leaving the country or simply disappearing in the wake of technological change and rising productivity."[198]

With regard to the 1970s, it is important to note that the central cities were areas of Black rebellions and political ferment. Black workers had organized against racism in the plants. The bosses wanted to move away from the centers of Black working-class power. The capitalists seized on deindustrialization and the revamping of industry to abandon the Black workers and their communities. The poverty in African-American communities outside the South was deliberately engineered by the government, the banks, and the industrialists—that is, the racist ruling class—throughout the entire period of migration to the North. This poverty and devastation was clearly outlined in the Kerner Commission Report as the underlying factor in the Black rebellions of 1968, numbering more than one hundred, which shook the foundations of U.S. capitalist society. But the bosses never made any real attempt to attack this poverty and devastation on any fundamental level. In fact, poverty in the Black community only intensified in the wake of the mass layoffs that began a decade later.

Globalization, outsourcing, and plant layoffs in the present period are eating away at the remaining unions, but also at nonunion jobs, sending Black unemployment up to an official 10 percent—more than twice the overall figure. However, 10 percent does not give a true picture of African-American unemployment, not only because the government undercounts but also because of the high proportion of Black workers who have given up looking for jobs.

In New York, scarcely half of African-American men age 16 to 65 had jobs in 2003, according to the Bureau of Labor Statistics' employment-to-population ratios for the city. This statistic is far more illuminating than the Bureau's official unemployment figures because it includes discouraged workers who have stopped looking for jobs and others who are not included in the unemployment figures. The findings showed that, out of the total employable population, only 51.8 percent of Black men and 57.1 percent of Black women had jobs. The percentage of Black men employed was the lowest since 1979.[199]

The proportion of the workers in general who have either become discouraged or who were never in the count in the first place, particularly young workers and workers who are just not counted because the government will not or cannot locate them, is undoubtedly much higher than the unemployment statistics show—particularly in inner cities and rural areas and especially among oppressed workers. The capitalist media have these figures available to them. But when the BLS announces the monthly unemployment and job reports, there is rarely any mention of the crucial employment-to-population ratios, which are far more representative of the plight of the workers.

Racism and low wages in the prison-industrial complex

The capitalist state in the U.S. consists of armed bodies to protect the exploiting class and suppress the poor and the exploited. Prisons are a principal institution of the capitalist state, along with the Armed Forces, the FBI, the Department of Homeland Security, the CIA, the police, and the courts. In the U.S., prisons are by and large concentration camps for the poor.

The prisons are filled with those who have acted out of desperation to survive; who have been victimized, demoralized, and marginalized by capitalist society; who either have no job, no future, no social support, or have been just plain framed up by the system. The aim of the prison system is to brutalize, to crush the human spirit and to punish those who rebel. The function of prison is not to rehabilitate but to debilitate.

As an instrument of a racist, exploiting ruling class, the state itself is racist and exploitative. Indeed, racism, repression, and super-exploitation intersect in the prison-industrial complex.

In the three decades during which the material conditions of the workers in the U.S. have declined, the prison population has increased by 300 percent[200] while the population as a whole has grown by only about 25 percent.[201] This disproportionate escalation of the prison population is the bosses' answer to capitalist restructuring, the spread of low wages, poverty, and the growth of the reserve army of unemployed. It reveals the intensification of racist arrest policies along with increasingly harsh prison sentences imposed by the legislatures and the courts.

Thus it is no accident that the world's so-called lone "super-power" in the age of globalization also has the world's largest prison population—both relatively and absolutely. There were almost 2.4 million prisoners in the U.S. at the end of 2006—1.6 million in state and federal prisons and another 723,000 in local jails. One in every one hundred of the 230 million adults in the U.S. is in jail. Another 5 million are on probation or on parole.

The fastest-growing prison population is among women. In 2006 a record high of 112,500 women were in federal and state prisons. If local jails are included, the number rises to 210,000. The female jail and prison population has grown twice as fast as the male inmate population since 1980; in 2006 it increased at the rate of 4.5 percent.

The United States has 5 percent of the world's population and 25 percent of the world's inmates.

The racist character of the state is reflected in the disproportionate use of the death penalty, racial profiling, and killings and assaults by police against African Americans. The broad statistics on imprisonment also show the depth and breadth of the racism. In 2006, 40 percent of all prisoners were African American and 20 percent were Latina/o. One in nine African American men age 20 to 34 was in prison. Black males had a 32 percent chance of going to prison at some point in their lives, Latino males had a 17 percent chance, and white males had a 6 percent chance. One in every 100 African-American women age 35 to 39 is in prison, compared to one in every 355 white women. However, the rate of imprisonment of white women is also growing.[202]

The system works methodically to increase the prison population and, at the same time, to create a growing captive labor force. Capitalist politicians declare a "war on drugs" and a "war on crime." In 1986 Congress passed a federal law mandating prison terms for crack cocaine use that were up to eight times as long as those involving powder cocaine.[203] About 90 percent of crack arrests are of African Americans while 75 percent of powder cocaine arrests involve whites. The refusal of Congress to soften this harsh, racist sentencing law resulted in a nationwide federal prison rebellion in 1996 as the prisons filled with Black youth.[204]

The banks facilitate drug dealing through money laundering and make profits on the deal. The police let the drugs flood into the oppressed communities and then make drug arrests. The legislatures pass drug sentencing and "three strike" laws. Pauperization of the people creates alienation and desperation. The courts hand down draconian sentences, even for petty, nonviolent offenses. The police, the prison-industrial complex, and the corporations that profit from the prison industry lobby for longer sentences, tougher parole, and harsher laws. The prison population grows and cheap labor becomes available for the prison system and for the bosses it serves.

Captive prison labor makes the class character of the state clear for all to see. The global search by capital for low-wage labor often winds up in super-exploitation inside the prisons. This phenomenon is as much a part of worldwide wage competition and low-wage capitalism as is the cross-border wage competition orchestrated by the transnational corporations.

The ruthless spirit of imperialist globalization seeks out unprotected labor everywhere. This is the spirit that engulfs the prisons. "For private business, prison labor is like a pot of gold," wrote Eve Goldberg and Linda Evans in 1997 in a pamphlet entitled *The Prison Industrial Complex & the Global Economy.* "No strikes. No union organizing. No unemployment insurance or workers' compensation to pay. No language problem, as in a foreign country. New leviathan prisons are being built with thousands of eerie acres of factories inside the walls. Prisoners do data entry for Chevron, make telephone reservations for TWA, raise hogs, shovel manure, make circuit boards, limousines, waterbeds and lingerie for Victoria's Secret. All at a fraction of the cost of 'free labor.'"[205]

The connection between the worldwide wage competition and prison labor was spelled out in a report by the National Institute of Justice, part of the U.S. Department of Justice, which urged employers to use prison labor to keep costs low.

"Companies are attracted to working with the prisons because inmates represent a readily available and dependable source of entry-level labor that is a cost-effective alternative to work forces found in Mexico, the Caribbean Basin, Southeast Asia and the Pacific Rim countries," said the report.[206]

The report described how Escod Industries, a division of a Fortune 400 company, used prison labor in South Carolina to assemble electrical cables, which were then sold to corporations like IBM and Northern Telecom. Escod had originally planned to have its work done in a Mexican *maquiladora*, but the state of South Carolina showed how total production costs could be kept to $6.04 an hour using prison labor.

A contract manufacturer that recycled Dell Computer parts brought the work back to the U.S. in order to use prison labor made available by Federal Prison Industries, Inc., the federal government's prison labor arm—known commercially as UNICOR. Federal prisoners, as of 2004, were paid anywhere from 23 cents to $1.15 an hour. And the prisons deduct expenses from these pitiful wages.[207]

UNICOR is a growing prison business that advertises operations including clothing and textiles, electronics, fleet management and vehicular components, industrial products, office furniture, recycling, and services (including data entry and encoding). As of 2007, 18 percent of federal prisoners, amounting to 21,250 inmates, worked for UNICOR.[208]

The generals in the Pentagon are basically businessmen in uniform and see all things through the eyes of the exploiting class. It is only natural that UNICOR, as of 2004, was the Pentagon's 39th largest contractor, supplying $400 million of materials and services to the military and $687 million overall.

Prisoners made 100 percent of battlefield head gear at Greenville, Illinois. In Marion, Illinois they worked on TOW and Patriot missiles. During the Gulf-War of 1991 they produced sandbags, blankets, night vision goggles, chemical gas detection devices and bomb components. In recent years they made everything from underwear and camouflage clothes to components for 30 mm and 300 mm battleship anti-aircraft guns. In 2002 700 prisoners at laundry facilities located in Texas, Florida and Alabama washed and pressed $3 million worth of military apparel. Prisoners at Edgefield, South

Carolina mend shirts and trousers. The federal prison factories operate three shifts a day, 24 hours around the clock.[209]

The use of captive labor in state prisons is widespread. At least forty states have business operations based upon prison labor, run by the state departments of corrections. The states lease prisoners out, set up manufacturing inside the prisons, contract out for piece work, and set up arrangements with privatized prison companies like Corrections Corporation of America or Wackenhut, which run state prisons on a contract basis for profit. These private prison firms, backed by Wall Street investment houses like Goldman Sachs, are notorious for brutalizing prisoners and squeezing the last penny of profit from them, either through forced labor, excessive fees, or cutting costs.

At least forty states have business operations based upon prison labor, run by the state departments of corrections

The California Prison Industry Authority, according to its Web site, has 5,900 inmates operating more than sixty service, manufacturing and agricultural industries at twenty-two prisons. They produce numerous items and "receive wages between $.30 and $.95 an hour, before deductions."[210]

Arizona Correctional Industries, a division of the Department of Corrections, has inmates producing a wide variety of services and products under three different programs. Under the program, which sells its products to governmental bodies, prisoners "may receive a wage of up to $.35 an hour." Another program pays $.35 to $.85 an hour. There are more than 2,200 inmates working in the prison system.[211]

Iowa, which sentences African Americans to prison at a rate 13.6 times that of whites, sends prisoners to work farms around the state, in addition to manufacturing. When they work in private industry they get the "prevailing wage," but are allowed to keep no more than 20 percent of their wages.[212]

The government witch hunt against undocumented workers has sent bosses looking to the prisons for substitute cheap labor. The immigrant prison population is the fastest growing part of the prison population in the U.S. When Arizona passed legislation in 2007 to fine employers for hiring undocumented workers, the bosses, particularly the farmers, inundated the Arizona Department of Corrections with requests for prison laborers. Arizona Correctional Industries, a division of the ADC, provided nine private agricultural companies, ranging from greenhouses to canneries, with prison labor. These companies hire prison laborers on a contract basis and pay them a minimum of $2 an hour. But 30 percent of these wages go to pay prisoners' room and board—so the wage is really $1.40 an hour.[213]

Examples of forced labor at the mercy of the state could be multiplied endlessly. The millions of hours of labor at near slave wages serves to drive down wages in the workforce generally in the particular occupation and region in which prison labor is applied. At the same time it is a reflection of what the capitalists really will do to the workers when they have the opportunity. Prison wages are a golden opportunity. They are as close to paying nothing as you can get, short of chattel slavery.

In fact, the prison labor system grew up in the South after the Civil War with the convict "leasing" system. Prisoners were leased to plantation owners as a substitute for chattel slavery. This system, which is really rooted in slavery, is thriving again in the 21st century—the age of imperialism and low-wage capitalism.

Mumia Abu-Jamal is a world-renowned Black journalist who has been on death row in Pennsylvania since 1982, having been framed up by the Philadelphia police. He is known as the "voice of the voiceless" and writes frequent commentaries on the political, economic, and social exploitation of prison labor, especially African-American labor. He wrote in 2005:

> In the prison context, we see the exploitation of globalism, in microcosm. Imprisoned workers work, quite literally, for pennies a day. In some states (like Texas) they work for nothing at all. They are super-exploited by excessive phone rates, which are but another hidden tax on the poor. This economic exploitation of prison labor is but a mirror of the political exploitation of prisoners, where they are counted in rural census populations, bringing federal monies to rural, conservative districts, where they, like many of their slave ancestors, were counted (albeit three-fifths) but had utterly no representation. Moreover, their home districts are further impoverished by their population losses and lost federal dollars, for housing, education and income maintenance.[214]

Monica Moorehead, editor of *Marxism, Reparations and the Black Freedom Struggle*, wrote that "a captive workforce can make super-profits for local, state and national governments—and slave labor can be pitted against other workers with better paying jobs."

"All the repressive arms of the state work hand in hand to build up this imprisoned army of the unemployed and the sky is the limit," says Moorehead, who highlights the threat to the labor movement and all workers by posing the question: "Shouldn't the unions make it their business to organize prisoners and demand union wages and conditions, so they can't be used as scab labor?"[215]

In fact, one of the principal demands of the inmates in the great Attica prison uprising of 1972 was for union wages. The Attica uprising was a political insurrection with anti-racist, anti-imperialist demands as well as demands for improved conditions. These crucial working-class demands apply today more than ever and must be taken up by the labor movement.

9

Globalization and immigration

Lenin on immigration · Searching for cheap labor at home and abroad · May Day 2006 in the U.S. · Latina/o immigrants pulled into low-wage labor force · Vast super-profits behind debate in U.S. ruling class · NAFTA and the crisis of Mexican workers and peasants · Remittances and the global migrant labor force

At the same time that Black workers have been pushed further and further into low-wage, low-income, and semi-employed status by capitalist industrial restructuring and globalization, Latina/o workers have also been increasingly pushed into the same low-wage status. The cause is long-standing racism against Latinas/os in general. But the situation is aggravated by economically forced immigration resulting from the impoverishment of Mexico, Central America, the Caribbean, and South America by U.S. transnationals and other imperialist corporations and banks.

The massive immigration into the U.S. of Latina/o workers and other workers of numerous nationalities over the last two decades is another effect of global capitalist restructuring and the worldwide wage competition designed to foster a "race to the bottom." The global restructuring of industry and services is meant to bring down the cost of labor to the capitalists worldwide by any and all means necessary. The massive incorporation of low-wage immigrant workers into the economies of Europe and the U.S. is the flip side of seeking cheap labor abroad.

Lenin on immigration

Before dealing further with current developments, it is worthwhile to go back to Lenin to see how the present struggle fits into the evolution of immigration under imperialism.

One of Lenin's important contributions to the study of imperialism was to show that it is not a policy, nor is it limited to global expansion. It is a form of society, a stage of capitalism. While Lenin's work concentrated on expansion abroad, it showed that the quest for territory, necessitated by the drive to acquire raw materials and spheres of influence, was driven by monopoly capital in its insatiable appetite for super-profits.

While the pursuit of super-profits is most often associated with foreign investment by big capital in underdeveloped colonial or neocolonial territories, it is also highly relevant to the question of immigration, particularly in the current stage of imperialism.

In his book, *Imperialism, the Highest Stage of Capitalism*, Lenin referred to the tendency of imperialism to divide the workers between the privileged and the lower-paid:

> One of the special features of imperialism connected with the facts we are describing is the decline of emigration from imperialist countries and the increase in immigration into these countries from the more [economically underdeveloped—FG] countries where lower wages are paid.[216]

Lenin went on to show the decline in emigration from Britain, France, and Germany and the increase in immigration from Austria, Italy, Russia, and other countries.

> According to the 1907 census, there were 1,342,294 foreigners in Germany, of whom 440,800 were industrial workers and 257,329 agricultural workers. In France, the workers employed in the mining industry are "in great part" foreigners: Poles, Italians, and Spaniards. In the United States, immigrants from Eastern and Southern Europe are engaged in the most poorly paid occupations, while American workers provide the highest percentage of overseers or of the better-paid workers. Imperialism has the tendency to create privileged sections also among the workers and detach them from the broad masses.[217]

Most important for the present discussion is that Lenin showed that migration of low-wage labor to the strongest, most prosperous capitalist countries was a special feature of imperialism. And secondly, he showed this in connection with the broader problem of the capitalist class stirring up chauvinism to set the higher-paid workers against the lower-paid immigrant workers from more oppressed regions.

Searching for cheap labor at home and abroad

Massive immigration and the slave trade were necessary to build up the foundations of the two social systems—capitalism and chattel slavery—that took root early in the thirteen colonies, during and after the invasion of European settlers that pushed the Native peoples from their land. After the settlers had either displaced or killed off the Native peoples, the natural rate of population increase was inadequate to supply the necessary urban and rural labor power essential to build up capitalism. Waves of migration to the United States took place in the middle of the nineteenth century, prior to the rise of imperialism. Each fresh wave of workers and farmers—from Ireland, Germany, Scandinavia, and other areas—met with brutal chauvinism and was forced to endure low wages and hard labor in both agriculture and industry. Later on, immigrants from southern and eastern Europe suffered similar hardships.

But what makes modern immigration a special feature of the later stages of imperialism is that the normal processes of plunder of the oppressed countries have set in motion a movement of impoverished masses toward the rich capitalist countries. Today's immigrant population is largely an oppressed population when it arrives here, because they come from countries and regions that were once ruled, directly or indirectly, by imperialism and colonialism, whether in Central America, Mexico, the Caribbean, South America, Asia, Africa, or the Middle East. Earlier immigrants were largely from the poorer sections of Europe; some were even semi-colonies. But despite initial persecution and hardships, the European immigrants were mostly white and, unlike present-day immigrants of color, were eventually permitted to assimilate into the oppressor nation. (One major exception was the large number of Chinese who suffered extremely harsh racism and oppression dating back to the early nineteenth century. They were not allowed to assimilate and still suffer racism today.)

Sections of the ruling class tolerate, encourage and take advantage of this influx of immigrants, not only for the purpose of filling a labor shortage or to settle territory, but also to artificially increase the reserve army of labor, an army of vulnerable workers who are forced to work at substandard wages. The principal aim of permitting and fostering immigration under imperialism is to greatly increase competition among workers and keep downward pressure on wages.

In this regard, immigration policy for imperialism, as part of the search for super-profits at home, is organically continuous with the process of the export of capital to the underdeveloped world. Importation of low-wage labor to serve the profit lust of the bosses at home is inseparable from finance capital scouring the globe for low-wage labor abroad.

May Day 2006 in the United States

The vast demonstrations that took place in cities throughout the United States on May Day, 2006, were a manifestation of an army of oppressed workers from around the globe, led by the Latina/o immigrant population.

The assembly of this population in the U.S. has taken place by the same process that has caused the international working class to grow throughout the rest of the neocolonial and underdeveloped world. Global imperialist finance capital, by its reorganization of capitalist production on a world scale, is concentrating unemployed, underemployed and impoverished rural labor, a vast reserve army of low-wage workers, into its plants and offices across the globe. In the process of exporting its manufacturing and service capital, it is multiplying and centralizing the working class. By this very process it creates the conditions for organized resistance against imperialism and capitalism. This demonstrates what Marx meant when he said that the capitalist class creates and is forced to develop its class antagonist, the working class.

With respect to Latin America and the Caribbean, the U.S. ruling class, by fostering immigration in the last three decades, has pulled together a scattered reserve army of poorly paid workers, many unemployed or underemployed, as well as impoverished or landless peasants suffering from the underdevelopment caused by centuries of colonialism and neocolonialism. This development was accelerated by globalization, which destroyed domestic economies in Latin America. It has concentrated these immigrants in the industries and cities of the United States to be super-exploited by the bosses here.

The mass demonstrations in 2006, and particularly the May Day boycott, showed this beyond a doubt. It was virtually a general strike. "Troqueros" shut down the largest U.S. port area in Los Angeles and Long Beach. Giant meatpacking plants across the country were paralyzed. The construction industry, the food service industry, and the fields and orchards of agribusiness were all affected. In a microcosm, the Bolivarian quest for continental unity was demonstrated by the massive unity of Latina/o immigrants on May Day in the streets of Los Angeles, Denver, Chicago, New York, and numerous other cities.

But in addition to Latina/o unity, what was stunning to the ruling class was the general unity of the immigrant population as a whole. The same exploitative process that has been inflicted upon Latina/os has been equally applied, if in lesser numbers, to workers from East Asia, South Asia, Africa, and the Middle East. They also came out for the May Day boycott.

In order to break up this massive movement before it could gain momentum, the Bush administration, using the Immigration and Customs Enforcement (ICE) division of the Department of Homeland Security, launched widespread and widely publicized raids on factories and sweeps of neighborhoods. Tens of thousands of immigrant workers have suffered ruthless deportation, the breaking up of families, and imprisonment in internment camps. Such tactics were designed to crush the movement before it could gain support and solidarity from the rest of the population. The anti-immigrant campaign was designed to expel enough workers and instill enough fear in the immigrant community to push back the organizing. The effect of the racist campaign was to make the immigrant population feel even more vulnerable.

At the same time that the bosses are "offshoring" and outsourcing production and services that can be divided into processes and shipped abroad to low-wage regions of the world, they are importing immigrants and forcing them into the low-wage jobs that cannot be offshored. Immigrants fill the jobs that must be done through personal contact or that cannot be moved abroad. This is imperialist "globalization" in search of super-profits pure and simple— except that they are garnered inside the borders of the United States.

Latina/o immigrants pulled into low-wage labor force

In the twenty-five years from 1980 to 2005, according to the U.S. Census Bureau, 20.1 million immigrants were admitted legally to the United States. It is impossible to gauge the accuracy of the estimates given for undocumented workers. But the Pew Hispanic Center, an immigrant population research institute, estimates that the undocumented population rose to between 11.5 million and 12 million in the same twenty-five-year period. This is a minimal figure. Thus, since the beginning of the 1980s the population of immigrants with legal status of one type or another, combined with the undocumented workers, has risen by more than 30 million. The number of immigrants is equal to 10 percent of the total U.S. population. The figures show that the influx has been increasing sharply since 1990, with the steepest rises in the last several years.

While the influx of immigrants as a proportion of the total population was highest in the years beginning with the 1890s up to 1914 (the last period of imperialist "globalization"), the absolute numbers of immigrants have reached unprecedented levels in the recent period— 7 million in the 1970s, 10 million in the 1980s, 14 million from 1991 to 2000 and 4 million more by 2004.

It is no accident that the surge in immigration coincides with both the imperialist neo-liberal offensive abroad and the anti-labor offensive at home conducted by U.S. capitalism

It is no accident that the surge in immigration coincides with both the neo-liberal offensive by imperialism and the anti-labor offensive conducted by U.S. capitalism. The recent wave of immigration began in the 1980s when the Reagan administration and the International Monetary Fund began their aggressive campaign of Structural Adjustment Programs (SAPs) and the dismantling of all semblance of economic autonomy of the oppressed countries. The era of the debt crisis and the consequent impoverishment of

Latin America, Asia, and Africa, especially, coincide with the increasing flow of immigrants to the imperialist countries.

The undocumented came in ever-larger waves during the capitalist restructuring of manufacturing, the shift in the economy to low-wage service jobs, and the union-busting campaigns of the 1980s and 1990s. One of the examples of the reduction in wages attributed to the super-exploitation of undocumented workers is the drastic reduction in wages in the meatpacking industry. What is not mentioned, however, is that the bosses broke the packinghouse workers' strike against Hormel, one of the largest meatpacking companies in the industry, when they destroyed Local P9 in Minnesota in the 1980s. The leadership of the labor movement abandoned that struggle and was in a general retreat during that period.

Second, it is not the undocumented workers who are responsible for the $9-an-hour wage. It is the packinghouse bosses. But it is also the union leaders, who for years abandoned their responsibility and ignored undocumented workers, leaving them to the mercy of the employers.

The degree to which the employers have eagerly drafted low-wage undocumented workers into the labor force is measured by figures compiled by the Pew Hispanic Center in March 2005. They estimated that 7.2 million undocumented workers were in the U.S. labor force and presented some of the highlights of the breakdown. [218] (See table on right.)

It is an extremely important fact that many of the jobs with a disproportionate number of undocumented workers—for example, butchers, fishery workers, poultry workers, and various construction trades, particularly roofers—are among the most dangerous in the country. And undocumented workers have great difficulty getting treated for injuries and receive little or no worker compensation benefits for accidents on the job.

This amounts to huge extra profits for the bosses over the course of a year. It is not just business owners who have an interest in keeping the flow of undocumented workers coming. Virtually every business, no matter how large or small, is in debt to the banks, and the bankers want to see that their loans are paid. For example, the homebuilding industry operates heavily on credit. The major role of low-wage immigrant workers in home construction adds to profit margins and makes loans easier to repay. Undocumented workers make businesses more profitable and the bankers know it.

Vast super-profits behind debate in U.S. ruling class

The legislative and political struggle within the U.S. ruling class over immigration reflects the conflict between the right-wing political establishment

Jobs of undocumented workers*

Percent of the workforce by category

OCCUPATION	No. of undocumented	% of total in occupation
Insulation workers	20,000	36%
Miscellaneous agricultural workers	247,000	29%
Roofers	93,000	29%
Drywall installers, ceiling tile installers	79,000	28%
Helpers, construction trades	40,000	27%
Butchers and other meat, poultry and fish processing workers	87,000	27%
Pressers, textile and garment workers	21,000	26%
Grounds maintenance workers	299,000	25%
Construction laborers	400,000	25%
Brick masons and stone masons	49,000	25%
Dishwashers	85,000	23%
Maids and housekeeping cleaners	342,000	22%
Painters, construction and maintenance	167,000	22%

The list continues in descending order to include, among other occupations, packers (176,000), vehicle cleaners (85,000), carpet and floor installers (66,000), cooks (436,000), parking lot attendants (12,000), upholsterers (13,000), sewing machine operators (51,000), food preparation workers (128,000), and laundry and dry-cleaning operators (30,000). In each of these occupations, undocumented workers make up more than 15 percent of the workforce. In general, these are all low-paying jobs to begin with and undocumented workers are forced to take below-scale wages.

* Based on data from a Pew Hispanic Center research report of March 7, 2006. See endnote 218.

and the bosses who rely heavily on undocumented workers, and immigrant labor in general, to work at low wages. It is not that the bosses who employ undocumented workers mind having a racist political climate against immigrants. When an atmosphere of fear and intimidation exists, it keeps those workers more vulnerable. But these employers and their supporters are all for some kind of guest worker program that will keep the supply of labor-power flowing in. Thus, until now, they have been opposed to legally interfering with the flow of workers, especially when the capitalist economy was expanding.

The employers in construction, agriculture, the textile and apparel industry, meatpacking, and many service industries have been in a struggle against the political campaign of the right wing of the ruling class, which waves the banner of immigrant bashing alongside anti-Black racism, slogans against abortion, and crusades against same-sex marriage and lesbian, gay, bi, and trans rights. The right wing comes into conflict with the employers of undocumented workers because its program calls for border fences, expulsion, and choking off immigration.

So long as there is capitalist expansion, the employers will be for a vigorous guest worker program, as were the Chamber of Commerce and the *Wall Street Journal* in 2007. But let there be a capitalist downturn with an unemployment crisis and the employers can easily unify with the political right wing around a program of not only scapegoating undocumented workers but calling for harsh repressive measures in order to ward off any move toward anti-capitalist unity among the working class. The union leadership and the progressive movement in general needs to be on guard and begin preemptively to counter the anti-immigrant tide that is rising The most progressive forces in the labor movement are calling for class unity and solidarity in action with undocumented workers as the only way to defend all workers.

NAFTA and the crisis of Mexican workers and peasants

The predominance of Mexican workers among the immigrant population requires a special comment on the so-called North American Free Trade Agreement. Neo-liberal economic aggression escalated under the Clinton administration. It is a matter of direct cause and effect that the largest spike in immigration from Mexico to the United States took place in 1995 and 1996 in the wake of NAFTA. Immigration has flowed to the U.S. in rising numbers ever since.

Many jobs in the United States were lost as a result of offshoring by U.S. corporations. One estimate puts the number of jobs lost from 1994 to 2002 because of NAFTA at 900,000.[219] But what the U.S. working class and the population in general must understand is the corporate invasion of Mexico and the consequent suffering of the Mexican masses that was also part of the offshoring process.

When NAFTA was first instituted on January 1, 1994, the Zapatistas led an armed rebellion in defense of the indigenous people of the Mexican state of Chiapas and against the incursion of U.S. agribusiness. The agricultural giants were already engaged in a campaign to undermine Mexican agriculture and replace many foodstuffs with crops shipped from the United States. The fears that provoked this rebellion were entirely justified.

NAFTA put small Mexican farmers in competition with giant U.S. and Canadian exporters. Under NAFTA the capitalist government of Mexico agreed to withdraw long-standing price supports, credit, and technical assistance for Mexican peasants. Meanwhile, corn and beans, the staple of the Mexican diet, were being subsidized in the U.S. and shipped south. To gain control of the market, U.S. corn was sold at prices 20 to 30 percent below the cost of production. According to Jeff Faux, "Between 1993 and 2002, roughly two million farmers were forced to abandon their land."[220] From November to May every year, a million Mexicans now work as migrant laborers inside their own country.

Many of the internal migrants can earn nothing at home because there are no paying jobs. They survive on beans and corn that they plant around their houses and the families migrate together. "Everyone works," wrote Faux. He cited one journalist: "There are neither schools nor health care and often not even the most minimal housing."[221]

In 1995, one year after the implementation of NAFTA, the Mexican peso collapsed. The collapse arose from financial speculation in Mexican bonds, primarily by Wall Street sharks. The prices were bid up in anticipation of NAFTA. When the Mexican government could not pay the debt on the bonds, the economy collapsed. Wrote Faux: "It was the steepest economic crash [in Mexico] since the Great Depression. In 1995, GDP per capita fell 9 percent, wages fell 16 percent, domestic consumption fell 10 percent, and business investment dropped by almost a third. The formal unemployment rate, which vastly understates joblessness, doubled."[222] Then President Ernesto Zedillo, working to pay the northern bankers, cut social services, education, and health care. Half the Mexican population was already in poverty and this just deepened it.

U.S. corporations benefited not only by displacing Mexican farmers but also by driving many of the workers impoverished by the economic collapse into *maquiladoras* on the Mexican border. A *maquiladora* is a factory that can export duty-free to the U.S. as long as it uses U.S.-made parts. These are assembly-line sweatshops that line the U.S.-Mexican border. During the years 1993 to 2003, Mexico lost 100,000 non-*maquiladora* jobs, while 540,000 workers were driven into the *maquiladoras*.

NAFTA and U.S. corporate offshoring that had started even earlier produced the same wage-depressing effect on Mexican workers that they did on

U.S. workers. In 1975 Mexican wages were about 23 percent of U.S. wages; in 1993-94 just before the formal enactment of NAFTA, Mexican wages were 15 percent of U.S. wages. By 2002 they had sunk to 12 percent of U.S. wages.[223]

With 50 percent of the population living in poverty, conditions have gotten worse. In 1994 the minimum wage (at that time $4.20 per day) bought 44.9 pounds of tortillas. In 2003 it bought 18.6 pounds. In 1994 it bought 24.5 liters of gas for cooking. In 2003 it bought 7 liters. Thus worldwide wage competition promoted by capitalist globalization created not only wage competition between U.S. and Mexican workers but wage competition within Mexico itself by driving up unemployment and rural displacement.

It should also be noted that the Mexican working class, after having been subjected to the invasion of U.S. offshoring capitalists and put to work in the *maquiladoras* at wages averaging less than 10 percent of U.S. wages, themselves became the victims of further wage competition. When Mexican wages rose slightly, the bosses began moving their factories to China, where wages were even lower. Between 2002 and 2003 some 200,000 jobs were moved out of the *maquiladoras*.[224]

Workers in the U.S. must understand that the very same corporations that are lowering wages, taking away benefits, and laying off workers here—that is to say, the capitalist enemies of the U.S. working class—are the architects of even greater suffering for the Mexican workers. Furthermore, workers in the U.S., Mexico, and China were all being manipulated by U.S. corporations into wage competition in order to increase the profits of the transnationals.

Each working class faces the same common enemy—whether it is General Motors, Ford, Eastman Kodak, or Motorola. The only way out of this race to the bottom is to unite across borders to face the bosses with a common front of resistance. And it is the workers in the imperialist countries, in the oppressor countries where the architects of this divisive policy are centered, who must take the initiative and reach out to the super-exploited workers around the world.

The bosses in the United States have made "border security" against undocumented workers a major political issue, driven by racism and chauvinism. But no one is raising border security for oppressed countries against the invasion of capital, which flies across national boundaries to exploit the workers and nations of the world. Because no country in the underdeveloped world has border security against finance capital or the underdevelopment and poverty that it brings in its wake, immigration and the defense of immigrants, documented and undocumented, must become a life-and-death issue for the working class, not only in the United States but in France, Germany, Britain, Belgium, Spain, and other big capitalist countries. This is a looming world question in the present age of imperialist globalization.

Remittances and the global migrant labor force

As a global source of labor, migration has grown significantly since Lenin first referred to it as a feature of imperialism and of the monopolies in their quest for low wages. On the one hand, the revolutions in cell phone technology and electronic banking, as well as advances in transportation, have facilitated migration on a global basis.

Senior journalist Jason DeParle wrote a major article for the *New York Times Magazine* ironically entitled, "A Good Provider Is One Who Leaves." Stating that an estimated 200 million migrants were spread across the globe, he pointed out that they were supporting a population much larger than themselves, perhaps amounting to more than half a billion people. DeParle wrote: "Were these half-billion or so people to constitute a state—migration nation—it would rank as the world's third largest."[225]

It is estimated that emigrants sent $300 billion back to their countries of origin in 2006

The article was centered on the Philippines, but showed in general how thoroughly the earnings and remittances of the tens of millions of migrant workers are integrated into and essential to the restructured, low-wage world capitalist economy. It is estimated that emigrants sent $300 billion back to their countries of origin in 2006.

According to DeParle, commercial banks in Turkey and Brazil use the expected remittances from abroad as collateral on bank loans. Banks campaign to get families of emigrants who have gone abroad to open up bank accounts and have the remittances wired through the accounts rather than sent directly to the families. The Philippines, with 90 million people, is fourth in the world in remittances—behind China with $25 billion, India with $24 billion, and Mexico, also with $24 billion. There are 22 countries in which remittances from emigrant workers exceed 10 percent of the gross domestic product, including Haiti with 23 percent and Lebanon with 22 percent. These funds ultimately wind up supporting the payment of debt by the oppressed countries to the financiers in New York, London, Paris, and Berlin.

Filipino workers go all over the world and have become the second-largest immigrant population in the United States. One in seven of all Filipino workers is employed abroad. The $15 billion a year in wages and salaries they send home represents one-seventh of the gross domestic product of the

Philippines. One million Filipino workers went abroad in 2006. In fact, the current Greek word for maid is *Filipineza*.

African emigration is a little-covered issue in the United States. But the Straits of Gibraltar, along the sea path from Africa to southern Europe, is known as "the biggest mass graveyard in Europe." An untold number of Africans, fleeing the desperate poverty imposed by neocolonialism, die crossing the Sahara desert or trying to get to Spain by boat.

If the $300 billion the emigrants send home in one year represented one-quarter to one-third of their paychecks, it would mean that they earned in the neighborhood of a trillion dollars in wages and salaries. And if they were paid a trillion dollars, the profit their labor-power contributed to the world capitalist economy would be at least in the hundreds of billions and possibly more, depending on the average rate of exploitation of immigrant labor.

10

Late 1970s:
Attack on unions begins

**The importance of unions • Listening to boardrooms, Reagan ambushes
PATCO • 'PATCO scenario' takes off • Globalization and the 'fear factor'**

Under capitalism, in the absence of unions, the conditions of workers are decided by their individual bargaining power with the boss and whatever social and labor legislation exists to provide benefits and legal guarantees. Furthermore, the extent and enforcement of any legal guarantees and benefits are themselves determined by the class struggle.

For workers in the United States, legislative protections and benefits for the working class as a whole are minimal. Everyday conditions of life depend entirely on the relationship of forces between the workers and the boss on the job. No provisions exist to prevent plant closings or downsizing or to take care of workers who have been laid off. No laws guarantee vacations, sick time, paid holidays, or other benefits. At best there is minimum-wage legislation, which was won through struggle but has been allowed to sink so far below poverty level that it is scandalous. Social Security for the elderly and disabled is another limited victory for the workers, but it often falls below the poverty level. Whether there is an eight-hour day with a forty-hour week is completely dependent on the will of the employers, who have instituted twelve-hour days and forced overtime, and have lowered wages so that workers have to extend their hours on the job or work two and three jobs in order to live.

The importance of unions

It is in this light that the fundamental significance of unions must be viewed, regardless of the character and practice of the leadership. Class organization determines whether workers get living wages that enable the support of a family or even of an individual worker; whether they get paid vacations, when they can take them, how long the vacation lasts, and if it is broken up; how much, if any, paid sick time they get; whether they are covered for extended illness, for themselves or dependents; whether they have decent health insurance or low-quality, high-cost health insurance or no health insurance at all; whether they have fixed-benefit pensions, 401-K's with or without employer matching, or no retirement benefits at all; paid maternity or paternity leave; limitations to stress on the job; any degree of control over their work shifts, forced overtime, shortened hours, any say over their assignments on the job, the right to resist abuse by supervisors, the right to safety on the job, training, advancement, seniority rights, any grievance procedure at all, or even limited job security, etc. All these issues and others, which are so crucial in the lives of workers, are determined by whether or not they have any organized power to set conditions. Without any organization, they work "at will"—meaning the will of the boss.

In the 1960s and 1970s, struggles for national liberation, civil rights, women's rights, lesbian, gay rights, immigrant rights, the rights of seniors, and the rights of the disabled had, to a limited extent, won legislation intended to overcome discrimination against the oppressed in hiring, wages, and access to education. (The struggle for bi and trans rights did not emerge until later.) These struggles also forced the government to spend some money to alleviate poverty. Over the last three decades, however, a war against the unions has been accompanied by a simultaneous and overlapping war against all progressive social formations in the United States.

It is a shameful abdication by the labor leadership of the AFL-CIO that it forced the workers to face this capitalist offensive with one hand tied behind their backs. It refused to use the potentially immense social and political power available to the unions and all workers. Had the leadership over the last three decades mobilized the vast infrastructure and financial resources of the labor movement in this battle—while also embracing the existing struggles against racism and national oppression, sexual and gender oppression, and of the undocumented workers as essential components of labor's cause—the relationship of class forces under U.S. capitalism could be far more favorable to the working class today.

The union struggle has broad economic and social ramifications. The experiences of the last three decades show that the conditions of the unions are bound up with the conditions of the multinational working class, with the oppressed, and with the fate of communities everywhere. Just as the upsurge in the 1930s and the victory for industrial unionism resulted in major advances for the working class as a whole, by the same token the undermining of the unions over the last three decades has had a highly detrimental effect on the overall conditions of the broader working class, as well as the middle class.

As has been shown, because Black workers struggled against the racism of the union leadership as well as the companies, some were able to rise out of menial positions and get union jobs at union wages with benefits and job security. But the destruction of the manufacturing union jobs then pushed hundreds of thousands of Black workers back into lower-paying positions and increased poverty in the Black community.

The same is true for Latina/o workers in agriculture, textiles, food, and commercial services. From the United Farm Workers to the Farm Labor Organizing Committee, winning union representation has raised wages and conditions, which become endangered with the undermining of the unions in general.

In 1972 the Coalition of Black Trade Unionists (CBTU) was created within the AFL-CIO. This formal recognition was imposed upon the labor hierarchy by the growing weight and significance of the organized Black working class. It followed a period of general upsurge by rank-and-file Black workers in the plants, notably the Dodge Revolutionary Union Movement (DRUM) in the auto industry, which fought racism on the job and in the union itself.

The creation of the Coalition of Labor Union Women (CLUW) in 1974 also represented forced recognition by the labor leadership of the strides made by women workers. The movement for equal pay, for seniority rights, and for respect flowing out of the women's movement and into the workplace saw economic gains for women. But the destruction of union jobs and the lowering of wages generally has meant that women entered the workforce *en masse* under the worst conditions and now constitute a vast, low-wage sector.

The same is true for lesbian, gay, bisexual, and transsexual workers. The establishment of Pride at Work as an officially sanctioned institution within the AFL-CIO in 1994 was also the result of decades of struggle. As a result, explicit provisions forbidding discrimination on the basis of sexual orientation were written into union contracts for the first time in history. But the elimination of union jobs diminishes both the economic and social position of lesbian, gay, bi, and trans workers. In addition to facing lower pay, they have no contractual basis from which to force employers to recognize their rights.

Communities across the country have been devastated by plant closings, downsizing, and concessions. The principal reason has been employer schemes to undermine the unions and all union-level wages. But whatever the cause, the communities, as well as both small and medium-size businesses, all suffer when workers' incomes go down. Bankruptcies abound. Income from local corporate taxes goes down or disappears and social services are reduced just when they are most needed. The poor and the oppressed suffer the most.

The significance of the unions stretches far beyond the organized labor movement, which sets the standard for the working class as a whole. During the post-World War II period up until the 1970s, wages generally went up as a result of collective bargaining agreements (not without constant strike struggles). The reason that companies like DuPont, Eastman Kodak, Sears Roebuck, IBM, Hewlett-Packard, Procter & Gamble, Metropolitan Life Insurance, and other giant non-union companies had to give raises, benefits, and job security in that period was in order to keep the unions out.

This most hostile, anti-labor ruling class was fully aware of the importance of the unions. Once the great struggles of the 1960s were over, and the bosses wanted to meet the challenge of their imperialist rivals who were introducing new technology and invading the world markets, the decision in the boardrooms was to open up the attack on their biggest obstacle, organized labor. By pushing back the strongest industrial unions—the unions that set the higher standard based on earlier struggles—the bosses laid the basis for opening up an assault on the broader working class.

Many concessionary demands were made on the unions in the 1970s but a major shot was fired at the United Steel Workers (USW) at the Campbell Works plant in Youngstown, Ohio, where the company laid off 4,100 workers and shut down the plant in 1977. These blows were continued throughout the 1980s.

Listening to the boardrooms, Reagan ambushes PATCO

Reagan gave a great boost to the anti-labor struggle in 1981 when he implemented Carter's plan to break the Professional Air Traffic Controllers Organization (PATCO) as an effective labor organization. He summarily gave the striking workers forty-eight hours to get back on the job after the beginning of their strike against onerous working conditions. When they refused, Reagan fired them all, hired permanent replacement scabs, already in place, and banned the striking workers from federal employment for life, effectively ending their careers.

Reagan basically ambushed a union that had distanced itself from the mainstream of the AFL-CIO. A small union of highly paid but overworked and highly stressed workers, it had incurred the ire of the labor leadership by endorsing Reagan for president in 1980. After he turned on the union, the

AFL-CIO leadership adopted the narrow, self-defeating policy of giving the striking PATCO workers only lukewarm support. They failed to realize that this act of class aggression by the capitalist state, led by the rabidly anti-union Reagan, required a mighty, unified response—a firm working-class rebuff.

What followed was a series of brutal attacks, during which the bosses were immeasurably assisted by mass unemployment in the early 1980s, caused by the most severe economic downturn since World War II. The downturn came in the midst of the opening phase of the technological revolution and advances in productivity pioneered in Germany and Japan that allowed the bosses greater freedom to install new job-killing technology.

From the post-World War II period up until the mid-to-late 1970s, most union contracts had resulted in wage and benefit increases. By the end of the 1970s and particularly beginning with the 1980s, contract negotiations became a defensive battleground for the workers. During the recession period of 1980 to 1983 the bosses used the collective bargaining process to turn the tables and eradicate the gains of the previous decades. They demanded wage freezes or wage cuts, pension freezes, pension cuts for retirees, cutting back or eliminating cost-of-living increases, reduced vacation days and paid holidays, and increased co-payments on health-care plans, among other things.

In addition, and perhaps more important for the future generations of workers, they inaugurated the two-tier system in hiring new workers. Workers who had been on the job and were paid the rates won in previous struggles would now be working side-by-side with "new hires" doing the same job but at sharply reduced wages, sometimes as low as half as much. The two-tier system negotiated in 2006-2007 between the UAW and the Big Three and Delphi, in the auto and auto parts industries, respectively, originated in the Reagan era.

Equally if not more important to the daily routine of the workers, the bosses sought at every turn to strengthen their control over the shop floor, demanding "flexibility," major changes in job classifications, staff reductions, prolongation of shifts, by-passing the seniority system, and overturning "past practices" established during periods when the unions were stronger.

The struggle for control over workplace conditions is vital to the well being of workers. It means some control over the speed, intensity, and everyday conditions of exploitation. Once the bosses began to take back control over all aspects of work, workplace stress and injury escalated in epidemic proportions.

Finally, the bosses sought to undermine pattern bargaining in auto, steel, meatpacking, trucking, and other major industries—in which the entire company or the entire industry would be bound by the same basic contract. This opened up the door to pitting locals against each other: different plants would compete with each other in making enough concessions to get more work, keep shifts going, or keep plants open.

Workers were whipsawed in an excruciating bind over and over again when confronted with the news from the company that it planned to shutter a plant. Instead of the unions mobilizing broad counterattacks against the wave of plant closings, each local had to hold its breath hoping that its plant would not be shut down. Meanwhile, they had to watch the sisters and brothers whose plant got the ax be shoved out of their jobs. This destroyed morale and solidarity within the unions. It heavily undermined class consciousness and led to further local concessions beyond those obtained through the general bargaining framework.

'PATCO scenario' takes off

In addition to eroding union positions through threats of plant closures and outsourcing, which were the big stick behind their hard-nosed concession bargaining, the bosses soon began to implement a more developed form of the PATCO scenario: force a strike, prepare to hire permanent scabs, mobilize the state, and either drastically weaken or altogether destroy the union.

As we discuss further in the next chapter, workers at Phelps-Dodge copper mines in 1983 faced massive state repression. The company led the post-PATCO campaign in the use of state violence to break an industrial union and fire striking workers for good. The meatpacking giant Hormel won a similar union-busting battle over Local P-9 of the United Food and Commercial Workers in 1985-1986.

The wave of union busting and concessions that began with the recession of 1980-1983 did not end with the return of economic growth. Concessions were extracted across the board in auto, steel, rubber, aluminum, airlines, supermarket chains, mining, trucking, local and state governments, newspapers, meat processing, and many other industries.

A multibillion-dollar industry of professional anti-labor "consulting" firms grew up. Modern-day Pinkerton spies in business suits, they advised companies on how to get rid of existing unions and keep new ones from getting in. So-called temporary agencies, like Alternative Workforce and dozens more, supply scabs to big companies where the workers are on strike. Vance International's Asset Protection Team and others have supplied squadrons of thugs equipped as riot control forces, armed with handguns and M-16 rifles, to companies like Caterpillar, the Detroit News, Pittston Coal, and many others to protect scabs, intimidate workers, set up violent provocations, and then provide photographic evidence to courts so that unions can be fined.

Strikebreaking and union busting have continued apace. Unions came under siege in strikes literally forced on the workers at Caterpillar, Goodyear Tire, Staley Machinery, Greyhound Bus, the Detroit News, and International Paper, among the better-known struggles. Pressure on the unions was across the board in the airline industry. In 1991 the railroad workers went on strike against threatened layoffs and harsh scheduling changes. After striking for only eighteen hours, they were ordered back to work by Congress. The vote in the House was 400 to 5. The Senate motion was introduced by both conservative Orrin Hatch and liberal Ted Kennedy under the National Railway Act. After the strike, thousands of workers were laid off under new work rules.

In all these strikes and struggles the workers fought back militantly, showing a willingness to make the greatest sacrifices to defend their unions. They battled police and scabs. The workers' combativeness and creative tactics, their attempts to rally solidarity among communities and within the labor movement, kept their struggles alive as long as possible. But individual locals were in combat with giant multinational corporations that had vast resources and command over the state, while the unions were hamstrung by passivity and routinism on the part of the top leadership. The leadership squandered the greatest resource of the labor movement: the militancy and determination of the rank-and-file. At best it gave limited and half-hearted support to the struggles; at worst, it undermined and sabotaged them.

Hundreds of strike struggles also took place at smaller companies in communities throughout the country. These strikes never made it into government statistics because, under Reagan, the government stopped recording strikes of less than 1,000 workers. Union decertification proceedings filed with the National Labor Relations Board at the behest of the corporations by strikebreakers and non-union workers hired in the wake of strikes multiplied many fold. Tens of thousands of workers per year were fired for union activity during the 1980s. The practice continues to the present.[226]

Globalization and the 'fear factor'

In the latest phase of the anti-labor offensive, with a pickup in the pace of global capitalist restructuring and worldwide wage competition, the threat of offshoring has been added to the threat of permanent strikebreakers.

Offshoring is heavily directed at undermining unions. Companies hide this information wherever possible, but a study of the known instances of offshoring shows how much it is directed at unionized workers and how this trend has deepened over time.

A study presented to the U.S.-China Economic Security Review Commission presented findings on offshoring for the first quarter of 2004.[227] Based on company announcements and other confirmed reports, the study showed that almost 49,000 jobs were known to have been shipped abroad in that three-month period. Of those, 19,000 were union jobs—39 percent, even though the workforce in the private sector was only 8 percent unionized! Thus, a union job was five times more likely to be shipped overseas to a low-wage area than one that was non-union.

The union jobs included white-collar as well as blue-collar ones. And the number of jobs offshored in that period had doubled compared to the first quarter of 2001. The estimate of the report, conservatively based on verifiable figures, was that 406,000 jobs would be sent abroad during the year. For union jobs, if they continued to be destroyed throughout the year at the rate of the first quarter, it would mean the elimination of 158,000.

Companies drove trucks on their premises marked 'Mexico' during union negotiations

The impact of offshoring on the working class goes far beyond the actual number of jobs sent abroad. The fear of offshoring is a powerful weapon in the hands of the bosses, one that they use ruthlessly to intimidate workers, extort concessions, and undermine union organizing drives. Companies have resorted to such practices as having trucks driven onto the premises during contract negotiations with signs saying "For Mexico." The 2004 commission report gave detailed examples of this fear factor.

John Deere, a giant corporation that makes earth-moving equipment, in 2004 told UAW Local 450 at its Des Moines works in Ankey, Iowa, that it planned to shift forty assembly jobs to Monterrey, Mexico, unless the union could prove within 120 days that it could do the work more cheaply. The union had agreed to these terms in its contract. If the union failed, the jobs would be moved. The report did not state the outcome. But this kind of pressure on the workers and the union is really capitalist gangsterism—practiced by the class as a whole.

In 2002 the U.S. subsidiary of the German company Continental AG, a global auto parts and tire firm, told the United Steelworkers that its Mayfield, Kentucky, plant—one of several it had in the U.S.—was not "competitive" enough. Management said it would shut down the Mayfield plant and lay off 800 workers unless the union could propose a way to cut $35 million out of a payroll of $55 million. The company threatened to move production to its

San Luis Potosi plant in Mexico and it ramped up production at its plant in Malaysia. When the union could come up with "only" a $20 million cut in payroll, Continental shut down the plant. Furthermore, it used the shutdown in Mayfield to break a union drive at its Mount Vernon, Illinois, plant.

The concessions extracted from the UAW by the Big Three U.S. auto companies—General Motors, Ford, and Chrysler—are aimed at undercutting its rivals, Toyota being the biggest. Anticipating the intensified competition, Toyota is also trying to use the threat of offshoring to transfer the burden to its workers. In 2007 Toyota management in Georgetown, Kentucky, called workers to come in small groups to meetings on "Growing in a Changing Market." They were shown charts of the Big Three auto plants shut down in the U.S., followed by presentations on average wages, from Thailand to Mexico.[228] The message was calculated to forestall any resistance to the company's planned reductions in wages and benefits and to prevent the workers from thinking about joining the UAW, which has been trying to organize workers at Toyota and Nissan.

This threat has its counterpart in the service industries, where outsourcing is rampant as a practice of getting around unions or keeping them out. Food services, janitorial services, mailing services, and customer service, among others, are routinely outsourced by large firms to agencies that pay well below union scale and also below a living wage. The service unions have been struggling to combat this trend with some success, especially at hotels, commercial buildings, and university campuses. But the practice is still pervasive.

Lessons from the past for the future struggle

Decades of rank-and-file fight-back

Solidarity Day and beyond: Phelps Dodge, Hormel, Pittston, Int'l Paper, Greyhound, Decatur 'War Zone,' Las Vegas Culinary Workers, Detroit news-paper strike, UPS Teamsters, GM Flint, L.A. Justice for Janitors, N.Y. Transit Workers, May Day • State of the unions: glass half-empty or half-full?

The slide in union membership, the decline of wages, and the general deterioration of living conditions for the working class, as well as the increase in racism and national oppression, the wave of anti-immigrant at-tacks, and all the other setbacks during the last three decades and more, were not inevitable. They were avoidable.

The underlying relationship of class forces in U.S. capitalist society was not objectively so unfavorable to the working class that it had no way to overcome the anti-labor offensive. Nor is further decline inevitable, even in the face of capitalist crisis.

What has contributed to the feeling of inevitability about the retreat of the labor movement and the workers in general has been the steadfast refusal by the AFL-CIO leadership, including the Change to Win leadership that set up a parallel federation in 2005, to muster the latent power of the workers and the oppressed in a true test of strength with the ruling class.

To be sure, there are undoubtedly thousands of local union leaders, del-egates, shop stewards, labor council members, as well as rank-and-file mili-tants throughout the labor movement, in every part of the country, who have been straining at the bit to launch a fight-back. Such militancy has mani-fested itself over and over again in struggles during the 1980s up until the present day. What will revive the labor movement is when these forces are able to multiply, organize, and gain the upper hand.

The deadly conservatism of the present-day top labor leadership resem-bles in many ways the refusal of the old leadership of the American Federation of Labor (AFL), all the way up to and through the 1930s, to lead the struggle of millions of industrial workers who were crying out for organization. It was the workers themselves, with general strikes, sit-downs, shop actions, and other forms of struggle that broke through and worked around the old conservative leadership to achieve historic victories. As the present-day leadership becomes an unendurable obstacle to the workers' need to defend themselves against the bosses, it is inevitable that these leaders will be either by-passed or swept aside by a mass upsurge.

Solidarity Day and beyond

During the entire period of the anti-labor offensive, there have been numerous opportunities for the labor leadership to open up a counteroffensive by seizing upon the militant resistance of the rank-and-file workers against concessions and union busting.

A month after Reagan fired the PATCO workers in August 1981 and replaced them with scabs, the AFL-CIO leadership called a demonstration in Washington labeled Solidarity Day. The architect of the demonstration was the conservative head of the labor federation, Lane Kirkland, the successor to George Meany. It was the largest single demonstration of the U.S. working class until that time and was estimated at half a million. Workers came from all parts of the country, many of them traveling long distances yet refusing to fly out of solidarity with the fired air traffic control workers.

The entire labor movement came out. Black and Latina/o groups and women's groups were invited and came. So did farmers' groups, environmental groups, consumer groups, and community organizers. In a rare departure for the encrusted, reactionary, white male labor leadership, the "approved" slogans included ones from moderate anti-war, civil rights, women's, and voting rights groups, as well as demands for jobs. The progressive movement gravitated toward the power of the labor movement as an answer to the Reagan reaction.

The demonstration was timely. It came in the wake of the sharp anti-labor turn in the Democratic Party under the Carter administration followed by the endorsement of the drastic Reagan budget cuts by the Democratic Party leadership, which still controlled both houses of Congress. Democrats joined Republicans in passing cuts in school lunches, student loans, and across-the-board social welfare spending. Furthermore, the Reagan administration threatened to cut Social Security.

Solidarity Day had a challenging tone to it. Capitalist politicians were excluded from the platform. Even Kirkland declared: "We have come too far, struggled too long, sacrificed too much, and have too much left to do, to allow all that we have achieved for the good of all to be swept away without a fight. And we have not forgotten how to fight."

Coming out of Solidarity Day, the workers were inspired and fired up. The sense of strength in unity was at a high point. But behind the scenes the labor leaders were really fashioning a non-struggle, self-defeating agenda. For them the goal of the demonstration was to strengthen their hand in the Democratic Party. This was the strategic road taken by the bureaucracy to arrest the budget cuts and reverse the anti-labor atmosphere in Washington. Kirkland's demagogy about fighting back notwithstanding, the AFL-CIO donated $1 million to the Democratic National Committee and remained passive while the bosses escalated their anti-labor offensive.

This steady retreat and acceptance of concessions without a significant struggle of the working class was entirely unwarranted. The retreat ran directly in the face of numerous manifestations showing the desire and willingness of the workers to fight back throughout the entire period.

1983: PHELPS DODGE MINERS

Militant worker resistance to a dangerous challenge arose during the Phelps Dodge struggle in 1983. The company, a giant transnational monopoly, provoked the United Steelworkers and a number of other unions at its copper mines in Morenci, Ajo, and other towns in Arizona, as well as in Texas, into a strike by demanding across-the-board concessions. These included cuts in wages and benefits, an end to cost-of-living adjustments, and a two-tier system with lower wages and benefits for new workers. The company refused to follow pattern bargaining that the union had established in the rest of the industry.

The workers, who were mainly Chicanos, rebelled against concessionary demands. The company advertised for scabs in the newspapers. The workers answered this challenge by massing at the Morenci mine and other mining towns with pipes, bats, and chains to stop the scabs. They forced the company to shut down the mine. But "liberal" Democratic Governor Bruce Babbitt, who had been endorsed by the union, stepped in and set up a ten-day "cooling-off" period, after which, at the behest of Phelps Dodge, he organized a massive counterattack. He sent in Huey helicopters, hundreds of state troopers, the National Guard, tanks, and other military vehicles to protect the scabs.

Various local unions raised funds and tried to give solidarity, but the national USW and the labor leadership let the miners battle on alone against Phelps Dodge, which was not only one of the largest mining corporations in the world but was aided by the capitalist state. The company evicted the miners from company-owned housing, barred them from company-owned hospitals, wore the workers down, and broke the union. It set a precedent for attacks on mineworkers throughout the region.

1985: HORMEL MEATPACKERS

The struggle of the Hormel meatpackers of Local P-9, United Food and Commercial Workers (UFCW) in Austin, Minnesota, became a national cause within the labor movement and the progressive movement in general because the local decided to take a stand against concessions. In August 1985, after a wave of concessions, wage cuts, layoffs, and destruction of unions in the meatpacking industry, the workers of local P-9 rejected Hormel's demands for wage cuts. By a 92-percent margin they voted down a wage cut from $10.69 to $8.75 an hour—an 18-percent reduction in pay—and then initiated a boycott of Hormel. The UFCW leadership at first sanctioned the strike but later condemned it, ordered the workers back to work, and suspended the local.

The Hormel workers sent agitators to cities throughout the country and got material support from more than 3,000 locals. Movement activists and tens of thousands of unionists and local officials came to the area. Jesse Jackson compared the struggle to the one in Selma, Alabama. In April 1986, 6,000 labor activists from around the country came to Austin to try to shut down Hormel's operation with mass pickets and other forms of obstruction to block scabs.

Some 6,000 labor activists from around the country went to Austin to try to shut down Hormel's operation

The workers faced teargas, police attack, and arrests. Governor Rudy Perpich, a Democrat, sent in 300 National Guard troops against the strikers. But what made the defeat of the strike inevitable, a strike that lasted a year and a half, was the hostility of the national leadership of the UFCW and the refusal of the AFL-CIO to join the battle on a national basis in the face of company strike-breaking and the intervention of the state. This major confrontation, which had been brought on by Hormel, was recognized as a highly significant battle among the rank and file of the labor movement. The workers at Hormel and far beyond showed more than a willingness and desire to unite and fight back at great sacrifice. [229]

1989: PITTSTON MINERS AND CAMP SOLIDARITY

In 1989 miners at the Pittston mines in Virginia and West Virginia launched another struggle against concessions. This one lasted ten months. The UMWA called its strike headquarters Camp Solidarity. During four months more than 3,000 workers and activists came to help stop the scabs and lend support. When the court imposed fines on the union for mass picketing,

46,000 workers went out on a wildcat in eleven states. Workers and supporters occupied one mine for four days. It was dubbed Operation Flintstone after the Flint sit-down strike of 1937. The Daughters of Mother Jones, made up of miners' wives and daughters, women miners, and community supporters, occupied Pittston's regional headquarters in Lebanon, Virginia.

The miners had to face police and federal marshals and were subjected to mass arrest, injunctions, and $63 million in fines. At a critical point in the strike, the Industrial Council of New Jersey voted to ask the AFL-CIO for a one-day union stoppage in support of the Pittston workers. But the AFL-CIO did the opposite, advising state federations to stick to food banks and newspaper articles and remain within the contractual frameworks that forbid strikes.

In the end the union fought off most of the concessions on pensions and retirees' health. It was a victory for the workers, but one in which they had to compromise. The AFL-CIO leadership refused to spread the strike and rally the workers as a whole to support this massive show of worker militancy and self-organization. Once the strike was settled in January of 1990, after intervention by the George H.W. Bush administration, there was no attempt to maintain the momentum of the struggle against concessions.

1987-1995: INTERNATIONAL PAPER, GREYHOUND, DECATUR 'WAR ZONE'

There were numerous other struggles during this period. Some were won, most were lost, but all involved militant resistance by the workers. The local unions were left to fight major corporations, most with worldwide holdings and deep pockets, without the support of the national labor leadership. These locals had to rely on their own efforts to rally solidarity from other locals and communities around the country.

The workers at International Paper waged militant struggles in Maine and Pennsylvania in 1987 to stop concessions. Greyhound workers belonging to the Amalgamated Transport Union (ATU) fought concessions with militant struggle in 1990. They occupied bus terminals, battled scabs and police all across the country, and occasionally took even more forceful measures.

The "war zone" struggles in Decatur, Illinois, referred to the battle of three local unions against Caterpillar, Staley, and Bridgestone/Firestone between the years 1993 and 1995, all in the same city at the same time.

The Staley workers waged a dynamic and determined struggle. They had answered concessions with a "work-to-rule" campaign but were finally forced out on strike. After being locked out, they sent contingents of "road warriors" around the country and created a support and solidarity network. The three unions banded together eventually, but were unable to get the required national mobilization of the AFL-CIO to push back against the corporate war for concessions. The bosses were in a common front against all three unions but the labor movement would not mount a corresponding front to push back.

1992-1998: CULINARY WORKERS, LAS VEGAS

During the same period, Culinary Workers Local 226, affiliated with the Hotel Employees and Restaurant Employees (HERE, now merged into UNITE HERE), carried on a militant organizing campaign at the big gambling casinos in Las Vegas. Earlier, the existing unions had been broken when big financial operators moved in to take over the casinos. The campaign to rebuild the unions was based upon empowering the low-paid immigrant and African-American kitchen workers and maids and establishing stewards and leadership committees in all the departments. The union carried out strikes, mass marches, and sit-ins and negotiated a major agreement in 1989 that considerably lifted the standard of living of the workers.

The struggle against one of the holdout casinos, the Frontier, was a legendary battle and a landmark in recent union history. It lasted six and a half years. There were picket lines twenty-four hours a day, seven days a week. In 1992 the union organized a march across the Mojave Desert to Los Angeles. The next year, a solidarity march from Los Angeles to Las Vegas met up with a demonstration of 20,000 that shut down the famous strip there.

The strike was supported by the solidarity of the rank and file. Non-striking members of Local 226, also low-paid workers, voted to increase their dues so those on strike could get benefits of $200 a week. The national union strongly backed the strike. The company finally surrendered in 1998 in the face of unbreakable solidarity and militancy. During the strike the union continued its organizing drive. The union has inspired others and lent assistance to organizing drives in hospitals and the building trades in Nevada.

Based on the militancy of the rank and file, their willingness to sacrifice, brave arrest, and take risks, and the high consciousness of worker solidarity, Las Vegas has become a center of union revival in a period of anti-labor reaction.

1995-1997: DETROIT NEWSPAPER STRIKE

During the Detroit newspaper strike against concessions, which lasted from 1995 to 1997, six unions representing workers at the Gannett and Knight-Ridder newspaper empires militantly battled a lockout and scab herding. The potential for a landmark victory against concessions was considerable, given that the strike took place in the center of unionism in the Midwest and the workers were determined not to give in.

The critical moment in the strike took place early on as the Detroit working class flexed its muscles. The 2,000 striking workers were joined by reinforcements from the Detroit labor movement. The workers set up mass picket lines at the printing plants, fought the police and scabs for hours at a time, and stopped production. A court then issued an injunction establishing a ten-picket rule. The local labor leadership made the critical decision to back down in the face of a court injunction against mass picketing.

In spite of the injunction, groups of 1,000 workers set up lines at distribution centers every Saturday night and fought the cops for three months, either stopping or cutting down the crucial Sunday newspaper distribution. But the leadership called off these picket lines.

Instead of escalating the struggle, the union leadership bowed to the courts. From then on the billionaire news empires won the war of attrition and the strike was finally called off in February 1997. The fight to restore the locked-out workers shifted to the National Labor Relations Board and the courts, where the relationship of forces was unfavorable, especially once the pressure of the workers' struggle was gone.

Even after the strike was called off, there was a chance to revive the struggle. In July 1997, the AFL-CIO brought 100,000 workers from forty-five states and Canada to descend on Detroit to demand restoration of the jobs of the locked-out workers and removal of the scabs. The mass march that took place was a demonstration of potential working class power, but it was censored out of the national news by the capitalist media.

This was an opportune moment to revive a genuine struggle. It was not hard to mobilize such a massive demonstration because Michigan, headquarters of the Big Three automakers, had been devastated by plant closings and concessions for more than fifteen years. Signs saying "No Scab Newspapers" were in thousands of stores, on lawns, and in every union hall in Detroit, including the UAW, where the auto workers were also under pressure to make more concessions. While the unions in the Decatur "war zone" had been defeated, the masses of unionized workers were eager to show their desire to fight back.

Calls and petitions for massive demonstrations of the labor movement and even for a one-day general strike had surfaced early in the strike.[230] * But

---

* In a keynote speech to a strike strategy conference at Wayne State University on December 7, 1996, David Sole, president of UAW Local 2334, noted: "Just as in the 1930s, not every strike today can become an historic test of wills, a critical political confrontation. But the Detroit newspaper strike can. We are in labor's stronghold with 350,000 union members in the southeast Michigan area. The unions here have enormous resources of personnel, funds, equipment, lawyers, media. ... Ten union locals, some of the biggest in the UAW, as well as locals on strike, even voted to support the call for a general strike to back the newspaper strike."

the AFL-CIO leadership waited a year and a half to call a mass demonstration—and then it was **after the strike was called off**. They made it a purely symbolic gesture rather than a call to arms.

Most of these struggles were defensive ones, against concessions. They remained defensive and had to fight against overwhelming odds. The official labor leadership of the AFL-CIO and the dozens of international unions that make it up let each struggle remain as an isolated guerrilla action of individual locals fighting against big capital, which had the state and the banks behind it.

1997: UPS TEAMSTERS

The strike against United Parcel Service (UPS) was a powerful one that fought to reverse concessions, which had begun in 1982. The company had won the right to create a two-tier, part-time system of employment. In August of 1997 the 185,000 members of the UPS division of the Teamsters union waged a fifteen-day strike that electrified the labor movement and the working class as a whole. Despite compromises made in the final settlement, it was understood, rightly so, as the first major victory for a significant section of the working class after two decades of defeat and retreat.

The strike was led by Teamsters President Ron Carey, who had democratized the union during his tenure. It was won by meticulous planning for a genuine class struggle, bringing in the rank-and-file at every stage. The struggle was popular in the union movement and among the working class as a whole because it was projected as a struggle against part-time and low-wage work—not just for UPS workers, but for the working class as a whole. Sixty percent of the 185,000 UPS workers were part-time workers who earned only $9 per hour, as opposed to $19.95 an hour, plus benefits, for full-time workers.

The UPS strike was projected as a struggle on behalf of the working class as a whole against low wages and part-time work

The UPS Teamster leadership prepared for the strike for over a year. In formulating their bargaining position, the leadership of the UPS division sent a questionnaire to all 185,000 workers asking for their views on the most important issues. Full-time jobs were the overwhelming priority for the workers. In addition, 10,000 of these workers were receiving part-time pay but were working thirty-five hours or more a week.

The union collected 100,000 signatures on a petition supporting its demands. It distributed the union's position at workplaces, sports events, and other sites long in advance. It prepared a strong strike apparatus.

Once the negotiations were underway, the union sent a video to all UPS shop stewards to keep them up to date. During the strike, the union updated its Web site every few hours, faxed bulletins to Teamster locals, and set up a toll-free hotline for strikers.

The negotiations were to begin in July of 1997 but rallies were organized around the country beginning in March and continued to multiply up until the strike deadline. Carey had even gone to Germany and France and worked with the UPS unions there to support the strike. When the UPS rank-and-file marched into battle they were thoroughly unified, highly organized, and prepared for struggle against a ruthless corporate giant with a world empire.[231]

The strike was won through a major test of strength between labor and capital. The AFL-CIO leadership supported the strike and John Sweeney promised to back the Teamsters' strike benefit fund with $10 million a week. During the strike President Bill Clinton was under pressure—from not only UPS but also Wall Street—to invoke the Taft-Hartley Act. The strength and broad popularity of the UPS workers pushed the Clinton administration back, even though Clinton finally pressured a settlement and leaned on the union to compromise. Nevertheless, the UPS workers forced the company to agree to turn 10,000 part-time workers into full-time employees, won raises for the lower-paid workers, and warded off an attack on pension funding.

The forward momentum of the workers' struggle arising out of the UPS strike was soon undermined, however. Immediately after the strike, the government framed up Carey on charges of illegally funneling funds to his union election campaign fund. A federal court cleared him of all the charges, but a so-called Independent Review Board got Carey barred for life from running for Teamster office.

This board had been set up by the Justice Department in 1989 to oversee the Teamsters. It was headed by William Webster, a former director of both the CIA and the FBI. The Democratic National Committee cooperated with the frame-up, despite the fact that the AFL-CIO leadership, including Carey, had poured hundreds of millions of dollars into getting Clinton elected.

Fearing a government attack, the AFL-CIO leadership left Carey to face the frame-up and ouster alone. Instead of standing up and challenging the government to indict the entire top leadership of the union movement, and preparing the rank-and-file to defend the leader who had launched the biggest union challenge to big business in two decades, they abandoned the struggle. The forward momentum gained by the militant mass struggle of 185,000 workers, backed by workers everywhere, soon died down. What the mass struggle had won was diminished by the craven retreat of the leadership.

1998: GENERAL MOTORS, FLINT

The strength of the mass struggle of the workers was also demonstrated in a "selective strike" by two auto parts plants that virtually shut down General Motors in 1998. The strike was called by two UAW locals at GM parts plants in Flint, Michigan: the Flint Metal Center and Delphi Flint East Complex. These plants and others in the region were under extreme pressure from the company to speed up production. Plant-closing threats were out in the open. In fact, on Memorial Day, GM began to move parts-making equipment out of the Delphi plant. Grievances over health and safety issues mounted even as outsourcing was eliminating jobs.

But the strike was precipitated by the immediate fear of plant closings and was fueled by the fact that GM had reneged on a pledge, made in return for concessions, to invest $180 million in modern equipment at the metal plant.

On June 5, 2,400 workers at the metal plant went out on strike, to be followed by 5,800 Delphi workers the next week. The metal plant produced doors, hoods, fenders, and other metal parts while the Delphi plant produced speedometers, spark plugs, filters, and other parts used in the production of almost every GM car in North America.

What followed was a hard-fought, fifty-three-day strike, the longest at GM in thirty years. It shut down more than one hundred plants in the U.S., Canada, and Mexico, including twenty-seven of twenty-nine assembly plants. Some 190,000 workers were off the job. The company lost production of 50,000 autos, $3 billion in after-tax profits, and $12 billion in sales, "the heaviest losses ever incurred by an American company in a strike, at least before adjusting for inflation."[232] The striking workers had the solidarity of the rest of the workforce. During the strike by the Flint workers, many other locals asked permission to go on strike but were denied by the national leadership.

During the 1998 strike GM brought the UAW to court for violation of the contract for the first time since 1937. The national contract only allowed plant-level strikes over outsourcing, speed-up, and health and safety issues. The company contested the right of the union even to bring up the issue that GM had reneged on promises of investment; it was looking for an injunction on that basis. GM management wanted to crush any form of say-so by the union as to how the company disposed of its capital. And it wanted a pretext for an injunction.

When it was over, the company got concessions on its speed-up of welders, but it had to promise not to shut down the Delphi plant and another assembly plant in Flint, as well as parts plants in Indianapolis and another in Dayton, at least until 2000. It also agreed to invest the $180 million, which it had claimed in court was outside the jurisdiction of the union. The parts-making equipment was returned to the plant.

The hopes of Wall Street that GM would deliver a knockout blow to the union were dashed. The steadfastness of the workers stood in the way. The workers were elated at having staved off the assault by the company on jobs, but they were not under any illusions that the victory was decisive. They had lived to fight another day and were preparing for an even bigger battle for the 1999 contract.

Neither side had expected such a momentous struggle in 1998. But the company dug in and the union dug in because GM had openly threatened jobs, on top of imposing grinding conditions that ate away at the health and safety of the workers. In the end, both sides blinked, but the workers got a temporary reprieve from plant closings and retained the ability to fight another round.

The key to the strength of the strike was its ability to disrupt GM's "just-in-time" production system. Such systems had been instituted all over capitalist industry and retailing—from Dell Computer to Caterpillar to Wal-Mart. Advances in transportation, communications, and computerized inventory tracking had made it possible to reduce inventories to the absolute minimum. This meant lower costs, faster turnover of capital, and, thus, more profits. But the "just-in-time" production and retailing was predicated on labor peace. The Flint parts plant workers revealed a critical GM weakness: no inventory and a highly specialized division of labor, so that parts from two plants alone could idle most of GM's North American empire.

However, there were ominous signs, even before the ink on the settlement had dried. As part of the agreement ending the struggle, there was a provision stating that both sides would meet regularly as a way to rebuild their relationship in order to avoid future confrontations.

The workers had collectively given up hundreds of millions of dollars in pay and stayed out almost eight weeks. They were anticipating that there would be a national follow-up on the question of job protection and shop issues. But the UAW leadership went in the opposite direction. Anticipating GM's demands in the upcoming national negotiations for expanding plant closures and threatening offshoring and more outsourcing, the leadership was building bridges to the company instead of preparing for an even greater struggle. In fact, the UAW leadership ignored the show of strength by the workers in 1998 and signed on to another round of concessions and tradeoffs in the 1999 contract. This laid the basis for further plant closings and layoffs.

One lesson that emerged from the selective strikes of 1998 was that the workers, after years of demoralizing retreats by the UAW, were nevertheless ready to fight if they were given the union's go-ahead and support. In fact, there had been more than two dozen local strikes in preceding years, including a seventeen-day strike in Dayton, Ohio, that shut down most of GM. The 1998 strike was by far the largest and most hard-fought in decades and it showed that the workers were **willing to fight**. It made clear that they could mount a successful challenge to the company if it was **a company-wide shutdown**. The strike also demonstrated that **preventive struggle by the rank-and-file mobilized for battle** was the only defense against plant closings, not handing over concessions.

2000: JUSTICE FOR JANITORS, LOS ANGELES

Workers in the Service Employees International Union (SEIU), mainly immigrants, showed their militancy during the Justice for Janitors campaign against the commercial real estate industry in Los Angeles that began in the late 1980s and culminated in a major strike in 2000. They carried out strikes; waged militant corporate campaigns in which they crashed boardrooms and marched onto golf courses; held mass marches with civil disobedience and blocking traffic. They endured mass arrests and beatings, faced SWAT teams, and defied the brutal, racist Los Angeles police. They organized major networks of community support and won important contracts against giant real estate interests.

Rank-and-file organization and militancy was the essential ingredient in their victories. The willingness and ability of the SEIU leadership in Los Angeles to organize the ranks, support their militancy, and mobilize union and community support was decisive. The workers were chambermaids, porters, cooks, clerks—the lowest-paid service workers.

The union disregarded company contracts signed by the landlords with outsourcing firms and battled the owners directly. These contracts skirted legality by allowing management to hire workers below union scale, without benefits or protections of any kind, to do the same work they had been doing before. The local leadership of the SEIU got around these legal loopholes and, by directing their struggles against the real enemy, defeated this dangerous outsourcing tactic.

Nor did they get bogged down in National Labor Relations Board electoral machinery but simply signed up the workers and demanded recognition. The union victories over a period of more than a decade were fueled by the energy and determination of the workers themselves, many of whom had battled dictatorships and political repression in their native countries—Mexico, El Salvador, Guatemala, and Haiti, among others.

Whatever the merits of the settlements, they improved the conditions of the workers. But the key point is that the workers showed their willingness over a period of a decade to risk arrest, deportation, and material hardship, once they were organized for struggle and could see the possibility of victory.

Furthermore, the janitors' victories strengthened the labor movement in Los Angeles and the whole region among immigrant workers as a whole and spread to other cities around the country.

2005: TRANSIT WORKERS, NEW YORK

This argument and historical precedent also apply to the New York City transit strike of bus and subway workers, which had national significance because it was carried out at the center of power of Wall Street and because it was an attempt to draw a line against concessions. The workers were up against New York State's Taylor Law, which forbids strikes by public employees.

Meeting such a challenge takes great effort. There are great risks and any such struggle must be well prepared and well grounded in the support of the workers, because it inevitably involves coming up against the capitalist state. But it begins with a readiness and determination of the leadership to resist as much as possible when the occasion arises.

In December 2005 the occasion was forced upon Transport Workers Union Local 100 in New York City by the Metropolitan Transit Authority, an authority set up by New York State to watch over the interests of bondholders. The union leaders, under Roger Toussaint, and the rank and file were prepared to stand firm against the MTA's demands, despite the almost certain risk of harsh penalties. The two-and-a-half-day strike pitted the 33,000 members of TWU Local 100, who are 70 percent Black, Latina/o, or Asian, against the forces of Wall Street, the governor, the mayor of New York, the courts, and the hostile capitalist media. It had national significance precisely because it was a challenge to the labor-hating, racist ruling class in the heart of their financial center and because the union was bucking a decades-long national trend of concessions by the labor movement.

The workers were being persecuted under an internal system of company discipline, to the point where one out of every three workers had been "written up" in the prior year. The MTA was moving to eliminate and combine jobs. Working conditions, especially on the subway tracks, were harsh and unhealthy. The workers were chafing under a general atmosphere of harassment and disrespect.

As the contract expiration neared, the MTA suddenly demanded a two-tier system of retirement benefits—tripling the contribution extracted from newly hired workers to 6 percent from 2 percent—and an extension of the retirement age from 55 to 62. The MTA said this was non-negotiable. The leadership was confronted with a stark situation—concessions or a strike. The rank and file were overwhelmingly ready to strike and the leadership body voted strike by a large majority.

The workers voted strike in the face of draconian sanctions under the Taylor Law: fines for each worker of two days' pay for each day on strike, possible fines for the union of a million dollars a day, and loss of dues check-off rights.

The strike ended after three days in a limited victory and a mixed result for the union. But the union won a victory in that the MTA had to back off the two-tier pension system, the fundamental issue of principle. The workers got a 10.5 percent raise over three years, maternity stipends, a paid holiday for Martin Luther King Day, plus a pension refund of thousands of dollars for nearly two-thirds of the members. In return for the MTA taking the two-tier system off the table, the compromise was a 1.5 percent contribution by all the workers to the health-care fund.

An unprincipled opposition in the local campaigned against the contract, which was defeated by just seven votes. Later on, the same contract was submitted to the membership and overwhelmingly accepted. The critics who had originally sunk the contract aimed their fire at Roger Toussaint, the president of Local 100. But, in reality, the overwhelming factor in any compromise forced on the union was the refusal of the city's AFL-CIO labor leadership to bring to bear the power of the organized working class.

These leaders offered symbolic support but failed to react to the serious crisis for the TWU created by the MTA. The crisis required broadening the struggle in order to have a significant impact on the outcome. Local 100 was defending not only its own union position but that of the labor movement in the city. Instead, the labor leadership acted as an instrument to transmit pressure against the union to end the strike and return to class peace.

TWU International President Michael O'Brien issued an open letter telling the workers to cease all strike activities and return to work. This went far beyond the mere formality by which union leaders protect themselves legally from charges of inciting an illegal strike. It was part of a vicious factional struggle against Toussaint, in addition to carrying on the tradition of class collaboration.

But the intervention of the International was largely ignored by the workers, save for a small group factionally aligned with it. It could easily have been overcome by solidarity in action from the rest of the labor movement.

Toussaint declared from the outset that the union would defy the demand for two-tier pension payments. The defiance was put in terms of standing up against the national trend of concessions. Furthermore, he made clear that Local 100 would not be party to setting a two-tier precedent that could then be imposed on all the municipal unions in the city.

The same day that the court imposed a $1-million-a-day fine on the union, Toussaint said, "There is a higher calling than the law. That is justice and equality." He invoked the legacy of Martin Luther King Jr. and Rosa Parks, both of whom had defied racist laws: "If Rosa Parks had answered the call of the law instead of the higher call of justice, many of us who are driving buses today would instead be at the back of the bus."

The union also showed that the MTA itself was in violation of the Taylor Law. Under the law, the MTA was authorized to bargain only over "salaries, wages, hours and other terms and conditions of employment, provided however, that such term shall not include any benefits provided by or to be provided by a public retirement system.... No such retirement benefits shall be negotiated pursuant to this article, and any benefits so negotiated shall be null and void."

Pension benefits for public workers are determined in the New York State Legislature and not by the MTA. Thus, the MTA's demand for a two-tier pension system or any pension system was a clear violation of the Taylor Law. Considering the circumstances, even though the strike was forced at the last minute, the situation was rife with possibilities for mounting a struggle that could have challenged the enforcement of the Taylor Law, if not the law itself.

The fundamental circumstance was the overwhelming unity of the rank and file, which was militantly behind the strike and stood up to the MTA, to Wall Street, to the governor, to the mayor, and to the capitalist media, which vilified the strikers. (At the time of the first contract vote, an opportunist faction created confusion over the concession on health care, which broke the hard-fought unity attained during the strike.)

The union had a powerful legal basis to declare the MTA in violation of the law with respect to its two-tier pension plan demands. The law itself declared the MTA's proposal "null and void." The application of the law to the local could be clearly challenged on that basis.

The union also had a powerful economic argument that it was acting not only on its own behalf, but on behalf of all the unions subject to the Taylor Law. There was a direct material basis for union solidarity.

The TWU had a powerful moral/political motivation for invoking the name of Rosa Parks. Parks had recently passed away and her birthday had been celebrated all over the city. Her example had been held up by the capitalist media and in every corner of the progressive community. Her mug shot after her arrest in Montgomery, Alabama, had been proudly displayed as a symbol of resistance. This resonated deeply and widely in the city, particularly in the Black community.

The strike took place at the height of the winter holidays shopping season. Most major retailers make up to 50 percent of their annual sales during this period. It would not take long before the commercial interests in the city and other employers would feel it.

There was no way the MTA could hire scabs to replace the 33,000 bus and subway workers. The option that had been used by bosses for the past decades to extract concessions was not available.

Despite the hardships it caused, the strike was extremely popular among the masses, for a variety of reasons: the demands for respect on the job, the fight to stop givebacks on pensions, and the fact that the union was 70 percent Black, Latina/o, and Asian in a city with a majority of oppressed people. These factors gave the strike an underlying source of support, despite claims to the contrary by the capitalist media. People in the city walked long distances, crossed bridges, and found ways to get to work.

Arguments can be made about the timing and circumstances of the return to work and the final settlement. But such arguments pale into insignificance in comparison to the need to examine the objective conditions of the strike and the behavior of the broader labor leadership in the city, which became prostrate before the Taylor Law.

'I don't need anyone standing on the sidelines holding my coat; I need someone to take off their coat.' Roger Toussaint, President Local 100 TWU

In a conference call two days into the strike, with forty union officials and the Local 100 leadership on the phone, the entire drift of the discussion was to pressure the union to end the strike. Toussaint expressed the tenor of the conversation during the call, when everyone was offering verbal, symbolic support on the one hand and trying to bring an end to the struggle on the other hand.

Toussaint is said to have declared: "I don't need anyone standing on the sidelines holding my coat, I need someone to take off their coat."[233]

Instead of taking off their coats and getting behind the class struggle, the labor officials acted as intermediaries, offering a compromise to Mayor Michael Bloomberg and the MTA. While Toussaint and the rank-and-file transit workers were refusing to bow down to the Taylor Law and were prepared to make major financial sacrifices in order to stand up to the bosses, the top labor leaders were quivering in their boots over the escalating struggle and were terrified into submission by fear of the Taylor Law.

As we showed earlier, during the United Parcel strike of 1997, John Sweeney, president of the AFL-CIO, had strengthened the struggle of the workers by openly pledging $10 million a week to the strike fund of the Teamsters UPS division and its president, Ron Carey. One basic gesture that would have shaken the MTA and the capitalist establishment during the transit workers' strike and strengthened the hand and the position of Toussaint and the TWU workers would have been a pledge by the New York City Central Labor Council or by a coalition of unions to support the transit workers with funds to carry them through the struggle and to help defray the cost of fines to the union, should they be levied.

Instead of becoming the high priests of compromise, they could have seen the situation as an opportunity to open up a political and propaganda struggle to weaken the ability of the MTA to apply the Taylor Law. They could have mobilized rallies and mass marches and used a variety of creative tactics. Above all, instead of pushing Toussaint to settle, they could have mobilized the ranks of the labor movement to blanket the city, explaining in simple language the cause of the transit workers and the unjust, illegal nature of the Taylor Law.

Many legal arguments and illustrations could have been elaborated. For example, by depriving workers of their right to withhold their labor, the Taylor Law nullifies the only leverage workers have in collective bargaining. With its onerous fines and sanctions, the law requires hundreds of thousands of workers to enter negotiations with a gun to their heads. The law makes the bargaining process inherently weighted in favor of the bondholders and other investors. Such a campaign could have made the Taylor Law the issue in the struggle and weakened support for it, limited its application in the strike, and laid the basis for future efforts to overturn it altogether by bringing these arguments to the attention of the masses.

It was incumbent upon the leadership to weigh the political, economic, and tactical advantages of the workers in the struggle against the onerous Taylor Law. It could not be left to Local 100 to fight alone. It required a class-wide approach of the workers in the metropolitan region to counterbalance the forces arrayed against the union. But the relationship of forces between the workers and Wall Street in the struggle against the Taylor Law was never tested. The labor movement fatalistically accepted the legal boundaries established by the bosses on government workers instead of trying to change the legality by facts on the ground.

Of course, not every situation lends itself to an open challenge to anti-labor laws and judicial rulings. But the mindset of any genuine, class-conscious leadership of the workers must always be preparation for challenging the restrictive and repressive aspects of bourgeois legality in favor of extending workers' rights. Emphasis on lobbying and electing "pro-labor" bourgeois politicians, as a substitute for fighting the bosses, will do nothing at all but sow illusions. The only path is that of mass mobilization in the class struggle.

2006: THE GREAT MAY DAY GENERAL STRIKE

The May Day strike/boycott of 2006 brought millions of immigrants out on the streets in cities and towns, large and small, from coast to coast to protest repressive legislation against undocumented workers. The largest ports in the country, in Los Angeles and Long Beach, California, were almost completely shut down. Meatpacking chains in the Midwest and South had to close. Businesses closed or had reduced staffs. School attendance dropped as students poured into the streets. The working class tide of immigrants, led by Latina/os, but including immigrant workers from Asia, Africa, the Caribbean, and the Middle East, flowed through the streets of Los Angeles, San Diego, Sacramento, San Francisco, Seattle, Denver, Houston, Kansas City, Milwaukee, Chicago, New York, Atlanta, Orlando, Tampa, Miami, and many other cities.

This was the largest mass political action by workers in the United States in recent history. It was a combination strike/boycott/demonstration. It was not only a protest against the attacks emanating from Congress and the right wing against undocumented workers, but also a demand for expanded rights and an end to repression. The demonstrations were originated by grassroots organizers in Los Angeles and were called on May Day because it is International Workers' Day and because the millions of undocumented and documented immigrants come from countries where the May Day tradition is strong and class consciousness is high.

In centers of immigrant working-class strength, such as California, and among unions with strong immigrant memberships, the local or statewide labor movement officially supported and participated in May Day. In almost all cases it was because of the weight of the immigrant workers in their organizations. The AFL-CIO could have taken a great step forward for solidarity had it gone beyond mere paper endorsement and called out all the workers to support May Day.

The AFL-CIO had made a step forward in 1997 when it reversed its long-held reactionary policy opposing immigrant workers and instead officially supported immigrant rights. Service sector, laborers, carpenters, and other unions actively began organizing immigrant workers, including the undocumented. Therefore, participation in May Day, which was a demonstration for immigrant rights, would have been consistent with this program.

Millions of undocumented workers and their families came out of the shadows to defend their rights. In doing so they risked being fired or other forms of reprisal on the job. In addition, they lost pay and risked exposing themselves to eventual deportation. Students risked being penalized at school or even being suspended. In general, they rose to the occasion in the belly of a racist society. This kind of energy and heroism should have been actively supported. Furthermore, it was an opportunity to educate the labor movement on the question of solidarity.

Despite turning out millions of workers and their families, the immigrant movement was largely left on its own. The abstention by the labor movement, as well as by a large section of the anti-war movement, from participating in and supporting May Day was noted by the administration and the capitalist state, which then took the decision to unleash a harsh, racist counterattack. Soon after May Day, highly publicized raids by Immigration and Customs Enforcement (ICE) agents began on businesses and immigrant communities around the country.

The failure by the broader labor and progressive movement to mobilize was a missed opportunity. This left a wide-open door for government repression. The key to strengthening the labor movement is building class solidarity with oppressed sectors of the working class. In this case the vast majority were Latina/o, but immigrants from every continent participated in the mass demonstrations.

May Day offered a rare, important moment to broaden the fight against the torrent of anti-immigrant scapegoating and racism emanating from Congress and to show working-class strength against media demagogues like Lou Dobbs, right-wing talk radio hosts, and fascist groups like the Minutemen. It was a moment to educate the workers as a whole about the need to improve the conditions for immigrant workers in order to keep them from being so vulnerable to super-exploitation. It should have been put in the context of "An injury to one is an injury to all." It was also a chance to improve international solidarity with the workers in the home countries of the immigrant workers, who had their own demonstrations on May Day.

The great May Day outpouring showed that the campaign by the bosses to spread wage competition, worldwide and in the U.S., has begun to backfire. It has brought renewed energy, primarily in the immigrant sector of the labor movement. Those in the vanguard of the revitalization have been the low-paid workers—largely Black, Latina/o, and Asian, many of them un-documented, and including women in large numbers.

State of the unions: glass half-empty or half-full?

There is an enormous preoccupation, both in the capitalist media and within the labor and progressive movement, over the decline of unions in the United States—justifiably so. It is certainly true that the last decades have seen a decline in both the absolute number of unionized workers and in their relation to the total workforce. No one feels this more acutely than union leaders and the rank and file themselves. And no one takes more comfort in this fact than the bosses.

To dwell upon this with fatalistic resignation and to harp on the weakening of the labor unions, without pointing out their potential for struggle, is to demoralize the workers and the movement. The capitalist media, when they cover the unions or the labor movement, seldom fail to mention that in the last thirty years the labor movement has gone from over 30 percent of the workforce down to 12 percent.

But the working class must have an objective, independent assessment of the present situation and where things stand in order to fight its way back. The first thing to note is that, while there has been a decline, the fact is that the combined membership of the AFL-CIO (more than 9 million as of 2005) and Change to Win (close to 6 million) still amounts to over 15 million workers in the organized labor movement. Furthermore, there are studies showing that millions more workers want to be in unions, perhaps as many as 50 million.[234]*

There are 33 unions each with more than 100,000 members. Five of these unions have more than a million members each. Many more have at least 50,000 members apiece. There are hundreds of Central Labor Councils across the country and tens of thousands of local unions. And the unions have combined financial resources in the billions of dollars.

In short, in spite of the heavy erosion of strength over the past decades of capitalist offensive and working-class retreat, there still remains a widespread infrastructure that can potentially be utilized to mobilize workers both inside and outside organized labor and the communities at large. It is sufficient to

---

*According to Freeman, who did a study of workers in the private labor force in the mid-1990s and another one in 2005, the "results suggest that if workers were provided the union representation they desired in 2005 then the unionization rate would be about 58 percent, up from 44 percent estimated from the mid-1990s." In 2005, according to the *Statistical Abstract of the United States, 2007*, Table 616, the employed private labor force was 111.6 million. Calculating 58 percent of 111.6 million comes to about 65 million. Subtracting the already unionized 15 million workers leaves 50 million unorganized workers who want to be in unions.

play a crucial role in the revival of the class struggle and the building of a mighty working-class fight-back movement.

The greatest weakness in the infrastructure of the unions exists in the South and to a lesser extent in the Southwest. But under conditions of united, militant mass struggle, carried out in conjunction with the struggle against racism and national oppression and in solidarity with immigrant workers, this challenge can be met.

In any such assessment, the importance of initial numerical strength should not be overestimated or made the predominant factor. Perhaps the two most important factors in the assessment are, first, the willingness of the rank and file, both organized and unorganized, to struggle and, second, the presence of leadership that is devoted to prosecuting a militant, class-wide struggle.

Historical comparisons can be useful in this regard. The period in which the working class in the U.S. made its last great leap forward was one of militant struggle that culminated in the formation of the Congress of Industrial Organizations (CIO) in 1935 and the organization of mass production industries into industrial unions. Service industries were also organized during this period, although that has gotten less attention.

The heroic victories of the workers over big capital were accomplished by a labor movement that had suffered devastating losses during the prior era, the so-called "roaring twenties"—losses that continued in the early years of the Depression.

The era of prosperity for the bosses in the 1920s had been one of union busting for the workers. Membership in the AFL plummeted from 1920 to 1930, going down from just above 4 million to 2.7 million. The section of the workforce that was organized dropped from 17.5 percent to 9.3 percent. Almost all unions lost *In the early nineteen thirties, on the eve of labor's greatest battles, union membership had dropped to 9.3 percent*

membership during this period. Then came the Depression and AFL membership dropped even further, to 2.3 million. Some unaffiliated unions also lost membership. The number of strikes dropped drastically—until 1933.[235, *]

The principal union behind the CIO was the United Mine Workers (UMW), led by John L. Lewis. Its membership had shrunk from half a million in 1919

---

* Divergent estimates exist regarding the size of the organized workforce in this period. They range from more than 5 million in 1920 to different figures for 1933. This is probably due to the fact that there were independent unions, including unions organized by the Trade Union Unity League, under the guidance of the U.S. Communist Party. There were also large numbers of workers in company unions; some government statisticians may have included them in their figures. In any case, all sources agree that the losses from 1920 to 1933 were devastating and left the organized part of the workforce well under 10 percent of the total.

to under 80,000 in the early 1930s.[236] Union treasuries were starved. When the Committee for Industrial Organization—which became the Congress of Industrial Organizations after being expelled from the AFL—was formed in 1935, it began with a treasury of $15,000, contributed in $5,000 chunks by the UMW, the Amalgamated Clothing Workers of America (ACWA), and the International Ladies Garment Workers Union (ILGWU). As the CIO progressed by attracting militant workers, it relied heavily on the treasury of the UMW.

From a numerical and financial point of view, the organizers of the CIO were in a far inferior position to today's AFL-CIO, given the present resources available. What was the difference? The rank and file of the workers were mobilized for struggle because of the Depression; strikes were carried out **in spite of mass unemployment**. In many cases the unemployed were organized to support strikers. It was the willingness and desire of the workers to struggle that overcame the numerical, organizational, and financial disadvantages of those unions and leaders willing to support mass organizing.

It would be entirely unrealistic to compare the present-day period to the days prior to the creation of the CIO. Two million workers went on strike in 1933 and 1934 alone. There were municipal general strikes in San Francisco, Minneapolis, and Toledo in 1934. Today, after three decades of an anti-labor offensive, the atmosphere and mood among the working class is not comparable to the aggressive, class-struggle atmosphere of the earlier period.

The objective factor in the present unfavorable relationship of class forces is the development of high technology and the implacable hostility of the bosses and their brutal tactics: using permanent scabs, outsourcing, offshoring, labor spies, union-busting consultants and goons, police actions, court injunctions, fines, illegal firings of pro-union workers, anti-labor rulings and endless stalling by the NLRB, and threats and intimidation of all sorts.

However, the ruling class was equally hostile to the labor movement for generations before the upsurge of the thirties.

Today the all-important subjective factor, the mood of the majority of the workers and their morale about the class struggle, is entirely attributable to the long retreat of the labor leadership and its failure to launch an appropriate fight-back. The leadership has no control over the bosses and their determination to launch an offensive. But it does have control over its own ability and willingness to fight back and the responsibility to devise ways of answering the bosses. It is clear that, at the top level, this leadership has not had the will or the desire to launch an adequate struggle.

12

Reviving the struggle

Two earlier periods of great struggle: CIO expanded workers' rights, African-American struggle overturned unjust laws • Labor's failure to fight racism undermined struggle • Stirring examples of rank-and-file control: San Francisco general strike, Making CIO leaders support the struggle, Woolworth sit-down and Wal-Mart today From class struggle to witch hunt • Rank-and-file support against reaction

As the U.S. enters a period of economic crisis, there is an opportunity for all those interested in building a working-class movement to act pre-emptively and prepare to stop the inevitable attempts by the corporations and the banks to make the working class bear the burden brought about by the profit system.

The enormous polarization of wealth in the past decades is well known. The fabulously wealthy, those corporations and banks that have accumulated trillions of dollars and their government in Washington, should be compelled to pay for the crisis. As a result of three decades of attacks on the multinational working class, there is now an underlying potential to build a powerful workers' movement that can fight to bring about this result.

The masses are entering a period of impending capitalist crisis more impoverished, more in debt, more insecure and bereft of any resources that might cushion the blows of a downturn than in decades. Conditions are growing ripe for a rank-and-file resurgence of class struggle and for a merger of the class struggle with the struggles against racism and for self-determination for oppressed peoples.

Two earlier periods of great struggle

Two great periods of advance for the workers and the oppressed in the U.S. took place in the past three quarters of a century: the first during the Great Depression for sections of the organized workers, the second in the post-World War II period for the African-American population and oppressed people in general.

Both periods were characterized by widespread struggles that arose from below. Each struggle began as a series of separate battles that grew in number and scope and ultimately expanded into a generalized, widespread movement that pushed the ruling class back.

Each period began with a defiance of unjust laws and practices that had been imposed by the bosses and the political establishment. Each opened with the determination of a section of the masses to gain fundamental rights by seizing them in struggle. Nothing less will turn the contemporary situation around.

CIO EXPANDED WORKERS' RIGHTS

The culminating victory of industrial unionism in the 1930s was the great Flint sit-down strike of 1937, in which the workers occupied the GM Fisher Body plants for forty-four days. They fought off the police and defied injunctions. The Women's Auxiliary of the United Auto Workers fought against scabs and the police. The strikers faced down the National Guard. They were bolstered by in-the-streets solidarity from the labor movement throughout the region, which sent workers to walk the picket lines and beef up flying squadrons and the mass lines of defense. The struggle was given financial support by the United Mine Workers, Rubber Workers, Amalgamated Clothing Workers, and many other national unions. In the end they defeated General Motors, the largest industrial corporation in the country with over 260,000 workers, by forcing it to sign a contract obligating the company to recognize and deal with the union.

The legal basis for the recognition had been established in law two years earlier, when the right to form a union became federal law for the first time in U.S. history under the National Labor Relations Act (NLRA) of 1935. That law itself was the result of rebellious strikes and unionization campaigns that were growing more widespread throughout the early 1930s. But the giant industrialists in steel, auto, rubber, electric, and machinery declared the right to organize a union to be an unconstitutional violation of their property rights and simply ignored the law. They continued to bust union drives and to ignore unions that had overwhelming recognition among the workers in the plants.

This is similar to the way the bosses ignore labor law today. They create elaborate systems to unearth union sympathizers and illegally fire them on false pretexts; they fire on-the-job union organizers or sympathizers at the first sign of an organizing drive; they subvert union elections by intimidation, with lies, and by forcing workers to attend anti-union meetings; they use labor spies; they ignore grievances until they pile up endlessly. They also create unsafe working conditions and violate other protective laws. Now, just as then, only the struggle can make capitalist legality serve the workers.

The upsurge began to subside in 1938. By that time it had won, in addition to the right to organize, many other rights including Social Security, welfare, the eight-hour day and forty-hour week, time-and-a-half for overtime, abolition of child labor, and unemployment insurance.

The decline of the struggle from below began in 1938 with the second phase of the Depression, which weakened the workers. The Roosevelt administration began preparing for World War II. Sensing the weakness brought on by the renewal of the Depression, the government clamped down on the labor movement. Strikes were broken and sit-downs were outlawed. The social democrats and the right wing of the labor leadership of the CIO pushed out many communist and socialist militants who had been the heart and soul of the organizing drives and were the most anti-racist elements among the white workers.

The official union leaders were drawn into the War Labor Board and the War Production Board. They became enforcers of a "no-strike pledge" during the war, much to the discontent of the workers, who carried out hundreds of wildcat strikes as the bosses took advantage of the enforced class peace to speed up production and pile on the profits. Historic gains had been made by the Depression-era struggles, but the pre-revolutionary mood that had existed was eradicated during the war. The stage was set for a long period of business unionism and class collaboration, resulting in an historic retreat of the labor movement.

AFRICAN-AMERICAN STRUGGLE OVERTURNED UNJUST LAWS

When Rosa Parks refused to give up her seat on a bus in Montgomery, Alabama, in December 1955, she defied a longstanding racist practice. It was the beginning of the Montgomery Bus Boycott. This segregationist practice was overturned by mass mobilization and self-organization of the African-American population of Montgomery in the face of a white supremacist establishment. It forced the local capitalist establishment to order the authorities to revoke segregation in the public transportation system.

Important legal struggles had been waged against segregation alongside many local struggles. But in the landmark case of *Brown v. Board of Education*, the Supreme Court in 1954 ruled that segregated schools were unconstitutional. Nevertheless, the racist establishment dug in and defied the ruling. The Montgomery Bus Boycott brought the struggle against segregation from the courts to the streets, defying the age-old racist custom that had had the force of law because it was enforced by the state.

This began an era of escalating struggle which swept across the South, attacking one racist institution after another: segregated public facilities of all types; white-only primaries that excluded Black candidates; taxes, tests, and plain terror that kept African Americans from voting, and segregated schools at all levels. Injunctions were defied. People young and old stood up to police clubs and dogs, water hoses, KKK nightriders, and terrorist bombers. There were sit-ins, Freedom Rides, voting rights campaigns, and the growth of armed self-defense organizations—like the Deacons for Defense that originated in Louisiana and the local chapter of the NAACP headed by Robert Williams in Monroe, North Carolina. These organizations were set up to protect the communities from the KKK. Pitched battles were fought from Birmingham, Alabama, to Cambridge, Maryland.

The struggle spread to the North and rebellions against racism, poverty, unemployment, and police rule in African-American communities. Many of the rebellions had insurrectionary components to them, particularly in the Los Angeles Black community of Watts and in Detroit. Alongside these struggles, African-American militants organized campaigns and job actions against racism in the factories, from Detroit to Mahwah, New Jersey. There were rebellions of Black troops in the military, prison uprisings, and many other forms of struggle.

The Civil Rights movement, which started during the Eisenhower administration and continued into the Nixon years, broke up the witch-hunt atmosphere of the 1950s. As the African-American struggle expanded and escalated over time, it helped fuel the struggles of the Chicana/o people, Puerto Ricans, Asians, Native people, the women's and lesbian and gay struggles, and the disabled movement. It attracted the more revolutionary elements of the anti-war movement.

Among the many important developments of that period, one of the most significant was the revival of the Native movement of resistance. It began with the founding of the American Indian Movement in 1968 and the occupation of Alcatraz Island in 1969. It continued with the Longest Walk across the country in 1972 on the Trail of Broken Treaties and the occupation of the Bureau of Indian Affairs in Washington, D.C.

This movement culminated in 1973 in the momentous and heroic armed occupation of Wounded Knee and the claiming of sovereignty over the sacred Black Hills on the Pine Ridge reservation in North Dakota. The occupation was put down by a massive show of state force. (The frame-up and life imprisonment of AIM leader Leonard Peltier was an act of revenge by the FBI and the courts for this rebellion.)

All these struggles shook the capitalist establishment to its foundations while the U.S. was engaged in an imperialist war adventure in Vietnam.

The Black liberation struggle did much to undermine Washington's racist war effort. It also won historic concessions along the way—the Civil Rights Act, the Voting Rights Act, and affirmative action. The last was also a concession to the women's movement and other struggles of the oppressed. The Black liberation struggle forced the ruling class to temporarily spend money in the community in the so-called War on Poverty. However, the tide of the Black liberation movement and other movements of the period was finally pushed back by relentless repression. Among the many targets of repression, one of the most prominent was the Black Panther Party. It electrified the country and attracted widespread support among African-American youth with its organization for self-defense, combined with its program to serve the people. The Panthers were systematically destroyed by the FBI through assassination, frame-ups, infiltration, and a host of other dirty tricks carried out by the government's "counter-intelligence" program (COINTELPRO), which was nothing but a secret police and provocateur operation.

During both periods the elemental driving force was the direct action by the masses, who disrupted the normal functioning of the capitalist system

Both the labor movement in its militant period and the African-American struggle changed laws, overturned previous court rulings, expanded the legal and political rights of the workers and the oppressed, and improved the lives of masses of people. They tested the strength of large sections of the masses against the strength of the ruling class. In the process they pushed the entire ruling class back into a posture of retreat and concessions.

Both periods of struggle created lasting gains, in spite of significant erosion later of what had been accomplished. And during both periods the elemental driving force was the protracted, widespread confrontation and direct action by the masses, who disrupted the normal functioning of the capitalist system, both in the workplace and in the streets.

Labor's failure to fight racism undermined struggle

As the capitalist economy heads into a new period of economic crisis, it is important to remember that both of these historic victories also arose out of periods of crisis. The struggle of the organized labor movement arose out of the economic crisis of the Depression. The struggle of the African-American people created a crisis for the system of racist oppression, which affected all aspects of life—social, economic, and political.

In looking ahead to the approaching period, which holds the prospect of both crisis and opportunity, it is important to look back at the past failures of the white labor leadership to support the struggle of the African-American people. This failure to forge unity by resolutely fighting racism and national oppression during the formation of the CIO and during the later African-American struggle for civil rights, equality, and liberation imposed sharp limitations on the ultimate achievements of both struggles. This also goes for the labor leadership's relationship to the Latina/o population, as well as to Asian and Native peoples.

During the formation of the CIO, the most progressive forces in the struggle were anti-racist and fought for Black-white unity. The official position of the CIO in the early days was one of treating all workers equally. This was opposed to the AFL, which openly defended the right of local unions to exclude Black workers. Thus, the position of the CIO was a step forward in the labor movement. Many Black leaders campaigned for the CIO and many Black workers were won over to the unions for that reason, even though there were many violations of the CIO program of equal rights to join a union.

As progressive as the CIO position was, it was a far cry from taking the struggle against racism and discrimination to all walks of life, including especially the entire rotten, segregated structure of the South. Many organizers in the South who were communists and socialists, and individual unions such as the Meatpackers, the United Electrical Workers (UE), the Food, Tobacco, and Agricultural workers, who were under leftist leadership, did campaign against racism there in the face of great danger.

But the CIO itself could have strengthened the appeal of the labor movement immeasurably by combining the right to organize with the struggle against racism. A large number of Black workers had migrated to the North, the Midwest, and the West Coast, in addition to the millions in the anti-union South.

Of course, such a policy could have caused divisions in the CIO because of strong racist hangovers among many white workers. And it might have led to difficulties in organizing in some areas. In the long run, however, to struggle against racism would have strengthened organizing efforts in both the North and, all importantly, in the South. In this way, the newly invigorated, militant working-class movement could have overcome the legacy of abandonment of the Black population by the labor officialdom that had lasted, with the exception of the Knights of Labor, from the post-Civil War era until the founding of the CIO in 1935.

After World War II, during the Civil Rights movement and the Black liberation struggle, the labor movement was either aloof or outright hostile. Rosa

Parks and Dr. Martin Luther King Jr. carried on their struggle with, at best, token support from the major unions. Smaller unions made up of low-paid, oppressed workers gave what support they could, but the vast resources of the AFL-CIO were never deployed in support of the sit-ins, the marches for voting rights, or even the organizing campaign of the Memphis sanitation workers, whose cause Dr. King took up just before he was assassinated.

The leadership of the AFL-CIO was hostile to the Black Power movement, to the Black Panther Party, and to the Black liberation struggle in general. The UAW leadership carried out a hostile campaign against the Dodge Revolutionary Union Movement and other sectors of Black workers who organized against racism in the auto plants. The teachers' union in New York City organized an infamous strike in 1968 against the efforts by the Black community in the Ocean Hill-Brownsville section of Brooklyn to institute community control of their schools. The United Federation of Teachers struck on the grounds of defending the seniority of white teachers who had been dismissed after the African-American administration of an all-Black school district determined that they were incompetent. Thus the teachers' union put narrow trade union rights ahead of the right of self-determination of the African-American community.

The class truth is that institutional racism, unemployment, poverty, segregation, low wages, and police brutality are all rooted in the schemes of the capitalist class to get super-profits by keeping oppressed people down. But this same capitalist class is the exploiter of workers both inside and outside the unions. Racism and oppression are not only an economic strategy but also a political strategy to keep the class divided.

Today, however, as the coming period of crisis descends upon the working class and the communities across the country, there is an opportunity for the multinational working class to rectify this historic division. There is a growing basis to combine the class struggle with the struggle against racism and national oppression—as well as all other forms of oppression—in one class-wide battle, providing the militant rank-and-file workers can assert their leadership over the unions.

Stirring examples of rank-and-file control

Throughout the last thirty years, workers in the United States have shown a great willingness to fight when confronted with corporate aggression. Whenever the leadership at any level has given the workers a chance to battle concessions, the ranks have taken up the challenge. They have fought police, company goons, and scabs. They have risked arrest and injury, made great financial sacrifices, risked personal health, family stresses and strains, and many other hardships. In the South they have faced racist authorities in anti-union, so-called "right-to-work" states. They have walked picket lines for great lengths of time, sat in, and traveled long distances to create networks of solidarity. Sometimes they have had the support of the top leadership. Most of the time the higher-ups have refused to muster the forces needed, dragged their feet, sat it out, or displayed open hostility.

What the rank-and-file have not been able to do is either force the union leadership to fight in a manner necessary for victory or take charge of the struggle from down below. As the U.S. and the working class face another economic crisis, it is worthwhile to recall aspects of the crisis of the 1930s, which fueled the struggle of the mass of workers and either forced the leaders to sanction and support major battles or swept them aside so that the true representatives of the ranks could take over the reins.

1934: SAN FRANCISCO GENERAL STRIKE

Examples from the past are not necessarily blueprints for the future. But they can be instructive about what is possible and point in a general direction. In labor history the San Francisco general strike of 1934 is one of the legendary struggles of the period. It was an epic battle, in which police killed two workers and injured many.

The strike originated in a struggle between the longshore workers and ship owners. There were many issues—including demands for recognition of the union, a six-hour day, thirty-hour week, and an increase in hourly pay—but the central demand of the dockworkers

The convening and empowerment of a rank-and-file convention was the foundation of the 1934 San Francisco general strike

was to rid themselves of a corrupt hiring system run by the bosses. Company hiring agents would arbitrarily decide on a daily basis who would work and who would not as workers assembled for shape-up.

The shape-up was called the "slave market" by the workers. The fundamental issue of the strike was to establish a hiring hall system run by the union. This would abolish company favoritism and discrimination as well as rotate the available jobs in order to more evenly distribute income.

The strike itself is a well-known milestone in labor history. But some of the important details are less known and are interesting in light of present problems and what can be anticipated as the economic crisis deepens.

The longshore workers in San Francisco knew that the International Longshoremen's Association (ILA) leadership, under President Joseph Ryan, as well as the local president, Lee Holman, were non-struggle and conservatives. In February, as the workers were preparing for negotiations, the San Francisco local under Harry Bridges called a West Coast rank-and-file convention. **Paid officers of the union were excluded as delegates. The convention lasted ten days and formulated the bargaining position independent of the conservative leadership.**[237]

This consolidation and empowerment of the ranks was the foundation for all that followed. When the top leadership maneuvered to take over the bargaining process, the rank-and-file convention passed a resolution requiring any agreement be submitted to the workers for approval. When the president of the local, Holman, made statements against the militant leadership, he was fired by the ranks. When the company rejected the union's demands, the union set a strike date.

President Franklin Delano Roosevelt himself intervened to try to cool things down. When Roosevelt's mediator tried to compromise with the waterfront bosses by giving them joint control over the hiring hall, the ranks rejected the idea. The union ignored telegrams from Ryan and the Labor Department not to strike and went out on May 9. The strike spread to ports along the West Coast.

What followed is also instructive and food for thought for the present day. Once the longshore strike began, within days nine more maritime craft unions began to formulate demands and walked out. They had been suffering demands for concessions during the Depression and had piled up grievances of their own. The longshore union took the innovative initiative to form a **Joint Strike Committee of 50**, five delegates from each union, with Bridges at the head. They pledged to support each other's demands and not to go back without a joint settlement. Another crucial act of solidarity that gave the strike an enormous boost was the fact that **the Teamsters resolved not to haul scab freight** in defiance of their local leadership. The Teamsters later went out in support of the maritime strike.

When Ryan and the ILA leadership tried to end the strike by getting the unions to submit to arbitration, the tactic was rejected. When Ryan negotiated a rotten compromise, that offer was rejected. Finally, on June 16, Ryan actually signed a compromise agreement, in violation of the rank-and-file convention resolution requiring submission of any agreement to the membership. The next day mass meetings were called all along the coast. Ryan was booed off the stage in San Francisco and **the strikers took the right to negotiate away from the Executive Board and turned it over to the Joint Strike Committee.**

The struggle progressed in stages, with the workers fighting the cops and scabs for weeks. On July 5, the police attacked 2,000 workers trying to stop scab trucks from opening the port. Pitched battles took place lasting hours. Two strikers were killed and more than one hundred were wounded. The National Guard was ordered in, with machineguns and armored cars. A mass funeral for the murdered workers brought out tens of thousands from the labor movement. Soon afterward the sentiment for a general strike swept the labor movement of San Francisco.

The Central Labor Council was pressured, against its will, into calling a general strike, but retained control by creating a Strike Strategy Committee with a conservative leadership. On July 15 more than 125,000 workers from sixty-five unions went out in San Francisco and Oakland. At the beginning of the strike San Francisco was largely shut down, save for a limited number of restaurants and emergency services permitted by the strikers.

The ruling class launched a full-scale counterattack. Federal, state, and local officials red-baited and violence-baited the strike. The entire capitalist media organized a coordinated, frenzied anti-strike barrage. Additional National Guard troops were sent in. Organized right-wing vigilante squads launched attacks on union offices and radicals in coordination with the police.

The conservative labor leaders predominating in the Strike Strategy Committee began to allow more and more economic activity to go on. They ultimately took control of the negotiating process and overruled the unions in the original Joint Strike Committee. The strike was called off on July 31 under tremendous ruling-class pressure. The ILA and the maritime unions had to submit to arbitration and were forced to compromise. The longshore workers gained recognition and raises but were forced to accept a version of joint control over the union hiring hall. Nevertheless, the union had come out strengthened and within a year it gained full union control over the hiring hall.

It is noteworthy that this historic struggle was carried out by longshore workers who were Black, white, and other nationalities under the leadership of Harry Bridges, who was elected chairman of the Joint Strike Committee of 50. They based themselves on meeting the needs and the will of the rank and file and relying on their fighting strength. This leadership created a new form of strike committee, in which many unions pledged to stick together and build new bonds of solidarity. It was when the rank-and-file leaders of the Joint Strike Committee lost control over strategy and bargaining to the conservative leadership of the appointed Strike Strategy Committee that the strike began to decline.

It is also important to note that it took two months of bloody fighting, a general strike, and the solidarity in action of 125,000 workers, who tied up all of San Francisco, to win even a limited victory in a strike that had started with just 12,000 longshore workers. Once they dared to fight back, it took this great effort to save them from being overcome by the combined forces of the ruling class.

In the general strike, the San Francisco Industrial Association representing big business, the San Francisco Chamber of Commerce, and a committee of the entire capitalist media headed by the Hearst papers, orchestrated a vicious media strike-breaking campaign against the workers.

The San Francisco struggle illustrated the imperative need for broad class solidarity in any important strike. The foundation of the general strike was the takeover of the union by a leadership that genuinely represented the needs of the rank and file and was willing to stand up to pressures from top union officials, the company, and the capitalist government. It was one of an untold number of struggles—including the general strikes in Toledo and Minneapolis—that also showed how the role of the rank and file is crucial when the workers are faced with intransigent resistance and aggression from big capital.

1934-1938: MAKING CIO LEADERS SUPPORT THE STRUGGLE

In a number of municipal general strikes in 1934, the rank and file under radical and militant leadership were able to take control of their locals and of the struggle. In each case, this drew the support of the majority of the rest of the workers in their cities.

In the formation of the CIO, a rebellion of the industrial workers occurred as economic activity began to revive around 1934. The mass of the industrial workers were unable to take control of the great national industrial unions that arose out of the struggles on the ground. But they were able to precipitate a split in the national leadership of the American Federation of Labor and gain the financial and organizational support of a section of that leadership, led by United Mine Workers President John L. Lewis.

The leaders of the AFL, which was based upon the narrow craft unions, were sitting atop a declining organized labor movement with their hands folded, even as a strike upsurge and demands for organization were rocking the mass production industries. Struggles in auto, rubber, textiles, machine shops, radio, meatpacking, and many other industries resulted in a torrent of requests from the industrial workers for charters from the AFL. Many charters were granted, but the leadership turned its back on actually organizing the mass of these workers—aside from offering to organize skilled workers, who were a minority in the plants, into the craft unions.

The struggle of the ranks broadened on the ground and forced the issue. There were short, rapid sit-downs in the Detroit and Cleveland auto plants in 1935, mainly over line speed-up. But in 1936 matters erupted. During that year there were sit-downs in every rubber factory in Akron, Ohio, the center of the U.S. rubber industry, where every major corporation had facilities.

The sit-downs were part of spontaneous efforts by the workers to get recognition for the Rubber Workers union. Bureau of Labor Statistics records for 1936 show forty-eight sit-down strikes involving 87,817 workers. In 1937 there were 477 sit-down strikes involving 398,177 workers. In 1938 fifty-two such strikes involved 28,749 workers.[238]

This upheaval of the industrial workers appealed to a section of the AFL leadership. There were only a few unions in the AFL organized on an industrial basis. But the leading industrial unions in the AFL with significant memberships—the United Mine Workers, the International Ladies Garment Workers, and the Amalgamated Clothing Workers of America—had no interest in preserving craft organization.

The revival and expansion of the union movement depended upon organizing the millions of workers in the mass production industries. These union leaders saw the workers in struggle and the opportunity to rejuvenate the movement. They seized upon the situation and sent funds and organizing staff to assist the struggles already begun by the workers. It was the workers themselves who opened the way for the leadership to get behind the struggle.

1937: WOOLWORTH SIT-DOWN AND WAL-MART TODAY

One of the main features of the new low-wage capitalism today is the creation of millions of low-paid retail jobs. This is typified by Wal-Mart, the largest employer in the United States. The idea put forth that this vast section of the working class is beyond organization is really self-justification for the narrowness and lethargy of the present labor leadership. In this connection, it is worthwhile to take time to look back to the 1930s and a nearly forgotten chapter in the history of that period. It pertains to the 1937 Woolworth sit-down strike, which became nationally known at the time. This strike sparked a wave of rank-and-file sit-down rebellions, which led to organizing around the country in retail, hotels, restaurants, laundries, etc. The account of this strike and its aftermath has been preserved by Dana Frank as a chapter in the book *Three Strikes: Miners, Musicians, Salesgirls, and the Fighting Spirit of Labor's Last Century.*[239]

Here are some of the highlights of this episode.

The victory of the UAW over General Motors through the sit-downs at the Fisher Body plant in Flint was concluded on February 11, 1937. The GM strike had idled 112,000 workers. Days after it was over, a strike wave in Detroit involved laundry workers, cleaning women, high school students working as delivery workers, and others in sit-downs.

On February 27, sixteen days after the GM victory, more than a hundred young women workers at one of the forty Woolworth stores in the city stopped work, ushered the customers out, shut the doors, and called the manager to come to a conference with all of them. They demanded raises, time and a half for more than forty hours, company pay for uniforms, lunch allowances, breaks, recognition of the Waiters and Waitresses Union, and hiring only through the union. The union had only one staff person there. None of the women had ever been in a union before.

The audacity of the strikers can be appreciated by the fact that they were up against the largest retailer of the era. In 1937 Woolworth's had more than 2,000 stores in the U.S., Canada, and Cuba. It had 737 stores in Britain and eighty-two in Germany. "It was," in the words of Frank, "like striking Wal-Mart, the Gap, and McDonald's all at the same time."

It employed 65,000 workers, almost all young women. It was viciously anti-union. And it had a racist, white-only hiring policy. Woolworth's had a policy of deskilling its labor force. Says Frank, "Woolworth's formula is the same one used by McDonald's, Circuit City, and other big chains today. If the job is sufficiently deskilled, a huge potential labor pool opens up, and if turnover rates are high, so much the better—managers can then pick and choose." Most importantly, the management picked young women who had few options on the job market, who were more likely to work temporary, and who "in theory, were less likely to unionize."

The sit-down strike lasted a week, until March 5. It broke into the media during the first few days. The Hotel Employees and Restaurant Employees (HERE) union was called in by the strikers—**after** they sat down. During the course of the strike the cooks' union supplied meals, the musicians' union supplied entertainment. Hotel workers from all around the city came to the site to picket and show solidarity.

UAW head Homer Martin came to Woolworth's to pledge union support. The head of the Detroit and Wayne County AFL showed up at the strike the first day. He held out a hand of solidarity to the CIO-affiliated UAW in support of the strike and donated money. The head of UAW Chrysler Local 7 showed support. The national president of HERE announced plans to come to Detroit to put the international behind the strike. It was settled before he arrived.

Five hours after the strike started, Kresge, Woolworth's biggest competitor, raised its workers' wages from $14 a day to $17. All over downtown Detroit, bosses were giving the workers raises in an attempt to stave off similar sit-downs.

The union shut down a second store with a sit-down strike and threatened to spread the strike to all forty Woolworth stores. Support flowed in from around the country. The Retail Clerks in New York started a solidarity campaign.

In Detroit itself, sit-downs spread among thousands of local workers, from waitresses to kitchen workers to cafeteria, hotel, and factory workers. On March 4 U.S. Steel capitulated to the Steel Workers Organizing Committee. While this drew all the headlines, on March 5 the biggest retail giant in the world caved in and the Woolworth workers won all their demands, including the union shop. The union won a uniform contract for all 40 stores in Detroit, which covered 2,500 workers.

The effects of the strike rippled for a year. In Detroit, there were sit-downs at Lerner's, at Federated Department Stores, and numerous other downtown stores. In New York City, the retail clerks sat down at five H.L. Green stores. In East St. Louis, Illinois, workers got a uniform contract covering Woolworth's, W.T. Grant, Newberry, and Kresge stores throughout the city. A similar victory took place among retail workers in Akron, Ohio, site of the first major sit-down strikes among the rubber workers. Some 1,500 workers at thirty-three Woolworth stores in St. Louis got a contract.

By year's end, chain variety stores, grocery and department stores had been organized in St. Paul and Duluth, Minnesota; Tacoma and Centralia, Washington; Superior, Wisconsin, and San Francisco.[240]

In Seattle, wrote Frank, "three thousand clerks in twenty-three stores, including Sears, J.C. Penney, Frederick & Nelson's, the Bon Marché, and Lerner's won not only the forty-hour week but a pay increase 'estimated to increase the income of the employees by at least one half-million dollars.' Over sixty years later, unions today in department stores all over the country owe their existence in part to the Woolworth strike."[241]

'Over sixty years later, unions today in department stores all over the country owe their existence in part to the Woolworth strike'

This is an important struggle in the history of the workers' movement. Wal-Mart is no more anti-union today than Woolworth's was in 1937. This struggle shows that it is not the structure of the retail industry that determines whether or not it can be organized but the climate of the labor movement, the general level of struggle in the country, and its effect on the rank-and-file.

From class struggle to witch hunt

During the organizing drive for the Congress of Industrial Organizations, communists, socialists, and other radicals were the heart and soul of the actual organizing staffs on the ground. The CIO leadership, and John L. Lewis in particular, knew that the CIO could not be built without them. They were veterans of many struggles and devoted to the working class. Lewis had voted for Herbert Hoover in 1932 and had engaged in many attacks on Communist Party members in the past, but for entirely pragmatic reasons he relied on the energies and skills of leftists in the struggle to organize.

But once the CIO was established, things changed. It began to shift from relying for its strength on the militant struggle of the workers to carving out arrangements with the bosses and the government, especially during and after World War II. In the post-war period, Washington and the Pentagon opened up the Cold War against the Soviet Union. Red-baiting became the order of the day. The international campaign to vilify socialism and communism was accompanied by a drive to root out all communists and progressives from any significant positions in society. Red-baiting dominated all politics and social life.

The right wing and the social democrats had control of the CIO leadership. This leadership, coming out of its collaboration with the ruling class during the war, fell in line with the anti-communist orientation of the ruling class. It completely suited their own narrow needs to root out militancy and eradicate the class-struggle spirit that had animated the unions in the formation of the CIO. Thus the leaders of the rank-and-file struggle, the progressive, radical, and anti-racist forces, were at first pushed back from positions of influence in the labor movement. And as McCarthyism and the general post-war witch hunt against communists and progressives took off, the CIO bureaucrats started their own internal anti-communist campaign, led by top officials.

The Taft-Hartley Act, enacted in 1947, demanded that all union officials disavow membership in the Communist Party. This gave a legal pretext for the witch hunt inside the CIO. Eleven unions with a total of 1 million members were expelled or driven out of the CIO. Most of them had leaders who were either members or sympathizers of the CP. Witch-hunt "trials" and kangaroo courts were set up comparable to the government's House Un-American Activities Committee (HUAC) hearings, which targeted the CP

leadership and progressives throughout U.S. capitalist society. Those targeted were the most militant, anti-racist unions with the most class-conscious
leadership.

Whatever errors the CP had made in politics and tactics, the ferocious assault by the CIO leadership had nothing to do with any CP deviations from
the politics of communism or working-class leadership. In fact, the CP had
supported the no-strike pledge during the war and subordinated the need for
an independent political road for the working class, giving all-out support to
Roosevelt and the Democratic Party. But these were not the concerns of the
top CIO leaders. They were motivated by the desire to crush any remnant of
communism, class-consciousness, and militant, anti-racist struggle within
the labor movement.

What happened to the expelled unions during the witch hunt and afterward
is important for what it says about the close relationship between the rank and
file, the class struggle, class-consciousness, and the union leadership.

The leaders of unions that were witch-hunted—like Harry Bridges of the
Longshore Workers (ILWU), James Matles of the Electrical Workers (UE),
and Ben Gold of the Fur and Leather Workers—were able to stand up during
the "trials" and still survive as leaders because they had built a strong rank-
and-file foundation based upon the class and anti-racist struggle and, in the
case of the UE especially, on the organization of women workers. Despite all
the scurrilous accusations about being agents of the USSR and being disloyal
and unpatriotic, the ranks did not desert them because of the right-wing
political attacks.

But the unions that were expelled or driven out of the CIO had lost their
status with the National Labor Relations Board and were subject to decertification because of the principled refusal of their leaders to sign a loyalty oath.
The CIO leaders began raids on the expelled unions in an attempt to destroy
them and created rival unions with charters and resources.

Rank-and-file support against reaction

It is significant that the CIO leaders were unable to make any inroads
against Harry Bridges and the ILWU in San Francisco, site of the great general strike, despite the fact that Bridges was red-baited in the vilest manner.
Bridges was suspended as regional director but the ranks of the union stood
firmly behind him, based upon his history of standing up to the bosses. It is
no accident that, in the present period, ILWU Local 10, Bridges' own local,
which now has Black leadership, remains among the most progressive, anti-
racist unions in the country.

Another significant union expelled during the witch hunt was the United Electrical, Radio and Machine Workers (UE). It had half a million members. It was strong in organizing workers in radio factories and other electrical appliance industries. Women made up a significant portion of its membership and it was an anti-racist, militant union with CP presence in the leadership. The union was severely damaged by the CIO leadership, especially the federation's red-baiting secretary-treasurer and president of the UE, James B. Carey, who fingered leaders of his own union for the FBI and HUAC. Carey and the CIO authorized the creation of a rival union, the IUE, to raid the UE. Between the witch hunt and the raids, this strong pillar of the CIO was much reduced.

Nevertheless, the UE survived the storm and still exists today as a progressive union. It has collaborated with Black Workers for Justice in the South under extremely difficult circumstances, fighting for the rights of government workers in the anti-union, right-to-work states. It was one of the first unions to reach out to Mexican workers in the border factories called *maquiladoras* and establish international collaboration against NAFTA and globalization.

Other expelled unions also demonstrate how difficult it was for the CIO leaders to overcome them, because they had the support of the ranks based on fighting the bosses and fighting racism. The Food, Tobacco, Agricultural, and Allied Workers (FTA) linked their organizing campaigns during the 1930s to racial justice in Memphis, Tennessee, and Winston-Salem, North Carolina. The union also led in gender equality. The International Mine, Mill, and Smelter Workers insisted on full racial equality in its locals in Red Mountain, Alabama, going up against many racist elements within the union as well as the racist, ruling-class establishment. Both these unions were influenced by communists and both were witch-hunted.

Official CIO red-baiting and the general anti-communist hysteria in the country whipped up by the ruling class were not enough to undermine the progressive, militant unions, however. Despite the witch hunt of Mine, Mill, the CIO had to create a rival union in the Red Mountain region and join in a vicious race-baiting campaign in a bloc with the Ku Klux Klan before it could finally defeat Mine, Mill in the region in 1949.

In order to prevail, the CIO leadership in 1950 actually destroyed Local 22 of the FTA in Winston-Salem, where the union had a strong biracial organization at the R.J. Reynolds tobacco factory. The only way FTA Local 22 could be defeated was through the combination of raids by a rival union and red-baiting by the mayor of Winston-Salem. The final result was no union at all.[242]

These experiences show that in order to build unions that can stand up to the bosses, withstand racism and other reactionary attacks, and weld together the membership for struggle, it is essential that the leadership fully reflect the interests and demands of the rank-and-file workers and that it be devoted to pressing the struggle forward to its fullest possible extent. The lessons of the past cannot be applied mechanically to the present and the future, but the coming crisis cannot be successfully confronted without empowering the militancy, the dedication, and the organization of the multinational rank and file of the labor movement.

13

High tech undermines old forms of class organization

**Limitations of craft unionism • Assembly line brought industrial unions
Rising tide of deskilled jobs • Breakup and dispersal of working-class centers
Growing retail proletariat • Marx's law of wages confirmed, with a vengeance**

The working class in the United States is facing a crisis that will bring to light the urgent need for a leap toward class-wide organization. This crisis of the labor movement is taking place in the framework of the global restructuring of capitalist production and services, which had already pushed tens of millions of workers and oppressed to the edge of mass pauperization, **even before the onslaught of the new economic crisis.**

Technological innovation is a constant under capitalism. Ever since its earliest beginnings, each generation of capitalists has sought to more thoroughly exploit the workers, most often through the introduction of more efficient, more productive equipment. The general tendency of innovation is to build the skills of workers into machines and thus eliminate or reduce the need for skilled labor. If workers are skilled, the idea is to eliminate them altogether or reduce their skills. In the past several decades, automation, robotization, software applications, and many other technological innovations have accelerated this process by leaps and bounds.

What is the consequence for the workers and their class organization of these continuing waves of technological attacks? The historical effect of leaps forward in capitalist technology is to undermine gains in union organization made in previous periods, or to shrink effective labor organization and isolate it within limited spheres.

Precisely because the aim of the bosses is to continually deskill jobs, the general skill level of the majority of the working class tends to go down historically. Once capitalism attains a relatively high level of development and the application of science and technology to production becomes general, the proportion of the lower skilled to the higher skilled workers rises. This is sometimes gradual, but at times of technological breakthrough it can occur in leaps. This is inherent in capitalist development.

Each new wave of technology is directed by capital precisely at eliminating the highest-paid jobs and the areas in which labor organization has been most successful. Its tendency is to drive down the price of labor power—that

Each new stage in capitalist technological development requires greater and greater working-class solidarity, wider and wider organization, and more unified struggle

is, wages. The most pervasive methods of accomplishing this are to destroy union jobs; to deskill jobs, making it easier to replace one worker with another with minimal to no training, which will increase competition among workers; or to direct capital towards new low-skill, low-wage, high-profit industries and avoid unions altogether.

For the working class this means that each new stage in capitalist technological development requires greater and greater class solidarity, wider and wider organization, and more unified struggle to overcome the ever-increasing tendency by the bosses to widen the competition among workers, both at home and abroad.

Limitations of craft unionism

The primary accomplishment of the 1930s in the United States was the creation of industrial unionism. Industrial unionism meant that everyone in a company, from the porters to the most highly skilled workers, would be included in one union and would get the rights and benefits that came with union organization and collective bargaining. Industrial union organization had been on the historical agenda for decades before these types of unions actually came into being as the predominant form of class organization.

The basis for industrial unionism was the growth of mass production industries and the concentration of capitalist ownership over giant enterprises. In the period after the Civil War, as U.S. capitalism was developing and expanding, there were parallel developments in the class struggle involving both craft organization and the struggle for industrial organization. A spontaneous national uprising of railroad workers in 1877 was crushed by the use of federal troops. In 1894, a groundbreaking attempt to organize an industrial union of railroad workers, led by Eugene Victor Debs, was also defeated by the bosses.

In the early stages of the union movement, the bosses were as hostile to craft unionism as they were to industrial unionism. The famous Homestead steel lockout of 1892 was directed against the skilled workers in the industry.

The union was crushed in an armed struggle between the workers and an army of Pinkerton agents—company goons.

It was skilled trades workers fighting for union recognition who carried out most of the successful strikes of that period, which were won only after bitter battles. The advantage of the craft workers in the struggle was precisely their skill and the relative difficulty of replacing them with scabs—in other words, they were better able to overcome competition among the workers. Printers, typographers, pressmen, carpenters, bricklayers, electricians, construction workers, plasterers, painters, machinists, etc., were able to get union recognition. In most instances they gained the right to train apprentices (thus further limiting competition), resist technological innovation, and enforce work rules.

Where there were mass production industries in mining, textiles, and clothing, industrial unions were able to form. But the predominant form of organization, based upon the early stages of industrial capitalism in the United States, was the craft form. Craft unions were the basis of the American Federation of Labor (AFL), which formed in 1886.

Despite its origins in militant struggle, the AFL largely turned its back on industrial unionism. Samuel Gompers, its founder, refused to back Debs in the 1894 Pullman strike. This was a turning point that led to the defeat of the first significant struggle for industrial unionism.

For half a century after the founding of the AFL, its leadership, with minor exceptions, rejected not only industrial unionism but any form of radicalism or political struggle on behalf of the working class. The leadership insisted that only those workers with craft skills could be allowed into the union movement. If workers in a mass production industry wanted to organize a union, the unskilled or semi-skilled would not be eligible while the skilled workers would be allotted to the particular craft union that had jurisdiction over their skill. What was even more injurious to working-class solidarity and organization was that the AFL, under the guise of recognizing "union autonomy," gave charters to racist, white-only locals.

Assembly line brought industrial unions

After the turn of the century, it was the development and steady expansion of mass production technology, principally the assembly line, and with it the absolute and relative growth of the semi-skilled and unskilled industrial proletariat that eroded the foundation of craft unionism as the predominant form of working class organization. The contradiction between craft unionism and industrial mass production erupted with the great wave of strikes and sit-downs of the 1930s. The stranglehold of the reactionary, privileged craft union leadership and all its exclusiveness, open racism, and narrow rejection of all forms of class solidarity was utterly defeated by the newly created industrial working class.

Craft unionism as an organizational form could not possibly encompass the many millions of production workers who had poured into the labor force over the preceding three decades. The giant corporations that had emerged could only be defeated by mass struggle, including plant occupations and sit-downs, as well as widespread class solidarity and support. The narrow methods of fighting for craft unions could not be applied to the new corporate giants with their industrial empires. However, it took three decades of capitalist development and a capitalist economic crisis to force the breakthrough of a higher form of organization and struggle.

Thus the development of the productive forces not only changed the character of the working class, but also required new forms of class organization and class struggle. With the impending present-day crisis in the era of globalization, the working class is approaching a similar conjuncture in its history. Just as in the 1930s, it will become apparent that things cannot go on in the old way.

Rising tide of deskilled jobs

At the beginning of the twentieth century the majority of autoworkers were skilled crafts workers. The introduction of the assembly line and new machinery sharply reduced the proportion of skilled autoworkers to semi-skilled and unskilled. But even with the introduction of the assembly line, skilled jobs such as painting and welding were plentiful in the auto industry. Today, with robotization, welding and painting jobs no longer exist. Fine machining was another skilled craft that survived the assembly line. Automated processes now produce machine parts to the highest tolerances.

Computers have absorbed many skills affecting millions of office jobs. Many jobs no longer exist that once required such skills as accurate typing, stenography, bookkeeping, editing, and spelling skills. These occupations used to employ millions, mostly women. Clerks in charge of inventory, ordering supplies, shipping, and other jobs that required significant periods of training, the accumulation of detailed knowledge, and the use of judgment have been replaced as their jobs were simplified by technology or wholly automated. Legal secretaries, tax preparers, fast-food cooks, and numerous other service occupations have been greatly deskilled by computerized technology.

Furthermore, tens of millions of new unskilled jobs have been created. The number of students getting out of colleges seeking skilled jobs far exceeds the number of skilled jobs that exist. This not only forces the new generation of college-educated workers to take jobs below their skill levels, it also throws them into the general competition for semi-skilled or unskilled jobs available. This all adds up to lower and lower wages.

In other words, this new state of pauperization of the working class is conditioned by the new scientific-technological phase of capitalism and the spread of this phase to include the entire globe.

Breakup and dispersal of working-class centers

Part of the union-busting process has involved the deindustrialization of the great urban centers with concentrations of workers. Working-class neighborhoods have either been broken up or left to deteriorate. Plants and offices devoted to auto, steel, meatpacking, rubber, and customer service industries, among others, have been dispersed to low-wage, non-union areas, often in rural or suburban communities. This process has especially affected Black workers and other oppressed workers in urban proletarian centers across the country.

The application of technology has broken up the giant, vertically organized industrial plants, particularly in large industries like steel and auto. This has undercut the concentrated power of workers. It used to be that every part of the process of production of an automobile, from beginning to end, took place in a giant factory or in factories located in close proximity to each other. Now the process has been broken up; parts and sub-assemblies are made in widely separated locations, from one end of the globe to the other.

Giant steel mills that went from purifying iron ore with coke all the way to turning out finished steel have been broken up and replaced by mini-mills, which can be placed almost anywhere. It was the technological assault by the bosses that opened up this general downsizing, in addition to outsourcing and offshoring. The capitalists will undoubtedly take advantage of the coming crisis, as they have done in earlier ones, to institute further job-destroying technological advances.

Another significant development is the transformation of the anti-union, right-to-work South from a textile center into a major industrial and food-processing area. Almost all the auto companies transplanted from Germany and Japan have facilities in the South. Much outsourcing by corporations located in other regions of the United States goes to the South.

With the growth of finance capital and technology, large concentrations of service workers can be found in banks, insurance companies, brokerage houses, and technology firms, among others. These companies are in the process of breaking up the concentrations of workers into smaller units and outsourcing or offshoring some of them to low-wage areas in the U.S. and abroad. There is a permanent state of insecurity among millions of so-called "back-office" workers and even more specialized technology workers.

Thus, in both manufacturing and offices, the workplaces are being broken up into smaller units, relocated to isolated areas or anti-union states, and disbursed over wider and wider geographic areas, including abroad.

The growing retail proletariat

Another prominent economic feature of capitalist restructuring is the growth of low-wage retail service industries. Wal-Mart is now the largest private employer in the U.S., with 1.2 million workers. The growth of retail chains, fast food chains, hotel and restaurant chains, apparel chains, bookstore chains, drug store chains, call centers, janitorial services, low-wage health service jobs, and many others confronts the working class with new strategic challenges of historic proportions.

The growth of these chains, which are largely non-union on a nationwide basis, despite pockets of organization in some of the larger cities (and even that is at very low wages), has to be viewed from two different sides. On the one hand these chains represent tens of thousands of workplaces spread all over the country. Organizing them presents major problems for the labor movement in its present state.

On the other hand, these chains have concentrated millions of workers into intermediate units. Many of these retail jobs were previously dispersed in tens of thousands of small, local stores and family businesses, each with only a few workers. They were generally outside the pool of workers who could be organized. Wal-Mart, Barnes & Noble, Home Depot, etc., have put an enormous number of these local stores out of business. Of course, workers or members of their families expelled from industry or other higher-paying jobs fill many of these lower-paying retail jobs just to survive.

Whereas a small bookstore, local lumberyard, or hardware store might have anywhere from three to fifteen or twenty workers, the average Wal-Mart, depending upon whether it is a regular store or a superstore, could employ several hundred workers. The same goes for Home Depot, Lowe's, Barnes & Noble, the Gap, etc. Thus millions of workers who were once hidden away in tiny shops have been brought out of isolation and into the larger social division of labor of U.S. capitalism. They now form part of the general proletariat.

What has brought this new sector of millions of low-wage retail workers into being? Software makes it possible to track every sale of every item at every cash register from thousands of stores in the retail empires. These sales are linked with inventory systems involving tens of millions of items daily. Barcode scanning is used not only to track sales but also to track the location of shipped items, down to the last box.

Communications and tracking systems follow boxes from the plane or ship to the airport or port, from there to the truck or train, all the way to the shelf. Supertankers, jumbo jets, computerized port machinery, GPS tracking of trucks—all are part of the so-called "logistics" system of globalized capitalism that allows for "just-in-time" delivery at each stage in the transit of commodities and just-in-time retailing. This is modeled after Toyota's infamous "lean" manufacturing, adopted by corporations worldwide, that speeds up workers and squeezes every last second of labor time out of them.

Marx's law of wages confirmed, with a vengeance

Marx showed that the value of labor power is determined by its complexity. Simple labor power, unskilled labor, has the lowest price; more complex labor has a higher price. The entire tendency of capitalism is to reduce complex labor to simple labor and thus reduce wages. To be sure, this requires an increase in the number of very highly skilled and higher-paid workers to create and develop the labor-saving technology. But because their technological products serve to either reduce or eliminate skilled work, high-skilled jobs are a smaller and smaller proportion of the total jobs available and the number of less-skilled jobs grows proportionately larger.

Under capitalism the proportion of lower-skilled jobs to high-skilled jobs goes up with the advance of technology

This has enormous implications for the future of the class struggle in the United States and the entire capitalist world.

It is an axiom of Marxism that, in the absence of working-class organization, competition among workers will allow the bosses to reduce wages in the direction of the absolute minimum necessary to survive—and, if they can get away with it, below the survival level. The weaker the organization of the workers, the greater the competition among them and the lower the wages will be. This is the law of wages under capitalism, which can only be overcome by organization to block or reduce the competition among workers.

The lower the level of skills of the workers, the easier it is for the bosses to replace one with another and the greater the competition among them. The scientific-technological revolution, by reducing the skills of the working class, has laid the basis for the new era of pauperization and universal low-wage capitalism. However, it is also laying the basis for a broad rebellion and the struggle to find new forms of class-wide organization.

Because the labor movement in the U.S. has been in retreat for thirty years, it has failed to hold back this tendency for wages to sink toward the absolute minimum. Thus, the bosses have gained greater and greater momentum in reducing the standard of living of workers, while piling up enormous profits.

But as capitalism heads toward a new period of economic crisis and instability, the workers will be compelled to create new forms of organization and class struggle to counter the crisis, just as they did during the Great Depression of the 1930s.

Successful militant strategies and tactics from the previous periods will have to be revived and refined. But these methods will have to be combined with new and higher forms of organization and class struggle and class solidarity in order to deal with the new crisis and the restructured form of low-wage global capitalism.

14

Building a broad
working-class movement

Struggle against racism and oppression—key to class unity • One-third of
U.S. working class from oppressed nationalities • Katrina disaster called
for working-class action • Women's and LGBT issues are workers' issues
Union cities and urban struggle • Need for other workers' organizations
Marx on unions as organizing centers for the whole class • The Million
Worker March Movement • For a militant, unified labor movement • For
coordinated class-wide struggle

It is important to overcome the current conception in the labor movement
that the struggle of the broad masses outside the unions is somehow off-
limits. To be sure, every labor leader nowadays has learned that it is necessary to link up with the community in some way. This has become a matter
of survival in many instances. But the concept is based **primarily upon
getting the community to help the union**.

Campaigning for social services, to the extent that the AFL-CIO carries
it on, is restricted for the most part to legislative lobbying. There is nothing wrong with lobbying, but it is a totally secondary, subordinate method.
Mass mobilization and struggle is the primary lever when it comes to winning real, meaningful concessions that meet the needs of the people. To
build a powerful workers' movement in this country, bridges of struggle
and support for the mass of the people must be forged.

To take the broadest view of the potential strength of the working class
and organized labor, it is essential to take into account not only the 15 million workers in the unions plus the 50 million workers who say they want a
union, but the hundreds of thousands of activists and community organizers in cities and towns across the country.

The reservoir of strength from this vantage point includes the natural allies and potential members of a broad working-class movement that reaches out and gives leadership in the general struggle to meet the needs and raise the demands of the working class as a whole.

This potential force includes the masses of unorganized workers, the under-employed, and the unemployed struggling to survive. It includes the communities of workers and their families being devastated by home foreclosures and evictions; the groups that have been fighting for immigrant rights; the "living wage" movement; the struggles for universal health care; activists fighting homelessness and demanding affordable housing; neighborhood groups fighting to improve the schools. There are thousands of groups around the country—local, regional, and national—that have been fighting against racism and national oppression, sexism, and gender oppression. They include the anti-war movement; groups fighting to save the environment from devastation by corporate polluters; and opponents of police brutality, the death penalty, and the prison-industrial complex.

All these movements are struggling against the corporate enemies of the working class that are behind the union-busting, the forced concessions, the layoffs, the plant closings, outsourcing, offshoring, and worldwide wage competition. All the reactionary institutions of capitalist society ultimately can be traced to a common enemy—the ruling class—whether they be the profiteering pharmaceutical and insurance companies blocking universal, affordable health care; the oil, coal, and other industrial enemies of the environment and the workers alike; the corporate-financed right-wing enemies of abortion rights and same-sex marriage; or the housing and real estate industry, giant hotel chains, and agribusinesses that live off the low-wage exploitation of undocumented workers.

The workers in the unions and their families dwell in the communities and are themselves the victims of greedy landlords, unscrupulous mortgage brokers, price-gouging food chains, and highway robbery by HMOs and insurance companies. Their children are forced to go to run-down schools. They are faced with unaffordable college education. If they are Black, Latina/o, Asian, or Native, their children or they themselves are confronted with racist police and other forms of discrimination.

The community needs to feel a bond with the unions, and that can only come through support by the labor movement for their struggles. The importance of this can be seen during strikes, boycotts, or other labor campaigns, when community support is crucial.

The unions must not stand aside and remain aloof or indifferent to the vast economic and social needs of the workers as a whole. The deepening stage of low-wage capitalism, with all its attendant suffering for the workers and the oppressed, cries out for the intervention of the labor movement.

The struggle against racism and oppression—key to class unity

"An injury to one is an injury to all" has been a time-tested slogan, together with "United we stand, divided we fall." They refer to the need for union and worker solidarity and express the determination of the workers to combat the never-ending and multifaceted divisive attempts by the bosses to set up competition among them.

The key to broad working-class unity lies in the ability of a significant sector of the white workers and the union leadership to oppose the various forms of racism and national oppression directed at oppressed people—not just at the workers on their jobs, but in everyday life among the population overall.

In the era of low-wage capitalism and particularly in the developing economic crisis, the question of workers' unity will become paramount. In an economic crisis, layoffs and shutdowns break down the organization of the workers, isolate them from one another, and intensify the competition for jobs. A crisis is likely to sharpen the question for the working class and all progressive society of fighting racism and national oppression—a question that has been the Achilles' heel of the labor movement in the U.S. since it began.

The trade unions and the broader workers' movement will face the greatest challenge, but perhaps also the greatest opportunity in history, to achieve broad class unity that reaches across race and nationality. Overcoming the historic, subjective divisions will be a Herculean task. But the objective basis for a strong, multinational united front of the workers has never been stronger.

U.S. working class: over one-third comes from oppressed nationalities

The foundation of this favorable objective situation begins with the changes in the U.S. population and consequently the changes in the composition of the working class. The population of the U.S. by the year 2005 was 296 million, of whom 98 million, or **one-third**, was categorized as "non-white." They were either African American or came mostly from communities formed by people from oppressed and formerly colonized countries. The official breakdown, according to the Census Bureau, was: almost 42 million Latina/os, 36.3 million African Americans, 12 million Asians, 2.3 million Native Americans and Alaskans, 405,000 Native Hawaiians and other Pacific Islanders, and 4.8 million people of more than one "race."[243]

No figures were available for Africans, nor was there a classification for people from the Caribbean who don't speak Spanish or English—i.e., Haitians, among others. Of course, the U.S. government notoriously undercounts oppressed peoples, partly out of plain racism and partly in order to minimize the population count in some districts to reduce their political representation and their access to those government funds that are allocated based on population.

The composition of the working class also reflects globalization and the bosses' search for cheap labor. In 2005, according to the Bureau of Labor Statistics, out of a labor force of 149 million, 43.3 million were from oppressed nationalities and national minorities. The breakdown was 6.5 million Asians, 17 million African Americans, and 19.8 million Latinas/os. These figures do not count Native Americans, Asian Pacific peoples, or people of more than one race.

Furthermore, the labor force consists of people who are both employed and unemployed. But to be classified "unemployed," you have to have looked for a job during the four weeks before the interview. Masses of oppressed people who couldn't find jobs have, by this definition, ceased to be part of the labor force. Furthermore, given that the population as a whole is one-third people of color, and that oppressed people are far more likely to be in the working class than in the middle class or the ruling class, it is highly likely that they are a **greater proportion of the working class than they are of the population as a whole.** In other words, it is highly likely that oppressed workers are **more than one-third of the working class**.

These broad statistics understate the true potential weight of Black, Latina/o, Asian, and all oppressed nationalities in the workforce. Even though the oppressed workers are more than one-third of the labor force nationally, they are majorities in the cities and metropolitan areas throughout the country. In 2005 the oppressed represented a majority in 10 percent of all 3,100 counties in the U.S. But, more important, they were a majority in one-third of the most populous counties, which include the suburbs. Thus, oppressed workers are not only heavily concentrated in the cities but are also being drawn into the suburbs in the search for jobs.[244] They also predominate in agriculture, of course.

The objective basis for achieving a strong degree of class unity is two-fold: on the one hand is the increasing number and proportion of workers from oppressed nationalities in the working class; on the other is the declining economic status of the vast majority of white workers.

Of course, Black, Latina/o, Asian, and Native workers must also counter all attempts by the racist ruling class to divide them from one another.

As white workers are cast down further and further in the direction of low wages and are more subject to layoffs, unemployment, mounting personal debt, and general economic hardship, they move closer to the **economic status** of the oppressed. This forms the objective basis for closer collaboration and unity in the struggle. And it is in the workplace, in common conditions of exploitation, that the need and the pressure for unity becomes urgent in times of battle.

But oppressed workers and all oppressed people in the U.S. live twenty-four hours a day in the **political status of special oppression.** They are super-exploited, getting lower wages than white workers for comparable jobs. They are cast into the worst jobs. They suffer most from any economic downturn because their margin of survival is, on average, far more tenuous than that of white workers. They are the last hired and first fired when it comes to higher-paying jobs. Statistics show that in everything from personal wealth to incidence of preventable diseases, life expectancy, infant mortality, housing conditions, educational opportunity—that is, in virtually every indicator of economic well-being—oppressed people suffer from a status inferior to that of whites.

They also suffer from disproportionate rates of imprisonment, execution, and victimization by police and are subject to constant racial abuse. Furthermore, Black, Latina/o, Asian, and Native peoples are vastly underrepresented at all the levels of political power—from governors, senators, and judges to the highest echelons of the federal bureaucracy and the executive, not to mention the police forces and other repressive agencies of the capitalist machine. This is the essence of special oppression.

The **objective** basis currently being established for unity—that is, the downward leveling of white workers along with all workers—comes about as a result of the automatic processes of capitalist development. It is the result of global restructuring and technological assault. But the **subjective** basis of solidarity does not come about automatically. On the contrary, it must be fought for tenaciously by advanced, class-conscious workers and revolutionaries. White workers must shoulder the primary responsibility for forging unity—working wherever possible with oppressed workers.

In fact, the deeper capitalism sinks into crisis, the more the ruling class will be prone to intensify racism and divisive scapegoating. We have already seen this in the vicious campaign against undocumented workers. This makes the conscious struggle for unity all the more crucial.

Racism and inequality in the U.S. today must be recognized as the legacy of oppression that began shortly after the Pilgrims landed in 1620. It began

Racism and inequality in the U.S. today are the legacy of oppression that began shortly after the Pilgrims landed in 1620 with the removal of whole Native nations and hundreds of tribes from their lands by genocidal violence, the spreading of disease, treachery, and betrayal. The brutal system of chattel slavery and the plantation system were built upon lands stolen from the Native people and populated through the African slave trade.

Two-thirds of Mexico was annexed by military invasion. Chinese workers were imported to build the railroads and perform other labor on the West Coast. Filipino and Latin American workers were brought to work in agriculture and the canneries. Latin American and Caribbean workers and peasants migrated to the U.S. to escape the poverty and oppression imposed on their countries by U.S. big business, backed by U.S. troops and sustained by U.S. puppet governments. In the recent era of advanced globalization and the race by the bosses for low wages, in skilled and unskilled jobs alike, the immigrant population has risen substantially.

The result of this history is that the U.S. is not one nation, all patriotic declarations to the contrary. In addition to being divided into classes, U.S. society contains within its borders a dominant, oppressor nation of whites controlled, structured, and manipulated by the white ruling class, together with a multitude of oppressed peoples of various nationalities who are subject to constant oppression—economic, social, and political.

This steady subjugation and oppression of various nationalities carried out over a period of centuries has been accomplished with the acquiescence of the white majority of the oppressor nation. To be sure, there have been white revolutionaries, radicals, liberals, and progressives who have opposed this oppression and sometimes lost their lives on that account. But in terms of fundamentally changing the relations between the oppressed and the oppressor through solidarity, the resistance to racism has been vastly overwhelmed by ruling class pressure and influence at all levels of the white population—which has been for the most part either apathetic, acquiescent, or outright complicit.

Thus it is the task of the white workers and the organized labor movement as a whole to win the trust of and build bridges to oppressed workers, to end their isolation in this racist society. And this can only be done by bold deeds.

Katrina disaster called for working-class action

For example, a great step forward could and should have been taken to strengthen class unity in the wake of the Katrina disaster. It was the moment for an all-out emergency mobilization of the labor movement to give aid and assistance to the African-American population of New Orleans and the Gulf Coast. There were many obvious avenues of support available, provided the workers were properly motivated.

With the horrors of Katrina on television for days on end, the mass sympathy for the Black population of New Orleans could have been converted into working-class action. This should have been the time to send emergency transportation brigades, medical brigades, construction brigades, etc., as part of a mass mobilization demanding immediate government funds and other measures to deal with the crisis.

Most importantly, financial, material, and political support should have been extended unconditionally to the African-American forces in New Orleans and throughout the South to help underwrite the massive campaign needed to rebuild and thus to make the right of return of the survivors materially possible. A political mobilization raising the demands of the African-American population and directed at the capitalist government in Washington was called for. In this way the labor movement could have helped the Black population gain leverage and helped level the playing field in the struggle with the capitalist state and big business to determine the fate of New Orleans and the Gulf Coast.

Such aid would have immeasurably strengthened local and regional forces in their struggle to prevent the ruling class from taking advantage of the disaster to permanently remove large sections of the Black community and turn New Orleans into a haven for gentrifying real estate developers. Such assistance would have been a concrete exercise in supporting the right of the African-American people to self-determination.

In the wake of the Katrina disaster, a dramatic and highly favorable opportunity existed to educate white workers about the legacy of slavery, about the removal and separation of families. The racism of the Bush administration and the ruling class, which was unfolding before everyone's eyes, could have been related to the more general racism in society as a whole, including among the bosses at the point of production.

Similar arguments can be made about the historic May Day Boycott of 2006 by millions of immigrant workers. The labor movement, and most of the progressive movement, for that matter, threw away an opportunity to build solidarity in the struggle against the Bush administration and against reactionary demagogues trying to foment suspicion and hostility toward undocumented workers, blaming them for budget cuts, the decline in social services, the overcrowding of schools, and so on.

Plans for the May Day demonstration were known long enough in advance to begin an educational campaign about how the hardships caused by budget cutbacks are the result of giveaways to the corporations—especially the trillion dollars handed over to the military-industrial complex for the wars in Iraq and Afghanistan and the tax cuts for the rich. This elementary education could have laid the basis for a large section of the labor movement to march side by side in solidarity with the millions of immigrants who came out on International Workers Day in cities throughout the country in 2006.

To be sure, such acts of solidarity require a relatively high level of class-consciousness. It is easy to point out what was needed and another thing to get it done. It would be completely counter-productive to merely criticize the labor bureaucrats for what they have not done and let it go at that. To do so would lead to cynicism and demoralization; it could turn activists away from the labor movement and from the workers in general.

Genuine Marxists strive to find any and all paths to the struggle of workers against capitalism. They do not throw up their hands in frustration, but rather seek those theoretical and practical avenues to prepare for future openings for struggle. That is why it is necessary to see social phenomena in their development, including the labor movement. The objective conditions that have reinforced the separation of the organized working class from the struggle against racism and national oppression are being demolished by capitalism itself. Just as the relatively privileged position of the higher-paid white male workers has been the economic basis for the conservative labor leadership, it has also been the basis of racism or indifference to oppression.

The new generation of white workers, the "second tier," so to speak, which is coming into the workforce under the new harsh conditions of restructured, globalized, ruthless, low-wage capitalism in crisis, will be far more amenable to an appeal for solidarity as a matter of survival than were the older generations, which grew up in the era of imperialist prosperity, with its relatively high wages and job security. In a crisis, moreover, many older workers can be awakened to struggle.

Furthermore, when the class struggle heats up, oppressed workers—who combine the energy of the struggle against racism with resistance to class exploitation—will emerge inevitably as a major force in the leadership and a crucial part of the vanguard in the class struggle. The prospects for unity in the period now on the horizon pose the greatest challenges. They also present the greatest possibilities for making strides forward.

Women's and LGBT issues are workers' issues

Sexist attitudes that emanate from every avenue of capitalist propaganda and cultural conditioning pave the way for the special oppression of women. Women are routinely paid less than men—both when doing the same work and in so-called women's occupations.

Rarely referred to today, despite all the capitalist demagogy about "spreading democracy," "perfecting democracy," ad nauseam, is the fact that Congress never passed the Equal Rights Amendment (ERA), a simple amendment to the U.S. Constitution declaring women to have equal rights.

The amendment consists of just three sentences and has repeatedly been introduced in Congress since 1923. It was put in motion and actually passed both houses of Congress in 1972, at the height of the women's movement. But it was shelved in 1982 because it failed to get the required passage by three-quarters of the state legislatures.

> *The capitalist class has such a profound interest in women's oppression that it blocked a constitutional amendment affirming equal rights*

The operative first part reads: "Section 1. Equality of rights under the law shall not be denied or abridged by the United States or by any State on account of sex."

The capitalist class has such profound interests in women's oppression that it blocked the passage of this elementary statement of democratic rights, which affects one-half of the population.

While biology determines the fact that women bear children, the women's movement has long fought to abolish the idea that "biology is destiny." But society determines women's role in child rearing and housework, as well as their overall social and economic status. The capitalist patriarchy forces women into the role of providing unpaid labor in child rearing. Women bear the primary burden of bringing up the next generation of workers with endless hours of unpaid labor taking care of children and the household. The socially useful labor they perform, labor without which society would cease to function, is treated as purely personal, uncompensated labor. This problem is thrust upon the family, both working class and middle class. But it falls most heavily upon poorer working-class households, and particularly on Black, Latina/o, Asian, Native, and Arab women, who are doubly oppressed.

When women enter the labor force to be exploited by some boss, capitalist society does not relieve them of the enforced role of also providing the unpaid labor of household work and child rearing. Social labor at the workplace is piled on top of the personal labor expected and performed at home. This has been referred to as the "second shift." And in the new era of low-wage capitalism, women often work a "third shift," with added responsibilities having to take care of grown children, the elderly, and other extended family members who cannot find jobs, have lost jobs, become ill, gone into debt, or run out of retirement funds.

These social roles are applied to women whether they have children or not, whether they fit into the stereotypes of what women should do and look like or not. In fact, lesbians, bisexual, and transsexual women are often singled out for the most extreme harassment and violence precisely because they do not conform to the social roles patriarchal society prescribes.

The legacy of slavery in the United States and the racist, sexist treatment of African-American women, as well as the super-exploitation of immigrant women from Asia, Africa, Latin America, and the Middle East, all find their expression in the targeting of these women for the lowest-paid, most menial jobs and for sexual exploitation.

The onset of a right-wing reaction after the upsurge of the women's movement of the 1960s was reflected in the steady assault on abortion rights and all reproductive rights, the epidemic of violence against women, including battering and widespread sexual abuse and harassment, the growing trafficking in women and girls, and all forms of oppression of women—economic, social, and political.

These are all issues that must be on the agenda of the workers' movement.

The "feminization of labor" is a worldwide phenomenon, most prevalent in sweatshops around the globe. This phenomenon, which arises out of the capitalists' search for low-wage labor, has become more and more pronounced in the U.S. with each passing year. In 2006, when official figures put the labor force at 151 million, 70 million or over 45 percent were women. According to the latest figures, 44 percent of the organized labor movement is made up of women.

This growth in the number of women workers, organized and unorganized, is bound to bring more and more women into the leadership of the workers' movement and expand its agenda to include both economic and political rights for women. No genuine working-class movement can succeed or progress without taking up all the demands for women's rights and equality that are needed to free women from the age-old oppression that has relegated them to second-class social status.

The oppression of lesbian, gay, bi, and trans (LGBT) people is directly derived from the patriarchal idea that men and women have narrow, prescribed roles, with women (and children) being the property of the man. Anyone not conforming to these narrow roles is labeled an outcast and targeted for special abuse and violence. Like the women's liberation movement beginning in the 1960s, the gay liberation movement sought to win rights for lesbian, gay, bi, and trans people and educate the population about this special oppression. Demands for equal pay, an end to discrimination and gay bashing, rights for partners, and gay marriage were put on the agenda for the working-class movement to take up. The fight for health-care rights in the midst of the AIDS crisis also became a matter of life and death.

Statistics on wage and income discrimination against the LGBT community are difficult to obtain because the Census Bureau does not gather data on sexual preference or gender identification in its questionnaires. This puts the LGBT community at a disadvantage in proving discrimination. In a similar way the French government, claiming that everyone in France is equal, refuses to collect statistics on nationalities of French residents, so that the oppressed can never prove racist discrimination.

Since the 1990 U.S. Census was taken, limited concessions have been made by using roundabout methods. In 1990 it was permitted to designate same-sex partners in a household. However, if the partners claimed they were married, the sex of one partner was changed and the partners were designated as heterosexual married couples. In 2000, the Census Bureau changed the process and allowed both "spousal" same-sex couples and unmarried same-sex couples to be classified as same-sex households. [245]

The undercount is vast. Lesbian or gay people living alone, regardless of whether they are single or in a relationship, are not counted. Bi and trans people have no classification. In addition, many LGBT people may be fearful of identifying themselves on a government form.

Nevertheless, despite limited statistics, researchers have been able to uncover that lesbian and gay families live in 99.3 percent of all counties in the U.S. There were 601,000 lesbian and gay families officially reported. Researchers are struggling to get economic statistics to clarify the picture. For example, one UCLA study in 2005 showed that same-sex couples with children have an average household income $12,000 lower and a home ownership rate 15 percent lower than heterosexual couples with children. This is significant because more than 39 percent of same-sex couples in the U.S. age 25 to 55 are raising children.[246]

Other findings include the fact that partnered gay men earn $3,000 a year less than men partnered with women.[247] In 1999 lower-educated partnered gay workers had annual incomes averaging $600 below straight men in the eleven states that protect against discrimination. But in the rest of the states, where there is no protection against such discrimination, gay workers earn an average of $5,700 less than heterosexual workers.[248]

These limited and scattered findings indicate the economic discrimination faced by the LGBT population. They also contradict the stereotypes that are often reinforced in the mass media that gay men are better off economically than straight men and that the LGBT population in general has more disposable income because they do not have children—neither of which is true.

If the slogan of the working class movement is "an injury to one is an injury to all," then the fight for women's and LGBT rights is an integral part of that struggle.

Union cities and urban struggle

When John Sweeney first became president of the AFL-CIO in 1995, he raised hopes for a labor revival by uttering phrases like "I'd rather block bridges than build bridges," meaning he would rather engage in militant struggle than build bridges to the employers. Among other things, he proposed to create "union cities" built around state and city central labor councils. The councils would become the center of alliances between the labor movement and various community organizations. The proposal had the sound of wanting to establish the unions as a center of united struggle in the cities.

Many progressive and militant organizers took it seriously and attempted to promote the concept. In a number of cities alliances were built with the community to aid in organizing drives and the struggle for living wage legislation. Attempts were made to create a pro-union, pro-worker political environment. But the AFL-CIO, despite the urgings of some local leaders, never really got behind the idea with anything like the resources that it needed. It frequently emphasized getting electoral allies as the primary method of making gains for the workers.

Like many militant-sounding slogans, the concept of "union cities" was never actually aimed at building the kind of struggle really needed in the cities. The cities were impoverished by decades of service cutbacks, layoffs and plant closings, racism, police brutality, invasion of drugs into the oppressed communities, declining schools, decay of housing, etc. Even a limited form of the concept was implemented only in a few cities.

But this idea, or some modified version of union cities, has vast potential in the hands of militant rank-and-file workers and community leaders. The urban centers hold the greatest concentrations of workers and are the places where their relative strength is also greatest. As the crisis of capitalism deepens, they are becoming more and more centers of poverty, unemployment, low wages, hunger, police brutality, and overall oppression.

Local and state governments stand by as foreclosures and evictions proceed. Layoffs and plant closings continue to devastate communities while mayors and city councils claim to be powerless to stop the onslaught. Constitutional and legal arguments can be easily established that require the authorities at every level of government to take preventive measures in order to avert either natural or social disasters that threaten the population.

When the people face dire circumstances but the authorities are derelict in their duties to protect the population against assaults by corporations, banks, mortgage companies, and landlords, it is entirely legitimate and fitting that a workers' movement use direct means to assert their democratic rights and mobilize militant resistance to combat layoffs, foreclosures, evictions, hunger, or other suffering.

Properly applied, the implementation of "union cities" or a similar concept could proclaim the right to food, to housing, to a job, to health care. It could be a rallying cry to the people to enforce those rights.

According to the federal government, as of 2005, almost 40 million people were in families that suffered from so-called "food insecurity."[249] These people are disproportionately Black, Latina/o, Asian, and Native, but also include millions of poor white workers and are disproportionately children. In cities where people are hungry and cannot afford food, yet supermarkets and warehouses are filled with it, it is perfectly legitimate to demand that food be made available to all at affordable prices.

In recent years municipal and state governments have been spending more than $30 billion a year to entice companies to set up shop within their boundaries. In every city, industrial corporations of all types, big-box chains like Wal-Mart, and real estate interests and developers have been given billions of dollars in subsidies in the form of tax abatements, wage subsidies, gifts of public land, lowered income taxes, free construction of special infrastructure, cash payments, and so forth.[250] In the struggle of different localities to attract businesses, state and city governments dole out massive "incentives." Companies have been given legal waivers, favorable zoning, promises of low wages, and all the advantages necessary to exploit the workers and the community as a whole. State and local governments have offices of special representatives whom they send out to woo big business at home and abroad with giveaways that are ultimately paid for by the masses in the communities.

These corporations, after getting rich in the communities they were bribed to move into, can then decide to bust or damage the unions, lay off workers, or just pick up and leave—abandoning the community in crisis. A movement led by the workers but involving all sectors of the community would have every right to stop the layoffs and closing of plants. A broad alliance between the unions and all elements of the community could carry out the kinds of militant mass mobilizations necessary to enforce not only the right to keep jobs in the community, but also to open up jobs for the unemployed.

Workers and their families have a legitimate claim to their homes or apartments based not only upon years of payments but also on the general right to housing, which must be established as a fundamental human right. Workers have a right to be shielded against predatory lenders and landlords.

Need for other workers' organizations

As the economic turmoil deepens, the urgent need is to keep the rich, the corporate profiteers and financial parasites from pushing the crisis of capitalism onto the backs of the workers. The fight against unemployment, poverty, hunger, evictions, racist scapegoating, imprisonment of the poor, and so on will become paramount.

But the struggle of the workers does not arise on schedule or according to a plan. The tempo and direction of the crisis are what determine when and where the struggle will break out and what needs arise for working-class organization. No one can predict just what forms the workers' movement will take; it may be highly multifaceted. This is most likely to be the case at the beginning of the struggle, before it is possible to create a centralizing or coordinating force.

Of course, on the one hand the labor movement has the resources, the numbers, and the organization to play a significant role in creating the kind of solidarity and unity so necessary to launch a wide social movement capable of countering the attacks coming down on the people. On the other hand, the labor leadership may be a conservative obstacle to the masses at the very moment they are in dire need of organizations to fight for their needs and push back the bosses' attacks.

Tens of millions of workers are not in unions; millions more will not even have jobs and thus will not have access to a union. These workers are for the most part the poorest and most oppressed among the masses.

Unemployed workers, particularly during an economic crisis, need to fight for jobs or for income for themselves and their families. Organizations demanding jobs or income will arise outside the unions. If a worker has been unemployed for a long time or is trying to enter the labor force for the first time but cannot get a job, then that worker is not eligible for unemployment insurance. The capitalist government and the corporations must inevitably be held responsible.

During the 1930s the Communist Party helped organize the Unemployed Councils. The councils were established after demonstrations in most major cities on March 6, 1930, under the slogan "Wages or Work—Don't Starve, Fight!" Some estimates claim that over a million people participated around the country. Pitched battles were fought after police attacked the demonstrations. When the councils were formed soon after, they organized the unemployed as well as struggles against eviction. Many tens of thousands of families were put back in their homes through these mass actions.

In the nineteen thirties many tens of thousands of evicted workers were put back in their homes by mass action

There were other organizations and struggles. In 1932 an estimated 20,000 World War I veterans, most of them jobless, camped in Washington for six weeks demanding early payment of promised bonuses from the government. The Bonus Marchers were attacked by the U.S. military, under the command of Gen. Douglas MacArthur.

The Sharecroppers Union in the South united poor Black and white sharecroppers against the Southern landowners despite racism and even lynching.

A nationwide campaign was conducted in the 1930s to save the Scottsboro defendants—nine young Black men ranging in age from twelve to nineteen who were framed up on charges of raping a white woman.

In more recent times the United Farm Workers (UFW), a merger of Chicano and Filipino agricultural workers' associations, waged a long struggle to get contracts in the fields in the 1960s, despite the indifference of the AFL-CIO and the outright hostility of the Teamsters leadership. The UFW used boycotts, demonstrations, and strikes and pioneered in developing a base within working class communities. Agricultural workers were excluded from coverage by the National Labor Relations Act of 1935 which meant that their right to organize was not protected under the law. The struggle forced the government to establish the Agricultural Relations Board in 1974 to enforce labor laws for agricultural workers.

The National Welfare Rights Organization in the late 1960s and 1970s fought to protect and expand the rights of millions of workers forced onto public assistance because of the lack of jobs and childcare. The NWRO filled a vacuum left by the labor movement, which ignored this section of the working class.

Organizations sprung up defending the rights of domestic workers, also disregarded by the labor leadership. These low-paid, mostly oppressed women workers were excluded from coverage under the National Labor Relations Act. They were also excluded from the Fair Labor Standards Act until 1974 after pressure from domestic workers organizations. The movement fought for standard contracts with domestic-worker employment agencies. These struggles are still alive today and they belong on the agenda of labor.

Workers' centers, day laborer organizations, and numerous other organizations have been established outside the official labor movement as a result of the historic neglect of immigrant workers, documented and undocumented.

Freedom unions, beginning with the Mississippi Freedom Labor Union, were formed in the South by the Student Non-Violent Coordinating Committee (SNCC) during the Civil Rights movement. Black caucuses were formed throughout industrial unions in the 1960s to combat racism by the companies and union leadership. Dodge Revolutionary Union Movement (DRUM) led the struggle against Chrysler and the UAW. It was followed by other UAW caucuses which formed the League of Revolutionary Black Workers (LRBW).

A present-day example of a working class organization that plays a vital role in the workers' struggle but reaches beyond the labor movement is the Black Workers for Justice (BWFJ) operating out of North Carolina. The BWFJ traces its roots to organizations like the LRBW. It is instrumental in the organization of the United Electrical, Radio, and Machine Workers of America (UE) Local 150 and pioneered the organization of public sector workers in the "right-to-work" state of North Carolina. State law makes it illegal for any government worker to join a union.

BWFJ has tirelessly promoted the struggle for the reconstruction of New Orleans and the Gulf Coast in the wake of Hurricane Katrina. It promotes the struggle for reconstruction as a fight for African-American self-determination and class power for the Black working class majority in New Orleans, the Gulf Coast, and the South in general.

The group took the initiative to forge the African American/Latino Alliance including the Farm Labor Organizing Committee (FLOC), North Carolina Occupational Safety and Health Project and the Raleigh Postal Workers Union. The vital struggle for Black-Brown unity grew out of the need to unite the Black workers with the growing number of Latina/o immigrants in the state. The need for such unity has proven to be even more important with time as the witch-hunt against undocumented workers has escalated along with ruling class schemes to sow divisions.

The BWFJ has historically linked civil rights with workers' rights. While the BWFJ organizes with UE it also supports the struggle of other unions. It helped the UFCW win a historic victory over the Delta Pride Catfish Company in Indianola, Mississippi, by forging alliances with community and civil rights groups. Indianola is the place where the White Citizens Councils were founded to give the KKK a legal face to oppose the Civil Rights Movement. The 1990 Delta Pride catfish workers' strike of mainly Black women was the largest strike in the history of Mississippi.

BWFJ led a campaign for the sanitation workers in Raleigh, North Carolina, and organized in the universities. It has also supported the UFCW fighting the viciously anti-labor Smithfield company in the struggle to organize oppressed workers in the largest pork factory in the world.

BWFJ runs schools of political and general education for workers. It views the South as part of the globalization process and part of the "global south." The BWFJ has pointed out time and again how the failure of the labor movement to organize the South has led to runaway shops, a steady stream of outsourcing to union-free, low-wage territory. Japanese and European investment flows into the South to compete with U.S. capital in super-exploiting U.S. workers. It has waged a political campaign against the right-to-work laws in North Carolina and has generally set an example for working class solidarity within the framework of fighting for the rights of the African-American working class and attempting to promote the organization of the South.

In the crisis now unfolding, a revitalized workers' movement, in order to be effective, will have to draw in all the sectors that have either been left out or marginalized. All workers' movements and working-class communities must have a place in the struggle that takes into account their particular needs, without being subordinated or subjected to bureaucratic leadership. This includes the fight for jobs, for income, for the right to a home and food. Occupations, mass demonstrations, strikes, and every form of struggle will be required. This is the road to a renewed workers' movement encompassing the unions and the far broader sections of the working class whose fighting spirit must be mobilized on the basis of addressing their needs.

Marx on unions as organizing centers for the whole class

Karl Marx delivered an address to the General Council of the International Workingmens' Association (the First International) in 1866. Included was a section on "The Future of the Unions." This passage, along with many others, is as relevant today for the labor movement as it was back in 1866 when it was first delivered.

> Apart from their original purpose, they [the unions] must now learn to act deliberately as organizing centers of the working class in the broad interest of its **complete emancipation**. They must aid every social and political movement tending in that direction. Considering themselves as acting as the champions of the whole working class, they cannot fail to enlist the non-society men [the unorganized—FG] into their ranks. They must look carefully after the interests of the worst paid trades, such as agricultural

laborers, rendered powerless by exceptional circumstances. They must convince the world at large that their efforts, far from being narrow and selfish, aim at the emancipation of the downtrodden millions.

–**Karl Marx** *from "Instructions for the Delegates of the Provisional General Council" delivered at the Geneva Congress of the First International, September 1866.*[251]

Karl Marx directed this passage to the advanced workers of the time in Europe. He was attempting to intervene in the developing trade union movement, which was reviving and growing after the defeat of the revolutions of 1848 and the subsequent suppression of the workers.

This was the early stage of the union movement and the dominant forces were primarily workers in the skilled trades. The earliest General Council of the First International was made up of tailors, shoemakers, carpenters, furniture makers, weavers, a mason, a watchmaker, a musical instrument maker, and a hairdresser. The powerful force behind the International was the London Trades Council, representing numerous organized trades in what was then the center of world capitalism and colonialism. It was not only the development of the unions and the class struggle that caused Marx to intervene, but also growing internationalism. It was the workers themselves who initiated the International. Marx became the heart and soul of it after the workers declared their intentions.

The genesis of the move toward international solidarity was the importation of strikebreakers from continental Europe by the English capitalists. The wages of craft workers were lower on the Continent. French workers had not yet gained the right to organize. In November 1863, the English workers drew up a letter to the French workers. This is an excerpt:

> A fraternity of peoples is highly necessary for the cause of labor, for we find that whenever we attempt to better our social condition by reducing the hours of toil, or by raising the price of labor, our employers threaten us with bringing over Frenchmen, Germans, or Belgians and others to do our work at a reduced rate of wages; and we are sorry to say, that this has been done, though not from any desire on the part of our continental brethren to injure us, but through a want of regular and systematic communications between the industrial classes of all countries. Our aim is to bring up the wages of the ill-paid to as near a level as possible with that of those who are better remunerated, and not to allow our employers to play us off one against the other, and so drag us down to the lowest possible condition, suitable to their avaricious bargaining.[252]

On September 28, 1864, workers from Paris brought the French reply to be presented to a packed St. Martin's Hall in London. After the English letter was read, the French read their reply. Here is a short excerpt:

Industrial progress, the division of labor, freedom of trade—these are three factors which should receive our attention today, for they promise to change the very substance of the economic life of society. Compelled by the force of circumstances and the demands of the time, capital is concentrating and organizing in mighty financial and industrial combinations. Should we not take some defensive measure, this force, if not counter-balanced in some way, will soon be a despotic power. We, the workers of the world, must unite and erect an insurmountable barrier to the baleful system which would divide humanity into two classes: a host of hungry and brutalized people on the one hand, and a clique of fat, overfed mandarins on the other. Let us seek our salvation through solidarity.[253]

The trade unionists who formed the First International were not communists. There were many tendencies represented. Marx was admired and became a major figure in the proceedings once he joined, but very few adhered to Marxism. Marx's task was to frame a program for the International, acceptable to all the various tendencies, that would push the movement forward, not only in the direction of internationalism, but also in the direction of mobilizing a class-wide movement that would go beyond the limited confines of the trade unions, as they were then constituted.

Marx declared that the future task of the trade unions was to reach out to the poor and the oppressed, the lowest paid, the unorganized, and push forward political and social movements that would aid in the emancipation of the working class as a whole.

Marx was fully aware of the need for a working-class political party to lead the struggle for power. In his inaugural address to the International in 1864, he lauded the simultaneous progress being made in England, Germany, France, and Italy in the formation of a workers' political party. He had no intention of substituting the unions for the party. But he was appealing to the unionists to expand their view. Marx regarded the unions as the fundamental nucleus of class organization of the workers. He was trying to steer the union leaders in the direction of becoming the center of a broad workers' movement to promote the political and social aims of all workers.

Marx's projection was unrealized at the time. The First International was created in the era just prior to the expansion of British imperialism, which would see Britain's colonies converted into vast sources of raw materials for its industrial machine and British monopolies expand on the international arena.

The rise of British imperialism and the super-profits that flowed to its industrial capitalists laid the basis for the bribery of the upper stratum of the British working class, the growth of the labor aristocracy, the supremacy of narrow trade unionism, and the cooptation of the unions by the Liberals and then the Labor Party. In fact, in the 1867 Reform Law, when voting rights were expanded to include the workers, some of the most important trade union leaders shifted away from the class struggle. They not only sought parliamentary careers but they also promoted elections as the fundamental instrument of progress for the workers.

While Marx's criteria for the success of the trade union movement were not limited to its ability to gain improvements in wages and conditions, he regarded fighting for the economic needs of the membership as necessary and fundamental.

In the same "Instructions for the Delegates" cited above, he wrote about the early days of unions:

> Capital is concentrated social force, while the workman has only to dispose of his working force.... The only social power of the workmen is their number. The force of numbers, however, is broken by disunion. This disunion of the workmen is created and perpetuated by the **unavoidable competition among themselves**.
>
> Trade unions originally sprang up from the **spontaneous** attempts of workmen at removing or at least checking that competition, in order to conquer such terms of contract as might raise them at least above the condition of mere slaves. The immediate object of Trades' Unions was therefore confined to everyday necessities, to expediences for the obstruction of the incessant encroachments of capital, in one word, to questions of wages and time of labor. This activity of the Trades' Unions is not only legitimate, it is necessary. It cannot be dispensed with so long as the present system of production lasts. On the contrary, it must be generalized by the formation and combination of Trades' Unions throughout all countries.[254] [Emphasis in original.]

Having explained the foundation of the unions, how they originate in the economic struggle, Marx goes on to describe their future role as that of building the broadest, class-wide, liberating workers' movement that participates in political and social movements and fights for the class as a whole.

Marx's expectation that the union movement would grow into a genuine mass movement of the workers was not realized because it came **on the eve of an era of growing stratification among the workers, of privileges granted to the upper layers of skilled trades and bourgeois pragmatic trade union narrowness,** which was the foundation for a bribed labor leadership. His projection, however, was anticipating the sharpening of class contradictions between the workers, especially in England, and the avaricious bourgeoisie. Instead, these clashes were softened by the growth of London's imperialist empire.

Let us fast forward to the present situation in the U.S. and talk about the future of unions in this country.

Marx's projection of what was needed for the working class is even more applicable in the U.S. today than it was in Europe in the 1860s. It is applicable precisely because the **working class today is facing a new era of draconian leveling downward of the vast majority of workers, and this coincides with the onset of a deepening economic and world crisis for Wall Street.**

The concerns of the French workers, in their letter read at St. Martin's Hall, were that "industrial progress, the division of labor, freedom of trade—these are three factors which should receive our attention today, for they promise to change the very substance of the economic life of society." They were remarkably prescient. They singled out some of the core features of capitalism that are still operative and shaping the world, albeit on a much larger scale.

In their contemporary application, "industrial development" translates into the scientific-technological revolution, automation, computerization, and so on. The "division of labor" has developed on a monumentally complex scale, allowing the bosses to create a worldwide wage competition based on a higher development of the socialization of production.

Their denunciation of the "freedom of trade" was directed against the ferocious capitalist competition for markets that manifested itself in improving technology, lowering skills, and lowering wages. The bosses used the argument for "free trade" in the same way that "competitiveness" is used against workers today. The difference is that today, capitalist competition is being carried out by giant imperialist monopolies struggling for world markets as they wreak havoc on the lives of workers, farm laborers, and peasants, from India to Mexico to North Carolina. The capitalist market, manipulated by the monopolies and dependent on the intervention of state power against the workers when need be, is used as a battering ram against the working masses everywhere.

The "substance of economic life" is being transformed in a negative direction daily and hourly for the workers and the oppressed, in the U.S. and everywhere on the globe, by these very same forces of capitalism. The form in which they play out has changed, but not their content. Salvation still lies in the solidarity of the workers of the world.

The Million Worker March Movement

Is the kind of trade union movement that Marx envisaged—when he urged those gathered around the First International to fight for the downtrodden, the low-paid, and the unorganized and to be part of every social and political movement—merely a hypothetical abstraction?

In fact, the embryonic development of such a movement manifested itself, with a clear political vision from an advanced sector of the labor movement, during 2004. The Million Worker March Movement (MWMM) came forward with an independent working-class program during the spring of that year, in an attempt to galvanize sections of the union movement and the entire progressive, radical, and revolutionary movement. The MWMM issued a call to build a movement and unite in a demonstration in Washington in October around the slogan "Organizing in Our Own Name and Putting Forth an Independent Workers' Agenda."

The MWMM coalition was initiated by Black leaders from Local 10 of the International Longshore and Warehouse Union in San Francisco, which has the largest African-American membership on the West Coast. The local is also the most racially diverse in the area, including Blacks, Latinas/os, Asians, and women. It was joined by Black and other progressive unionists from around the country.

Local 10 has a militant history of anti-racism and international solidarity. It has been in the vanguard of the struggle for economic and social justice. It refused to unload cargo from apartheid South Africa beginning in 1977, including a ten-day boycott of the Nedlloyd Kimberly ship in 1984. In 1978 the union refused to load bomb parts going to the fascist dictatorship in Chile, thus exposing U.S. military aid to the Augusto Pinochet regime. In 1981 the ILWU imposed an embargo on military cargo for the U.S.-backed death squad regime in El Salvador and later joined a boycott of Salvadoran coffee.[255]

Local 10 organized solidarity for the world-renowned African-American political prisoner, journalist, and liberation fighter Mumia Abu-Jamal, known as the "voice of the voiceless." He has been on death row since 1982 after being framed up by the Philadelphia police. After Hurricane Katrina, Local 10 organized the shipping of containers of clothing and other supplies to New Orleans, raised funds, and invited survivors to speak in the Bay Area and the Pacific Northwest. On May 1, 2008, Local 10 initiated within the ILWU a one-day general strike of West Coast dockworkers against the war in Iraq.

Local 10's roots were in the historic 1934 San Francisco general strike referred to earlier, led by Harry Bridges. In this sense the MWMM represents a direct historical continuity with the legacy of the 1930s and the high point of the labor movement.

Despite a boycott and sabotage by the AFL-CIO leadership at all levels, the MWMM call reverberated among important Black trade unionists and progressive labor councils. Among its supporters were the Black Workers for Justice, with a twenty-five-year record of organizing in racist right-to-work states of the South, especially North Carolina and South Carolina; the Teamsters Black Caucus and Teamsters Local 808 out of New York City; AFSCME

District Council 1707 representing low-paid social service workers, a majority of them African-American and Caribbean women; the Coalition of Black Trade Unionists; the Charleston (South Carolina) Labor Council; the Farm Labor Organizing Committee; the San Francisco Day Laborers, and many others in the California Bay Area and New York State.

The Million Worker March Movement called for the workers to establish their own political identity

There was also support from a limited number of other areas, including the anti-imperialist wing of the anti-war movement, some peace groups, student groups, academics, religious progressives, and celebrities such as Danny Glover and Dick Gregory.

The MWMM put forward a detailed set of elementary democratic demands. What made their program noteworthy was the fact that it called for the workers to establish their own political identity as workers and that it went far beyond the narrow political horizons of the AFL-CIO leadership. It claimed the right and necessity of the workers to demand a say in all aspects of capitalist politics and economics—from Social Security to war to the struggle over sexual preference, from a living wage for all to an end to global warming and the preservation of the ecosystem.

It called for the repeal of the anti-labor Taft-Hartley Act as well as the repeal of the Patriot Act and the Anti-Terrorism Act. It demanded "universal, single-payer health care from cradle to grave" as "a right of all people." The MWMM demanded amnesty for all undocumented workers, an end to NAFTA, and an end to all racist and discriminatory acts, including those based on sexual orientation or gender in the workplace and in the communities.

The MWMM called for "an end to both the criminalization of poverty and the prison-industrial complex." It called for "guaranteed pensions that sustain a decent life for all working people." It aimed to "slash the military budget and recover trillions of dollars stolen from our labor to enrich the corporations that profit from war." Thus it introduced the important concept that when the capitalist government takes billions from workers' taxes and hands it over to the military-industrial complex, this is just another form, in addition to direct exploitation at the workplace, in which the ruling class steals workers' labor.

This was further elaborated in a subsequent demand to "extend democracy to our economic structure so that all decisions ... are made by working people who produce all value through their labor." This conception has unlimited application in the struggle for jobs, workers' rights on the job, and the right to keep workplaces open.

There were demands to fund "a vast army of teachers," a free mass-transit system, a national living wage, a program for affordable housing and an end to homelessness, and many other demands that affect the lives of all workers.

The program raised democratic political demands against oppression and reaction side-by-side with social and economic demands for the benefit of the broadest masses. No document such as this had emerged from any section of the labor movement in generations. It had a truly liberating aspect to it.

The demonstration itself fell short of expectations and the MWMM was unable to reach the considerable potential inherent in the appeal of its program. But this was largely because the labor leadership and the social democrats in the political movement were fanatically dedicated at the time to the election of John Kerry, the Democratic presidential candidate.

The MWMM demonstration was an implied declaration of independence from the Democrats. In fact, one of the factors that led to the calling of the demonstration was that the labor leaders were pouring hundreds of millions of dollars into the coffers of the Democratic Party at a time when the labor movement desperately needed to expand its organizing and support workers' struggles already in progress.

The labor leaders not only boycotted the march but engaged in sabotage by lobbying against it behind the scenes. Social democrats of all stripes outside the labor movement would have been hard pressed to disagree with any of the specific democratic demands put forward by the MWMM. Nevertheless, forces in the peace and "social justice" movements regarded an independent working-class movement as a challenge to the strategy of relying on the Democratic Party. They tightly withheld all support and stayed away from the march.

The MWMM was a bold affirmation that Black working-class leadership was ready to step forward with a highly progressive, comprehensive program for an independent working-class movement. Its demands were calculated to unite the workers with the community and the entire movement. It fell on deaf ears among the bureaucrats of the AFL-CIO.

Whether or not the MWMM and its program will be revived in its present form, sooner or later a similar current will have to reemerge among advanced forces within the labor movement. The labor leadership is slavishly dependent upon the Democratic Party and is squandering hundreds of millions of dollars of workers' dues in the 2008 presidential campaign. The leaders are throwing it away in the hope that they can get some voice in the future administration, after having been shut out by Bush for eight years.

But when the smoke clears, whoever gets into the White House, the attacks by the bosses on the workers and the oppressed will continue, particularly if the economic crisis deepens further. All the so-called "friends of labor" (if there are any left in the Democratic Party) will not substitute for the independent class struggle. As this becomes apparent after the elections are over, programs of the type initiated by the MWMM for an independent workers' movement will surely resurface.

For a militant, unified labor movement

The unfolding struggle in the United States must begin on its present-day foundations. But those foundations were established in the 1930s and have been significantly eroded since then. They will have to be fortified and extended in order to cope with restructured capitalism. An expansion of working-class unity and solidarity in the struggle must be the basis of any renewed foundation.

The formation of the CIO was a great advance over the craft unionism of the previous period. The CIO broke from the AFL and opened its doors to millions of lower-paid, less-skilled industrial workers. Despite this great advance, however, the CIO retained features developed under the AFL that were inherently restrictive of the class struggle, features that carried forward through the later merger of the AFL-CIO in 1955. These features still exist today, after the break-away from the AFL-CIO by Change to Win.

Under the AFL, the craft unions that were part of the federation operated largely independently of one another. Union autonomy was a cardinal rule and foundation of the federation. Its central functions were limited to issuing charters, ruling on jurisdiction, lobbying, and publicity. Each craft jealously guarded its turf.

When the CIO was formed, it expanded the central functions to include economic research, legislative and political lobbying, programs on civil rights, community and health services, and industrial safety—in addition to raising financial support for organizing. But, like the AFL, each of the industrial unions had virtual autonomy and looked after its own narrow interests.

There was no attempt among the union leaders to move toward a confederation in which the mode of operation was coordinated action in the class struggle. This conception, which has been adopted with great success in Europe, Asia, and Latin America, was anathema to leaders of both the CIO and the AFL. The CIO adopted the same narrow, every-union-for-itself attitude. Deals were made at the top when it came to parceling out jurisdiction. Raiding and competition also existed among the industrial unions.

The word "international" as a designation for a union merely referred to the fact that U.S. unions also had Canadian affiliates. The working-class internationalism implied by the name was not practiced. On the contrary, the CIO and later the AFL-CIO gave aid to the ruling class, working with the CIA and various bourgeois subversive organizations in the war against communist, socialist, and all progressive unions abroad.

Despite official recognition that the old Cold War AFL-CIO policies were reactionary, the present AFL-CIO leadership works with the congressionally supported National Endowment for Democracy. The AFL-CIO leadership worked with the State Department in 2001 through its Solidarity Center, to strategize with the CTV, a reactionary, corrupt union in Venezuela, to undermine the government of President Hugo Chávez. The CTV organized destabilizing strikes leading up to the U.S.-backed coup of April, 2002. In Iraq, the Solidarity Center coordinated with the Bush foreign policy by supporting a union that was on the puppet Governing Council appointed by U.S. viceroy L. Paul Bremmer.

International trade union solidarity means supporting progressive unions, anti-imperialist unions, and respecting the rights of unions, especially in the oppressed countries, to self-determination.

For coordinated, class-wide struggle

In U.S. capitalist society, 150 million workers make everything run twenty-four hours a day, seven days a week. This puts them in a strategic position to not only push back against capital, but to overturn capitalism altogether. Even from the point of view of just pushing back the bosses and defending their position within the framework of capitalist society, however, the strategic power of the working class has not been exercised. The battles fought in the recent period against the onslaught of the capitalist class have been fought largely as **isolated events.**

In the coming crisis a class-wide defense is going to be necessary. The vast majority of the class, organized and unorganized, is going to be under further attack. This means abandoning the obsolete and self-defeating fragmentation of the labor movement and unifying it in life, not just in name, to stop the onslaught and turn the situation around.

It would be utopian to expect the present leaders to abandon their class collaborationist posture and suddenly turn toward class struggle on their own. The development of organizational structures that will aid class solidarity will have to come out of the living struggle, in the same way that the dockworkers of 1934 created the Joint Maritime Strike Committee. The joint committee reached across crafts and brought together unions that had been at war with each other to unite in common struggle against the ship owners. This time around, joint, coordinated struggle will have to be on a citywide, region-wide, national or international scale, depending on the circumstances.

Contrast the course of the San Francisco general strike to the struggle in the "war zone" in Decatur, Illinois. During the Decatur struggle in the mid-1990s, locals from three different major unions in the same city battled three powerful corporations—Caterpillar, Bridgestone/Firestone, and Staley—to stop concessions. The unions involved were the UAW at Caterpillar, the Rubber Workers at Bridgestone/Firestone (which merged with the United Steel Workers during the strike), and the Allied Industrial Workers at Staley (which merged with the International Paper Workers during the strike). The UAW and Rubber Workers unions had been founders of the CIO and pioneers of the sit-down strike. They had won their battles with the indispensable aid of class solidarity.

The situation in Decatur was difficult. Deindustrialization had brought high unemployment to the area. Without resistance, it was easy for the companies to recruit scabs. From the separate standpoint of each union, the situation might have been bleak. But a coordinated struggle by the three national unions backed by the labor movement in the Mid-West would have given a far greater chance of turning the situation around and preventing a humiliating and demoralizing series of setbacks.

The same reasoning applies to the Detroit newspaper strike, which took place in the heartland of the UAW. Rank-and-file sentiment for a one-day general strike was widespread when this was proposed by an ad hoc committee during the struggle. There are other strikes that could have been strengthened by the unified action of the labor movement: the transit strike in New York City, the grocery workers' strike in southern California, and many more.

Often a struggle cannot be won if restricted to one or a few workplaces. Sometimes it cannot be won even if restricted to a single company or a single industry. In the era of monopoly capital and giant corporate empires, in which major corporations are intertwined with one another and with the banks, any struggle of significance is not just between the company and an isolated contingent of workers in a local or a district, or even in an entire major union like the UAW, the Steel Workers, or the Service Employees. In most cases, the workers are up against a company with financial support, and even the smallest company has behind it the capitalist state—the police and the courts, always in reserve when needed.

This speaks to the fundamental need for strategies that mobilize the necessary strength of the working class sufficient to counteract the far-reaching advantages of the bosses, with their deep reservoirs of support inherent in the structure of U.S. capitalism.

The most pressing need is for union solidarity in the form of sympathy actions, be they sympathy strikes, partial strikes, mass boycotts, militant demonstrations, occupations, and/or mass picket lines, not only including other unions but with unorganized workers and communities.

The general strike is a form that has not been used since the Seattle general strike of 1919 and the San Francisco, Minneapolis, and Toledo general strikes of 1934. While it is reckless and infantile to casually toss around the slogan of general strike when there is no basis for it, nevertheless, it must always be on the minds of leaders of the struggle when the situation calls for it. Short-duration general strikes, or strikes of specific sectors of the labor movement, have been major weapons in the class struggle in Europe. The general strike in France of 10 million workers in 1968 showed the power of the working class and challenged French capitalism itself.

It is undeniable that at the present time the working class is falling back from blows inflicted by the bosses. And it is obvious to all that the present leadership is, at best, fighting a rearguard action of trying to minimize those blows; at worst, it is complicit in the ruling-class offensive. Many local union leaders, lower-level officials, shop stewards, and rank-and-file militant workers are in a combative mood, but at the same time are being forced into a defensive posture and retreat by the labor leadership.

But the coming crisis is bound to breed resistance. New, militant leaders will inevitably emerge and gain the upper hand. No one can foretell at what point the working class will reach the point at which it is propelled to engage in offensive action. But there is a rich history of struggle to draw upon in the coming period.

One of the most important lessons from the history of the 1930s and earlier is that the bosses' interpretation of the rights of workers cannot be allowed to stand as the limit of the class struggle. It is not possible to unleash the power of the workers **so long as the capitalist class is allowed to define the legal rights and limitations of the forms of struggle of the working class.**

15

Class struggle
and capitalist legality

Taft-Hartley and 'right-to-work' laws: illegal brakes on workers' rights
Human Rights Watch on repression of U.S. labor • Unequal 'protection' for
unions • Legality follows struggle • Plant occupations and the right to a job

Putting aside for the moment the reluctance of the top labor leaders to
initiate a new level of united struggle, the labor movement has been held
tightly in check by the Taft-Hartley Act of 1947 and the so-called "right-to-
work" laws authorized by Taft-Hartley. These anti-union laws exist in more
than twenty states in the South and Southwest.

Taft-Hartley, 'right-to-work' laws: illegal brakes on workers' rights

The Taft-Hartley Act criminalizes class solidarity and militant struggle,
among other things. It is a legal barrier to the kind of effective class struggle
that is needed to end the long period of retreat of the labor movement. This
fact cannot be avoided indefinitely. For the labor leadership to ignore this, after
having denounced Taft-Hartley as the "slave labor law" when it was first enacted, leaves the working class chained in silence by this anti-labor legislation.

The Taft-Hartley Act was passed after World War II, during the early period
of Cold War reaction. It was the bosses' chance to reverse much of the National Labor Relations Act of 1935, known as the Wagner Act, which protected
workers' rights. Taft-Hartley was also used to outlaw many of the tactics used
in the class struggle that had brought victory to the CIO in the 1930s.

In fact, the law was not written by legislators. It was written "sentence
by sentence, paragraph by paragraph, page by page, by the National Association of Manufacturers," according to Representative Donald O'Toole of
New York, commenting at the time, as quoted in *Labor's Untold Story*. The
book also documents how lobbyists and lawyers for General Electric, Allis-
Chalmers, Inland Steel, Chrysler Corporation, and Rockefeller interests participated in writing the bill.[256]

For sixty years this law has hung over the heads of the workers like a sword of Damocles. We have already discussed the anti-communist oath in the Taft-Hartley Act that was used to witch-hunt militants out of the labor movement. The law also gives the president of the United States the right to seek a court order forcing an eighty-day so-called "cooling-off period" if a strike is determined to negatively affect the economy. Once an eighty-day back-to-work injunction is issued, the workers and the union come under judicial oversight and are subject to fines and even imprisonment for doing anything in the nature of resistance, such as slow-downs. If the strike was in protest of onerous conditions, then the workers must continue to submit to those conditions. If the bosses are preparing an assault on the union, the injunction gives them time to perfect the assault, slow down the momentum of the workers, sow division, and stonewall the union in negotiations.

George W. Bush used the eighty-day cooling-off injunction against the West Coast longshore union (ILWU) in 2002, but not to end a strike. It was to force the workers to go back after a two-week lockout by the Pacific Maritime Association (PMA), a group of eighty shippers and port operators. The PMA had locked out the dockworkers after refusing to bargain over safety and its forced introduction of job-killing technology, a violation of union rights. When the lockout failed to break the workers' will and holiday season freight began piling up on the docks, Bush used Taft-Hartley and threats to send in the military to bolster the PMA and giant retailers like Wal-Mart, Home Depot, Target, and Best Buy, which had formed the West Coast Waterfront Coalition to fight the union.

The ILWU had been subject to Taft-Hartley injunctions before and had a record of going out on strike when the eighty days were over. The union held firm and forced the company to back up in the final settlement. But the menace of the Taft-Hartley Act suddenly and dramatically surfaced as a harsh reminder to the entire labor movement.

Taft-Hartley also abolished the closed shop, under which a company could hire only union members. It allowed companies to charge unions with "unfair labor practices," which it defined as including basic union tactics such as sympathy strikes of one union with another, most wildcat strikes, and "quickie" or other hit-and-run strike tactics and slowdowns. It banned what it called secondary boycotts of companies not directly involved in a labor dispute.

It outlawed the all-important tactic of mass picketing that "blocks entrances" or "coerces" scabs. The law compelled the unions to stop spontaneous or "wildcat" strikes under threat of fines.

Taft-Hartley directs the handling of grievances toward the National Labor Relations Board and away from the shop stewards. A backbone of industrial unionism was the practice of militant shop stewards standing up to the foremen or other company representatives directly in the workplace. Together with wildcat strikes, the shop steward grievance process was the heart and soul of workplace militancy.

Under the Taft-Hartley Act grievances are redirected to a remote, time-consuming NLRB process. Stewards wind up filling out grievance forms for the NLRB instead of fighting for the rank and file right in the workplace. The whole process allows the companies to stall the unions endlessly. Many workplaces have hundreds of grievances backlogged at the NLRB.

The Norris-LaGuardia anti-injunction act of 1932 had taken the power of injunction away from the federal government. This was an important victory that limited corporate access to anti-labor judges, who had been issuing injunctions against strikes, picketing, and even language and gestures used by picketers. But Taft-Hartley gave back the broad power of injunction to the NLRB and the president and even required its use by the NLRB against unions.

Under the Wagner Act companies had been legally required to remain neutral during organizing drives. Taft-Hartley gave corporations, under the rubric of "free speech," the right to interfere in union drives with anti-union campaigns.

The law opened up a wide array of situations in which companies could sue unions for damages. It let courts administer huge fines for violations of injunctions or of the law itself and allowed companies to tie up unions in lengthy and costly legal proceedings.

One of its most significant features, which had an enormous impact on workers all over the country, was the provision allowing states to pass so-called "right-to-work" laws, thus making it difficult to organize the unorganized. Such laws have been passed in over twenty states in the South and Southwest, making these regions of the country havens for runaway shops and corporations from all over the world seeking non-union, cheap labor.

The Taft-Hartley Act governs the legality of labor relations in the U.S. However, its provisions have not been invoked frequently during major strikes in recent years. When Bush used the eighty-day cooling off period against the ILWU in the 2002 lockout of the dockworkers, it was the first time in thirty-one years that it had been used. Thus, the law has not been that widely publicized. But it has had an invisible impact on the fate of the unions and the condition of the workers in the U.S., organized and unorganized.

This law applies to every situation in which the class struggle could potentially break out. It acts to frighten conservative leaders and also to restrain militants. The prospect of huge fines, jail time, and union disqualification lurks behind every attempt of the workers to wage effective struggle. The union leaders are legally obliged to obey injunctions that prohibit mass picketing, leaving the membership to watch as scabs have free access to their jobs.

When frustration breaks out over unsafe conditions, company abuse, line speed-up, or other kinds of contract violations, and grievances lie on a pile of papers at the NLRB, wildcat strikes break out. The local union leaders are in the excruciating position of having to choose between suffering injunctions, fines, or other harsh penalties by the capitalist state or becoming the enforcers of discipline over the ranks. This form of state intimidation hovers over the labor movement permanently as an unseen but overwhelming factor in the struggle.

Human Rights Watch on repression of U.S. labor

Human Rights Watch did a comprehensive study of the legal rights of workers in the United States in 2000 and produced a major report entitled *Unfair Advantage*.[257] HRW is a bourgeois organization that alternates between serving imperialism, as in hostile reports on Cuba, and exposing imperialism for its conduct in Iraq or at the Guantanamo prison camp. It devoted one section of its report to "Worker Solidarity and Secondary Boycotts."

HRW found that in nearly every country, by which it was referring to the big capitalist countries in Europe and Japan, "secondary action," meaning solidarity and sympathy strikes and boycotts, "is lawful so long as the primary dispute is lawful and so long as the secondary action is carried out within the bounds of that country's regulations. The United States, however, has imposed a blanket prohibition on solidarity action."

The report does not mention that other regulations, such as outlawing mass picketing, are just as restrictive of the workers' rights as the outlawing of solidarity actions. But it does show that the Taft-Hartley Act's "ban on workers' solidarity is so absolute and the punishment is so swift and resolute that workers rarely test the law's harsh strictures."

The report compares labor law in the U.S. to that in Europe and Japan, as well as to the guidelines established by the International Labor Organization, a conservative bourgeois labor organization under the auspices of the United Nations. In its comparison the report not only discusses solidarity actions but also the right of companies to bring in permanent scabs—or "replacement workers," as they are euphemistically called. It shows that the right of companies to hire scabs to permanently take workers' jobs vastly undermines the right to strike, as well as to organize unions.

The report is rife with case studies about the denial of workers' rights all over the country. Two examples of the tyranny of the bosses under striker replacement law should suffice. The report cites a letter circulated to all employees by management at the Precision Thermoform and Packaging Company in Baltimore, Maryland. The letter said that the law "provides that an employer can CONTINUE TO OPERATE AND HIRE NEW EMPLOYEES TO PERMANENTLY REPLACE THE EMPLOYEES WHO ARE OUT ON STRIKE. If this happens, as it frequently does, the replaced strikers have no jobs to ago back to when the strike ends." [258] (Capitalization in the original.)

The HRW report gives the example of "captive audience" meetings, such as those described by a worker at the Smithfield Foods plant in Wilson, North Carolina. "They kept talking about they can get rid of us for good if we ever went on strike," Robert Atkins told the HRW interviewer.

Says the report,

> The permanent replacement threat is not only raised in organizing.... [M]anagement threatens replacement during collective bargaining negotiations more often than unions threaten to strike.
>
> The United States is almost alone in the world in allowing permanent replacement of workers who exercise the right to strike. Some of the United States' key trading partners take a polar opposite approach. In Mexico, for example, federal law requires companies to cease operations during a legal strike. Permanent replacements are also prohibited throughout Canada. In Quebec, even temporary striker replacements are banned, and a company may only maintain operations using management and supervisory personnel. In most European countries the law is silent on the subject because permanent replacements are never used and the very idea of permanent replacement of strikers is considered outlandish. [259]

Workers in the heralded U.S. 'democracy' live under the most repressive labor laws in the developed capitalist world

The labor movement tried to get anti-scab legislation passed during the Clinton administration. It passed in the House but was defeated in the Senate. Unlike during the titanic struggle to pass NAFTA, in which he went to the wall, calling in all his favors and blocking with Newt Gingrich, Clinton just let the anti-scab law die.

The HRW report puts into perspective the legal situation for unions and the unorganized in the U.S. It shows that workers here in the great, heralded "democracy" live under the most repressive labor laws in the developed capitalist world.

The first time that permanent scabs were used in the U.S. was the late 1970s. But their use has been widespread from the 1980s until the present. The use of permanent scabs has a great deal to do with the decline of strikes, along with globalization and outsourcing. Unlike the seldom used Taft-Hartley anti-strike injunctions, this tactic has been used frequently and openly as a way of intimidating workers and their unions.

In times of capitalist stability, the Taft-Hartley Act remains largely in the background with regard to strikes and solidarity actions. Its principal effects are unseen by the broader movement because just having the law inhibits struggles or may keep them from breaking out altogether. Its provisions are like invisible walls that contain or suppress working-class militancy and solidarity through legal threats and intimidation. It has a chilling effect on every significant struggle.

In order to push back this historic offensive of capital, seen in both Taft-Hartley and the practice of using permanent scabs, the unions and the entire working class will have to raise the level of struggle in this country with greater class-wide organization and coordination and new strategies and tactics. It is extremely important from a political point of view for the labor movement to put the repeal of Taft-Hartley high on its agenda and to expose and agitate against it among the workers.

One thing is for certain. The law won't be abolished by lobbying or legislative methods until the working class has overridden it in life. But as the economic crisis deepens and the workers see the dire need for new levels of unified class action and solidarity, Taft-Hartley and the "right-to-work" laws will have to be challenged and ultimately overturned.

Unequal 'protection' for unions

As the struggle develops and the workers expand their solidarity, they will have every legal right to challenge these unjust anti-labor laws. These laws violate the basic democratic rights of workers; they are illegal restrictions, unconstitutional, and in violation of international norms.

Much can be said about the limitations of the National Labor Relations Act (NLRA) of 1935 and some of its negative effects on the struggle. Nevertheless, Section 7 of the NLRA stated unequivocally the basic gains made in that period of labor upsurge:

"Employees shall have the right to self-organization, to form, join, or assist labor organizations, to bargain collectively through representatives of their own choosing, and to engage in other **concerted activities** for the purpose of collective bargaining or other **mutual aid and protection**." [Emphasis added.]

You don't have to be a labor lawyer or a legal expert to see that, from a purely constitutional point of view, the Taft-Hartley Act is a complete violation of the Fourteenth Amendment, which made it illegal to "deny any person ... equal protection of the laws." This amendment was passed to protect the civil rights of freed slaves. Since a Supreme Court ruling favoring the railroads in 1886, corporations have been legally declared to have the rights of "persons."[260], * This is the legal basis used to declare that a corporation's "right to free speech" allows them to sabotage union drives with force-fed, pro-company propaganda.

To say that sympathy strikes, secondary boycotts, and other forms of class solidarity are illegal is an abrogation of a fundamental workers' right, won through blood and sacrifice and affirmed in the NLRA, to carry out "concerted activities" whose aim is "mutual aid and protection."

The bosses have the right to get "mutual aid" from other bosses—who buy their products, for example, and thus aid them with revenue while workers are losing pay by being out on strike. Big capitalists get lines of credit from the banks in preparation for and during strikes, and thus engage in "concerted activity" against the workers. But workers are forbidden to ask for or receive "mutual aid and protection" through the "concerted activities" of other unions in the form of sympathy strikes or boycotts, etc.

The Taft-Hartley Act provides endless ways for harsh injunctions, huge fines, jail sentences, disqualifications, loss of rights, etc., to be imposed upon the workers. There are no fines, jail sentences, or loss of rights for the bosses under the law. At worst, they have to give back pay or cease and desist from some practice, and this happens often months or years after the violation of workers' rights has occurred.

Since Taft-Hartley leaves corporations free from any harsh penalties, which are imposed only against the workers, and since the bosses are allowed to get support from other sections of their class (and the capitalist state) while

---

* "Corporations gained personhood through aggressive court maneuvers culminating in an 1886 Supreme Court case called *Santa Clara County v. Southern Pacific.* Until then, only We the People were protected by the Bill of Rights, and the governments the people elected could regulate corporations as they wished. But with personhood, corporations steadily gained ways to weaken government restraints on their behavior—and on their growth. After steady progress over the decades, they made huge strides in the 1970s through Supreme Court rulings that awarded them Fourth Amendment safeguards against warrantless regulatory searches, Fifth Amendment double jeopardy protection, and the Sixth Amendment right to trial by jury. These blunted the impact of the Clean Air Act, the Occupational Safety and Health Administration Act, and the Consumer Product Safety Act, which were enacted to protect workers, consumers, and the environment." Tom Stites, "How Corporations Became 'Persons.'" (See endnote 260.)

workers are forbidden from getting vital support from other sections of the working class, this law has a blatantly discriminatory class character. The workers have every legal right to override it, just as Black people had every right to override the blatantly discriminatory segregation laws.

It can be shown that the fundamental labor law in the United States, the National Labor Relations Act, was written specifically to outline the protection of workers from the bosses. This legislative purpose was illegally undermined by an "unfriendly"—in fact utterly hostile—amendment which turned it into its opposite. Taft-Hartley turned much of what was a labor rights law into a law to defend the bosses against the workers.

Furthermore, the Taft-Hartley amendment to the NLRA was written behind closed doors by representatives of the biggest corporations at the time, whose interests were diametrically opposed to the basic interests of labor. On that ground alone this law should be ruled null and void.

As for the permanent scab replacement provision, it is clearly in total contradiction to the right to strike, without which collective bargaining becomes completely one-sided in favor of the company. It says to workers you have the right to strike if you are willing to lose your job and your livelihood. It gives the bosses the right to completely override the right to collective bargaining, as established in law, by firing strikers whose goal is to force the bosses to obey the law and engage in legitimate collective bargaining.

The right wing of the capitalist class praises so-called "strict constructionist" reactionary judges who want to overturn reproductive rights or affirmative action or any legal provision that benefits the masses and was won over years of struggle. Don't the workers have the right to be "strict constructionists" in the progressive sense of the phrase, by refusing to recognize laws that overturn their basic rights? There is probably a great variety of legal grounds to use in asserting workers' rights, including the Thirteenth Amendment against involuntary servitude, the First Amendment covering the right of association, and other legal rulings. But the reassertion and expansion of workers' rights can only be achieved by mass struggle, just the way the laws protecting the workers were achieved in the first place.

Legality follows struggle

During the early part of the nineteenth century, unions themselves were outlawed as a "conspiracy." As unions progressed and the conspiracy laws fell by the wayside, the bosses took anti-trust laws, which were supposed to be used against big business, and used them against union organizing on the grounds of "restraint of trade." Even after unions won recognition based on their own strength, the right to organize and bargain collectively was never recognized by the bosses. Each union had to win its individual battle. The bosses could legally wage a no-holds-barred war against union organizing or to break a union already formed.

It was the workers' own struggle in the 1930s that vastly expanded their rights and upended all previous anti-labor legislation and judicial rulings by winning passage of the Wagner Act of 1935—although it did not apply to agricultural workers and domestic workers, who are the lowest paid and most harshly exploited. But even after the Wagner Act was passed, the bosses acted as though it never existed. They completely disregarded the legal right to organize prescribed in the Wagner Act.

The workers' own struggle in the 1930s vastly expanded their rights and upended all previous anti-labor legislation and judicial rulings

According to that law, employers were not supposed to oppose attempts by workers to organize unions and to engage in collective bargaining. But the bourgeoisie kept the old legality in place *de facto*. Contrary to law, the bosses used every tactic available to stop industrial union organizing. That was what led to the sit-down strikes of 1936 and 1937, including the Flint sit-down strike. That strike broke the back of General Motors' anti-union resistance and hastened the victory of the UAW and the CIO. It was only **after** the victory of the CIO, **after** U.S. Steel, GM, Chrysler, Firestone, and the other big industrialists had thrown in the towel, that the Supreme Court finally declared the Wagner Act constitutional, late in 1937.

Sam Marcy, in *High Tech, Low Pay*, dealt with the question of the class struggle and bourgeois legality in writing about the lessons of the 1930s. His analysis is worth quoting at length.

> Great changes in strategic and tactical approaches develop slowly. They are most often the product of a long line of evolutionary development which includes not only phases of slow growth but leaps and giant forward strides.
>
> The first such struggle was for the right "to think unthinkable thoughts," to think of organizing the workers. It had been regarded as a conspiracy— any combination of workers to organize a union, even to conduct meetings, had been regarded as illegal.
>
> That won, the next struggle was over the right to openly proclaim the need for organization and the right to strike. But the thing to remember is that **the strikes came before striking was legalized**. That's the lesson of the 1930s.[261] [Emphasis in the original.]

Plant occupations and the right to a job

The strike weapon has been central to the struggle of the workers since the early days of resistance to capitalism. Withholding labor power is the fundamental lever against the exploiters. And the strike has always been most effective when the capitalists are expanding production and have an urgent need to keep the plants running in order to meet orders. This happens in a period of capitalist upturn.

But what happens when the capitalist economy is being ravaged by the scientific-technological revolution? What happens when the bosses are straining at the bit to replace workers with machines? What happens in the era of downsizing, the outsourcing of jobs to non-union, low-wage areas, and the offshoring of jobs to low-wage countries? And what happens when the growth of the capitalist economy generates fewer and fewer jobs and the reserve army of the unemployed grows? Above all, how do the workers devise strategies and tactics for a period of full-scale capitalist downturn, when there is mass unemployment?

Marcy discussed the question of the problems of the strike weapon during periods of capitalist downturn. His observations on strikes apply today.

He asked back in 1985,

> What if there are attempted lockouts, what if the employers **force** a strike during a period of capitalist recession?

> The vast transformation which the structural framework of capitalist industry is undergoing makes new forms of struggle absolutely indispensable or the workers must become captives of management altogether. These new forms of struggle are an outgrowth and development of the older forms and an advance on them.

> What's needed is not to abandon old militant methods but to recognize that conventional, traditional weapons—including the indispensable strike weapon—have to be refined and supplemented by new methods, which include the right to seize, occupy, take over, and operate plants, equipment, and machinery.[262]

What has been at stake during the entire period of layoffs and downsizing has been the right of the workers to their jobs. We must recall the assertion by Luis Uchitelle that between the early 1980s and 2004, an estimated 30 million workers were permanently laid off from full-time jobs. That figure has risen by several million since then.

The question is how to put a stop to this bloodletting by the bosses. The issue before the working class and the unions especially is do workers have a right to their jobs? As the creators of the wealth of the bosses do the workers not have equity, do they not have property rights to the wealth that they have created? By what right can they be deprived of that property?

The labor of the workers has created the wealth that has been invested and reinvested over and over again to create the plants, the offices, the mines, the hospitals, etc. Having created all this property, workers should have a property right to their jobs. In simpler terms, workers have "sweat equity" in their jobs and in the workplace as well.

Having created all this (corporate) property, workers should have a property right to their jobs

They have every right to prevent the bosses from depriving them of their jobs as a matter of defending their property rights. The right to occupy a workplace to prevent closings and layoffs must be established as a fundamental right of the working class. Possession of the plants should be viewed as nothing more than asserting the property rights of the creators of the wealth that built those plants. The capital of the owners is nothing more than accumulated labor of the workers, for which they have not been paid. Seen in this light, the seizure of the workplace by the workers in defense of their jobs is nothing more than laying claim to property that they have created.

If workers occupy the workplace to defend their jobs, it means the bosses are separated from the property, instead of the workers. This creates conflicting claims, but possession of the workplace establishes a strong claim by the workers to the property right in their jobs in order to keep working and getting paid union wages.

Instead of the workers being out on the street trying to get their jobs back, the bosses are kept outside and have to deal with the workers from a weakened position.

Such a strategy raises many questions and there are many that must be crossed once such a struggle is undertaken. But it is most important to begin the struggle. Under the conditions of mass working-class resistance, the workers will deal creatively and militantly with the challenges, as they have in the past. To be sure, such a tactic cannot be contemplated unless it gets widespread support and active solidarity from the labor movement and the community. Once the ruling class is confronted with an organized class-wide movement of the workers to expand their rights, things that seemed impossible in times of retreat will be attainable, and more.

Under conditions of downsizing, offshoring, outsourcing, and technological innovation, collective bargaining has in many instances been reduced to concessions bargaining. The number of strikes has drastically declined because of the threats of shutting down, moving away, or scab herding.

The fear of strikes is totally understandable among the workers. But without having use of this essential tool of the labor movement, they are put in the position of having to accept concessions or risk losing their jobs. In this situation, the labor movement must consider adding to its arsenal of weapons the support of work-place takeovers by unions when they are faced with demands for concessions backed by company threats of layoffs or scab herding. The battle cry to establish this must be **the right to a job**! The right to occupy the workplace is directly linked to the right to a job. And support for these rights should not be limited to union workers but extended to any unorganized workers, should it catch on as it did among the service workers in 1937 after the Woolworth sit-down.

A discussion of this topic is a critical matter for the unions and the entire working class. Marcy noted that extending the right of the workers to seize and occupy the workplace "is a logical and inevitable phase in the struggle of the labor movement, as imperative a necessity and as vital to the existence of the trade union movement as any of the preceding phases in its history."

It is possible to multiply recent examples where plant seizures, with the support of the labor movement and the community, could have saved a dire situation from becoming tragic for the workers. In the future such occupations could lead to a reinvigoration of the workers' struggle as a class. An economic crisis will pose this alternative again and again.

16

Class consciousness and class struggle

Challenging the capital-labor relationship · UAW concessionary contracts of 2007
Breaking through the bosses' ideology · Globalization and international solidarity · The
end of capitalist stability and social peace · New phase of permanent crisis for workers
Socialism the only way out

The indoctrination of generations of workers with bourgeois concepts of society has become a significant factor in the class struggle. Concepts such as "middle-class" workers and "working families" or "common interests" between workers and employers are repeated daily by the media, politicians, teachers, academics, religious figures, and labor leaders.

According to bourgeois sociology, individuals in society are classified in multiple groups, roles, and categories such as labor, middle class, professionals, blue-collar, white-collar, consumers, homeowners, etc. This profusion of categories in bourgeois sociology skirts the fundamental class divisions and antagonisms in society between the workers and the bosses. This indoctrination is calculated to cloud any scientific conception of the class nature of society. Above all, it is meant to keep the workers from an understanding of this antagonism that would lead to class action against their antagonist, the capitalist class.

As class tensions beneath the surface of U.S. capitalism continually heighten, the terms "middle-class jobs," "middle-class workers," and "working families" are repeated more and more often, as though the propagandists for the ruling class are struggling harder and harder to keep a class conception of society from emerging in a moment of impending capitalist crisis.

Bourgeois economists want to categorize the population according to income level instead of by relationship to the means of production. If a worker has gone from a $60,000-a-year unionized industrial job to a $30,000-a-year job in a non-union machine shop, then that worker is supposed to think that he or she has fallen out of the middle class into the "lower class."

In the case of the union worker who might earn $60,000 a year, the class truth is that the worker was never in the middle class, but rather is a member of the working class whose degree of exploitation is probably limited by being in a union. Once cast out by one boss and then hired by another at a lower, non-union wage, the worker is subject to the same relationship of exploitation, but at a different intensity.

The worker has gone from the higher-wage proletariat to the low-wage proletariat. The constant is that the worker has to find a boss who will buy her or his labor power. The worker is a wage slave who provides surplus value to the boss in the form of unpaid labor and must go from capitalist master to capitalist master selling labor power for the highest price possible or, in hard times, at any price she or he can get. If there is no capitalist buyer, the worker faces unemployment and crisis.

On the other hand, if the income of a small business owner with three or four workers drops from $100,000 a year to $25,000 a year, that owner is still middle class, regardless of income. He or she is a petty exploiter, deriving income from surplus value, and is in neither the ruling class nor the working class. There are numerous individuals in capitalist society who regard themselves as middle class because they have jobs with relatively high incomes and amenities. But if they sell their labor power to a boss, if they produce surplus value, they are workers—a fact that is more and more sharply being driven home to them with downsizing, layoffs, wage competition, and economic crisis.

Of course, there are such things as white-collar jobs, homeowners, consumers, a middle class, etc. But these categories are a false starting point from which to analyze the social structure under the system of capitalist exploitation. An office clerk may wear the same white collar as a manager—whose job it is to see that the clerk gives every last minute of labor time to the boss. The clerk has sold her or his labor power to the boss and the supervisor is there to see that this labor power is as thoroughly exploited as possible. The superficiality of the category "white collar" will be revealed the moment the clerk and other workers demand a raise, try to organize a union, or go on strike. The white-collar manager will be on the side of the boss trying to crush the white-collar workers on the picket line. (Of course, this does not refer to workers who, because of some added responsibility, are artificially classified by management as supervisors in order to make them ineligible for overtime pay or union membership.)

The term consumer can be applied to both a middle manager at a Hilton hotel and to a maid who cleans the rooms. But the maid's power of consumption depends upon her wages and the degree of exploitation enforced by the middle manager. The middle manager is paid out of the surplus value, or profit, made from the unpaid labor of the maid. The manager is beholden to the owners of the Hilton chain. The manager represents capital and the maid is part of the proletariat. Their class interests are diametrically and irreconcilably opposed to one another.

The bourgeois classifications of white collar, consumer, etc., group people in the same category whose class interests are opposed. The relationship of exploitation puts people the bourgeoisie claims to be the same in a highly tense, antagonistic relationship. An exploiting consumer and an exploited consumer are objectively opposed to one another. This antagonism is embedded in the structure of capitalism, which is divided into bosses and workers, those with property and those without. It is this relationship that makes the class struggle a permanent feature of capitalist society—a struggle that must eventually break out into open class warfare.

This ideological assault to stop the emergence of class consciousness comes at a time when workers are being forced by the capitalists into making concessions, are being laid off, are losing their homes, and in general are under attack from all directions by the propertied class. As the dependence of the workers on the owners of the means of production and the financiers becomes more and more apparent, as the gulf between the owners and non-owners of private property is widening, the paid mouthpieces of the ruling class are rushing to cover over this gulf with false terminology.

Ideological clarity about the capital-labor relationship would be a tonic to the workers and give them a scientific framework within which to understand their position and change their strategy and tactics accordingly.

The most favorable circumstances for ideological clarity are when the living struggle demands it. The present economic crisis is putting the kind of pressure on the workers that lends itself to the beginning of class consciousness among the most advanced and active workers who want to find a way out of their dilemma through organization and struggle. It leads to basic consciousness of the antagonism between the workers as an exploited class and the bosses as an exploiting class.

Challenging the capital-labor relationship

In order to fight management it is necessary to reject the ideological framework of management. Even within the framework of the capitalist system, the workers in their present situation cannot move forward in any significant way unless they challenge the labor-capital framework. The workers will have to challenge some of the basic prerogatives of capital and the ideology of the supremacy of the capitalist market and the rights of capitalist property. Indeed, when the UAW workers seized the plants in Flint, when the hundreds of thousands of workers carried out successful sit-downs in 1936 and 1937, they challenged the property rights of the bosses. It was the only way they could win.

Over the past three decades, the bosses have been using the argument of the need to "remain competitive" as their wedge against the workers in the struggle for concessions. However, in the unfolding economic crisis, the argument of "competitiveness" may be combined with the assertion that shutdowns and layoffs are necessary because the company must maintain profitability and prevent losses.

The question of profitability must be subordinated to the right of the workers to jobs and income. The workers have the right to take over their workplaces and operate them with government or corporate subsidies, if necessary. Workers have the right to demand jobs programs to deal with their crisis as a class.

The capitalist government gives hundreds of billions in subsidies to the military-industrial complex, to corporate firms for research and development, to build infrastructure for corporations, and so on. Workers have a right to demand that this largesse, this charity to the corporations, be redirected to meet the needs of the workers in a crisis.

When the capitalist system utterly fails to meet the most elementary needs of survival for millions of workers, then the workers have the right to deal with the crisis by defying capitalist methods and beginning to establish their own legal rights and their own power on the ground. This will require struggle but it will also demand that the workers get beyond the basic assumptions of capitalism so that their struggle can be effective.

To continue with the question of class-conscious ideology, consider the universal argument of the capitalist class used against the workers about the need "to remain competitive." Why do the bosses constantly bring this up in labor negotiations (assuming the workers have a union)? It is a clear statement that the one who wins the capitalist competition is the one with the lowest labor costs. Thus, in order for the capitalist in company A to beat out the capitalist in company B, the workers in company A have to out-compete the workers in company B by allowing their wages to be cut below the others —and/or submitting to speed up or other "productivity" measures.

The capitalists in company B then go to their own workers and tell them that in order to remain competitive with company A, which has just reduced its labor costs by cutting wages or benefits, the workers in company B have to at least match those cuts. And so it goes in the race to the bottom. This is the trap the workers are in if their representatives buy into bourgeois ideology at the bargaining table and remain within the capital-labor framework imposed by the bosses.

One example of this can be clearly seen in the non-union auto plants, like Toyota, that have been operating in the South. They have been paying near union wages in order to keep the union out. Now that the Big Three are establishing the two-tier system and pushing their health-care costs on to the union, Toyota has warned its workers that cuts are coming. It has told the workers that it is now going to pay according to the local wage scale, which is very low in the "right-to-work" South, instead of basing wages on industry scale.

Accepting the bosses' notion that labor must subordinate its demands to the overriding necessity of capital to remain competitive and profitable is a self-defeating ideology. The workers cannot be guided by it. Such arguments completely tie the fate of the workers to the perils of the capitalist market.

The notion that labor must subordinate its demands to the needs of capital to remain competitive and profitable is a self-defeating ideology

To unravel this problem ideologically, it is first necessary to restate the fundamental Marxist truth that the substance of profit is surplus value. And surplus value consists of unpaid labor. Profits are directly proportional to the unpaid labor of the workers. As was pointed out earlier, the wage form of payment itself hides this fact. Nevertheless, higher profits are derived from additional unpaid labor. It means that more surplus value is extracted from the hides of the workers. By the same token, if the workers are paid more for their labor, the profits of the bosses are lowered proportionally. This absolutely reciprocal relationship is what lies behind the irreconcilable antagonism between workers and bosses.

Another way of saying it is that the lower the wages and benefits of the workers, the faster they have to work, the more "productive" they are forced to be, then the greater is the time they are working for free and the more they are exploited. It is not just that they don't get "fair" wages when wages go down. No wages are fair under capitalism, because all wages entail handing over free labor to the capitalists. The bosses then use the money from this unpaid labor to further expand exploitation and get richer. Reductions in wages or benefits (benefits are nothing more than deferred wages) mean handing over more free labor time to the bosses.

To hold the workers responsible for the profitability of capital is to **demand that they agree to intensify their own exploitation to solve the crisis of their exploiters**. This must be explained to the workers. They can easily comprehend it.

There are times when concessions may have to be given because the situation is very unfavorable for the workers. But the idea that concessions must be made so the boss can be "more competitive" chains the fate of the workers to the capitalist market.

When put this way, it is easier to argue for new strategies that break with the destructive strategies of the past, which put the workers in the untenable position of having to choose between concessions and job loss. Acceptance of the political and ideological premises of capital traps even the most militant workers, those who reject the concessionary positions of the leadership and want to fight. They find themselves in the defensive position of merely trying to limit the damage of the concessions. Others wind up resigning themselves to the class-collaborationist arguments of the leadership, who are basically transmitting the arguments of the bosses.

The question should be posed: Why must the exploited sacrifice their wages, their benefits, their working conditions, and their very jobs in order to maintain the continued prosperity of the exploiters, who have lived off the wealth created by the workers in the first place?

UAW concessionary contracts of 2007

The concessionary UAW contracts of 2007 are prime examples of the bankruptcy of accepting the bosses' premises. In these contracts, the Big Three automakers obtained breakthrough concessions from the UAW under President Ron Gettelfinger. It was a planned retreat by the leadership in which they relentlessly pursued a strategy of alleged job security in exchange for concessions. The contracts were sold to the majority of the members on the basis of fear of plant closings and offshoring. The resistance to these contracts and the resentment of a significant minority, especially in Chrysler, was played down or covered up. The so-called "job security" promised in the contracts is bound to be ephemeral, but the concessions, unless overturned by the rank and file, are hard and fast.

In the UAW contracts, as in all union contracts that deal with job security, there is always a loophole giving the company the right to override any agreement to keep plants open if confronted with "legitimate business reasons," "market conditions," the need "to remain competitive," to protect the solvency of the company, or similar language.

The two things that have been constant in the last twenty-five years of the UAW's relations with the Big Three auto companies have been the loss of jobs and concessions. In 1979 there were 725,000 UAW workers at GM, Ford, and Chrysler. By 2008, there were 178,000. Over the period of the last eight contracts, in spite of pledges of job security, 547,000 jobs have been lost. Within a few months of signing the 2007 contracts, all three companies announced layoffs and have also reneged on other parts of the agreements.

In the latest round of contracts with the UAW, basic walls for worker protection, walls that had been weakened over time, were finally breached altogether—including the end of company responsibility to maintain the retirees' health-care funds, introduction of a two-tier wage system, and the substitution of annual raises for annual one-time bonuses.* As any worker can tell you, bonuses come and go. Many other dangerous concessions were made on work rules and laid-off workers' income protection (job banks), among others.

The UAW had been the strongest remaining bastion of industrial union power in the U.S. and was the foundation of the CIO in the 1930s. It established the highest standard for union workers in the country. But management and Wall Street have battered it into line with the broad parameters of concessions forced upon much of the labor movement during the brutal course of the anti-labor offensive.

For example, the UAW agreed to and promoted the policy of the giant auto companies to engage in massive buyouts of the older generation of higher-paid workers while at the same time initiating a two-tier system in which newly hired workers are paid far less than the retiring generation. In this, the union bureaucrats became instruments of a broad strategy by the Big Three and Wall Street to transform auto from a high-wage to a low-wage industry.

The auto industry is still the largest manufacturing employer in the United States and the UAW is the largest industrial union. That makes these concessions extremely significant. It would be one thing if the concessions were forced on the union after a struggle that ended up in a stalemate and the

---

* Financial responsibility to maintain the retirees' health-care fund has been lifted from the company and transferred to the union, under the so-called Voluntary Employees' Beneficiary Association (VEBA). The company makes a one-time contribution in setting up the fund, which the union will take over. The contributions by the companies are far less than their present liabilities and also include stocks and securities, along with cash. Thus, aside from the insufficient funds to begin with, the fund is at the mercy of stock and bond markets. The two-tier hiring system is another fundamental breach, in which a large proportion of the new hires will earn half what the present generation makes.

union, unable to prevail, then moved to cut its losses. But in this case, concessions the bosses could never obtain by opening up a struggle with the workers were imposed through bargaining with the labor leadership.

The contract was sold on the basis of keeping the company competitive in order to avoid job loss. But the very idea is utterly absurd. In the first place, the Big Three **compete with one other,** not just with Japanese and German companies. So why help GM compete against Ford and Chrysler? Won't that put Ford and Chrysler workers out of work, as well as other autoworkers?

Non-union autoworkers in Japanese-owned auto plants all over the South are just trying to stay alive. Instead of agreeing to lower wages in the Big Three, a concerted union drive should be made to intensify the organizing efforts in the South in order to get union wages for the workers in the Japanese-owned companies.

We have already given the extreme example of whipsawing, when workers in one plant are forced into competition with another plant and make local concessions in order to win the award of work dangled in front of them by management.

What has happened is that sections of the union leadership are being so thoroughly absorbed into the capitalist system that they are gradually turning the unions into their opposite. The original purpose of unions, as pointed out long ago by Marx and Engels, was to interfere with, to block, to combat the competition among workers; to unite them against capital; to free them from being set against one another and their wages reduced to a subsistence level, or below. This was the historic role of unions. This is what the great strikes of the last hundred years were about. The goal of the sit-down strikes of the 1930s was to represent all the workers in a company and in an industry in order to abolish the forced competition of unorganized workers against one another.

It is this competition among workers, the ability to play them against one another in the struggle for jobs and the means of life, which has been the basis of the rule of the capitalist class. In this era of concessions bargaining, much of the top union leadership has objectively become an instrument by which the unions themselves are assisting the bosses in fostering competition among workers worldwide.

This situation threatens the unions' very existence and must be turned around. It will persist as long as the workers accept the logic of capitalism— that profit is the only goal of production, that markets are the governing factor that determines the fate of labor, and that exploitation is an unbreakable social relationship.

What is happening in the auto industry has happened throughout the economy. It has been the line of the bosses in industry after industry, organized or unorganized, manufacturing, transportation, or service.

Breaking through the bosses' ideology

In the coming crisis, propaganda and agitation along economic lines will be an integral part of promoting the class struggle and directing it toward a class-wide offensive. The goal is class solidarity and allowing the workers to break out of the narrow restrictions of the capital-labor framework.

The bosses have obstructed the class struggle at every turn with outrageous and arbitrary legal restrictions and red tape—bans on solidarity strikes, injunctions, tearing up labor laws meant to protect the workers, etc. Agitation for freedom of action to defend the interests of the working class, the creators of all wealth, over the interests of the exploiters who appropriate that wealth for their own private property, must be made the priority.

The bosses' wall of ideology promoting competitiveness, profitability, and the sanctity of capitalist property must be breached by sound working-class concepts such as the right to a job, the right to have a decisive say in bankruptcy hearings, the right to stop the removal and shutdown of workplaces, the right to housing, etc.

Strategies and tactics must be developed to expand the rights of the workers as the ruling class prepares to unload the disasters created by capitalism on their backs. During the entire period leading up to the present crisis, and now more than ever with the crisis deepening, **there is no other practical way for the workers to successfully fight back other than to upset the entire present web of capitalist restrictions. Ordinary means—individual strikes alone or even large-scale strikes—are insufficient in times of a downturn.**

That being said, at the same time it must be pointed out that the level of class consciousness required of the fighting vanguard of the workers goes far beyond simply understanding capitalist exploitation and the political and economic rights of the workers.

To overcome the evils of capitalism and build a just society, free of exploitation, racism, and discrimination, it is necessary to engage in daily struggles of every kind on every front. But these struggles must be directed toward the ultimate goal of placing all of society on a new basis, one that does not just mitigate exploitation, oppression, and war, but eliminates them altogether. The aim must be to create a society based upon human need and not profit. Such a goal can only be achieved by the complete revolutionary destruction of the capitalist social order and the building in its place of the only social system that can replace it, a system based on human need and not profit: the system of socialism.

It was Lenin, the architect of the first successful socialist revolution in history, who fought for this conception at the beginning of the twentieth century. He argued for the creation of a revolutionary party, which ultimately became known as the Bolshevik Party.

Lenin argued strenuously for bringing socialist, political class consciousness to the workers as a highly important task, along with carrying on economic agitation, strikes, and demonstrations, all of which he put forward in the groundbreaking pamphlet "What Is to Be Done?" written in 1902.

While Lenin's co-thinkers in the movement of the time had thrown themselves into the economic struggle of the workers, he argued:

> It is not enough to **explain** to the workers that they are politically oppressed (no more than it was to **explain** to them that their interests were antagonistic to the interests of the employers). Agitation must be conducted over every concrete example of this oppression (in the same way that we have begun to conduct agitation around concrete examples of economic oppression). And inasmuch as **this** oppression affects the most diverse classes of society, inasmuch as it manifests itself in the most varied spheres of life and activity, industrial, civic, personal, family, religious, scientific, etc., etc., is it not evident that **we shall not be fulfilling our task** of developing the political consciousness of the workers if we do not **undertake** the organization of the **political exposure** of the autocracy **in all its aspects**? In order to carry on agitation around concrete examples of oppression, these examples must be exposed (just as it was necessary to expose factory abuses in order to carry on economic agitation).[263] [Emphases in original.]

At the time, the socialist movement was fighting against the tsarist autocracy, the final, antiquated, political holdover from the era of feudalism, whose regime was being undermined by capitalist modernization, rebellions among the students, and the growing working class. The struggle of the day was to overthrow the autocracy and establish a democratic regime that would make it easier for the workers to struggle for power.

Yet Lenin insisted that, side by side with the struggle for bourgeois democracy, it was necessary to conduct the struggle for socialism among the proletariat. He castigated the reformists who called themselves socialists but wanted to restrict themselves to fighting for economic reforms.

Conditions in the United States at the turn of the twenty-first century are certainly drastically different than conditions were in tsarist Russia a century earlier. But in spite of those differences, this is a truth that has lasting value for the present day.

The ruling class in the U.S. has evolved a complex array of weapons in the struggle against the workers and the oppressed. They are meant to fortify the system of exploitation and require **a socialist political explanation** in order to keep the struggle against the bosses on target. To be effective, class-consciousness among the workers means consciousness of the ruling class and the way in which it camouflages its interests.

Class consciousness among the workers means consciousness about the ruling class and the ways in which it camouflages its interests

For example, racism, scapegoating of undocumented workers, and demonization of Black and Latina/o youth result in a direct economic/profit advantage to the bosses, because they can discriminate by paying lower wages to oppressed people. But the economic advantage to the bosses cannot be separated from the poisonous political effects of racism. It is a basic political weapon calculated to divide the workers, to stir up white workers and direct their hostility toward oppressed people and away from the capitalist class.

For white workers to defend affirmative action in employment, in the sphere of education, or elsewhere, not only compensates oppressed people for past injustice, it also **welds class solidarity, which is of immeasurable importance in the struggle of the workers as a whole to expand jobs and opportunity for everyone**.

The same is true in regard to the practice of paying women less than men and keeping them in the lowest-wage job categories. The bosses gain outright economic advantage by paying women less than men. And the capitalist class as a whole justifies this practice by promoting demeaning ideas about the worth of women's work.

In addition, the ruling-class "right-to-life" ideology declares that women have to surrender their right to control their bodies. This reinforces sexism and the oppressed status of women in a patriarchal, capitalist society. It strengthens backwardness, diverts the real underlying class issues, and divides the workers, creating enormous stress on poor women, who have the least access to abortion and reproductive rights.

In fact, the poverty enforced by capitalism deprives women and the working-class family of **the right to plan their families, including the right to have children and bring them up in a healthy, supportive environment,** with child care, health care, housing, stable income, opportunities for education, etc.

The bigoted, right-wing opposition to same-sex marriage and to lesbian, gay, bi, and trans people is similarly an attempt to direct hostility away from the system and create in the minds of the workers imaginary threats, while denying the fundamental democratic right to freedom of sexual preference and gender identification. Meanwhile, the working class is faced with **real threats** at every turn, twenty-four hours a day, seven days a week, from every form of capitalist exploiter—whether it is the boss, the landlord, or the price-gouging supermarkets, oil companies, credit card loan sharks, parasitic mortgage bankers, etc.

The broad economic class interests of the workers cannot be separated from **the political struggle** against all forms of oppression. These forms of oppression, which occur outside the immediate sphere of capitalist exploitation, must be exposed as essential weapons of the capitalist class enemy.

Class consciousness means understanding that the war-makers, the military contractors, the oil companies, and the same big corporations and banks that are oppressing and exploiting the workers are the forces behind the slogans "war against terrorism," just as they were behind the so-called "war against communism."

Wars, occupations, and interventions are aimed at securing profits and exploitation abroad in the same way that layoffs, cutbacks, fraudulent mortgages, reductions in health care and benefits, loss of job security, etc., are aimed at securing profits at home. The concept of "national interest" is a smokescreen to cover the interests of the transnational corporations and the Pentagon.

The general conception of "democracy" in the U.S. is also a smokescreen to conceal the fact that democracy exists only for the corporate billionaires who control the political process through the two capitalist political parties. To secure their interests, the rich fight it out behind the scenes in Washington and in the state houses and city halls of the country. Meanwhile, corporations exercise a dictatorship at the work place and determine conditions in the daily lives of more than 150 million workers and their families. Every four years the workers get to choose which group of capitalist politicians will rule.

The only way that the workers can truly express their political will, openly and plainly, without deception or demagogy, and fight for their interests in an organized way as an exploited class is to have their own revolutionary socialist party. The workers' party must not only be independent of the capitalist parties, but independent of all influences of the capitalist class. This means not only leading in the fight against the injustices of capitalism in the workplace, on the streets, and in the political arena, but also leading the struggle to replace capitalist exploitation altogether.

Such knowledge and analysis is necessary to combat bourgeois ideology and cannot be derived from the direct confrontation with the bosses at the workplace. It would fly in the face of historical experience and of Marxism to think that, even under conditions of furious class-wide struggle, the workers would somehow automatically come to highly class-conscious conclusions. Political class consciousness has to be fought for, alongside the economic struggle.

Globalization and international solidarity

Capitalist global restructuring has elevated the need for international class solidarity to the highest level. Many unions have attempted to organize across borders in the recent period, on a limited basis.

The United Electrical Workers (UE) has pioneered collaboration with unions in Mexico. UNITE organized in the *maquiladoras* in Mexico, Central America, and the Caribbean. HERE has organized hotels in various cities around the world. SEIU has organized commercial properties internationally. The Teamsters have also done international organizing.

The Steelworkers defeated a lockout at a plant in Ravenswood, West Virginia, by organizing internationally. The United Food and Commercial Workers and the Communication Workers of America have also attempted cross-border organizing. Recently, the Steelworkers merged with unions in England, Canada, Ireland, and Australia in order to strengthen their hand against the growing international steel monopolies.

While there are considerable difficulties in cross-border organizing, whatever efforts have been made are a step in the right direction. But the efforts lag far behind the necessities of the present situation. And, more importantly, they have been carried out largely from the top and from the point of view of getting workers around the world to help organizing drives of unions in the U.S.

Of course, it is important to try to get international solidarity for workers' struggles here. But the efforts have to lead to general class solidarity with workers abroad, especially in the oppressed countries. The rank-and-file have to be motivated and made conscious of the conditions and the problems of the workers in Mexico, Thailand, Guatemala, Indonesia, India, etc.

The idea of international solidarity must be brought to the ranks of the labor movement in an uncompromising way. This is the only way it can really be achieved in practice. Raising this kind of perspective would involve advanced thinking, dedication, and sacrifice. But workers in the U.S. will not be able to respond to appeals for international solidarity until they break the stranglehold of conservative, limiting strategies and tactics that come from business unionism. A precondition of real international solidarity is that it be reciprocal. That is why it is so necessary to move toward class-wide struggle and class consciousness.

The general concept that workers abroad are "stealing" the jobs of workers in the U.S. has to be fought and defeated by any labor leadership that hopes to lead the workers out of the morass of the worldwide competition being promoted by the capitalist class everywhere, but in the U.S. in particular.

The idea that the problem is "free trade" muddies up the question and conceals the underlying class issue. Bashing China and Mexico just feeds bourgeois thinking and is another form of promoting competition for jobs among workers in different countries.

The problem is the freedom of the bosses to roam the globe in search of opportunities for low-wage exploitation, for union-free environments, and for impoverished workers who need jobs. The problem is that the bosses are allowed to take wealth created by the workers and invest it wherever they please, shutting down workplaces or reducing shifts at will.

When the capitalists close down a plant to send it abroad where they can pay the workers even lower wages, it is the bosses who have stolen the jobs, not the workers in the other country. The boss is the thief. The capitalist is taking advantage of the unemployed workers or peasants who desperately need jobs and have been living on a few dollars a day. These impoverished workers are not the culprits.

The best and only way to keep the bosses from stealing the jobs is to stop them from closing down. If it takes a plant occupation, an industry-wide strike, or a more general offensive by the workers, struggle is the only way to stop the epidemic of plant closings and layoffs. And the best way to reduce low-wage competition from workers abroad is to **help those workers organize to improve wages and conditions.**

The present-day labor leaders would do well to recall the words of the English workers, quoted earlier, to their low-paid French counterparts: "Our aim is to bring up the wages of the ill-paid to as near a level as possible with that of those who are better remunerated, and not to allow our employers to play us off one against the other, and so drag us down to the lowest possible condition, suitable to their avaricious bargaining."

If Ford, GM, Delphi, IBM, AT&T, or any other capitalist corporation has the money to invest in a plant somewhere else, the workers should remind them that that money represents the wealth these workers created. The workers have a fundamental right to have their say in how that wealth is used. They have a right to insist that it be used to raise the conditions of all the workers in the company or the industry.

Furthermore, the workers here must understand that the workers of Mexico, India, Thailand, Guatemala, or anywhere else have low wages and are impoverished because of the centuries of plunder by the corporations that also exploit the working class in the U.S. and in other imperialist countries. If Ford or Delphi workers in Mexico are getting one-tenth the wages of autoworkers in the U.S., the mission should be to help bring the wages of the Mexican autoworkers closer to U.S. industry standards, not to take away their jobs.

In cross-border organizing, it is also important to remember that the U.S. is regarded around the world as an oppressor and exploiter of the world's people. The top union bureaucrats in this country have long been identified with the capitalist government here, with the CIA and its dirty tricks. As we pointed out earlier, even though the AFL-CIO has disavowed this practice, it was involved in supporting the right-wing forces in Venezuela opposed to President Hugo Chávez. For that reason, any form of intervention by a U.S. institution, including the official labor movement, may be regarded with suspicion.

International solidarity requires shedding all vestiges of domination, any connection with the U.S. imperialist government in Washington, and stretching out the hand of the labor movement to **assist the workers in other countries to raise themselves up**. It must not confine its organizing efforts to getting support for an immediate struggle here. This is particularly important if the workers abroad are in struggle with the corporate rulers in Washington. Only true class solidarity can succeed.

There is a long way to go from where U.S. workers are now to international consciousness. But there are two fundamental reasons having to do with the development of international capitalism that will exert greater and greater pressure on the U.S. working class and will open the way for advanced working-class thinkers to help their class move in the direction of proletarian internationalism.

The first is the new world division of labor in capitalist production and many services. Technology has made capital more mobile, production more global, and workers more closely woven into a socialized, interconnected network than ever before in history. Without international working-class organization, the bosses can manipulate this network to their advantage.

The second factor is the concentration of wealth and growing monopolization, both in the manufacturing and the service sectors. In addition to global steel companies and auto companies, there are now global chains of hotels, casinos, resorts, real estate empires, retail stores, supermarket chains, food services, health care, etc. Vast corporate property is being swallowed up by giant holding companies bankrolled by finance capital and concentrated into global empires. The concentration of ownership drives the unions in the direction of international organizing. Fighting an international corporate giant on a national basis alone leaves it free to continue to make profits abroad that it can use to fight the workers. Conversely, shutting the company down internationally increases the leverage of the workers in any given country.

To achieve the level of internationalism sufficient to check the divisive schemes of the bosses, a significant section of the working class will have to come to see itself as part of a worldwide class, an exploited class, with a common worldwide class enemy, the capitalist ruling class. In addition to understanding their condition as workers in a company or an industry, or as U.S. workers, under the right conditions of a high level of class struggle and guided by a class-conscious leadership, they will be able to see that they have a commonality with the workers of the world, whether in India or Italy, Russia or Brazil, Mexico or China, Nigeria or Egypt. That commonality, despite differences in nationality, language, history, and culture, and despite drastic differences in economic condition, derives from the common condition of wage slavery. From this common class condition flows a common class interest in opposing and ultimately overturning capitalism.

A significant section of the U.S. working class must come to see itself as part of a worldwide exploited class

Of course, just as it is necessary for white workers in the U.S. to appreciate the need to take the initiative in establishing solidarity with oppressed workers at home, in the same way workers in the U.S., the most privileged country in the world based upon generations of plunder, must lead the way in establishing international solidarity with workers in countries that have been oppressed by colonialism and imperialism.

But genuine class consciousness does not consist only in understanding the economic relations between workers and bosses, i.e., understanding capitalist exploitation as such. Understanding it as an economic system, including understanding the nature of capitalist crises, would be a great step forward for the workers in the U.S. It is all-important to promote a combative class attitude of "us versus them," workers against bosses.

The end of capitalist stability and social peace

At the present moment the capitalist financial authorities are trying desperately to control an uncontrollable system—capitalism. Capital must expand, capitalists must seek profit wherever they can get it: in a tiny sweatshop, in a transnational corporate manufacturing empire, or in the wildest, riskiest, most fraudulent financial speculations. The unquenchable thirst for profit drives the system. It always has and always will as long as capitalism exists. At best, the rulers have learned how to manipulate the system to postpone the day of reckoning. But when the contradiction between private property and the socialized means of production grabs them, when overproduction overtakes the system, they are powerless to prevent a crisis. Their answer is to unload it on the backs of the workers.

Despite the extraordinary development of science and industry, of space-age technology and digital wonders, the capitalist system at the dawn of the twenty-first century behaves in the same fundamental way that it did in 1825, during the first capitalist crisis of overproduction. Profits pile up. Fortunes are made. Then markets collapse. Profits shrink. Workplaces shut down. Workers are thrown out and left on their own. This in a nutshell is the bare bones of every capitalist crisis. Except that this time, as in the 1930s, it is not just a cyclical crisis but a crisis of the system.

The scientific-technological revolution has propelled capitalism and imperialism into a new stage that is beyond their control. The collapse of the USSR and the opening up of China have cleared the way for the uncontrollable spread of rapacious exploitation to every nook and cranny of the globe.

New phase of permanent crisis for workers

It is important to be objective about the present mood of the workers and their level of working-class consciousness and not mistake future possibilities and goals for the present situation. But it is also important to ponder the future. As capitalism goes more deeply into crisis, the profit system itself will become more and more vulnerable to criticism among the workers. Layoffs, evictions, hunger, poverty, will be increasingly enforced against the millions by laws and institutions designed openly and specifically to guard and enforce private property.

Under conditions of crisis, the irrationality of capitalism, which puts profits before people, will become manifest on a society-wide scale. No amount of bourgeois propaganda will be able to cover it over. Even in the preliminary stages of the crisis there is already an opening to carry on anti-capitalist and socialist agitation among the workers, provided it is connected to the living struggle, illuminates the lines of battle, and is done artfully.

The previous period of capitalist stability is about to come to an end. The material basis for this long period of backwardness and retreat is being undermined by capitalism itself. The new phase of worldwide wage competition and restructured global low-wage capitalism is now entering a period of economic crisis. At the outset it has the earmarks of a deep and widespread crisis as it spreads throughout the financial markets of the world. It appears that all the efforts to put off the general crisis of capitalist overproduction by extending credit and pumping money into the economy are stretched to the limit.

But whether it all comes crashing down in the immediate future or the bourgeoisie is able to temporarily rescue the situation by further financial manipulation, capitalism has entered into **a new phase of permanent crisis for the working class.** Given the enormous leaps forward in the productivity of labor and the rate of exploitation, even periods of capitalist upturn are characterized by "jobless recoveries." Fueled by debt, they no longer revive even the mildest form of prosperity for the working class.

The consciousness and the mood of the U.S. working class at present cannot be the criterion from which to judge the future of the struggle. The present is the product of the past. The historical conditions that shaped the present consciousness of the workers and the current forms of the class struggle are rapidly coming to an end. The conditioning factors of the recent period were the monopoly of economic, political, and military power of U.S. imperialism after World War II and its protracted war against the USSR and the socialist camp, known as the Cold War.

The scientific-technological revolution fueled a qualitative intensification of economic rivalry among the giant monopolies, carried out at the expense of the workers of the world. This corporate rivalry has confronted the workers with conditions not experienced since the 1930s.

Drastic changes in conditions lead to drastic changes in mood and consciousness. To be sure, consciousness lags behind events. But eventually it must catch up. The potential for struggle within the working class must not be viewed in light of the previous period or the present, but in light of what the consciousness will be once it reflects the new conditions of crisis that are deepening every day.

Socialism the only way out

Nothing can change the facts about the overriding contradiction governing all of modern society. This contradiction is between, on the one hand, the private ownership of the world's vast means of production by a tiny minority of fabulously wealthy corporate financiers who operate the entire system for profit, and on the other, the highly developed, interdependent, socialized, global production process set in motion twenty-four hours a day by the labor of the world's working class under increasingly onerous conditions. Nothing can change the fact that capitalism has entered a new stage in which more and more layers of the working class are pushed into conditions of poverty and near poverty and face job loss, eviction, foreclosure, hunger, health crises—all clearly arising out of the capitalist profit system.

It is scientifically correct to assert that socialism is the antithesis of capitalism, its only form of negation. There is no other historically possible resolution of capitalism's fundamental contradictions. Socialized ownership must be brought into correspondence with socialized production, thus enabling the socially planned use of the world's productive and natural resources. The antagonistic social relations created by capitalism, the final form of private property, weigh oppressively on the vast majority of humanity.

Imperialism in the age of the scientific revolution is expanding and deepening exploitation and oppression on an unprecedented scale. What is referred to as "globalization" is in fact the expanded export of capital and the use of cutthroat trade by giant transnational corporations to pile up huge profits at the expense of the people of the world. In short, it is a phase of intensification and widening of the imperialist plunder of the globe.

This process of expanded global exploitation, which is proceeding at breakneck speed due to modern high technology, has profound consequences at home and abroad and is rapidly developing the groundwork for the next phase of the world historic struggle for socialism.

Imperialist war in the 21ˢᵗ century

Three stages of imperialist war • 'Regime change' from Clinton to
Bush • Colossus with feet of clay • Peace, an interlude between wars
Expand or die

No analysis of imperialism would be complete without a discussion of
the systemic tendency of imperialism toward war. While an extensive
treatment of this tendency is not the focus of the present work, nevertheless, imperialism's warlike character and dependence on militarism could
well create a deep social crisis and instability in the United States. Therefore, it is important to discuss some of the salient characteristics of imperialist militarism over the last 130 years.

Three stages of imperialist war

The imperialist powers have engaged in constant wars of aggression during the century since monopoly became the dominant force in the capitalist
world. Wars have been waged by almost all the imperialist powers regardless
of the type of political administration: liberal democratic or conservative,
social democratic or monarchist or fascist.

The period of imperialist war began with the war of 1898, known as the
Spanish-American War, in which the U.S. captured the Philippines, Cuba,
and Puerto Rico. Since that time there have been ceaseless imperialist wars
with millions upon millions of casualties and untold destruction. The permanent war drive has persisted in different forms through dramatically different historical periods: first, the period of inter-imperialist wars from 1898 to
1946; second, the period of war between the socialist and imperialist camps;
and third, the war for reconquest of the globe since the fall of the USSR.

WAR TO REDIVIDE THE WORLD

In his work *Imperialism,* Lenin noted that a fundamental feature of imperialism was the complete division of the globe into colonies and "spheres
of influence," ushering in a permanent struggle to divide and redivide the

globe. Military conflict among the imperialists over spheres of influence predominated until the end of World War II, which was in many ways a continuation on an expanded scale of World War I. In the first war, the German imperialists had lost their colonies in Africa to the British. Britain and France also had divided up the Ottoman Empire in the Middle East.

In World War II German imperialism tried again to force its way onto the world stage, this time in an alliance, called the Axis, with Japanese and Italian imperialism. The Axis powers were decisively defeated, but Britain and France were also exhausted by the war. The question of who would dominate the imperialist camp—the issue underlying both world wars—was finally settled when the United States emerged as the preeminent imperialist power. It took charge of reorganizing its capitalist rivals and the entire capitalist world under its domination.

WAR BETWEEN SOCIALIST AND IMPERIALIST CAMPS

During World War II, the USSR not only survived a massive invasion by German imperialism but went on to defeat the Nazi fascist armies, albeit at great cost. In China, the Communists built an army of workers and peasants to resist the invasion by Japanese imperialism. After the war, the struggle continued on a class basis against the landlords and the capitalists allied to the imperialists—called the comprador bourgeoisie. When the Chinese Revolution triumphed in 1949, and it became an ally of the USSR and Eastern Europe, there emerged a socialist camp consisting of almost one-third of the world's people.

Triumphant, nuclear-armed U.S. imperialism put an end to a 50-year period of inter-imperialist war when it mobilized the forces of world capitalism for an all-out struggle to contain the further expansion of both the socialist camp and national liberation struggles in Africa, Asia, and Latin America that were threatening to overthrow colonial and neocolonial rule, and eventually roll back and destroy the forces of socialism and liberation.

The old driving force of war, the inter-imperialist struggle to redivide the globe, was superseded by a struggle between two class camps representing two irreconcilable social systems—socialism and capitalism. The Korean War, the Vietnam War, the CIA-financed wars against liberation movements in Angola, Mozambique, Nicaragua, and El Salvador, the "Bay of Pigs" invasion of Cuba, and many other conflicts were all part of the global imperialist war against socialism and national liberation. The Cold War, which was in reality a class war, turned into many small hot wars, with the threat of world war always looming in the background under the banner of anti-communism.

The period following the collapse of the USSR in 1991, instead of ushering in a new era of peace, as much of the world expected, saw the irrepressible war drive of imperialism surface anew as a struggle to reconquer territories lost during the previous era of socialist revolution and national liberation struggles. The bourgeoisie was determined to prevent other countries from breaking away from imperialism.

Before the Bolshevik revolution, as Lenin had pointed out, almost the entire globe was under the direct or indirect rule of one imperialist power or another. Beginning with the creation of the Soviet Union, capitalism lost its sway over one-sixth of the earth's surface. The geographical sphere of imperialist domination contracted steadily for 74 years, primarily in Europe and Asia, but also in the Middle East, Africa, and Latin America. The period after the collapse of the USSR was the first time that imperialism had expanded geographically since the so-called scramble for Africa at the end of the nineteenth century.

This is not to say that inter-imperialist warfare is now permanently ruled out. Under changed relationships of forces, other imperialists would not hesitate to challenge Washington. The uneven development of the imperialist powers, particularly the growing strength of Germany and Japan in relation to U.S. capitalism, is an additional motivation for the Pentagon to use military force as a way to intimidate its rivals, to show who is boss, and to insure that U.S. imperialists get the lion's share of the loot—as, for example, in the U.S.-led NATO war against Yugoslavia.

But, for the foreseeable future, the military dominance of the U.S. ruling class seems unchallengeable in the military sphere. Thus inter-imperialist struggle has been confined to the economic and diplomatic spheres. If the European and Japanese imperialists seek to build up their military forces at the present, it is not for the purpose of challenging the Pentagon militarily but in order to gain some independent leverage to participate in the reconquest of the world without having to rely so heavily on Washington.

'Regime change' from Clinton to Bush

The new orientation of the imperialist war drive toward reconquest did not spring whole from the minds of George W. Bush and the so-called neo-cons. It was first codified under the Clinton administration in relation to Iraq. In fact, the term "regime change" was first written into law in 1998 under pressure from the right. Regime change in Iraq was explicitly demanded in a 1998 letter to Clinton signed by, among others, Donald Rumsfeld and Paul

Wolfowitz. It was then carried out in practice by the Clinton administration with sanctions and bombing against Iraq and a merciless, unprovoked air war against Yugoslavia, the last even semi-independent country in central and southern Europe, which had retained elements of socialism after the era of President Tito.

The concept of regime change was expanded by the Bush administration in its "National Security Strategy" doctrine of September 2002, when it generalized the right of U.S. imperialism to impose "regime change" and to engage in so-called "preemptive warfare." Bush openly targeted Iraq, Iran, and the Democratic People's Republic of Korea in his infamous "Axis of Evil" speech.

While he did not explicitly target socialist Cuba in the speech, the Bush administration has done everything it could to overthrow the government and restore the old colonialist regime. It has also used subversive measures against Venezuela, Bolivia, Ecuador, and other governments seeking to break with imperialism

Bush's "Nuclear Posture Review" announced the adoption for the first time of the "first-nuclear-strike" policy and revised U.S. military doctrine to integrate tactical nuclear strikes into battlefield plans together with conventional warfare. Alongside the change in doctrine, Bush issued orders to target seven countries for potential nuclear attack.

At the same time, in a less publicized way, the Pentagon was also modernizing its strike force in the Pacific region by constructing a theater anti-missile system. It was building up its bases in Central Asia on the southern flank of Russia and China and redeploying forces from Western Europe to Eastern Europe and the Balkans.

It is worth noting that in March 1992, after the collapse of the USSR and toward the end of the Bush I administration, an internal Department of Defense document called the "Defense Planning Guidance" declared the intention of U.S. imperialism to rule the world and warned that no power or combination of powers should even think about challenging Washington or the Pentagon. It was written by Paul Wolfowitz, at that time deputy to Secretary of Defense Dick Cheney, and "Scooter" Libby, who was later convicted in the case involving CIA agent Valerie Plame. All three men signed off on the document.

Parts of this document were leaked to the *New York Times*, but the full document has never been made public. During the following administrations of Bill Clinton and George W. Bush, there occurred a significant evolution of the forward strategy doctrine of U.S. imperialism—from that of static rule to one of expansive reconquest, that is, "regime change."

The reactionary slogans of the era of reconquest have been fashioned to ensnare the masses in the post-Soviet period: "the war against terrorism," the need to eliminate or prevent "weapons of mass destruction," the campaign to "spread democracy" and "stamp out tyranny," etc., are being taken up by the entire capitalist media and political establishment as general slogans for the time. These slogans were being circulated before 9/11, but took on full force thereafter.

Such slogans, of course, are all directed against the governments of countries that have broken away from imperialism in the last century or against movements and countries that are fighting for their liberation now. This ideological offensive in the era of reconquest is equivalent to the anti-communist crusade of the Cold War era. Its cries of "godless communism," etc., were a smokescreen for the attempt to whip up prejudice and conceal the class character of the struggle between the two camps of socialism and imperialism.

When the USSR, the German Democratic Republic, and Eastern Europe collapsed, imperialism regained access to over one-fifth of the globe. The imperialist powers also had a freer hand in exploiting many bourgeois, semi-independent countries that had leaned on the USSR and the socialist camp for assistance in countering the aggressive attempts at neo-colonial penetration by imperialism. However, there still remained significant portions of the globe not under the control of imperialism. Washington has since set its sights on the reconquest of those parts of the world retaining any form of independence that could pose an obstacle to the advance of monopoly capital.

Thus, while the form of the imperialist war drive has changed over time with the changes in the world situation, and the relationship of forces on a global scale has shifted, the fundamental nature of the war drive as first explained by Lenin is as true today as in his time. Its goal is to secure and expand the profits of monopoly capital, whose drive to accumulate capital is irrepressible.

Colossus with feet of clay

In planning for the war on Iraq, then Secretary of Defense Donald Rumsfeld developed a doctrine that reflected his military views in support of the 2002 "National Security Strategy" document, the strategic doctrine of reconquest as made public by Bush. The Rumsfeld doctrine was tested in Iraq but was part of a global strategy and plan for "military transformation" promulgated at the outset of the Bush administration. Its essence was to use a combination of high-technology guidance systems, from land, sea, air, and space, to coordinate highly lethal, highly accurate strikes that would create "shock and awe" to knock out or fatally weaken a regime. It relied heavily on limited ground forces, with an emphasis on highly trained Special Forces that could be rapidly deployed across the globe to consummate the conquest.

On the face of it, this doctrine was tailor-made to demonstrate that U.S. imperialism has the capacity to embark on its campaign of reconquest. The Rumsfeld doctrine consciously tried to overcome the fatal weak point of U.S. imperialism—how to deal with the masses at home and abroad—by concentrating on what he considered to be its strong points: high technology and overwhelming military power.

In light of the disastrous consequences in Iraq and the utter failure of the Pentagon to anticipate a sustained and powerful resistance to the U.S. occupation, this doctrine may seem now to have been based on a delusion. But it did have a clear purpose from the point of view of imperialist strategy. It was calculated to show that the U.S. military, using high-tech, high-explosive firepower and limited ground troops, could conquer the world by knocking out regimes that opposed it without having to resort to military conscription—the draft. Its goal was to achieve imperialist conquest abroad while maintaining social stability at home.

The failure of the Rumsfeld doctrine in the face of the Iraqi resistance confirms a characterization of imperialism that Lenin made during the struggle of the Bolsheviks to hold on to power. In October 1919, Lenin addressed the progress of the war against the imperialist armies of intervention and the domestic counter-revolutionary forces besieging the revolution on all sides:

> Victory in war goes to the side whose people has greater reserves, greater resources of strength and greater endurance.
>
> We have more of all these qualities than the Whites, more than the "all-powerful" Anglo-French imperialism, this colossus with feet of clay. We have more of them because we can draw, and for a long time will continue to draw, more and more deeply upon the workers and working peasants; upon those classes which were oppressed by capitalism and which everywhere form the overwhelming majority of the population....
>
> Our enemies, whether the Russian or the world bourgeoisie, have nothing remotely resembling this reservoir; the ground is more and more giving way under their feet; they are being deserted by ever greater numbers of their former supporters among the workers and peasants.[264]

It was precisely to minimize the role of the masses that the Rumsfeld doctrine was formulated. It shows that while Bush, Cheney, and Rumsfeld (and now his successors at the Pentagon) underestimated the role of the masses, nevertheless their strategy was to do everything militarily and technologically possible to get around the problem of mass resistance to a draft at home and a wider war in Iraq, Afghanistan, and beyond.

In Iraq, things turned out just as Lenin predicted. The resistance, despite being faced with overwhelming firepower, with tens of thousands rounded up and imprisoned, thousands of fighters killed, and despite being divided within itself, draws deeply upon the Iraqi masses while the U.S. invasionary force grows exhausted and the "ground is more and more giving way under its feet."

When the smoke clears in Iraq, or perhaps before, the imperialists will have to go back to the drawing board. Washington and the Pentagon are going to have to refashion their military approach.

The question facing the anti-war movement is this: Will the U.S. ruling class, seeing its vulnerability in Iraq, Afghanistan, and Iran, declare that its ambitions are beyond its resources and retreat into a less belligerent and expansive mode? Or will it move in the direction of further military adventurism?

The developing confrontation with Iran is a case in point. The Pentagon is bogged down in Iraq and Afghanistan. The Bush administration and its chief military strategists have been humbled. The great, "all-powerful" colossus, to use Lenin's term, has been held at bay. The Bush administration is now in the position of having to restore Washington's status of invincible superpower.

Thus, there is constant talk of a nuclear strike on a non-nuclear developing country like Iran, which is not even at war with the U.S. Such a horrific prospect, had it been contemplated during the Soviet era, could never have been uttered in public. (It was revealed after the Vietnam War that Henry Kissinger, Nixon's secretary of state, threatened the Vietnamese with nuclear attack several times during "peace" negotiations. But that fact was never allowed to see the light of day at the time.)

Whether the U.S. will actually use nuclear weapons or carry out an unprovoked military attack on Iran is not known. But the fact that the Pentagon is brandishing nuclear threats is a sign not only of military madness but of desperation and ultimately of strategic weakness in the struggle to reconquer the world.

Peace, an interlude between wars

A cardinal tenet of Leninism is that war in the era of imperialism is inevitable. Periods of peace are only interludes of preparation for new wars. The entire bloody history of imperialism has borne out this thesis. The aggressive posture of Democrats and Republicans alike towards the rest of the world is a daily demonstration in the political sphere of how deeply rooted in ruling-class society is this tendency toward military adventure, big-power chauvinism, and domination.

The dominant forces that drive imperialism, as Lenin pointed out, are the largest and most powerful monopolies—such as Big Oil, the military-industrial complex, the transnational banks, etc. It is necessary to fortify the movement on this question and to continue to strategize about reaching the workers with an anti-militarist message.

This is especially pertinent to the question of maintaining the independence of the movement and the working class from the imperialist-controlled Democratic Party and any other political movement tied to imperialism. The question of a peaceful evolution of imperialism resolves itself down to the issue of whether capitalism can soften its economic contradictions and function in opposition to the laws of capitalist accumulation and the drive for the maximization of profit. But these are irrepressible forces that drive the ruling class toward war, whether they want it or not.

Expand or die

The struggle to penetrate and reconquer the globe is not a choice by the ruling class, any more than was the earlier struggle to redivide the globe, which resulted in two world wars, or the struggle against the socialist camp that threatened thermonuclear war and caused major wars of imperialist aggression in Korea and Vietnam. Any particular war may appear as a matter of choice. But the consistency of the war drive over the period of a century shows its deeply rooted character. All these wars were driven by the organic need of imperialism to expand or die.

These military adventures were the result of the underlying pressure to find new spheres of investment, raw materials, and markets for the dynamically developing productive forces of world capitalism, which long ago outgrew the confines of the nation-state. The pressure for war comes from the inner contradictions of the massive development of productive capacity, which always outstrips the slow development of consumption under capitalism, inevitably resulting in capitalist overproduction, the contraction of capitalist exploitation, the shrinking of profits, and mass unemployment—or depression.

War is a disruptive and potentially destabilizing event for capitalism. Most of the bourgeoisie, save the military-industrial complex, would undoubtedly prefer peace to war. Peace with class oppression is the best possible scenario for the bourgeoisie, for it guarantees the uninterrupted, "peaceful" exploitation of labor and piling up of profits. But even those in the ruling class who prefer peace will go to war if it is the only path available to continue to expand their profits and forestall or divert an economic crisis of capitalist accumulation. It is the ruling class that controls the state. It is the ruling class that will make the decisions on war and peace until the working class takes that state out of their hands and constructs its own.

Acknowledgments

Low-Wage Capitalism originated as a discussion paper. The task of elaborating it into a fully developed work evolved over time and could not have been accomplished without the dedicated assistance of Deirdre Griswold and Naomi Cohen, who collaborated on its editing and paid close attention to every aspect of the writing. Lallan Schoenstein designed the cover and the overall graphic style of the book. Cheryl LaBash both proofed and copyedited the manuscript and Paddy Colligan did final reference and fact checking, as well as proofreading.

Needless to say, the division between editorial and technical work was blurred on many occasions. The editors paid attention to details of copyediting and proofreading, while the copyeditor and proofreaders used their editorial and political understanding to make valuable suggestions.

I am grateful to Berta Joubert-Ceci who translated into Spanish a summary of the book for presentation at the IV International Conference on "The Work of Karl Marx and the Challenges of the 21st Century," held in Havana, Cuba, in May 2008.

Thanks to Monica Moorehead, editor of *Marxism, Reparations and the Black Freedom Struggle*, for suggestions on the prison-industrial complex section. Thanks to Clarence Thomas of the International Longshore and Warehouse Union (ILWU), Local 10, for his suggestions on the section dealing with Local 10 and the Million Worker March Movement. Thomas is a leader of the MWMM and an organizer of the West Coast dockworkers' general strike against the war in Iraq on May Day, 2008. Thanks also to Martha Grevatt, author of a soon-to-be published work on the General Motors sit-down strike of 1936-37, who pointed out the little-known history of the very important women's sit-down strike of 1937 at Woolworth's. Thanks also to Shelley Ettinger, who made important suggestions for the section on lesbian and gay income, and to Leslie Feinberg, author of *Stone Butch Blues* and other works, who gave literary input and suggestions on the characterization of the family.

Of course, the author takes full responsibility for the treatment of those subjects in this book.

Bibliography

ABU-JAMAL, MUMIA. "Greeting to Global Women's Strike," 2005. Assata Shakur Forums, accessed on May 28, 2008, www.assatashakur.org/forum/mumia-abu-jamal/4051-global-womens-strike-2005-a.html?t-4051.html.

AVERY, SUSAN. "Suppliers are global partners at Boeing." *Purchasing Magazine Online,* January 12, 2006, www.purchasing.com/article/CA62979.html.

AZENMAN, N.C. "Record High Ratio of Americans in Prison." *Washington Post,* February 28, 2008.

BERGER, SUZANNE. *How We Compete: What Companies Around the World Are Doing to Make It in Today's Global Economy.* New York: Doubleday, 2005.

BERNANKE, BEN S. "Global Economic Integration: What's New and What's Not?" (Remarks at the Federal Reserve Bank of Kansas City's Thirtieth Annual Economic Symposium, August 25, 2006). Jackson Hole, Wyo. Board of Governors of the Federal Reserve System, accessed on August 28, 2006, www.federalreserve.gov/newsevents/speech/bernanke20060825a.htm.

BERNSTEIN, IRVING. *The Turbulent Years: A History of the American Worker, 1933-1941.* Boston: Houghton Mifflin, 1970.

BLINDER, ALAN S. "Offshoring: The Next Industrial Revolution?" *Foreign Affairs,* March/April, 2006.

BOUSHEY, HEATHER, SHAWN FREMSTAD, RACHEL GRAGG, and MARGY WALLER. "Understanding Low-Wage Work in the United States." The Mobility Agenda, Center for Economic and Policy Research, March 2007, www.cepr.net.

BOYER, RICHARD O., and HERBERT M. MORAIS. *Labor's Untold Story.* New York: Marzani and Munsell, 1965.

BRADSHER, KEITH. "The G.M. Settlement: The Overview." *New York Times,* July 29, 1998.

BRECHER, JEREMY. "Resisting Concessions." *Z Magazine,* March 1998, www.zmag.org/zmag/viewArticle/12731.

BRONFENBRENNER, KATE, AND STEPHANIE LUCE. "The changing nature of corporate global restructuring: The impact of production shifts on jobs in the U.S., China, and around the globe." Washington, DC: US-China Economic and Security Review Commission, 2004. Report submitted to the U.S.-China Economic and Security Review Commission. University of Massachusetts, Amherst, Oct. 14, 2004. Cornell University ILR School, digitalcommons.ilr.cornell.edu/cbpubs/15.

CHAN, SEWELL, AND STEVEN GREENHOUSE. "From Back-Channel Contacts, Blueprint for a Deal." *New York Times,* December 23, 2005.

CHANDRA, NAYAN. Transcript of an interview with Louis Uchitelle. The interview has the same title as his book, *The Disposable American: Layoffs and Their Consequences.* Yale Global interview, Yale Center for the Study of Globalization, May 11, 2006, YaleGlobal online. yaleglobal.yale.edu/display.article?id=88.

"Coming Up Short: A Comparison of Wages and Work Supports in 10 American Communities," *Wider Opportunities for Women (WOW),* Summer/Fall 2004.

DEPARLE, JASON. "A Good Provider Is One Who Leaves." *New York Times Magazine,* April 22, 2007.

EHRENREICH, BARBARA. *Nickled and Dimed: On (Not) Getting By in America.* New York: Henry Holt, 2001.

ELLIOTT, JEFF. "Prison Labor Boon for Employers, Report Says." *The Albion Monitor,* March 10, 1996, www.monitor.net/monitor.

Engardio, Peter, ed. *Chindia: How China and India Are Revolutionizing Global Business.* New York: McGraw-Hill, 2007.

---. "Online Extra: Penske's Offshore Partner in India." *BusinessWeek* Online, January 30, 2006.

"Factories Go South; So Does Pay," *Business Week*, April 9, 2007.

"Facts About Prisons and Prisoners." The Sentencing Project, accessed on May 28, 2008, www.sentencingproject.org.

Fantasia, Rick, and Kim Voss. *Hard Work: Remaking the American Labor Movement.* Berkeley: University of California Press, 2004.

Faux, Jeff. *The Global Class War.* Hoboken, NJ: John Wiley & Sons, 2006.

Ferry, Jeff. "Flextronics: Staying Real in a Virtual World." *strategy+business*, Winter 2004.

Fishman, Charles. *The Wal-Mart Effect.* New York: Penguin Books, 2006.

Freeman, Richard B. "Doubling the Global Workforce: The challenge of integrating China, India, and the former Soviet Bloc into the world economy." Presentation on Nov. 8, 2004, Center for Global Development, www.iie.com/publications/papers/freeman1104.pdf.

---. "Do Workers Still Want Unions? More Than Ever." *Economic Policy Briefing Paper*, Feb. 22, 2007, www.epi.org.

Friedman, Thomas L. *The World Is Flat: A Brief History of the Twenty-first Century.* New York: Farrar, Straus and Giroux, 2006.

Gates, Gary. "Income of Gay Men Lags Behind that of Men Partnered with Women." Urban Institute, accessed June 24, 2008, www.urban.org/publications/900631.html.

Glover, K. Daniel. "Prison labor program under fire by lawmakers, private industry." *National Journal*, April 12, 2004. See www.govexec.com/story_page_pf.cfm?articleid=28221.

Goldberg, Eve, and Linda Evans. "The big business of prisons." August 13, 1998, Green Left online, accessed April 30, 2008, www.greenleft.org.au/1998/328/20614.

---. "The prison-industrial complex & the global economy." Prison Activist Resource Center, Berkeley, December 18, 1997, www.hartford-hwp.com/archives/26/152.html.

Greenhouse, Steven. "Yearlong Effort Key to Success for Teamsters." *New York Times*, August 25, 1997.

Harrison, Bennett. *Lean and Mean: Why Large Corporations Will Continue to Dominate the Global Economy.* New York: Guilford Press, 1994.

Head, Simon. *The New Ruthless Economy: Work and Power in the Digital Age.* New York: Oxford University Press, 2003.

Hill, Nicole. "With Fewer Migrant Workers, Farmers Turn to Prison Labor." *Christian Science Monitor.* August 22, 2007. AlterNet, accessed June 24, 2008, www.alternet.org/workplace/60497.

Human Rights Watch. "Unfair Advantage: Workers' Freedom of Association in the United States under International Human Rights Standards." www.hrw.org/reports/2000/uslabor.

"Hunger in America Rises by 43 Percent over Last Five Years," *ScienceDaily,* October 29, 2005.

Kelly, Kathy. "U.S. Prison Labor: Another Cog in the War Machine." May 7, 2004. AntiWar.com, accessed May 21, 2008, www.antiwar.com/orig/kelly.php?articleid=2494.

Kripalani, Manjeet, with Steve Hamm. "Open Season on Outsourcers: More Western giants are snapping up Indian companies that specialize in back-office operations." *Business Week*, April 17, 2008.

Krugman, Paul. "The Big Disconnect." *New York Times,* September 1, 2006.

Lenin, V.I. "Imperialism, the Highest Stage of Capitalism." *Collected Works.* Vol. 22. Moscow: Progress Publishers, 1964.

---. "Results of Party Week in Moscow and Our Tasks." *Collected Works.* Vol. 30. Moscow: Progress Publishers, 1965. Also available at www.marxists.org.

---. "What Is to Be Done?" *Collected Works*. Vol. 5. Moscow: Progress Publishers, 1975.

LEONDAR-WRIGHT, BETSY. "Black Job Loss Déjà Vu." June 4, 2004. *dollars&sense*, accessed October 29, 2006, www.dollarsandsense.org/archives/2004/0504leondar.html.

LEONHARDT, DAVID. "Our Safety Net Is Disappearing. What Will Follow?" *New York Times*, April 4, 2007.

LICHTENSTEIN, NELSON, ed. *Wal-Mart: The Face of Twenty-First Century Capitalism*. New York: New Press Books, 2006.

LIPTACK, ADAM. "U.S. Imprisons One in 100 Adults, Report Finds." *New York Times*, February 29, 2008.

LYNN, BARRY. *The End of the Line: The Rise and Coming Fall of the Global Corporation*. New York: Doubleday, 2005.

"Making Ends Meet: How much does it cost to raise a family in California?" The California Budget Project, revised November 2005. California Progress Report, www.cbp.org/pdfs/2005/0509mem.pdf.

MALLABY, SEBASTIAN. "Progressive Wal-Mart. Really." *Washington Post*, November 28, 2005.

MARCY, SAM. *High Tech, Low Pay*. New York: WW Publishers, 1986.

MARX, KARL, and FREDERICK ENGELS. *Manifesto of the Communist Party*. Peking: Foreign Languages Press, 1975.

MARX, KARL. *Capital*, Vol. I. Moscow: Progress Publishers, 1974.

MARX, KARL. *The First International and After: Political Writings*. Vol. 3. Ed. David Fernbach. London: Penguin Books in association with New Left Review, 1974.

MISHEL, LAWRENCE, JARED BERNSTEIN, and SYLVIA ALLEGRETTO. *State of Working America 2006/2007*. Ithaca, NY: Cornell University Press, 2007.

MITCHELL, BROADUS. *Depression Decade: From New Era through New Deal, 1929-1941*. New York: Rinehart, 1946.

MOORE, SOLOMON. "Justice Department Numbers Show Prison Trends." *New York Times*, December 6, 2007.

MOOREHEAD, MONICA, ed. *Marxism, Reparations and the Black Freedom Struggle*. New York: World View Forum, 2007.

NOYES, ANDREW. "Study: Gay parents poorer than straight ones." *PlanetOut Network*, September 23, 2005, www.gay.com/news/article.html?2005/09/23/2.

"Offshoring Backlash." *Global: Daily Economic Comment, Morgan Stanley Economic Trends*, February 13, 2004, www.rexialo.com/site/pdf/Offshore.pdf.

PALLEY, THOMAS. "Super-sized: What happens when two billion workers join the global labor market?" September 29, 2005, www.thomaspalley.com/?p=18.

PASSEL, JEFFREY. "The Size and Characteristics of the Unauthorized Migrant Population in the U.S., Estimates Based on the March 2005 Current Population Survey." Pew Hispanic Center, March 7, 2006; pewhispanic.org/files/reports/61.pdf /.

PETERS, JEREMY W. "Hardly a Union Hotbed, Toyota's Kentucky Plant Is a Test for Organizers." *New York Times*, September 4, 2007.

Pew Research Center. "U.S. Imprisons One in 100." February 28, 2008. Accessed April 29, 2008, www.pewcenteronthestates.org/uploadedFiles/One%20in%20100.pdf.

PUGH, TONY. "U.S. Economy Leaving Record Numbers in Severe Poverty." *McClatchy Newspapers*, February 22, 2007.

RACHIEFF, PETER. *Hard Pressed in the Heartland: The Hormel Strike and the Future of the Labor Movement*. Boston: South End Press, 1993.

RIAZANOV, DAVID. *Karl Marx and Friedrich Engels: An Introduction to Their Lives and Work*. New York: Monthly Review Press, 1973.

ROACH, STEPHEN. "More Jobs, Worse Work." *New York Times*, July 22, 2004.

ROBERTS, PAUL CRAIG. "The New Face of Class War." *Counterpunch*, Sept. 30/Oct. 1, 2006, *www.counterpunch.org/roberts09302006.html*.

ROBERTS, SAM, "Minorities Now Form Majority in One-Third of Most-Populous Counties." *New York Times*, August 9, 2007.

ROSEN, RUTH. "The Care Crisis." *The Nation*, March 12, 2007.

SAHADI, JEANNE. "Census Bureau reports a slight rise in 2006 incomes but as a group, households aren't doing as well as before the 2001 recession." *CNNMoney.com*, Aug. 28, 2007.

SCHLOSSER, ERIC. *Fast Food Nation*. New York: HarperCollins, 2002.

SCHMITT, JOHN, and BEN ZIPPER. "The Decline in African-American Representation in Unions and Manufacturing, 1979-2006." Center for Economic and Policy Research, Washington, D.C., March 2007, www.cepr.net/content/view/1062/8/.

"Showdown in Motown: the Detroit Newspaper Strike, 1995-1997." Unpublished compilation of articles that first appeared in *Workers World* newspaper, 1995-1997, written by trade union participants in the strike support effort: Kris Hamel, David Sole, Key Martin, Stephanie Hedgecoke, and Jerry Goldberg.

SHULMAN, BETH. *The Betrayal of Work: How Low-Wage Jobs Fail 30 Million Americans*. New York: New Press, 2003.

SMITH, DAVID M., and GARY GATES. "Gay and Lesbian Families in the United States." Urban Institute, accessed July 1, 2008, www.urban.org/publications/1000491.html.

"Special Report: The Future of Outsourcing." *Business Week*, January 30, 2006.

STITES, TOM. "How Corporations Became 'Persons.'" UUWORLD, www.uuworld. org/2003/03/feature1a.html.

"Study: Offshoring of U.S. Jobs Accelerating." Associated Press, May 18, 2004, www.msnbc. msn.com/id/5003753/.

TAGLIABUE, JOHN. "The Eastern Bloc of Outsourcing; Europe Finds Its Own Answer to Bangalore, and It's Growing Fast." *New York Times*, April 19, 2007.

"Thousands Apply for Jobs at New Wal-Mart." *Chicago Sun-Times*, January 26, 2006.

TONELSON, ALAN. *The Race to the Bottom: Why a Worldwide Worker Surplus and Uncontrolled Free Trade Are Sinking American Living Standards*. Colorado: Westview Press, 2002.

U.S. Bureau of Labor Statistics. Current Employment Statistics. www.bls.gov/ces/home.htm.

U.S. Census Bureau. *Statistical Abstract of the United States: 2007*. 126th ed. Washington, DC, 2006.

---. *Quarterly Report for Manufacturing, Mining and Trade Corporations*. 2006.

UCHITELLE, LOUIS. *The Disposable American: Layoffs and Their Consequences*. New York: Alfred A. Knopf, 2006.

---. "A Statistic That's Missing: Jobs That Moved Overseas." *New York Times*, October 5, 2003.

---. "End of the Line As Detroit Workers Know It." *New York Times*, April 1, 2007.

---. "For Blacks, a Dream in Decline." *New York Times*, October 23, 2005.

United Nations Industrial Development Organization (UNIDO). "Industry and Trade in a Global Economy with Special Reference to Sub-Saharan Africa." 2005, www.unido.org/ fileadmin/import/userfiles/puffk/ahghana5.pdf.

URBINA, IAN. "Hard Time in the Heartland." *Middle East Report Online*, September 30, 2003, www.merip.org/mero/mero093003.html.

"Visteon cuts jobs, shifts work abroad." *Detroit News*. Online, November 1, 2006.

WARREN, ELIZABETH, AND AMELIA WARREN TYAGI. *The Two-Income Trap: Why Middle-Class Mothers and Fathers Are Going Broke*. New York: Basic Books, 2003.

WELCH, DAVID. "Go Bankrupt, Then Go Overseas." *Business Week*, April 24, 2006.

WESSEL, DAVID, AND BOB DAVIS. "Pain from Free Trade Spurs Second Thoughts." *Wall Street Journal*, March 28, 2007.

"Work in American Prisons: Joint Ventures with the Private Sector." *The Albion Monitor*, March 10, 1996, www.monitor.net/monitor.

"Workplace Protection Linked to Higher Earnings for Less-Educated Gay Men." June 13, 2003. Urban Institute, accessed June 24, 2008, www.urban.org/publications/900632.html.

YELLEN, SAMUEL. *American Labor Struggles: 1877-1934*. New York: Monad Press, 1936.

ZEIGER, ROBERT H. *The CIO, 1935 to 1955*. Chapel Hill: University of North Carolina Press, 1995.

ZEIGER, ROBERT H., AND GILBERT J. GALL. *American Workers, American Unions: the Twentieth Century*. Baltimore: Johns Hopkins University Press, 2002.

ZINN, HOWARD, DANA FRANK, and ROBIN G. KELLEY. *Three Strikes: Miners, Musicians, Salesgirls, and the Fighting Spirit of Labor's Last Century*. Boston: Beacon Press, 2001.

Additional Internet Sources

Accenture Web site. See Fact Sheet, newsroom.accenture.com/section_display.cfm?section_id=160.

Arizona Correctional Industries Web site, www.adc.state.az.us/catalog.htm.

California Prison Industry Authority Web site, www.pia.ca.gov/.

Flextronics Web site, www.flextronics.com.

International Longshore Workers Union Web site, www.ilwu19.com/history/the_ilwu_story/contents.htm.

Iowa Prison Industries Web site, www:iaprisonind.com/, May 28, 2008.

Solectron Web site, www.solectron.com.

UNICOR Web site, www.unicor.gov.

Endnotes

Chapter 1 – Doubling the global workforce

1   Richard B. Freeman, "Doubling the Global Workforce: The challenge of integrating China, India, and the former Soviet Bloc into the world economy." Presentation to Center for Global Development, Nov. 8, 2004. www.iie.com/publications/papers/freeman1104.pdf.

2   Ibid.

3   Ibid.

4   Thomas L. Friedman, *The World Is Flat: A Brief History of the Twenty-first Century* (New York: Farrar, Straus and Giroux, 2006), p. 212.

5   Ibid., p. 10.

6   Ibid., p. 213.

7   Ibid.

8   Ibid.

9   Alan Tonelson, *The Race to the Bottom: Why a Worldwide Worker Surplus and Uncontrolled Free Trade Are Sinking American Living Standards* (Colorado: Westview Press, 2002), p. 53.

10 Ibid., p. 55.

11 Ibid., p. 53.

12 Thomas Palley, "Super-sized: What happens when two billion workers join the global labor market?" www.thomaspalley.com/?p=18, posted Sept. 29, 2005.

13 Ibid.

14 Ben S. Bernanke, "Global Economic Integration: What's New and What's Not?" Remarks at the Federal Reserve Bank of Kansas City's Thirtieth Annual Economic Symposium, Jackson Hole, WY, Aug. 25, 2006.

15 Ibid.

16 Ibid.

17 Ibid.

18 Ibid.

19 Suzanne Berger, *How We Compete: What Companies Around the World Are Doing to Make It in Today's Global Economy* (New York: Doubleday, 2005), p. 19.

20 Calculated from percentages given by Berger and dollar amounts given in World Trade Organization press release: "Trade growth in 2005 to slow from record 2004 pace," Oct. 27, 2005, www.wto.org/english/news_e/pres05_e/pr417_e.htm.

21 Tonelson, *Race to the Bottom*, p. 15.

22 Barry Lynn, *The End of the Line: The Rise and Coming Fall of the Global Corporation* (New York: Doubleday, 2005), p. 7.

23 Ibid.

24 Berger, *How We Compete*, p. 20.

25 Tonelson, *The Race to the Bottom*, p. 16.

26 Friedman, *The World Is Flat*, p. 244.

27 Karl Marx and Frederick Engels, *Manifesto of the Communist Party* (Peking: Foreign Languages Press, 1975), p.48.

28 Karl Marx, *Capital* (Moscow: Progress Publishers, 1974), Vol. I, p. 164ff.

29 Ibid., p. 524ff.

Chapter 2 – New global networks of exploitation

30 Friedman, *The World Is Flat*, p. 516.

31 Lynn, *The End of the Line*, p. 126.

32 Berger, *How We Compete*, p. 151.

33 Bennett Harrison, *Lean and Mean: Why Large Corporations Will Continue to Dominate the Global Economy* (New York: Guilford Press, 1994), p. 156.

34 Ibid., p. 158.

35 Berger, *How We Compete*, p. 83.

36 Friedman, *The World Is Flat*, p. 243.

37 Ibid., p. 447.

38 Berger, *How We Compete*, p. 147; Friedman, *The World Is Flat*, p. 244.

39 Berger, *How We Compete*, pp. 148, 212.

40 "Factories Go South; So Does Pay," *Business Week*, April 9, 2007.

41 David Welch, "Go Bankrupt, Then Go Overseas," *Business Week*, April 24, 2006.

42 "Visteon cuts jobs, shifts work abroad," *Detroit News* Online, Nov. 1, 2006.

43 Friedman, *The World Is Flat*, p. 227.

44 Berger, *How We Compete*, p. 211.

Chapter 3 – Supply chains: vassals of the lords of capitalism

45 Flextronics, "About Us," www.flextronics.com.

46 Ibid.

47 The Flextronics Web site in the spring of 2008 listed 138 locations where it had factories, including twenty-four in China, eleven in

Malaysia, four in Brazil, four in Mexico, two in the Czech Republic, five in Hungary, three in the Ukraine, three in India, four in Ireland, others in all the major imperialist countries in Europe, and ten in the U.S. See www.flextronics.com.

48 Flextronics Partners, op cit., www.flextronics.com/partners.

49 Jeff Ferry, "Flextronics: Staying Real in a Virtual World," *strategy+business*, Winter 2004.

50 Ibid.

51 Ibid.

52 Ibid.

53 Ibid.

54 Ibid.

55 Ibid.

56 Solectron, www.solectron.com.

57 Berger, *How We Compete*, p. 79.

58 Ibid., p. 29.

59 Ibid., p.148.

60 Susan Avery, "Suppliers are global partners at Boeing," *Purchasing Magazine Online*, Jan. 12 2006, www.purchasing.com/article/CA62979. html.

61 Friedman, *The World Is Flat*, p. 229.

62 Lynn, *The End of the Line*, p. 151.

63 Ibid.

64 Ibid., p. 131.

65 Ibid., p. 144.

66 Ibid., p. 145.

67 Ibid., p. 142.

68 Ibid., p. 152.

69 Ibid., p. 11.

70 Ibid.

71 UNIDO, "Industry and Trade in a Global Economy with Special Reference to Sub-Saharan Africa," 2005.

72 UNIDO, p. 5.

73 Ibid.

74 Berger, *How We Compete*, p. 186.

75 Ibid., p. 142.

76 Ibid., p. 191.

77 Ibid.

78 Harrison, *Lean and Mean*, p. 14.

79 Louis Uchitelle, "A Statistic That's Missing: Jobs That Moved Overseas," *New York Times*, Oct. 5, 2003.

80 Paul Craig Roberts, "The New Face of Class War," *Counterpunch* Online, Sept. 30/Oct. 1, 2006, *www.counterpunch.org/roberts09302006.html*. Roberts is a former assistant secretary of the Treasury in the Reagan administration, a writer for the *Wall Street Journal*, and a rogue conservative who

has turned against the Iraq war and flirts with populist politics.

Chapter 4–Offshoring: millions of service jobs at risk

81 Blinder quoted in David Wessel and Bob Davis, "Pain from Free Trade Spurs Second Thoughts," *Wall Street Journal*, March 28, 2007.

82 Alan S. Blinder, "Offshoring: The Next Industrial Revolution?" *Foreign Affairs*, March/April, 2006.

83 Wessel and Davis, "Pain from Free Trade," op cit.

84 Peter Engardio, ed., *Chindia: How China and India Are Revolutionizing Global Business* (New York: McGraw-Hill, 2007), p. 39.

85 Ibid., p. 44.

86 Ibid., p. 38; also see various articles from *BusinessWeek* and *BusinessWeek* Online between 2003 and 2005, cited in Chapter 3, "The New Global Paradigm."

87 "Study: Offshoring of U.S. Jobs Accelerating," Associated Press, May 18, 2004, www.msnbc.msn.com/id/5003753/.

88 Engardio, *Chindia*, p. 42.

89 Friedman, *The World Is Flat*, p. 24.

90 "Special Report: The Future of Outsourcing," *BusinessWeek*, Jan. 30, 2006.

91 Ibid.

92 Ibid.

93 Peter Engardio, "Online Extra: Penske's Offshore Partner in India," *BusinessWeek* Online, Jan. 30, 2006.

94 Manjeet Kripalani, with Steve Hamm in New York, "Open Season on Outsourcers: More Western giants are snapping up Indian companies that specialize in back-office operations," *Business Week*, April 17, 2008.

95 Accenture Web site, Fact Sheet, http://newsroom.accenture.com/section_display.cfm?section_id=160.

96 For this and the following information on Eastern Europe, see a lengthy article by John Tagliabue, "The Eastern Bloc of Outsourcing; Europe Finds Its Own Answer to Bangalore, and It's Growing Fast," *New York Times*, April 19, 2007.

97 Friedman, *The World Is Flat*, p. 32.

98 Wessel and Davis, "Pain from Free Trade," op cit.

99 Blinder, "Offshoring: The Next Industrial Revolution?" op cit.

100 Ibid.

101 Ibid.

102 Ibid.

103 Ibid.

Chapter 5–Marxism and globalization

104 V.I. Lenin, *Imperialism, the Highest Stage of Capitalism, Collected Works* (Moscow: Progress Publishers, 1964), Vol. 22, p. 257.

105 Ibid., p. 193.

106 Ibid., p. 283.

107 Marx, *Capital,* Vol. I, p. 424.

108 Lenin, *Imperialism,* p. 302.

109 Louis Uchitelle, *The Disposable American: Layoffs and Their Consequences* (New York: Alfred A. Knopf, 2006), p. 145.

110 Jeff Faux, *The Global Class War* (Hoboken, NJ: John Wiley & Sons, 2006), p. 78.

111 Uchitelle, *The Disposable American,* p. 36.

112 Lawrence Mishel, Jared Bernstein, and Sylvia Allegretto, *State of Working America 2006/2007* (Ithaca, NY: Cornell University Press, 2007), pp. 17-18, 211-212. Also Stephen Roach, "More Jobs, Worse Work," *New York Times,* July 22, 2004, and "Offshoring Backlash," *Global: Daily Economic Comment, Morgan Stanley Economic Trends,* Feb. 13, 2004.

Chapter 6–Where high tech is leading

113 Sam Marcy, *High Tech, Low Pay* (New York: WW Publishers, 1986), p. 10.

114 Ibid., p. 72.

115 Ibid., p. 60.

116 Ibid., pp. 60-61.

117 Ibid., p. 67.

118 Ibid., pp. 67-68.

119 Ibid., p. 68.

120 David Leonhardt, "Our Safety Net Is Disappearing. What Will Follow?" *New York Times,* April 4, 2007.

121 Louis Uchitelle, "End of the Line As Detroit Workers Know It," *New York Times,* April 1, 2007.

122 Engardio, *Chindia,* p. 51.

123 "Transcript of *The Disposable American: Layoffs and Their Consequences,*" *Yale Global* interview with Uchitelle by Nayan Chandra, Yale Center for the Study of Globalization, www.YaleGlobal.com, May 11, 2006.

124 Uchitelle, *The Disposable American,* p. 209.

125 Ibid.

126 Ibid., p. 210.

127 Ibid., pp. 131-137.

128 Lynn, *The End of the Line,* pp. 75-76.

129 Uchitelle, *The Disposable American,* p. 155.

130 Marcy, *High Tech, Low Pay,* p. xii.

131 Ibid., pp. 17-18.

132 Uchitelle, *The Disposable American,* p. 130.

133 Marcy, *High Tech, Low Pay,* p. 4.

134 "Thousands Apply for Jobs at New Wal-Mart," *Chicago Sun-Times,* Jan. 26, 2006.

135 U.S. Census Bureau, *Statistical Abstract of the United States: 2007* (126th Edition) Washington, DC, 2006. Table 971, "Gross Domestic Product in Manufacturing in Current and Real (2000) Dollars by Industry: 2000 to 2005." Source: U.S. Bureau of Economic Analysis: Survey of Current Business, May 2007.

136 Ibid., Table 980, "Manufacturing Industries—Employment by Industry: 1990 to 2005." Source: U.S. Bureau of Labor Statistics, Current Employment Statistics internet site, www.bls.gov/ces/home.htm.

137 Ibid., Table 989, "Manufacturing Corporations—Selected Finances: 1990 to 2005." Source: U.S. Census Bureau: *Quarterly Report for Manufacturing, Mining and Trade Corporations* released 2006.

138 Uchitelle, *The Disposable American,* p. 139.

139 U.S. Census Bureau, *Statistical Abstract,* Table 997, "Iron and Steel Industry—Summary 1990 to 2005."

140 Ibid., Table 1011, "Aerospace Industry Sales by Product Group and Customer: 1990 to 2006."

141 Ibid., Table 980.

142 Marcy, *High Tech, Low Pay,* p. xi.

143 Uchitelle, *The Disposable American,* p. 69.

144 Engardio, *Chindia,* p. 51.

145 Tonelson, *The Race to the Bottom,* pp. 39-40.

146 Lawrence Mishel, et al. *The State of Working America 2006/2007,* p. 169.

147 bid., p. 170.

Chapter 7– Globalization and low pay

148 Paul Krugman, "The Big Disconnect," *New York Times,* Sept. 1, 2006.

149 Heather Boushey, Shawn Fremstad, Rachel Gragg, and Margy Waller, "Understanding Low-Wage Work in the United States," The Mobility Agenda, Center for Economic and Policy Research, March 2007. Online at www.cepr.net.

150 Beth Shulman, *The Betrayal of Work: How Low-Wage Jobs Fail 30 Million Americans* (New York: New Press, 2003).

151 Paul Craig Roberts, "The new face of class war," op cit.

152 Uchitelle, *The Disposable American,* p. 66.

153 Eric Schlosser, *Fast Food Nation* (New York: HarperCollins, 2002), p. 69.

154 Ibid., p. 72.

155 Simon Head, *The New Ruthless Economy: Work and Power in the Digital Age* (New York: Oxford University Press, 2003).

156 Berger, *How We Compete*, p. 140.

157 Karl Marx, *Capital*, Vol. I, pp. 167-168.

158 Ibid., p. 168.

159 Ibid.

160 *State of Working America 2006/2007*, Table 1.8, "Median family income by family type, 1973-2004 (2004 dollars)," p. 55.

161 Barbara Ehrenreich, *Nickled and Dimed: On (Not) Getting By in America* (New York: Henry Holt, 2001), p. 213.

162 *State of Working America, 2006/2007*, Table 1.24, "Annual hours of work, husbands and wives, age 25-54, with children, 1979-2004, by income fifth," p. 91.

163 Elizabeth Warren and Amelia Warren Tyagi, *The Two-Income Trap: Why Middle-Class Mothers and Fathers Are Going Broke* (New York: Basic Books, 2003), p. 51.

164 Faux, *The Global Class War*, p. 197.

165 Marx, *Capital*, Vol. I, p. 373.

166 Jeanne Sahadi, "Census Bureau reports a slight rise in 2006 incomes but as a group, households aren't doing as well as before the 2001 recession," CNNMoney.com, Aug. 28, 2007.

167 Ruth Rosen, "The Care Crisis," *The Nation*, March 12, 2007.

168 Uchitelle, *The Disposable American*, p. 145.

169 Marx, *Capital*, Vol. 1, p. 168.

170 "Making Ends Meet: How much does it cost to raise a family in California?" The California Budget Project, revised November 2005.

171 "Coming Up Short: A Comparison of Wages and Work Supports in 10 American Communities," *Wider Opportunities for Women* (WOW), Summer/Fall 2004.

172 Ibid.

173 Tony Pugh, "U.S. Economy Leaving Record Numbers in Severe Poverty," *McClatchy Newspapers*, Feb. 22, 2007.

174 Ibid.

175 Ibid.

176 Ibid.

177 Ibid.

178 Nelson Lichtenstein, ed., *Wal-Mart: The Face of Twenty-First Century Capitalism* (New York: New Press Books, 2006), pp. 15 and 148.

179 Ibid., p. 268, Wade Rathke; "A Wal-Mart Workers' Association?: An Organizing Plan."

180 Ibid., pp. 268-269.

181 Charles Fishman, *The Wal-Mart Effect* (New York: Penguin Books, 2006), p. 235.

182 Ibid., p.15.

183 Lichtenstein, *Wal-Mart*, p. 176.

184 Fishman, *The Wal-Mart Effect*, p. 185.

185 Ibid., p. 186.

186 Lichtenstein, *Wal-Mart*, p. 26.

187 Fishman, *The Wal-Mart Effect*, p. 6.

188 Sebastian Mallaby, "Progressive Wal-Mart. Really," *Washington Post*, Nov. 28, 2005.

Chapter 8 – Sexism, racism, and low wages

189 Mishel et al., *State of Working America 2006/2007*, Table 1.8, op cit.

190 Mishel et al., *The State of Working America*, p. 128.

191 Ibid., pp. 298-299.

192 Ibid., p. 181.

193 Ibid., pp. 181-182.

194 John Schmitt and Ben Zipper, "The Decline in African-American Representation in Unions and Manufacturing, 1979-2006," Center for Economic and Policy Research, March 2007, Washington, D.C. Available online at www.cepr.net/content/view/1062/8/.

195 Louis Uchitelle, "For Blacks, a Dream in Decline," *New York Times*, Oct. 23, 2005.

196 Ibid.

197 Betsy Leondar-Wright, "Black Job Loss Déjà Vu," www.dollarsandsense.org, June 4, 2004. Leondar-Wright is the communications director at United for a Fair Economy and co-author of the UFE report "The State of the Dream: Enduring Disparities in Black and White."

198 Ibid.

199 Ibid.

200 Adam Liptack, "U.S. Imprisons One in 100 Adults, Report Finds," *New York Times*, February 29, 2008.

201 The U.S. population has grown from about 240 million in 1986 to 299 million in 2006. See *Statistical Abstract: 2007*, Table 2, and *New York Times Almanac*, 2008, p. 204.

202 The figures in this section are based on a 2007 Department of Justice report and a February 28, 2008, Pew Research Center study. They are cited in Adam Liptack, "U.S. Imprisons One in 100," see note above; Solomon Moore, "Justice Department Numbers Show Prison Trends," *New York Times*, December 6, 2007; and "Facts About Prisons and Prisoners," The Sentencing Project, www.sentencingproject.org.

203 N.C. Azenman, "Record High Ratio of Americans in Prison," *Washington Post,* February 28, 2008.

204 Eve Goldberg and Linda Evans, "The big business of prisons," Green Left online, August 13, 1998.

205 Eve Goldberg and Linda Evans, "The prison-industrial complex & the global economy," Prison Activist Resource Center, Berkeley, December 18, 1997. Online at www.hartford-hwp.com/archives/26/152.html.

206 Jeff Elliott, "Prison Labor Boon for Employers, Report Says," *The Albion Monitor,* March 10, 1996, www.monitor.net/monitor. Elliott cites "Work in American Prisons: Joint Ventures with the Private Sector," The report studied prison labor in California, South Carolina, and Connecticut.

207 K. Daniel Glover, "Prison labor program under fire by lawmakers, private industry," *National Journal,* April 12, 2004, www.govexec.com/story_page_pf.cfm?articleid=28221.

208 See UNICOR Web site, www.unicor.gov.

209 Ian Urbina, "Hard Time in the Heartland," *Middle East Report Online,* September 30, 2003, at www.merip.org/mero/meropo3003.html. Urbina is a former *New York Times* reporter and former associate editor of Middle East Research and Information Project. Also see Kathy Kelly, "U.S. Prison Labor: Another Cog in the War Machine," May 7, 2004, at www.antiwar.com/orig/kelly.php?articleid=2494.

210 California Prison Industry Authority Web site, www.pia.ca.gov/.

211 Arizona Correctional Industries Web site, www.adc.state.az.us/catalog.htm.

212 Iowa Prison Industries Web site, www:iaprisonind.com/htm/about/whatis.asp, May 28, 2008.

213 Nicole Hill, "With Fewer Migrant Workers, Farmers Turn to Prison Labor," *Christian Science Monitor,* Originally posted August 22, 2007.

214 Mumia Abu-Jamal, "Greeting to Global Women's Strike, 2005," www.assatashakur.org/forum/mumia-abu-jamal/4051-global-womens-strike-2005-a.html?t-4051.html, May 28, 2008.

215 Monica Moorehead, ed., *Marxism, Reparations and the Black Freedom Struggle* (New York: World View Forum, 2007), p. 152.

Chapter 9 – Globalization and immigration

216 Lenin, *Imperialism,* p. 282.

217 Ibid., p. 283.

218 Jeffrey Passel, "The Size and Characteristics of the Unauthorized Migrant Population in the U.S., Estimates Based on the March 2005 Current Population Survey," Pew Hispanic Center, March 7, 2006; online at www.pewhispanic.org.

219 Faux, *The Global Class War,* p. 130. The author cites an Economic Policy Briefing Paper of Nov. 17, 2003, Robert E. Scott, "The high price of 'free' trade: NAFTA's failure has cost the United States jobs across the nation."

220 Ibid., p. 134. Much of this section is based upon material in *The Global Class War.*

221 Ibid. Faux cites an article by George Thompson, "Made in Squalor," *New York Times,* May 6, 2001.

222 Ibid., p. 113.

223 Ibid., p. 136. Faux cites John Audley et al., *NAFTA's Promise and Reality* (Washington, D.C.: Carnegie Endowment for International Peace, 2003), p. 15.

224 Ibid., p. 136. Faux uses International Labor Organization and International Monetary Fund statistics. See also his footnote 22 on p. 264.

225 Jason DeParle, "A Good Provider Is One Who Leaves," *New York Times Magazine,* April 22, 2007.

Chapter 10 – Late 1970s: Attack on unions

226 Sources for the material in the preceding section are based partly on the author's direct experience and also on material and bibliographies in: Rick Fantasia and Kim Voss, *Hard Work: Remaking the American Labor Movement* (Berkeley: University of California Press, 2004) and Peter Rachieff, *Hard Pressed in the Heartland: The Hormel Strike and the Future of the Labor Movement* (Boston: South End Press, 1993).

227 Kate Bronfenbrenner and Stephanie Luce, "The Changing Nature of Corporate Global Restructuring: The Impact of Production Shifts on Jobs in the U.S., China, and Around the Globe," submitted to the U.S.-China Economic and Security Review Commission, Oct. 14, 2004. Congress created the commission in 2001.

228 Jeremy W. Peters, "Hardly a Union Hotbed, Toyota's Kentucky Plant Is a Test for Organizers," *New York Times,* Sept. 4, 2007.

Chapter 11 – Decades of rank-and-file fight-back

229 Jeremy Brecher, "Resisting Concessions," *Z Magazine,* March 1998, www.zmag.org/zmag/viewArticle/12731.

230 "Showdown in Motown: the Detroit Newspaper Strike, 1995-1997." Unpublished compilation of articles that first appeared in *Workers World* newspaper, 1995-1997, written by trade union participants in the strike support effort: Kris Hamel, David Sole, Key Martin, Stephanie Hedgecoke, and Jerry Goldberg.

231 Much of this information is from Steven Greenhouse, "Yearlong Effort Key to Success for Teamsters," *New York Times*, Aug. 25, 1997.

232 Keith Bradsher, "The G.M. Settlement: The Overview," *New York Times*, July 29, 1998.

233 Sewell Chan and Steven Greenhouse, "From Back-Channel Contacts, Blueprint for a Deal," *New York Times*, December 23, 2005.

234 Richard Freeman, "Do Workers Still Want Unions? More Than Ever," *Economic Policy Briefing Paper*, Feb. 22, 2007, at www.epi.org.

235 Broadus Mitchell, *Depression Decade: From New Era through New Deal, 1929-1941* (New York: Rinehart, 1946), p. 268.

236 Robert H. Zeiger and Gilbert J. Gall, *American Workers, American Unions: the Twentieth Century* (Baltimore: Johns Hopkins University Press, 2002), page 69.

Chapter 12 – Reviving the struggle

237 Samuel Yellen, *American Labor Struggles: 1877-1934* (New York: Monad Press, 1936), pp. 330-331.

238 Irving Bernstein, *The Turbulent Years: A History of the American Worker, 1933-1941* (Boston: Houghton Mifflin, 1970), p. 500.

239 Howard Zinn, Dana Frank, and Robin G. Kelley, *Three Strikes: Miners, Musicians, Salesgirls, and the Fighting Spirit of Labor's Last Century* (Boston: Beacon Press, 2001). In the section on Woolworth's from Chapter 2: "Girl Strikers Occupy Chain Store, Win Big: The Detroit Woolworth's Strike of 1937," title based on news headline.

240 Ibid., pp. 112-114.

241 Ibid., p. 114.

242 Robert H. Zeiger, *The CIO, 1935 to 1955* (Chapel Hill: University of North Carolina Press, 1995), pp. 284-287.

Chapter 14 – Building a broad working-class movement

243 BLS statistics compiled by Swivel; see www.swivel.com/data_sets/spreadsheet/1005277.

244 Sam Roberts, "Minorities Now Form Majority in One-Third of Most-Populous Counties," *New York Times*, August 9, 2007.

245 David M. Smith and Gary Gates, "Gay and Lesbian Families in the United States," Urban Institute, www.urban.org/publica-tions/1000491.html.

246 Andrew Noyes, "Study: Gay parents poorer than straight ones," *PlanetOut Network*, September 23, 2005.

247 Gary Gates, "Income of Gay Men Lags Behind that of Men Partnered with Women," Urban Institute, www.urban.org/publications/900631.html.

248 "Workplace Protection Linked to Higher Earnings for Less-Educated Gay Men," Urban Institute, www.urban.org/publications/900632.html.

249 "Hunger in America Rises by 43 Percent over Last Five Years," *ScienceDaily*, October 29, 2005.

250 Uchitelle, *The Disposable American*, p. 75.

251 Karl Marx, *The First International and After: Political Writings*, Vol. 3. Ed. David Fernbach (London: Penguin Books in association with New Left Review, 1974), p. 92.

252 David Riazanov, *Karl Marx and Friedrich Engels: An Introduction to Their Lives and Work* (New York: Monthly Review Press, 1973), p. 143.

253 Ibid., p. 145.

254 Karl Marx, *First International and After*, op cit., p. 91.

255 See www.ilwu19.com/history/the_ilwu_story/contents.htm.

Chapter 15 – Class struggle and capitalist legality

256 Richard O. Boyer and Herbert M. Morais, *Labor's Untold Story* (New York: Marzani and Munsell, 1965), p. 347.

257 Human Rights Watch, "Unfair Advantage: Workers' Freedom of Association in the United States under International Human Rights Standards," 2000, available at www.hrw.org/reports/2000/uslabor/index.htm.

258 Ibid., p. 285 of pdf version.

259 Ibid.

260 Tom Stites, "How Corporations Became 'Persons,' " see www.uuworld.org.

261 Marcy, *High Tech*, p. 144.

262 Ibid., p. 138.

Chapter 16 – Class consciousness and class struggle

263 V.I. Lenin, "What Is to Be Done?," *Collected Works* (Moscow: Progress Publishers, 1975), Vol. 5, p. 400.

Afterword: Imperialist war in the 21st century

264 V.I. Lenin, "Results of Party Week in Moscow and Our Tasks," *Collected Works* (Moscow: Progress Publishers, 1965), Vol. 30, pp. 71-75; also available at www.marxists.org.

Index

A

ABN AMRO, 43
Abu-Jamal, Mumia, 147, 242, 290
Accenture, 42-5, 294
Adidas, 31
Advanced Micro Devices (AMD), 9
affirmative action, 199, 256, 271
Afghanistan, 228, 286-7
AFL-CIO, vii, 7, 76, 82, 162-5, 173-81, 186, 189-90, 192, 194, 201, 221, 232, 235, 242-6, 275
Africa, 5-6, 11, 23, 28, 34, 60, 63, 85, 136, 151-2, 154, 160, 190, 230, 242, 282-3, 293
African American (Black), iv, 64, 66, 78, 82, 93, 101, 105, 109, 114, 119, 122, 126-7, 134, 137-42, 144, 147, 149, 163, 174, 178, 185, 188, 191-2, 195, 197-201, 204, 210-1, 217, 222, 224-5, 227, 229, 230, 233, 235-7, 242-4, 256, 271, 289, 292-3
African American/Latino Alliance, 236
AFSCME District Council 1701, 242-43
Agricultural Relations Board, 235
Aid to Families with Dependent Children (AFDC), 122, 134
AIDS crisis, 231
Airbus, 25-6, 31
Alcoa, 26
Allis-Chalmers, 249
Alternative Workforce, 166
Amalgamated Clothing Workers of America (ACWA), 194, 206
Amalgamated Transport Union (ATU), 177
America Competes Act, 38
American Express (AmEx), 40-41
American Federation of Government Employees (AFGE), 140
American Federation of Labor (AFL), 173-4, 193-4, 200, 205-7, 215, 245
American Postal Workers Union (APWU), 141
Angola, 10, 282
Anti-Terrorism Act, 243
anti-war movement, 191, 198, 222, 243, 287
Apple Computer, 26

Arizona Correctional Industries, 146, 294
Asia, 6, 21-2, 26, 28-30, 42, 63, 85, 97, 145, 151-2, 154, 190, 230, 245, 282-4
Asians, 136, 198, 223-4, 242
assembly line, iii, 21, 31, 75, 81, 132, 213, 215-6
Attica prison uprising, 147
Australia, 273
Austria, 29, 150
automation, 54, 75, 78, 82, 85, 139-41, 213, 241

B

Babbitt, Bruce, 175
Bangladesh, 7, 129
Barnes & Noble, 218
Barrett, Craig, 6
Bear Stearns, 69
Belgium, 159
benefits, vi-vii, 21, 34, 37, 57, 88-9, 93, 103, 106, 108, 114, 122, 134-5, 137-8, 154, 158, 161-4, 169, 175, 178, 180, 184, 186-7, 214, 256, 264-6, 272
Berger, Suzanne, 12, 14, 25-6, 31, 36-7
Bernanke, Ben, 8-10, 13, 19, 290
Best Buy, 87, 250
Black, see African American
Black Panther Party, 199, 201
Black Workers for Justice, 211, 236, 242
Blinder, Alan, 39-40, 45-48
Bloomberg, Michael, 188
Boeing, i, ix, 19, 25, 27, 31, 35, 290
Bolivia, 284
Bolsheviks, 10, 286
Bon Marché, 208
Bonus Marchers, 235
brain drain, 60
Brazil, 6-7, 20-1, 26, 28, 30, 33, 43, 159, 276
Bremmer, L. Paul, 246
Bridges, Harry, 203-4, 210, 221, 242
Bridgestone/Firestone 177, 247
Britain, 26, 55, 150, 159, 207, 239, 282
British East India Company, 50
Broadcom, 31

Fordism, 75
Forrester Research, 40-1, 43
France, 14, 29, 150, 159, 181, 231, 239, 248, 282
Frederick & Nelson's, 208
free market, 37
Freeman, Richard B., 4-6, 65, 192
French East India Company, 50
Friedan, Betty, 119
Friedman, Thomas, 6, 15, 19, 20, 23, 25, 31, 45, 47
Fur and Leather Workers, 210

G
Gannett, 178
Gap, the, xiii, 31, 36, 103, 207, 218
Gartner, Inc., 40
gay liberation, 231
General Electric (GE), 17, 22, 27, 30, 35, 37, 40, 42-3, 45, 91, 249
General Motors (GM), vii, 17, 24, 78, 84-5, 140, 158, 169, 173, 182-4, 196, 207, 257, 267-8, 274, 289
Genpact, 42-3
German Democratic Republic, 59, 66, 285
Germany, 9, 14, 20, 29, 44, 56, 66, 84, 92, 150-1, 159, 165, 181, 207, 217, 239, 283
Gettelfinger, Ron, 266
Gingrich, Newt, 134, 253
global restructuring, v, ix, 27, 33, 47, 85, 149, 213, 225, 273, 290
global warming, 243
globalization, 2, i-vi, viii-ix, xii, 1, 4, 6-8, 10, 12, 15-7, 26, 34, 38, 40, 45-6, 49-50, 54, 57-8, 60, 90, 100, 105, 107, 121, 136-7, 142-4, 149, 152-3, 158-9, 161, 167, 211, 216, 224, 226, 237, 254, 261, 273, 279, 290
Glover, Danny, 243
Gold, Ben, 210
Goldberg, Eve, 291
Goldman Sachs, 42, 146
Gompers, Samuel, 215
Goodyear Tire, 167
Great Depression, 65, 157, 195, 220
Greenspan, Alan, xiii, 8, 69-70
Gregory, Dick, 243
Greyhound Bus, 167
Guantanamo, 252

Guatemala, 185, 273-4
Guinea-Bissau, 10

H
H.L. Green, 208
Haiti, 159, 185
Hatch, Orrin, 167
health care, 3, 17, 47, 63, 65-6, 106-7, 115, 117-8, 124-5, 137-8, 157, 187, 222, 233, 243, 271-2, 275
Hewlett-Packard (HP), i, 19-20, 22-3, 28-9, 43, 92, 164
High Tech, Low Pay, 81, 91, 93, 257, 292
Hitler, 61
Holman, Lee, 203
Home Depot, 218, 250
Homestead steel strike, 75, 214
Hon Hai, 31
Hoover administration, 209
Hormel, viii, 154, 166, 173, 176, 293, 300
Hotel Employees and Restaurant Employees (HERE), 178, 207, 273
HSBC Securities, 41
Human Rights Watch, iv, 252, 291
Hungary, 14, 28-30, 33, 44
Hurricane Katrina, iii-iv, 221, 226-7, 236, 242

I
Iceland, 26
immigrant rights, 162, 190-1, 222
immigrant workers, v, x, xii, 121, 136, 149-52, 154, 185, 190-1, 193, 227, 236
imperialism, 1-2, ii, vi, 5, 9-11, 35, 49-54, 56-61, 63, 77, 79, 82, 85, 136, 147, 149-53, 159, 239, 252, 276-9, 281-8, 292
Imperialism, the Highest Stage of Capitalism, 51, 150, 292
INA-Schaeffer, 41
India, 4-9, 11, 14, 19, 23, 25, 28, 30, 40-3, 50, 55, 59-60, 159, 241, 273-4, 276, 291
Indian companies
    Bank of India, 23
    Infosys, 42
    Tata Consultancy Service, 42
    Wypro, 42
Indonesia, 6-7, 20, 26, 30, 50, 59, 129-30, 273
Industrial Council of New Jersey, 177
industrial revolution, vi, 8, 39, 75, 81, 94, 290
industrial unionism, 75, 162, 196, 214-5, 251

Mao Zedong, 54
maquiladora(s), 145, 157-8, 211, 273
Marcy, Sam, 81-5, 91, 93-4, 100-1, 257-8, 260, 292
Marks, Michael, 29
Marriott, 43
Martin, Homer, 207
Marx, Karl, 3, 13, 15-7, 49-51, 55, 79, 83, 85, 94, 105, 111-4, 118, 122, 131, 152, 219, 221, 237-41, 268, 289, 292-3, 305
Marxism, i-ii, v, 49-51, 67, 100, 147, 219, 239, 273, 289, 292
Marxism on
  anarchy of production, 34
  composition of capital, 84, 94
  constant capital, 32, 83-4, 94
  cost of labor-power, 113
  labor law of value, 17, 51
  law of capitalist accumulation, ii, 75, 93-4, 96, 101-2
  law of wages, iii, 213, 219
  price of labor-power, 114, 121-2
  rate of exploitation, 25, 48, 86, 90, 94-6, 98, 101, 160, 278
  rate of profit, ii, 75, 83-5
  super-exploitation, xiii, 5, 12, 19, 33-4, 36-7, 45-6, 52, 54-5, 121, 136-7, 143-4, 154, 191, 230
  super-profits, i, iii, 27, 30, 33-6, 42, 45, 47, 52, 54, 71, 84-5, 147, 149-51, 153-4, 201, 239
  surplus value, 27, 30, 35, 37, 45, 48, 70, 75-6, 83, 94-5, 98, 112, 131-2, 262-3, 265
  value of labor-power, 112, 114, 118, 121-2
  variable capital, 83-4, 94
  wage competition, i, v, ix-xiii, 1, 3, 12-3, 15, 17, 47, 57-8, 60, 79, 85, 98, 114, 121, 134, 137, 144-5, 149, 158, 167, 191, 222, 241, 262, 277
  mass production, 75-6, 81, 136, 193, 205-6, 214-5
Matles, James, 210
Matsushita, 22
Mauritius, 41
May Day, iii, viii, 149, 151-2, 173, 190-1, 227-8, 289
McCarthyism, 62, 209
McDonald's, 102, 110, 207
McKinsey Global Institute, 47, 102

Meany, George, 174
Merrill Lynch, 69
Metropolitan Life Insurance, 164
Metropolitan Transit Authority (MTA), 185-9
Mexico, v, xii, 5-7, 14, 17, 23-4, 28-30, 33, 43, 46, 129, 136, 145, 149, 151, 156-9, 168-9, 182, 185, 226, 241, 253, 273-6
Mexicans, 97, 157
Microsoft, 28, 40-1, 45
Middle East, 23, 63, 151-2, 190, 230, 282-3, 294
military-industrial complex, x, 78, 228, 243, 264, 287-8
Milliken, William, 78
Million Worker March Movement (MWMM), iv, 221, 241-5, 289
minimum wage, 95, 158
Minutemen, 191
Mississippi Freedom Labor Union, 236
MIT Industrial Performance Center, 12
Mitsubishi, 22
monopolies, i, 7, 10, 13, 15, 17, 19, 22, 27, 29-33, 35-8, 45-6, 51-2, 57, 77-8, 92-3, 129, 159, 239, 241, 273, 278, 287
Montgomery Bus Boycott, 197
Moorehead, Monica, 292
Morgan Stanley, 42, 44, 69, 292
Motorola, 27, 29, 158
Mozambique, 10, 282
MphasiS, 43

N

NAACP, 198
National Association of Letter Carriers, 141
National Association of Manufacturers, 249
National Bureau of Economic Research, 4
National Endowment for Democracy, 246
National Guard, 175-6, 196, 204
National Labor Relations Act (NLRA), 196, 235, 249, 254-6
National Labor Relations Board (NLRB), 167, 179, 184, 194, 210, 251-2
national liberation struggles, 11, 61, 282-3
national oppression, ii-iii, viii, 51, 66, 101, 133, 136, 162, 173, 193, 200-1, 222-3, 228
National Railway Act, 167
National Security Strategy, 284-5
National Welfare Rights Organization, 235

Q

Quanta, 31

R

R.J. Reynolds, 211
R.R. Donnelly & Sons, 43
racism, ii-iii, viii, 12, 57, 64, 66, 93, 106, 114, 133, 136-8, 141-4, 149, 151, 156, 158, 162-3, 173, 191, 193, 195, 198-201, 211-2, 216, 221-8, 232, 235-6, 269, 271
Radio Free Europe, 63
Ralph Lauren, 36
Rank, Mark, 126
RCA, 91
Reagan administration, 76, 78, 109, 153, 174
Reagan, Ronald, 76, 90, 123
recession, vi, 29, 38, 63, 69, 127, 141, 165-6, 258, 293, 298
Reebok, 31
reindustrialization, 86
Republicans, 174, 287
reserve army of labor, xiii, 10, 79, 94-5, 97, 151
Rhodia, 44
right to a job, iv, viii, 65, 249, 257-8, 260, 269
"right-to-life," 271
"right-to-work," iv, xii, 23, 30, 92, 125, 202, 211, 217, 236-7, 242, 249, 251, 254, 265
Roach, Stephen, 293
robotization, 54, 82, 84, 101, 213, 216
Rockefeller, 249
Romania, xii, 14, 26, 30, 44
Roosevelt administration, 197
Roosevelt, Franklin Delano, 203
Rosen, Ruth, 119-120, 293
Rubber Workers, 196, 206, 208, 247
Rumsfeld, Donald, 283, 285-286
Russia, ix, 6-7, 23, 25-6, 41, 43, 59, 61, 136, 150, 270, 276, 284
Russian Revolution, 10, 51, 65
Ryan, Joseph, 202

S

Sacco and Vanzetti, 61
San Francisco Chamber of Commerce, 205
San Francisco Day Laborers, 243
San Francisco general strike, 195, 202, 242, 247
San Francisco Industrial Association, 205
SAP, 44

Saudi Arabia, 42
Scandinavia, 151
Schaffer, Steve, 31
Schlosser, Eric, 110, 293
scientific-technological revolution, v-vi, xii, 10, 13, 53-5, 57, 77-8, 83, 90-1, 94, 101, 219, 241, 258, 277-8
Scotland, 23
Scott, H. Lee, 130
Scottsboro defendants, 235
Sears, 92, 164, 208
Seattle general strike, 248
Semiconductor Manufacturing International, 14
serfdom, 59
Service Employees International Union (SEIU), 184, 273
sexual orientation, 163, 243
Sharecroppers Union, 235
Siemens, 41, 44
Silicon Valley, 28, 60
Singapore, 9, 20-1, 26, 28, 30, 59, 129
sit-down strikes, viii, 206, 208, 257, 268
slave trade, 50, 150, 226
slavery, ix, 19, 48, 53, 56, 96, 136-8, 147, 150, 226-7, 230, 276
Slovakia, 25, 44
Smithfield, 237, 253
Social Security, 161, 174, 197, 243
socialism, iv, ix, 10-1, 29, 48, 50-1, 59, 61-6, 96, 103, 209, 261, 270, 278-9, 282, 284-5, 305
socialist countries, 59, 61, 63-5
Solectron, i, 27, 30-1, 294
Solidarity Day, iii, 173-5
Sony, 22, 29
South Africa, 6, 23, 28, 242
Soviet Union, *see* Union of Soviet Socialist Republics
Spain, 159-60, 305
Spanish Inquisition, 62
Spanish-American War, 57, 136, 281
special economic zones, 85
Sri Lanka, 129
Staley Machinery, 167
standard of living, x, 6, 54, 58, 63, 79, 86-8, 96, 107, 110, 114, 121-2, 125, 178, 220
Steel Workers Organizing Committee, 208

Department of State, x, 63, 246
Department of the Treasury, 106
Federal Bureau of Investigation (FBI), 143, 181, 198-9, 211
Immigration and Customs Enforcement, 152, 191
National Institute of Justice, 145
National Security Agency, 64
Supreme Court, 197, 255, 257
United States Steel, 90
United Steel Workers (USW), 164, 168, 175, 247
Union of Soviet Socialist Republics (USSR), v, xii, 4-6, 8, 9-11, 19, 25, 54, 59-67, 76-7, 83, 92, 94, 209-10, 277-8, 281-5

V

Valentine, Brian, 40
Vance International, 166
Venezuela, x, 246, 275, 284
Victoria's Secret, 145
Vietnam, 7, 10, 59, 61, 91, 199, 282, 287-8
Vietnam War, 91, 282, 287
Visteon, 24-5, 294
Voice of America, 63
Voting Rights Act, 199

W

W.T. Grant, 208
Wackenhut, 146
Wagner Act, 249, 251, 257
Waiters and Waitresses Union, 207
Wall Street, xiii, 26, 39-40, 42, 58, 61, 63-4, 69-70, 90, 92, 146, 156-7, 181, 183, 185, 187, 189, 241, 267, 294
Wal-Mart, ii, vii, 22-3, 26, 97, 105, 127-32, 183, 206-8, 218, 233, 250, 291-3
War Labor Board, 197
"war on poverty," 123, 199
War Production Board, 197
Warren, Elizabeth, 294

"weapons of mass destruction," 284
Webster, William, 181
Welch, Jack, 91
welfare reform, ii, 125, 133-5
Welfare Reform Act, 134
West Coast Waterfront Coalition, 250
West Germany, 66, 84
Western Europe, 29, 44-5, 66, 284
Westinghouse, 22
whipsawing, 268
White Citizens Councils, 236
white-collar jobs, 40-1, 262
Wider Opportunities for Women, 124-5, 291
Williams, Robert, 198
Wilson, Woodrow, 65, 253
Wolfowitz, Paul, 283-4
women workers, 97, 119-21, 133, 163, 207, 210, 230, 235
women's liberation movement, 231
women's rights, 162, 230
Woolworth sit-down strike, 206
Woolworth's, 207-8, 289, 301
Workers World Party, 81, 305
World Bank, 5, 11
world division of labor, 56-7, 275
World Economic Forum, 40
World War I, 61, 65, 137, 235, 281
World War II, 10, 60-1, 64, 89-93, 97, 117, 165, 197, 200, 209, 249, 278, 281-2

X

Xerox, 28-9, 110

Y

Yemen, 10
Youngstown Sheet & Tube, 90
Yugoslavia, 7, 283

Z

Zapatistas, 156
Zedillo, Ernesto, 157

About the author

Fred Goldstein writes on international and domestic affairs from a Marxist perspective and is a contributing editor to *Workers World* newspaper. The main themes in *Low-Wage Capitalism* were first presented for discussion at a conference entitled "Preparing for the Rebirth of the Global Struggle for Socialism," held in New York City in May 2006 and sponsored by Workers World Party.

The thesis was later presented, under the title "Colossus with Feet of Clay," at the International Communist Seminar in Brussels in May 2007 and was more fully developed for presentation at the IV International Conference on "The Work of Karl Marx and the Challenges of the 21st Century," held in Havana, Cuba in May 2008. The Havana presentation was translated into Spanish, reprinted online in Latin America and Spain, and widely circulated on the Internet.

fgoldstein@workers.org